Tyne after Tyne

Tyne after Tyne

An Environmental History of a River's Battle
for Protection, 1529–2015

Leona J. Skelton

Dedicated to James Anthony Thompson (1924–1995)

My Grandad, a proud Shipbuilder whose love for the River Tyne continues to flow in my Dad and in me

Copyright © Leona J. Skelton
First published 2017 by
The White Horse Press, The Old Vicarage, Winwick, Cambridgeshire PE28 5PN

Set in 11 point Adobe Garamond Pro
Printed by Lightning Source

All rights reserved. Except for the quotation of short passages for the purpose of criticism or review, no part of this book may be reprinted or reproduced or utilised in any form or by any electronic, mechanical or other means, including photocopying or recording, or in any information storage or retrieval system.

British Library Cataloguing in Publication Data
A catalogue record for this book is available from the British Library

ISBN   978-1-874267-95-9 (HB); 978-1-912186-25-9 (PB)

CONTENTS

Acknowledgements... x

List of Figures... xiv

Glossary... xvi

The Author.. xviii

Introduction... 1
    Overview 1
    River Historiography 12
    Methodology and Description of Chapters 25

Chapter 1. 'Hurting the River of Tine':
Protecting a Pre-Modern River Estuary, 1529–1850 34
    Introduction 34
    Early Modern Environmental Historiography 36
    The Need for Regulation 45
    The Foundations of Regulation 52
    The Character and Stringency of Regulation 56
    Conclusion 61

Chapter 2. 'Tinkering' the Tyne:
Increasing Demand for Structural Change, 1655–1855 64
    Introduction 64
    Ralph Gardiner's Petition, 1655 65
    The Great Floods of 1771 and 1815 71
    *The River Committee and Public Impatience for River Improvement,
        1832–1850* 75
    The Royal Commission of 1855 81
    Conclusion 87

Chapter 3. Creating a Grand and Deep River:
The Tyne Improvement Commission, 1850–1968. 90
- *Introduction* 90
- *The TIC's Structure and Purpose* 94
- *Docks and Piers* 97
- *Dredging for Industrial Progress* 101
- *Dredging for Resources* 109
- *Straightening the Channel* 116
- *Domestic and Industrial Wastes* 119
- *Testing and Attempts at Regulation* 128
- *The TIC's Intervention in Non-Tidal Reaches* 133
- *Conclusion* 135

Chapter 4. Fish in the Tyne:
The Tyne Salmon Conservancy, 1866–1950 138
- *Introduction* 138
- *The Tyne Salmon Conservancy's Work* 143
- *The Consequences of Scientific Progress* 147
- *Tackling the Estuary's Pollution* 151
- *Conclusion* 155

Chapter 5. Testing the Troubled Waters:
SCORP's Tyne Sub-committee and a Succession of Unsuccessful
Reports, 1921–1945 157
- *Introduction* 157
- *A Thousand Reports* 159
- *A Tyne Sewerage Scheme and the Joint Committee* 165
- *Unsuccessful Reports* 170
- *Conclusion* 174

Chapter 6. 'A Medieval Street of Squalor':
The Final Demand for a Clean-Up, 1950–1975 175
- *Introduction* 175
- *The 1950s on Tyne* 177
- *Final Demands for a Clean-Up* 181
- *The Tyneside Joint Sewerage Committee and the Howdon Plan* 185
- *Stories from before the Clean-Up* 187
- *Conclusion* 192

Chapter 7. Damming the Tyne:
The Creation and Impact of Kielder Reservoir, 1975–2015 . . . 194
Introduction 194
The Kielder Scheme and its Local Enquiries, 1972–1973 197
The Fish Pass Issue 206
Conclusion 209

Chapter 8. 'A Big River?':
Regeneration, Tourism and the Cultural Meaning of the Tyne,
1972–2015 212
Introduction 212
Iconography of the Newcastle-Gateshead Quayside 214
Creativity on Tyne 220
River Recreation 223
Ecological Responsibility 226
The Tyne's Indomitable Natural Independence 235
Stories from after the Clean-Up 237
Conclusion 244

Conclusion. 246

Bibliography. 255

Index 267

ACKNOWLEDGEMENTS

This study is the product of well over a hundred people's efforts, as well as my own. Above all, I would like to express my enormous gratitude to a keen river historian and lover of all things watery (especially if he can swim in them!). The University of Bristol's Professor Peter Coates conceptualised my post-doctoral research project, 'Degeneration and Regeneration on the Tyne: River Pasts, Presents and Futures, 1529–2015', with another environmental historian, Professor David Moon (University of York). Peter – whom I can almost forgive for continuing to think, in the face of all the evidence I've presented here, that his boyhood river, the Mersey, is just as important as the Tyne – installed and connected the Tyne case study into his Arts and Humanities Research Council (AHRC) project, 'The Power and the Water: Reconnecting Pasts with Futures' and kindly provided comments on an earlier draft of this book. Between 2013 and 2016, this project reconnected the severed ties between past activities and current and future environmental problems, taking an extensive tour across several aspects of the UK's energy and water infrastructure, ranging from the National Grid, to the Severn Barrage proposals, to renewable energy landscapes, to the Derbyshire lead-mining subterranean drainage channels known as soughs.

Back in March 2011, as I finalised my doctoral thesis on sanitation and environmental regulation in early modern British towns at Durham University, an innovative band of modern environmental historians, David Moon, Peter Coates and Paul Warde (Cambridge University) welcomed me into their previous collaborative AHRC project, 'Local Places, Global Processes'. Professor Georgina Endfield (University of Nottingham) joined the network soon afterwards and as co-investigator on 'The Power and the Water' project, her cultural geography perspectives have enhanced my research. They let an early-modern historian loose with a dictaphone, encouraged me to develop my growing expertise and experience in environmental history and introduced me to a truly global network of scholars in our field. I have never looked back as this intellectual network has continued to blow my mind, encouraging me to understand human interactions with water, rivers and reservoirs as two-way processes. I will always be extremely grateful to these inspiring and pioneering professors for setting my academic research career on a much more explicitly environmental history track.

I would also like to thank the AHRC for funding the research project and for realising the value of one of its intended main functions, to train the next generation of environmental historians, of whom I am now very fortunately one. Thanks also to the University of Bristol for supporting me as I conducted my two-year Tyne research project between 2013 and 2015 and also during the academic year 2015 to 2016, when their history department kindly provided me with an honorary research affiliation, including essential library access, while I wrote *Tyne after Tyne*. The Bristol History Department's wide-ranging lunchtime Environmental History Reading Group has been particularly valuable to me.

It has been a privilege and an honour to work alongside three truly inspirational fellow post-doctoral researchers within 'The Power and the Water' project. Dr Marianna Dudley's research into water recreation, how watery environments make us feel, how they encourage us to play and why this has changed over time has challenged me to think much more about feelings and emotions in relation to the environment, and about the physicality of our engagement with particular waterscapes. Dr Jill Payne's research into debates surrounding renewable energy landscapes has pushed me to think much more about aesthetics and why they dominate intense debates about alternative energy futures. Dr Carry van Lieshout's research into the subterranean landscape of the Derbyshire mining soughs, including her brave trawls in full caving gear through some of these little understood underground landscapes, has led me to analyse my historical research from a vertical as well as a horizontal perspective. My ideas and arguments have also been challenged and progressed by stimulating conversations and debates with our project Ph.D. students, Alexander Portch and Kayt Button, and I wish them the very best of luck in their future careers.

My engagement with several of the Tyne's current and future conservators, managers and regulators has been crucial to the production of this book. After having researched the Tyne's historical conservators merely through the documents they left behind, I was able to meet and discuss the Tyne's environmental problems with its current conservators in person. The particularly kind support of the environmental charity, the Tyne Rivers Trust, has enabled me to understand in substantial depth how my historical research can be reconnected to the environmental legacies which they work tirelessly to mitigate through a wide range of very impressive river restoration schemes that rely on a large cast of volunteers. Thanks to the whole team at Tyne Rivers Trust, but in particular to Dr Ceri Gibson (a chemist who now works at the Freshwater Biological Association), Susan MacKirdy (the Trust Director), Graham Holyoak (who oversaw their recent Water Voles Heritage Project) and Aidan

Pollard (their invaluable Fisheries Consultant). The Clean Tyne Project was also very helpful and its manager, Jayne Calvert of Gateshead Council, provided me with a very warm welcome when I embarked on the research in October 2013. Jayne has supported me throughout the project, particularly in terms of inviting the whole 'Power and the Water' team to ride their debris-collection vessel, the Clearwater, on our three-day 'Tyne Trip' in June 2014. Its captain and its skipper, Steve and Dave, possess an impressive knowledge of the river and their passion for the Tyne and for their work is very moving.

Northumbrian Water Ltd have provided me with information when I needed it, and kindly added a fascinating tour of their Waste Water Treatment Works at Howdon during our 'Tyne Trip'. I would particularly like to thank their Director of Research, Dr Andrew Moore and their Customer Engagement Officer, Lucy Denham, for their thought-provoking input into the project. Engaging with the Port of Tyne was particularly interesting after having ploughed through the very voluminous records of their predecessors, the Tyne Improvement Commission, and their environmental officer, James Wright, provided the whole project team with a very useful insight into their operations at Tyne Dock during our 'Tyne Trip'. I would also like to thank Dr Angela Connelly, of another AHRC-funded project, the Jetty Project, for sharing her research into public perceptions of and engagement with the Tyne's riparian art installations and the iconography of the Newcastle-Gateshead Quayside. And thanks also to the Environment Agency for providing me with a tour of the Kielder Salmon Hatchery.

The archivists at Northumberland Record Office at Woodhorn, at Tyne and Wear Archives in Newcastle's Discovery Museum and at the National Archives in London enabled me to navigate my way through a wealth of documents as I made sense of the Tyne's very complex history. The librarians of Newcastle's Literary and Philosophical Society were especially helpful. From the very bottom of my heart, I would like to thank the Geordies of Tyneside, and in particular the Geordies of Gateshead where I grew up, of whom I am extremely proud to be one. It has been a heartfelt honour to have written the history of my river. My intimate knowledge of the riparian places, of the people and of its history has acted as a springboard for the archival research into the details of the Tyne's story. In particular, I would like to thank the 36 people who allowed me to interview them about their own personal relationships with the river and how and why these have changed over time. Their poignant, surprising and important stories have rendered an otherwise highly administrative history of local and national river governance into an immensely more interesting and far deeper appreciation of how the river has made people feel, both when it bubbled with toxic gases and when it has thrived with flora and fauna. In particular, I would like to express my huge thanks to Tony Henderson, the Environment Editor of the Journal newspaper; Pearl Saddington, the manager of the Low Light Heritage Centre, where I mounted a public exhibition of my research in June 2015; Matt Hall, an amateur historian and the proudest Geordie I have ever met; and David Fraser, whose very deep knowledge of the Dunston Staiths has helped me a great deal. Thanks also to Gordon Ball, a professional photographer and friend, who took most of the photos in this book.

Last, but by no means least, I would like to thank my Dad, Alan J. Thompson, who grew up in Walker and North Shields and who was a keen member of Tynemouth Rowing Club in the 1970s and 1980s. And I am grateful to thank his Dad, James A. Thompson, a Tyne shipbuilder who worked as a Marine Engineering Turner and Fitter at several of the Tyne's riparian shipyards in the mid- and late-twentieth century including the famous Swan Hunters, known affectionately by those who worked there as Swans. My Grandad Thompson died in 1995 when I was only ten years old, but the industrial, manual and very highly skilled work that he conducted by the River Tyne, a river which has meant such different things to him, to my Dad and to me, has always inspired me. Whenever I reached a temporary impasse over the course of ploughing through seemingly endless stacks of documentary records, I remembered how much more physically demanding my Grandad's work was than my own in a comparatively luxurious set up of sitting comfortably at a desk in a warm archive. *Tyne after Tyne* is dedicated to my late Grandad Thompson with a great deal of respect, love and gratitude for sparking my initial interest in the river as a little girl in the late 1980s and early 1990s and for laying the immovable foundations of the immense pride I will have for my River Tyne, my Tyneside and my North-east England for the rest of my life.

LIST OF FIGURES

Figure 1. Map of the Tyne Catchment Area to show places referred to in the text (I am grateful to Tyne Rivers Trust for providing this map)....5

Figure 2. The Meeting of the Waters at Warden Rock, Northumberland (Photograph: Gordon Ball)....7

Figure 3. North Tyne Source Marker, Deadwater Fell, near Anglo-Scottish Border (Photograph: Gordon Ball)....12

Figure 4. Flood markers at the Boathouse Public House, Newburn (Photograph: Gordon Ball)....72

Figure 5. Tyne Improvement Offices, Bewick Street, Newcastle, opposite Central Station (Photograph: Gordon Ball)....95

Figure 6. The Mouth of the Tyne, showing the Black Middens in front of the north pier (Photograph: Gordon Ball)....100

Figure 7. The Black Midden Rocks in front of the north pier (Photograph: Gordon Ball)....101

Figure 8. Looking downriver at the Tyne from St Anthony's, Walker, 2015 (Photograph: Gordon Ball)....140

Figure 9. Dove Marine Laboratory, Cullercoats Bay (Photograph: Leona Skelton)....159

Figure 10. Wylam Bridge, 2015 (Photograph: Gordon Ball)....163

Figure 11. Grounds of Objection to Kielder Scheme submitted to Public Inquiry (1972)....202

Figure 12. Kielder Reservoir from Leaplish Waterside Park (Photograph: Gordon Ball)....205

Figure 13. Kielder Reservoir from below Bakethin Reservoir
(Photograph: Gordon Ball).............................. 206

Figure 14. The River North Tyne below Kielder Dam
(Photograph: Gordon Ball).............................. 211

Figure 15. Newcastle-Gateshead Quayside, 1983
(Photograph: G. Melvin). 215

Figure 16. Newcastle-Gateshead Quayside from the Gateshead
Millennium Bridge, 2015 (Photograph: Gordon Ball). 215

Figure 17. Newcastle-Gateshead Bridges
(Photograph: Gordon Ball).............................. 216

Figure 18. 'Seaside at the Quayside' (Photograph: Gordon Ball). . 216

Figure 19. Gateshead Millennium Bridge
(Photograph: Gordon Ball).............................. 217

Figure 20. Remains of Kittiwake Nests, Baltic Centre for
Contemporary Art, Gateshead (Photograph: Gordon Ball).... 234

Figure 21. Looking Upriver on the Main Tyne at Newburn
(Photograph: Gordon Ball).............................. 252

Figure 22. Looking Upriver to Newcastle from St Anthony's
(Photograph: Gordon Ball).............................. 252

GLOSSARY OF KEY TERMS AND ABBREVIATIONS

AONB	Area of Outstanding Natural Beauty, which has been singled out for special protection.
Bilge Water	A mixture of water, oily fluids, lubricants and grease, accumulating from interior spillage, rough seas or leaks in the hull, which collects in the lowest part of a ship (known as the bilge).
Catchment	An area of land that directs all of the water that lands on it to one single point, such as an estuary, sea or ocean.
Defra	Government Department for the Environment, Food and Rural Affairs, which is responsible for the countryside, agriculture and the environment.
Kelt	Salmon that has spawned.
LIA	Little Ice Age: a period between 1300 and about 1870 during which North America and Europe experienced much colder winters than they experienced subsequently in the twentieth century. During this period, rivers such as the Tyne and the Thames froze up and, during many severe winters, sections of them were unnavigable for periods of up to three months.
LWOST	Low Waters of Spring Tides, which today is known as MLWS (mean low water spring tides). These abbreviations are used as reference points for water marks and are the mean average of two successive low water marks during the 24 hours when the tide is at its lowest (once every semi-lunation of about two weeks).
LWONT	Low Waters of Neap Tides, now known as MLWN.
HWOST	High Waters of Spring Tides, now known as MHWS. The mean average of two successive high water marks during the 24 hours when the tide is at its greatest (once every semi-lunation of about two weeks).
HWONT	High Waters of Neap Tides, now known as MHWN.
NAA	Northumbrian Anglers Association, now known as the Northumbrian Anglers Federation.

NRO	Northumberland Record Office, Woodhorn, Northumberland.
Riparian	On or related to riverbanks.
SCORP	The central government's Standing Committee on River Pollution had several sub-committees which accumulated scientific evidence of the impact of pollution on rivers around the UK. All of the references to SCORP in this study refer to the work of its Tyne Sub-Committee (1921–1939), which produced approximately 1,000 reports on its experiments at its Dove Marine Laboratory in Cullercoats Bay, near the river mouth.
SSSI	Site of Special Scientific Interest, such as the Black Middens near Tynemouth.
Smolt	The young of salmon or sea trout at about two years of age when it exhibits the silvery colour of an adult and begins its migration out of the river in which it was born to live in the sea. They are sometimes also referred to as parr.
TIC	Tyne Improvement Commission, appointed by Act of Parliament in 1850 to improve the navigability, trade facilities and economic efficiency of the tidal reaches of the River Tyne and its tributaries. In 1968, it was disbanded and replaced by the Port of Tyne Authority.
TNA	The National Archives, Kew, London.
TSC	Tyne Salmon Conservancy, established in 1866 in Hexham, Northumberland, to enforce the Salmon and Fisheries Acts. It rarely interfered in the TIC's management of the estuary because the Tyne estuary was specifically exempted from the Salmon and Fisheries Acts which regulated pollution in 'streams'. However, its jurisdiction did cover the whole catchment. It was disbanded in 1950, when its work was taken over by the Northumberland and Tyneside River Board.
TWA	Tyne and Wear Archives, Discovery Museum, Newcastle on Tyne.

THE AUTHOR

An environmental historian of water, rivers and sanitation infrastructure, Leona J. Skelton is Vice Chancellor's Research Fellow in the Humanities at Northumbria University in Newcastle. Her work focuses on the two-way interactions between people and the environment, developments in environmental attitudes and regulation and how dramatic environmental change has shaped economic, cultural and social lives and livelihoods across northern England and Scotland between 1500 and the present day. Her first monograph was *Sanitation in Urban Britain, 1560-1700* (London: Routledge, 2015). Between 2012 and 2015, she contributed to two of Prof. Peter Coates' environmental history research projects as a Research Assistant: 'The Places that Speak to Us and the Publics we Talk with' and 'The Power and the Water: Reconnecting Pasts with Futures'.

INTRODUCTION

Overview

In 1950, the River Tyne Improvement Commission (TIC) celebrated its centenary. It had been appointed in 1850 by an Act of the UK Parliament to improve the navigability, economic efficiency and export capacity of north-east England's River Tyne. The river had long functioned as a nationally strategic port exporting, among other goods, very substantial volumes of coal down the east coast to London, around the Baltic Sea and elsewhere. Even in the seventeenth century, so much of London's coal was brought down the east coast by collier sailing ships that the fuel was known locally by Londoners as 'sea coal'.[1] The widely used idiom, 'carrying coals to Newcastle', synonymous with 'selling snow to Eskimos', continues to remind us of the enormous historical importance of the Tyne as a conduit for the export of coal. In the TIC's official centenary publication, tellingly named *A Century of Progress* (1951), the commissioners congratulated themselves and gave thanks to their predecessors for a job very well done indeed. The publication showcases a series of modern photographs of large-scale docks, productive shipyards and booming riparian industries, deliberately juxtaposed against engravings, by local artists James Wilson Carmichael and Charles Richardson, of the Tyne's romantic, mid-nineteenth-century riverscapes featuring sail ships, coal rowing boats known as keels, pastoral riverbank scenes devoid of industry, an angular meandering river course and great, treacherous waves wreaking havoc on fragile vessels as sailors struggled to overcome the awesome power of a much more natural river. Reminding readers that they were now part of a 'mercantile nation' and that commerce 'is our life blood', the commissioners admitted that the engravings

---

1. W. Cavert, 'The Environmental Policy of Charles I: Coal Smoke and the English Monarchy, 1624–40', *Journal of British Studies* 53 (2) (2014): 316. See also W. Cavert, *The Smoke of London: Energy and Environment in the Early Modern City* (Cambridge: Cambridge University Press, 2016).

'produce a nostalgic feeling at the loss of the scenic beauties of the lower reaches of the Tyne', but reassured them that ultimately this was a worthwhile and a fully justified sacrifice.[2]

As a result of 'this good work', even by the 1880s, the TIC had created the largest coal exporter and the largest centre of ship repair in the world, which as a builder of ships was second only to Glasgow's River Clyde. Moreover, the tonnage of the port's vessels exceeded even that of the River Thames, it came second only to that of the Mersey and accounted for an incredible one ninth of the UK's total shipping tonnage.[3] Consequently, by the late nineteenth century, the Tyne underpinned substantial regional economic prosperity, supporting a population of 850,000 people who called Tyneside home. In order to convey the enormity of their engineering achievements, the Tyne commissioners asked readers to imagine the very dramatic transformation that would be required to the Tyne's northern neighbour (and fellow renowned salmon river), the largely rural and undeveloped River Tweed which flows through Berwick near the Scottish border, to render it navigable for cargo vessels of 10,000 tons as far inland as Coldstream, some fifteen miles from the North Sea.[4] By comparing the Tyne of 1850 to their modern creation of 1950, the river commissioners told no lies and they did not exaggerate the very large, in their words 'startling', extent to which the river had been transformed. But they did tell its story from a very particular and arguably narrow viewpoint, seeing their work as a hard-won battle against the natural, powerful, unimproved and therefore shamefully wasted Tyne. They saw their sustained engineering and economic achievements as essentially having upgraded an inefficient natural system into a wide, deep and controlled channel that contributed crucially to the region's, and indeed to the wider UK's, economic prosperity.

While most environmental river histories have focused on the post-1800 period, this study analyses half a millennium of river management in order to incorporate early modern (1500–1800) attitudes to this natural resource as well as nineteenth-, twentieth- and twenty-first-century attitudes. It also reconnects, or dovetails, the river's pre- and post-1800 periods by discussing in depth the important strands of the river's history which bridge the artificial fissure caused by arbitrarily compartmentalising early modern and modern history. Sharing many of its chronological milestones with numerous other

---

2. The National Archives [hereafter, TNA], ZLIB 2/73: *Tyne Improvement Commission Centenary, 1850–1950: A Century of Progress* (1951), p. 3.

3. Ibid., p. 3.

4. Ibid., p. 3.

Introduction

industrial rivers, from the early nineteenth century, the Tyne was subjected to concerted economic, engineering and political initiatives to transform it into a much more controllable socio-technical system or environment. A schedule of large-scale 'improvements' was implemented from 1850 right up until the major clean-up of the river estuary which began in 1972. However, the attitudes, values and management styles of the TIC, which sought to control the river between 1850 and 1968, were as distinctly different from those of the Tyne's early modern conservators (1529–1850) as they were from those of the increasingly environmentally sensitive post-1972 managers of the river. *Tyne after Tyne* argues that today's conceptualisation of the river, celebrated as a success story by the national and local governors and others who regulate and manage it, prioritising flora's and fauna's perceived rights to thrive in a more natural, clean and environmentally healthy riverscape to which tourists flock above generating economic and industrial productivity, is no wider a perspective than that of the Tyne's earlier conservators. It is no wider than the perspective of the TIC, which prioritised creating a nationally strategic, functional and economically successful Port of Tyne (1850–1968). And nor is it any wider than that of the TIC's oligarchic predecessors, Newcastle's mayor and aldermen, who prioritised amassing profits, who were disinclined to invest their shipping and ballast tolls into restructuring the river and who regulated riparian development and the disposal of solid waste into the river very stringently to ensure the continued functioning of their monopolistic Port of Newcastle at the head of a liquid highway (1529–1850). In short, the period 1850 to 1972 represents an anomalous blip on the graph, during which the river was controlled and utilised increasingly as an economic system, or in Richard White's words as an 'organic machine', within a much longer-term period of working with the river as a natural system both before 1850 and after 1972, albeit with very different motivations in the respective periods.[5]

The historically specific meanings of the word 'conservation', from one century to the next, are the foundation stones of our changing relationship with the Tyne and they could perhaps serve as a neat summary of the Tyne's environmental story. In many respects, over the last five centuries, the widely different definitions of river 'conservation' have come full circle. Firstly, between 1529 and 1850, conservation in practice meant the careful and considered preservation of the river as an economic trading facility, a liquid highway. This was a time when the limitations of available technology, Newcastle Corpora-

---

5. R. White, *The Organic Machine: The Remaking of the Columbia River* (New York: Hill and Wang, 1995).

tion's disinclination to invest their profits into structural 'improvements' and quite stringent environmental regulations to maintain a sufficient depth of river water accommodated, or conserved, many of the Tyne's natural functions quite comfortably. Secondly, between 1850 and 1968, the TIC interpreted their role as river conservators in terms of enhancing as quickly as possible the river's navigability, industrial productivity and export capacity. Thirdly, and probably neither finally nor forever, today's environmentally sensitive Tyne Rivers Trust, Environment Agency, Northumbrian Water Ltd, Clean Tyne Project, Port of Tyne and riparian councils perceive the conservation of the river ultimately as a moral and ecological responsibility to protect the cleanliness of the river water and the plants and wildlife which inhabit it from human activities perceived as harmful and from non-native, invasive species which could threaten their survival and sustainability. Analysing long-term attitudinal changes, divergent perceived meanings of conservation and the very different motivating forces that have contributed to various conceptualisations of how to engage with the river enables us to appreciate the vulnerability and provisionality, and the potentially short-term survival, of our own understanding of how we should engage with the Tyne.

The River Tyne catchment covers approximately 2,936 square kilometres (1,134 square miles) of north-east England and the main Tyne, North Tyne and South Tyne measure 321 kilometres (199 miles) in length, excluding their many tributaries. The tidal estuary flows to and from Wylam, some 32 km (twenty miles) from the North Sea, between the large population centres of Newcastle on its north bank and Gateshead on its southern bank, 13 km (eight miles) from the sea, and between North and South Shields at the river mouth. The Tyne is quite a speedy river, with an average speed of 45 cubic metres per second. In December 2015, the aftermath of Storm Desmond enabled the Tyne to flow at an even faster rate of 1,700 cubic metres per second, which has only been beaten once since records began, during the Great Flood of 1771, which washed away several stone bridges including the old Tyne Bridge.[6] The North Tyne and the South Tyne, which meet to form the main Tyne at Warden Rock near the villages of Fourstones and Warden, two miles from the market town of Hexham in Northumberland, drain relatively sparsely populated areas. The North Tyne drains primarily Northumbrian moors and the South Tyne drains the North Pennines, the second largest of the forty Areas of Outstanding Natural Beauty in England and Wales. Some forty miles from their respective sources

---

6. H. Graham, 'Winter Storms leave River Tyne flowing at Record-Breaking Rates', *Chronicle Live* (15 Jan. 2016).

Introduction

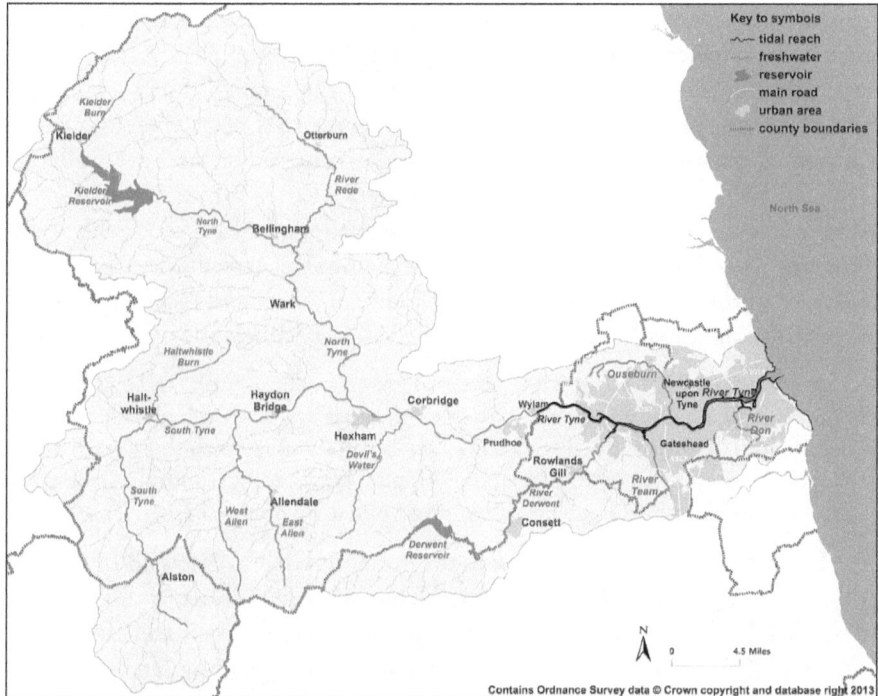

Figure 1. Map of the Tyne catchment Area to show places referred to in the text.
I am very grateful to Tyne Rivers Trust for the map of the Tyne catchment on which this is based.

and thirty miles from the sea, the spectacular confluence and the beginning of the main River Tyne, known locally as the Meeting of the Waters or Waters Meet, is a must-see site for anyone trying to understand the river, its character, its flow and its wildlife. The North Tyne flows south-east from Deadwater Fell near Kielder, Northumberland, and the Anglo-Scottish border. The South Tyne makes its way north from near Alston, high in the North Pennines, before turning sharply east towards Hexham. The confluence between the two main tributaries is a breath-taking natural compromise between the respective bodies of water, each possessing a different speed, colour and character of flow. Warden Rock is a popular beauty spot for many people living throughout the Tyne catchment (competing with equally popular sites such as the Collingwood Monument at Tynemouth and the regenerated Newcastle-Gateshead quayside) and it is easy to see why when you visit the site in person. Its relative isolation from roads, housing and other human distractions enables visitors to appreciate the soundscape of the waters' communications as eddies crash together and the waters make their journey henceforth in unison to the North Sea. It is from here that Tyne salmon head up either the North Tyne or the South Tyne in a purposeful manner to spawn and then die on the precise gravel beds where they once hatched. It is a popular place for anglers, and private rod licences are available.

In 1859, a librarian of the Royal Society, Walter White, visited Waters Meet on his tour of Northumberland as he walked from Alston along the South Tyne and then along the main Tyne to Tynemouth. After having 'to cross a few acres of turnips to get to the point where the South and North Tyne meet together in one broad stream', he described Warden Rock as

> A wild spot; a rough sandy bank, where coarse grass, gorse, thrift, and harebells intermingle at pleasure with scrubby alders, fronted by a sandy shingly slope, the dry margin of the river-bed not unlike a sea-beach. Looking at the long reach of North Tyne, you see a vista of sparkling ripples, bordered by woods that clothe the base of Warden Hill, on one side, and an obtrusive brick yard on the other.[7]

The brickyard has been demolished, but much of what White said in 1859 is still directly relevant to the scene today. The arable fields next to the Meeting of the Waters, around the villages of Fourstones and Warden, contribute to a view which many would perceive as an aesthetically pleasing landscape, but they produce cereals which cannot be sold for human consumption because harmful minerals such as lead, cadmium and zinc, which were flushed into the river during historically extensive metal mining in the South Tyne valley, are continually emitted from the river bed of the South Tyne into the river water and thence into the soil of the adjacent fields, literally poisoning the crops.

Tyne after Tyne emphasises that the Tyne, and the tributaries that have nourished its flow, has forged connections naturally between innumerable particular places, people, wildlife, activities and economies, for better or worse. In this respect, the Tyne is in fact a true historical agent of change and experience. This book is not an attempt to track rises and falls in the numbers and species of wildlife and plants. Nor is it designed to describe accurately and in minute detail the admittedly dramatic and important chemical changes that have occurred in its water. This is not a traditional historical geography of the Tyne river basin and it does not focus exclusively on the origins of modern nature conservation in the catchment, though this is not to say that these foci are not valuable to environmental history. This work stands on the shoulders of environmental historians, such as Christopher Smout, who have made significant

---

7. W. White, *Northumberland and the Border* (London, 1859), p. 41 (ch. 6).

Introduction

Figure 2. The Meeting of the Waters at Warden Rock, Northumberland (Photograph: Gordon Ball).

progress in deepening our understanding of natural history, the rise and fall of particular plant and wildlife species and the birth of modern environmentalism and conservation in northern England and Scotland.[8] This study is a history of the socio-environmental entanglements and the direct interactions between humans and one river system over five centuries. For its analytical framework, the leading lights and the parameters used to guide the development of this particular interpretation of the Tyne's fascinating story, the book draws heavily from Richard White's crystal clear and inspiring analogy,

> I mean to do more than write a human history alongside a natural history and call it environmental history. This would be like writing a biography of a wife,

---

8. C. Smout, *Nature Contested: Environmental History in Scotland and Northern England since 1600* (Edinburgh: Edinburgh University Press, 2000); S. Foster and C. Smout, (eds.), *The History of Soils and Field Systems* (Aberdeen: Scottish Cultural Press, 1994); C. Smout, *Scottish Woodland History* (Dalkeith: Scottish Cultural Press, 1997).

placing it alongside the biography of a husband and calling it the history of a marriage. I want the history of the relationship itself.[9]

Similarly, this study is indebted to Dale Porter's conceptualisation of the construction of the Thames Embankment in the nineteenth century, his observation that 'the environment, too, must be treated both as a relatively autonomous source of conditions and forces acting upon society and its physical surroundings, and as a product of sustained human intervention guided by historically circumscribed concepts'.[10] Porter encourages us to remember that human ways of perceiving and interacting with the environment 'are always mediated by intellectual, religious, political, economic, class and gendered filters'.[11] At the micro-scale, this book tells intimate stories about the relationships established, maintained and then discontinued between: Tynesiders and the Tyne, tourists and the Tyne, scientists and the Tyne, environmental inspectors and the Tyne, shipbuilders and the Tyne, salmon and the Tyne, kittiwakes and the Tyne, musicians and play-writers and the Tyne, local and national governors and the Tyne and between environmental charities, regulatory organisations and recreational groups and the Tyne. In each of these relationships, the two-way nature of interactions between all these historical agents and the Tyne itself is emphasised. Thereby, the river is the hub of all of these interactions.

The Tyne is interpreted as an independent force as much as possible, in the same way that Roger Deakin appreciated the independent flow of the Windrush, a tributary of the River Thames, as an active and independent character:

> All down this valley, the river snaked joyfully, unconstrained by anyone who might have thought they could put it straight on its exuberant, doodling course to join the Thames. It went its own way, like Shakespeare's dawdling schoolboy on his way to school. Like all running water, it wanted to turn everything into the image of its constantly undulating form. It worried at the river banks, hollowing them, rounding them into oxbows. If you made a very slow-motion stop-frame aerial film of a river's history, it would look like a swimming snake, or a writhing garden hose when water is run through it. Left to itself, a river will always meander.[12]

---

9. White, *The Organic Machine*, p. x.
10. D. Porter, *The Thames Embankment: Environment, Society and Technology in Victorian London* (Akron: The University of Akron Press, 1998), p. 10.
11. Porter, *Thames Embankment*, p. 11.
12. R. Deakin, *Waterlog: A Swimmer's Journey through Britain* (London: Vintage, 2000), p. 256.

Introduction

In a similar vein, though from a rather more pessimistic perspective of lament for a river's lost freedom, Charles Rangeley-Wilson tracked the Buckinghamshire River Wye, another tributary of the Thames, at Holywell Mead:

> I waded through the ephemeral flow [between culverted sections], this reminder of a long-buried life, around the northbound turn of the roundabout by the library and along the southern gutter of the A40 past Sainsbury's, over the underground confluence of the Hughenden stream and on past Bridge Street … until I reached the Venus de Milo willow where a foaming torrent plunged angrily into its subterranean coffin. … I don't know how long I stood rooted to that place feeling the dispossessed soul of the river surge through me, … what it must be like to have no recourse, to break out in ways you might hardly comprehend, let alone control … as the rain beat down and the river boiled and foamed at the gateway to its prison.[13]

While the study does not go so far as to personify the Tyne, it constantly emphasises its agency and its power to shape the course of history at both the micro and the macro level. At the macro level of historical development, this volume tracks and analyses the development in chronological succession, but with some substantial overlaps, of several new and different ways of conceptualising the Tyne and of using it and allowing it to influence society according to very particular attitudes and values.

As the book's title suggests, one new and different Tyne was created after another, after another, but it is important to emphasise the historically important ways in which the Tyne actively influenced the shape and direction of its own historical development. The Tyne, it is argued, shaped history just as much as, if not more than, those who sought to regulate and use the river in new and different ways for their own purposes. Throughout what we might perceive as a very long-term period of five centuries in human history – no more than a blink of an eye in the context of the Tyne's prehistoric origins – this powerful water force continued to shape its own historical pathways and to express itself in indomitable ways. It utilised its own flood plains, deployed its powerful flow to damage and undermine edifices projecting into its channel, moved debris downstream, altered its course, mitigated human engineers' efforts to alter its course and eroded the soil of some river banks to create erosion cliffs while depositing its sediment to enlarge others. Continuously over this period, from 1529 right through to the present, people organised themselves into successive and overlapping institutions that tried to conserve the river carefully, to

---

13. C. Rangeley-Wilson, *Silt Road: The Story of a Lost River* (London: Vintage, 2014), p. 195.

protect it from various historically specific definitions of 'harm' and to work with, instead of trying to control, its natural functions. The marked differences between their perspectives and priorities and those of the river's very different official conservators and managers defined the parameters within which people engaged with the river, added particles to its water, changed its course, altered the speed of its flow and intervened in its natural processes. In line with widely held misconceptions about other industrial rivers, many believe that the Tyne was used and abused maximally, and without any environmental regulation whatsoever – as a vast waste-disposal receptacle, as a source of fluvial power, as a liquid highway and as a supplier of resources such as fish and gravel – until the very recent rise of modern conservation in the 1960s. This book argues that, although environmental concern for the River Tyne has been expressed in different ways, in different historical contexts and as a result of very different motivations, it has nevertheless been constantly present to variable degrees throughout the entire period under discussion. Even during the reign of the TIC, for example, the Tyne Salmon Conservancy acted to protect the Tyne's fisheries.

Any of the new and different Tynes discussed in this study could have filled books in their own right, as could any of the book's themes such as sanitation, fish, recreation or industry. The wide scope of the book has necessitated some inevitable summarisation, but it is hoped that the broad bird's eye view of changing relationships with the Tyne over such a lengthy chronology, over the whole catchment and reconnecting all the various sub-themes together will produce the first total environmental history of the Tyne, perhaps inspiring others to produce more detailed case studies of particular themes or of shorter chronologies or geographical areas within the catchment, filling in some of the inevitable gaps of this overarching study. It is only by observing changing attitudes towards the environment over centuries, rather than decades, that we can see how transient our own relationship with the river might be in the long-term future. While very long-term river histories are rare, Stuart Oliver's ambitious article-length study of the use of the River Thames to power water mills from the eighth to the nineteenth century demonstrates the value of using such a chronology.[14] By analysing long-term changes in the uses of and engagement with the Thames, Oliver revealed that riverscapes have 'liquid materiality', which he defines as 'a mix of solidity and fluidity that is constructed and defined in contingent and (above all) local ways'.[15] This is also true of the Tyne. Stepping back to survey

---

14. S. Oliver, 'Liquid Materialities in the Landscape of the Thames: Mills and Weirs from the eighth to the nineteenth century', *Area* 45 (2) (2013): 223–229.

15. Ibid., p. 223.

Introduction

socio-environmental entanglement with one natural system over a relatively long chronology enables us to appreciate each phase of the river's history as equally narrow, equally vulnerable to being swept away and supplanted by a different framework and equally open to interpretation as morally or ethically right or wrong, progressive or wasteful, by particular human societies, and by different groups of people within those respective societies. Just as Victorian Tyneside harboured people who believed wholeheartedly in prioritising the health of the Tyne fisheries, so too does today's Tyneside incorporate those who believe in prioritising the development of an economically productive river, supporting fully employed humans above an ecologically healthy river within which wildlife and plant species flourish to their full potential. What will the Tynesiders of 2315 think of our prioritisation of salmon, recreation and oxygenated river water? What will their conceptualisation and use of the river look like? How long will our particular conceptualisation of the river survive and what might replace it? Could the Tyne Improvement Commissioners of the 1880s have envisaged the Newcastle-Gateshead quayside of today, where tourists take river cruises amid restaurants and pubs, an art gallery and a music hall as salmon leap under the bridges? And how would we react to the view from the Tyne Bridge in 2315? How would it make us feel? In essence, this book is an imaginative attempt to reconnect the severed ties across time and space linking those who have engaged directly with the Tyne over half a millennium.

This is, of course, impossible, but let us join an imaginary live debate about how to engage with the Tyne, about its meaning and the parameters of reasonable environmental regulation. Let us seat at that table today the character of the Tyne itself, some of its salmon, some seventeenth-century Tyne River Court Jurors, some nineteenth-century Tyne Improvement Commissioners, a 1920s biologist who tested the river's water for the Standing Committee on River Pollution, a mid-twentieth-century Tyne angler, shipbuilder and council planner and some twenty-first-century Tyne Rivers Trust Riverwatch volunteers, representatives of the Environment Agency and Northumbrian Water Ltd and a few tourists who happened to be visiting Newcastle-Gateshead quayside, or any other such diverse combinations of people and non-human agents who have engaged with the river. What would they disagree about, and would they agree on anything at all? Would it be an intense or a constructive debate and would it be possible for each of those historical agents to convey accurately their particular relationship with the river, the meaning it holds for them and their conceptualisation of what the river is for and how it should be used and regulated by human society? What would be the consequences of such a debate for the river? This book's primary aim is to construct a series of such debates virtually, anatomising discord and accord in relation to a plethora of Tyne issues, in order to revive, reconnect and reinvigorate the severed bonds and flows linking particular riparian places, issues and people across five centuries.

Figure 3. North Tyne Source Marker, Deadwater Fell, near Anglo-Scottish Border (Photograph: Gordon Ball)

River Historiography

Over the last two centuries, a profusion of books has been published on the River Tyne. Much of this writing is heavily narrative and focuses on the Tyne's dramatic transformation from a natural river to an increasingly unnatural, engineered and economically efficient river. It tends to focus on the river's lower, urban and tidal reaches, which hosted the bulk of riparian heavy industry and export trade infrastructure and activity. It is far too voluminous to cite in full here, though a representative selection has been footnoted chronologically below to give an impression of its content.[16] This literature generally celebrates

---

16. W. Armstrong, *Observations on the Improvement of the Navigation of the Tyne* (1836); M. Richardson, (ed.), *The Conservatorship of the River Tyne* (Newcastle, 1849); P. Dodd, *The Salmon of the Tyne and of the Dams* (1856); J. Palmer, *The Tyne and its Tributaries* (London, 1882); A. Watson, *The Tyne* (1889); R. Johnson, *The Making of the Tyne: A Record of Fifty*

Introduction

economic, mercantile and transportation history, and to a lesser degree historical geography, though there are a few examples which are especially relevant to the Tyne's environmental story, such as Michael Marshall's *Tyne Waters: A River and its Salmon* (1992) and R. Rennison's *Water to Tyneside: A History of the Newcastle and Gateshead Water Company* (1979).[17] The shape of the existing literature means that we know more about the shipyards and Tyne valley industries than we do about the river itself (its water, channel, bed and course). Two relatively recent accounts by David Archer, a local resident and water engineer – one about the rivers of Northumberland as a whole, *Land of Singing Waters: Rivers and Great Floods of Northumbria* (1992) and *Tyne and Tide: A Celebration of the River Tyne* (2003) – though extremely well informed and presenting an impressive breadth of detailed academic case studies of important themes, do not constitute environmental history. Peter Wright's recently published *Life on the Tyne* (2014) is yet another example of a book featuring the name of a river in its title whose focus is not the natural functions of the river itself, but rather

---

Years' Progress, with numerous views and portraits of those concerned in the development of the river (1895); W. Campbell, *A Century of Chemistry on Tyneside, 1868–1968* (Newcastle, 1968); F. Graham, *Bellingham and the North Tyne* (Newcastle: F. Graham, 1972); K. Groundwater, *Maritime Heritage: Newcastle and the River Tyne* (Newcastle: Silverlink Publishing, 1990); T. Rowland, *Waters of Tyne* (Warkworth: Sandhill Publishing, 1991); Anon., *The Mid-Tyne Villages of Northumberland: a History in Photographs of Ovingham, Ovington, Stocksfield* (Morpeth: Northumberland County Library, 1993); P. Dillon, *The Tyne Oarsmen: Harry Clasper, Robert Chambers, James Renforth* (Jesmond: Keepdate Publishing, 1993); T. Rowland and J. Thompson, *Waters of Tyne: A River Journey through History* (Warkworth: Sandhill Publishing, 1994); M. Marshall, *Turning Tides: a History of the Tyne and the Wear* (1997); H. Blakey, *Newcastle Potters and the Export of Earthenware from Newcastle on Tyne 1739 to 1796* (Stoke on Trent, 2001); J. Jonas, *Walking the Tyne: Twenty-five walks from mouth to source* (Newcastle: Ramblers' Association, 2001); I. Rae and K. Smith, *Swan Hunter: The Pride and the Tears* (Newcastle: Tyne Bridge Publishing, 2001); F. Manders and R. Potts, *Crossing the Tyne* (Newcastle: Tyne Bridge Publishing, 2001); R. Thornton, *The River Tyne from Sea to Source* (Newcastle: Zymurgy Press, 2002); R. French and K. Smith, *Lost Shipyards of the Tyne* (Newcastle: Tyne Bridge Publishing, 2004); R. Keys and K. Smith, *Tall Ships on the Tyne* (Newcastle: Tyne Bridge Publishing, 2005); V. Histon, *Unlocking the Quayside: Newcastle Gateshead's Historic Waterfront Explored* (Newcastle: Tyne Bridge Publishing, 2006); D. Keys and K. Smith, *Tales from the Tyne* (Newcastle: Tyne Bridge Publishing, 2006); H. Dobson, *Exploring the Tyne Valley* (Morpeth: Henry Dobson, 2007); K. Smith, *Queens of the Tyne: The River's Great Liners, 1888–1973* (Newcastle: Tyne Bridge Publishing, 2007); J. Shotton, *First, Famous and Forgotten Ships of the Tyne* (Newcastle, 2012); K. Smith and T. Yellowley, *The Story of the Tyne: and the Hidden Rivers of Newcastle* (Newcastle: Tyne Bridge Publishing, 2015).

17. M. Marshall, *Tyne Waters: A River and its Salmon* (London: H. and G. Witherby, 1992); R. Rennison, *Water to Tyneside: A History of the Newcastle & Gateshead Water Company* (Newcastle: Northumberland Press, 1979).

the social and economic activities played out on its banks and water, such as shipbuilding, coal export and other water trades, during the seventeenth and eighteenth centuries.[18] While Wright pays some attention to the variable depth of the estuary due to the tides, and the angular nature of the river's course, this is primarily a history of social and economic change in which the Tyne provides a geographical focus and crucially underpins the functioning of water trades but is nevertheless described as an object of human endeavour, certainly not as a true historical agent capable of expressing itself. The river flows through every chapter of *Life on the Tyne* effectively as a backdrop, albeit an essential one, to the bustling early modern city and port of Newcastle and all those who lived and worked there.[19] Yet, astonishingly, Wright has neglected to utilise any of the minute books of the Tyne River Court, extant from 1644 to 1834, which contain very detailed information about the regulation of interactions with the river water, bed, channel and course.[20]

Pioneering a new sub-field of Tyne literature, this study aims to reintegrate foreground and hinterland rivers, accomplishing this from the fully-fledged and fully self-conscious perspective of environmental history, which approaches the relationship between humans and the rest of the natural world as an interactive and symbiotic dialogue rather than in terms of one-directional impacts. This book connects what we have done to the river with what the river has done to us, and tells the dramatic and exciting story of that interaction over five centuries. Placing the river at its heart, it explores interactions between the Tyne and the humans and wildlife that have utilised its fluvial power and resources across its catchment area over the course of half a millennium. This study departs from both the previously dominant narratives of environmental change: the progressive narrative that equated change with improvement, and the declensionist narrative that equated change with loss and destruction. Moving purposely away from morally loaded notions of better or worse, and even dead, rivers, this book refocuses on the production of new and different rivers and fully situates this history of fluvial transformations within its political, economic, cultural, social and intellectual contexts. The book contributes to and underlines important insights derived from Richard White's study of the Columbia River in the US, as an 'organic machine', and Sara Pritchard's

---

18. P. Wright, *Life on the Tyne: Water Trades on the Lower River Tyne in the Seventeenth and Eighteenth Centuries, a Reappraisal* (Farnham: Ashgate, 2014).

19. Ibid.

20. Tyne and Wear Archives [hereafter, TWA], BC.RV/1/1–9: Tyne River Court Minute Books, 1644–1834.

Introduction

socio-technical analysis of the French River Rhone.[21] Both White and Pritchard argue that a river is also an energy system with agency, independent expressions and reactions and with the capacity to perform work. The Tyne, too, has demonstrated, and will continue to demonstrate, its power to thwart our ambitions as well as to nurture our economic, social and cultural lives. These sorts of connections between human and non-human sources of power and energy have been little studied in British environmental history.

The traditional interpretation of the late nineteenth-century relationship between the UK's largest industrial cities and London is typically expressed in the words of Stephen Daniels: 'with the evident loss of their [provincial industrial cities'] industrial power and cultural independence, and the ascendency of London as a self-consciously financial, imperial and regal capital, so they were reduced to provinces of a metropolitan core'.[22] This view unjustly marginalises the huge, national and strategic industrial, political and economic importance of several industrial cities, including Newcastle, Liverpool and Glasgow, well into the twentieth century. Despite their continuing national and international importance, John Sheail's ambitiously wide overview of Britain's twentieth-century environmental history features some fourteen pages which discuss the River Thames and only three that mention the River Tyne; astonishingly, the Clyde, Mersey, Wear, Severn and Humber are not mentioned at all.[23] Jonathan Schneer's observation that the Thames 'has been central to English life and therefore to British history' is of course indisputable, but several other British rivers also played similarly 'central' roles.[24] Several great northern British rivers, notably the Mersey, the Clyde, the Tyne and the Humber, which played very significant roles in Britain's industrialisation and arguably in that of the British Empire too, have been unhelpfully overshadowed by a profusion of histories of the River Thames. Insofar as it exists, British river history is very

---

21. White, *Organic Machine*; S. Pritchard, *Confluence: The Nature of Technology and the Remaking of the Rhone* (London: Harvard University Press, 2011).
22. S. Daniels, *Fields of Vision: Landscape Imagery and National Identity in England the United States* (Cambridge: Polity Press, 1994), p. 29. Daniels is currently researching the River Trent and, since 1994, has gone on to conduct further wide-ranging research on landscape and environment in relation to far broader UK geographies beyond London, including Northampton and Nottingham.
23. J. Sheail, *An Environmental History of Twentieth-Century Britain* (Basingstoke: Palgrave, 2002), see index.
24. J. Schneer, *The Thames: England's River* (London: Abacus, 2005), p. 289.

Thames-centric. The Thames dominates studies of river pollution.[25] It dominates studies of river channelisation.[26] And it enjoys a near-monopoly over studies of UK rivers from a socio-cultural standpoint.[27] Even in relation to pollution and evolving environmental attitudes, the Thames is the river of choice. For example, in Lawrence Breeze's *The British Experience with River Pollution, 1865–1876* (1993) – an account of the two mid-Victorian Royal Commissions (1865–68 and 1868–74) that investigated the problem of river pollution from industrial and urban sources, generated nine lengthy reports and led to the Rivers Pollution Prevention Act of 1876 that remained on the books until 1951 – the Thames receives a chapter and the Tyne one passing mention.[28] Yet, even as early as in 1651, William Ellis proudly emphasised the large scale and consequently national importance of Newcastle's coal exports by comparing it to Peru: 'England's a perfect world! Has Indies too! / Correct your maps: Newcastle is Peru'.[29] In-depth histories of other major British rivers, written from a deeply environmental perspective, are urgently needed if we are to move beyond the false, but widely perceived, primacy of Old Father Thames. The particular historical development of socio-environmental entanglements between people and the River Thames, the river's bio-physical flows, the environmental regulation which liberated and limited those flows and the cultural meanings of the river nurtured by the people who have engaged with it over the course of their lives create an important case study of the Thames in its own right. As a case study, the Thames can and should be used to inform wider British and international histories. However, a whole series of environmental histories of northern British rivers need urgently to be written to ensure that the Thames' very particular story is not allowed to flow through British environmental river history like the words running through a stick of seaside rock.

Taking the lead, in 2012, Christopher Smout and Mairi Stewart created an environmental history of Scotland's and Edinburgh's River Forth, the first truly environmental British river history.[30] Unusually, it discusses environmental

---

25. B. Luckin, *Pollution and Control: A Social History of the Thames in the Nineteenth Century* (Boca Raton, Florida, USA: CRC Press, 1986).
26. Porter, *Thames Embankment*.
27. P. Ackroyd, *Thames: Sacred River* (London: Vintage, 2008).
28. L. Breeze, *The British Experience with River Pollution, 1865–1876* (New York: Peter Lang, 1993).
29. W. Ellis, *News from Newcastle* (London, 1651).
30. C. Smout and M. Stewart, *The Firth of Forth: An Environmental History* (Edinburgh: Birlinn, 2012).

Introduction

regulation in the early modern period in significant depth, in two of eleven chapters. Indeed, its effective use of such an expansive chronology right up to the modern day inspired the long-term chronology of this book. Smout and Stewart compare and contrast the environmental impact of hunter gathering communities, of pre-modern industrialisation and of the heavy industrialisation of the nineteenth and twentieth centuries to track the 'lives and fortunes of many sensate and insensate beings other than ourselves'.[31] They convey very effectively the 'many aspects and many twists' of the changing political and legal ecological parameters within which the river has interacted with the humans, wildlife and plant species seeking to use its resources, inhabit its water and banks or to utilise the energy of its flow.[32] Its key strength is the inclusion of animals and plants as historical agents equally as important as the humans which also shaped the river's ecological story.[33] By emphasising the long-term historical development of progressive attitudes towards, stringent environmental regulation of and considered engagement with the River Forth, 'the great gaping mouth of Scotland', they lead the way towards an urgently needed much longer-term, certainly pre-1800, appreciation of two-way socio-environmental interactions and their intended and unintended consequences, the winners and the losers, within environmental history more generally.[34]

Also helping to counterbalance the relative domination of the River Thames in British river histories, Peter Coates' *Story of Six Rivers* includes yet another great northern river, the Mersey.[35] Coates attributes Liverpool's rise to become a world city primarily to the River Mersey, even comparing the relationship to that of Alexandria and the Nile.[36] However, he makes an important point about the crucial role of technology in transforming great rivers to create great riparian cities, noting 'many great cities rely for their greatness on great rivers, yet great rivers do not automatically make great cities'.[37] In many respects the inextricably linked histories of Liverpool and the Mersey share a great deal with the similarly inseparable histories of Newcastle and the River Tyne. It is hoped that by emphasising the enormous impact of rivers' environmental stories on the development of great British cities, more urban historians of river cities might

---

31. Ibid., p. 8.
32. Ibid., p. 277.
33. Ibid.
34. Ibid., p. 1.
35. P. Coates, *A Story of Six Rivers: History, Culture and Ecology* (London: Reaktion, 2013).
36. Ibid., pp. 161, 162.
37. Ibid.

be encouraged to join the cause. Perhaps urban historians could progress our understanding from an environmental perspective of how humans interacted with, used, abused, polluted, harnessed, engineered, damaged, protected and conserved rivers. Perhaps their expertise in relation to particular cities' historical developments could helpfully shed light on how the rivers running through them expressed themselves in response to human actions within very different political, legal, cultural and economic parameters. Coates' exploration of several new and different River Merseys (Mastered Mersey, Manufacturing Mersey, Mucky Mersey and Mercy on the Mersey) creates a framework that enables us to appreciate both the positive and the negative, the intended and unintended, characteristics, opportunities and challenges that defined the river in very distinct phases of its environmental story. By presenting the Mersey's history alongside five other rivers from around the globe (the Danube, Spree, Po, Yukon and Los Angeles River), Coates encourages us to use case studies of particular rivers, like this one of the River Tyne, to deepen our understanding of important differences, similarities and global patterns in the 'dynamic and reciprocal' relationships between rivers, people and human affairs.[38]

Leslie Rosenthal focused in depth on ten nineteenth-century legal nuisance disputes involving pollution into English rivers, including large industrial centres such as Birmingham, Leeds and Wolverhampton and much smaller places such as Tunbridge Wells and Harrogate. She used these legal cases to get to the heart of the very difficult decision-making process of providing adequate sanitation for rapidly expanding cities and smaller communities while simultaneously protecting the rights of private landowners and providing an acceptable standard of cleanliness and health in rivers and fisheries.[39] Rosenthal explains the very complex and often counter-productive administrative, legal, governmental and demographic frameworks in which these legal conflicts played out. And she highlights the similarly complex physical landscapes and riverscapes into which rapidly changing types of waste were discharged. Rosenthal explains how and why not one of the ten cases led to a sewer outlet being physically blocked from discharging into a river. *Tyne after Tyne* explains why the TIC sanctioned nearly all of the applications they received to construct new sewers through which to drain increasingly more untreated industrial and domestic waste directly into the Tyne estuary. As a detailed case study of one institution's attitudes towards sewage-disposal into one river estuary over 118 years,

---

38. Ibid., p. 162.
39. L. Rosenthal, *The River Pollution Dilemma in Victorian England: Nuisance Law Versus Economic Efficiency* (Farnham: Ashgate, 2014).

Introduction

it complements Rosenthal's deep study of several legal disputes in different locations. Rosenthal's work has a great deal to offer environmental historians of rivers, environmental regulation and urban settlements, as it provides a fully contextualised and detailed lens through which to deepen our understanding of the problematic and direct interactions between humans, their waste and rivers in a particularly challenging era of very rapid change.

Socio-cultural and economic histories of rivers have tended to reduce these powerful natural systems to little more than stages or backdrops on which or against which human histories have been played out. Very few of them pay attention to rivers' natural functions such as tides; their independent agency to use their flood plains or to divert their courses; or their integral and very long-established contributions to wider ecosystems, landscape and hydrological cycles. Schneer's focus on superficial events on, over or next to the Thames, such as King John signing the Magna Carta at Runnymede on the Thames in 1215 or the use of the river as a navigational aid by enemy German pilots in 1940, demonstrates that he has missed the point in terms of understanding how people have engaged directly with rivers and how rivers have engaged with people. His comment that 'great events have taken place on, or near, or above the river' fails to progress our understanding of the intimate, powerful and deep entanglements with the river's flows, power and wonder over time.[40] By reimagining the Tyne as an agent of history, as an important character no less worthy of deep biographical analysis than any military or political leader, we can release it from being studied as yet another object of human agency, or as a backdrop to human history, and instead understand the enormous role it played in an innumerable cast of people's, plants' and animals' lives. In a two-way process, the river interacted with many different local and national governors, various organisations of official conservators charged with managing and protecting its natural functions, the multitudes of people whose livelihoods depended directly on its flow and resources and the wildlife and plant species inhabiting the river's water and banks. The Tyne also interacted with the people who have drawn artistic inspiration from it and the informal groups which fought to protect the river water, channel, bed and course from a wide range of historically specific definitions of 'harm'.

This Tyne study, alongside Smout and Stewart's *Firth of Forth*, can serve as a template for a body of work on British rivers that shakes off the straitjacket of the Thames as well as traditional socio-cultural approaches to river history. There are many British rivers, including the Clyde, Humber, Severn, Tees,

---

40. Schneer, *The Thames*, pp. 288–289.

Wear, Lagan, Don, Tay, Dee and many more, whose exciting and historically important environmental stories are yet to be revealed. These rivers' stories should be fully integrated with those of the humans, animals and plants in which they have played such an integral role. They all need to be analysed in depth and installed into the global grid of environmental river historiography to identify important synergies, distinctions and common drivers for change before, during and after industrialisation. Globally, many environmental river histories have pushed the boundaries much further towards understanding the interactions between human society and rivers, encouraging us to think about these interactions in new and different ways, but these important and pioneering studies have been unable to engage directly with British case studies due to the lack of progress in the field of environmental British river history.[41]

As early as in 1995, Richard White contributed his conceptually pioneering *The Organic Machine: The Remaking of the Columbia River*, which foregrounded the overlaps between the human and the natural, emphasising that although humans have altered natural systems and resources substantially, nevertheless 'there is no easy way to disentangle the natural and the cultural' on the Columbia.[42] He suggested 'nature still exists … only altered by our labor', manifest in 'the steam with Emerson's boiler' and 'hidden in aluminium factories and pulp

---

41. There are also many article-length environmental history case studies of rivers from around the globe, including: D. Gilvear and S. Winterbottom, 'Changes in Channel Morphology, Floodplain Land use and Flood Damage on the Rivers Tay and Tummell over the last 250 years: Implications for Floodplain Management', in R. Bailey, P. Jose and B. Sherwood (eds), *United Kingdom Floodplains* (London: Westbury, 1998), pp. 92–115; D. Stradling and R. Stradling, 'Perceptions of the Burning River: Deindustrialization and Cleveland's Cuyahoga River', *Environmental History* **13** (3) (July 2008): 515–535; V. Taylor, 'Local History and the Environmental History of the River Thames, 1960–2010', *Transactions of the London and Middlesex Archaeological Society* **64** (2014): 79–92; V. Taylor, 'Whose River?: London and the Thames Estuary, 1960–2014', *London Journal* **40** (3) (2015): 244–271; W. Taylor, 'Misplaced Identities: Cultural and Environmental Sources of Heritage for the 'Settler Society' along the Swan River, Perth, Australia', *National Identities* **9** (2) (2007): 143–161. See also the publications of the Australian Parklands, Culture and Communities Project, which has undertaken some very detailed research into the crucial role played by socio-environmental interactions with the Georges River in the process of migrant communities' assimilation into Australian life: H. Goodall, D. Byrne and A. Cadzoe with S. Wearing, *Waters of Belonging: Arabic Australians and the Georges River Parklands* (Sydney: UTS ePress, 2012); A. Cadzow, D. Byrne and H. Goodall with S. Wearing, *Waterborne: Vietnamese Australians and Sydney's Georges River Parks and Green Spaces* (Sydney: UTS ePress, 2011).

42. White, *Organic Machine*, pp. xi, 111.

Introduction

mills'.[43] Christian Schwagerl's remarkably similar observation in his recent *The Anthropocene* (2014), that 'we are not separate from our environment ... each time we reach for our Smartphones, we are holding to our ear an assortment of rare metals that have come from dozens of different mines around the world!', only underlines the strong influence of *The Organic Machine* over the last two decades.[44] White highlighted that, although in previous ages humans had applied art and technology to the river, innovations such as wooden canoes relied on muscle or wind power whereas in the nineteenth century new machines such as steam-powered ships were sufficiently powerful to overcome the river's organic power.[45] Focusing on work and labour, White noted 'labor rather than "conquering" nature involves human beings with the world so thoroughly that they can never be disentangled'.[46] And in relation to the transition from pre-industrial, to industrial, to post-industrial work, explaining the cult of the wilderness and the development of national parks, he noted 'factories and cities took humans away from nature; leisure brought them back'.[47]

The influence on environmental attitudes of the transition from industrial to post-industrial work was investigated further in 2006 by Gregory Summers in his *Consuming Nature*.[48] Summers contrasted the experience of industrial work in paper mills around the Fox River, Wisconsin, USA, when engagement with nature was physically difficult and the river was a place of toil and harshness, against post-industrial office-based work, which involved far less direct engagement with the natural river system, alongside frequent recreational use of the river system as somewhere to relax and play. He argued that, by the post-industrial period, the lake had become somewhere of beauty, of fun and of physical comfort.[49] Summers makes a very important point that, without the development of consumer society, people would not be able to drive over to a lake in their cars and use sporting equipment such as boats and drysuits to ensure safe recreation on a lake whose beauty and cleanliness they only value

---

43. Ibid., p. 59.
44. C. Schwagerl, *The Anthropocene: The Human Era and How it Shapes our Planet* (London: Synergetic Press, 2014), p. 45.
45. White, *Organic Machine*, p. 31.
46. Ibid., p. 7.
47. Ibid., p. 34.
48. G. Summers, *Consuming Nature: Environmentalism in the Fox River Valley, 1850–1950* (Lawrence, Kansas, USA: University of Kansas Press, 2006).
49. Ibid.

because they play instead of working there.⁵⁰ The use of such equipment and the ability to enjoy such environments, he argues persuasively, is itself a product of the very consumerism which damages nature, against which conservationists protest so vociferously.⁵¹ As chapter eight explains in depth, on the Tyne, too, many recreational uses of the river are widely perceived by many, though not all, as more progressive and more environmentally sensitive than using the river to develop economically productive industries.

Matthew Evenden's work on the Canadian Fraser River in British Columbia, published in 2005, is an important case study, not only because the Fraser is the world's most productive salmon river and the third largest river flowing into the Pacific after the Columbia and the Yukon, but also because, unusually, the main river has remained undammed.⁵² Evenden contributed a remarkably detailed analysis of the impact of human activity on the salmon population, notably the development of the Pacific Railway, the damming of tributaries for Vancouver's electricity needs and the exploitation of the salmon by canneries situated near to the estuary.⁵³ As chapters four and five herein explain, the health of the Tyne salmon fisheries also dominated the intense debate from the 1920s to the 1970s over whether, when and how to clean up the Tyne. Further south in North America, John Anfinson contributed a political history of the Upper Mississippi in the nineteenth and twentieth centuries to explain how and why a conservation movement rose to challenge the dominance of the Corps of Engineers who managed and implemented large-scale engineering 'improvements' to enhance the river as a navigation facility.⁵⁴ From a largely administrative perspective, it tracks and analyses the complex interactions between a very powerful and natural river system and its conceptualisation by many as the key to developing the mid-west's economy to undermine the railroad's aggressive monopoly on transportation.⁵⁵ In particular, *Tyne after Tyne* draws from Anfinson's effective articulation of new and different rivers to evoke important differences between the changing riverscapes, the performance of natural functions and the socio-environmental relationships resulting from

---

50. Ibid.
51. Ibid.
52. M. Evenden, *Fish versus Power: An Environmental History of the Fraser River* (Cambridge: Cambridge University Press, 2004).
53. Ibid.
54. J. Anfinson, *The River We Have Wrought: A History of the Upper Mississippi* (Minneapolis: University of Minnesota Press, 2003).
55. Ibid.

Introduction

different human managers, administrative organisation, governance frameworks, political decisions and conceptualisations of the relationship between regional and national economy. In a very similar vein, Marc Reisner explains the complex political and administrative story of the fierce late nineteenth- and twentieth-century competitive battle between the Corps of Engineers and the Bureau of Reclamation to dam as many rivers as possible in the American West to keep pace with the increasing demand for water fuelled by irrigation farming, population increase and an insatiable desire for hydro-electric power.[56]

Moving back to Europe, Mark Cioc's *The Rhine: An Eco-Biography, 1815–2000* (2002) focuses solely on the modern era, and is organised administratively and politically around successive river managers, but Cioc argues powerfully that such political and administrative changes can have enormous consequences for the river's environmental health, even going as far as to liken the impact of the political changes of 1815 to the environmental changes of the last Ice Age.[57] Cioc focuses on the interactions between humans and the river as a natural system, highlighting, for example, that the vast sums invested into regeneration in more recent decades are 'nothing but reparation payments for two centuries of ecocide'.[58] Similarly, in 2010, Stefania Barca's *Enclosing Water: Nature and Political Economy in a Mediterranean Valley, 1796–1916* revealed the environmental story of Italy's River Liri.[59] Drawing from White's concept of a river as an 'organic machine', Barca notes that nineteenth-century industrialists were 'redefining the river as property, and materially enclosing it in the factory system', so that, she argues, 'they ended up manufacturing floods by the same means with which they were manufacturing woollens and paper sheets', emphasising that 'human history is also the history of the environment'.[60] Barca develops a concept of a 'mountain-and-river system' proto-industry and she describes and explains the complex process by which seventeenth- and eighteenth-century perceptions of the Liri as aesthetically beautiful, forceful and quasi-sublime gradually gave way in the nineteenth-century to a conception of

---

56. M. Reisner, *Cadillac Desert: The American West and its Disappearing Water* (New York: Penguin, 1993).

57. M. Cioc, *The Rhine: An Eco-Biography, 1815–2000* (Seattle, Washington, USA: University of Washington Press, 2002), p. 12.

58. Ibid., p. 5.

59. S. Barca, *Enclosing Water: Nature and Political Economy in a Mediterranean Valley, 1796–1916* (Cambridge: The White Horse Press, 2010).

60. Ibid., pp. 1, 4.

the river as a useful and essential part of an industrial, utilitarian vision.[61] She links this very effectively to the wider European history of the Enlightenment and the Improvement Project.[62]

Sara Pritchard's *Confluence: The Nature of Technology and the Remaking of the Rhône* joined this flourishing field in 2011, and is another work that draws on White's influential concept of an 'organic machine' and his concept that technology is nature and nature is technology.[63] Pritchard provides a very deep and detailed analysis of the enormous role that technological expertise, equipment and infrastructure played in the post-World War Two environmental story of the Rhone, whose technological transformation functioned as a focus for nation building and recovery within a riverine 'envirotechnical landscape'.[64] Pritchard highlights, importantly, how the French people noticed that, while the German state could destroy French bridges, roads, agriculture, towns and cities, it could not destroy the Rhone; thereby the river came to signify an environmental resistance to oppression, a natural symbol of enduring liberty in which the people and the river participated together.[65] The Rhone survived as a useable liquid highway when other forms of transport and connection lay in ruins.[66] This book follows Pritchard's lead in that she purposely and very effectively wrote France's history into that of the Rhone rather than telling the Rhone's story as a counterpart of France's wider national history. *Tyne after Tyne* also adopts Pritchard's metaphor of opening the 'black box' of a river's history in order to conceptualise the Tyne's conservators as pilots of the river, influencing manifold aspects of its water, bed, channel and course and being influenced by them in return.[67] Following Pritchard's template, this book takes us to the heart of how the Tyne's environmental history interacted with, underpinned and sometimes undermined wider regional and British history, in economic, cultural, social and political contexts. I am not merely seeking to extract the parts of north-east England's or the wider UK's history relating directly to the river, and tell those stories in isolation. Rather, I am trying to resurrect the dialogue, the bonds and the interactions that connected the region's and the country's historical development to that of the Tyne, thereby reconnecting

---

61. Ibid., pp. 5, 10.
62. Ibid., pp. 5, 10.
63. Pritchard, *Confluence*, pp. 1, 15.
64. Ibid., pp. 1, 15.
65. Ibid., p. xvi.
66. Ibid., p. xvi.
67. Ibid., pp. 2, 5.

Introduction

the river with the wider historical developments through which it flowed as it shaped and was shaped by that historical development over five centuries.

All these works rightly obfuscate and complicate the artificial boundary that many people draw between the human and the natural. This book stands on all their shoulders as it tries to emulate the best aspects of their methodologies in order to explain the interaction between humans and the River Tyne. It demonstrates the historical significance of the changing styles of these interactions over time, and the long-term impacts of changing political and environmental priorities in local and national government on the Tyne as an industrial river, a port, a liquid highway, a salmon river, an open sewer, a source of energy for mills, a regional icon, a recreational facility, a tourist attraction and a source of regional pride and artistic inspiration. What all environmental river histories demonstrate is that people's particular conceptualisations of a river, and thus the shape of their attempts to manage its natural functions, result from their first-hand physical experiences, through life, work and play. While the Tyne has always been used as a liquid highway throughout the last five centuries, its successive conservators and managers perceived it in markedly different ways, just as they physically used it very differently.

This Tyne study offers a contribution to the relatively new and growing body of environmental river histories by telling the very exciting and dramatic environmental story of one of Britain's truly great northern rivers. Just as Anfinson wanted to clarify 'the history of how the [Mississippi] river came to be in its current state' in order to 'place the debate over the river's future in a fuller context', *Tyne after Tyne* has been written with the intention of objectifying the Tyne's current and future conservators in the eyes of their successors in the long-term future. What will the people who manage the river in 200, 300 or even 500 years' time say, write and think about the actions of the Environment Agency, Northumbrian Water Ltd and Tyne Rivers Trust? By looking back over five centuries, it is hoped, people will be more inclined to look forward into a similarly long-term projection of the Tyne's future to imagine just how differently socio-environmental relationships between people and the River Tyne might be conceptualised then.

Methodology and Description of Chapters

Researching five centuries of one natural system's environmental history has necessitated very deep archival research into numerous regulatory organisations' records. Inevitably, therefore, the study has been shaped heavily by the administrative, political and legal jurisdictions, organisations and regulatory parameters that were designed to limit socio-environmental relationships between people and the Tyne at particular times. However, it is important to remain mindful that most of the extant archives are heavily engendered by the objectives of the employees (and their employers) who produced them. In short, they tend to tow official lines. Moreover, they tend to focus on noteworthy, official events and major changes rather than more prosaic, everyday life experiences and personal, yet deep and important, relationships between Tynesiders and their River Tyne. Some records were written by seventeenth- and eighteenth-century scribes working for the oligarchic Newcastle Corporation; others were written by the successive secretaries of the profit-driven Tyne Improvement Commission (1850–1968); or by those working for the national government's Standing Committee on River Pollution which was appointed to test the river water in the 1920s and 1930s. The minutes of the Tyne Salmon Conservancy (1866–1950), based upriver in Hexham, provide yet another very different perspective, transporting the researcher to a world of anglers who worked hard to install fish passes, to protect the Tyne's fish from pollutants and to restock rivers to ensure the continuance of commercial river fishing and their angling sport. The reports compiled after 1972 by regeneration planners, environmental researchers and local councillors are no less narrow and are similarly biased towards their priorities, their particular conceptualisation of the river and their ideological focus on non-human inhabitants of the riverscape. But in all these important records there is something missing: the gritty, the mundane, the real life experiences that demonstrate how the river's meaning changed as it wove its way through the lives and livelihoods of individuals, communities and the whole Tyneside region. It shaped quotidian experiences from day to day, year to year and decade to decade, as the river underwent unprecedented and dramatic change both environmentally and in terms of how it looked, sounded and smelled to the people who sensed and experienced it directly. This is why oral history interviews were conducted with local people living throughout the Tyne catchment and why, over the course of the research, very fruitful efforts were made to engage as much as possible with the organisations that manage and engage heavily with the river today, including Tyne Rivers Trust, the Clean Tyne Project, the Environment Agency, Newcastle Council, Gateshead Council, the Low Light Heritage Centre, Northumbrian Water Ltd and the Port of Tyne. Much of the research was conducted necessarily in local and national archive holdings, primarily at Northumberland Record Office (near Ashington, Northumberland), Tyne and Wear Archives (Newcastle) and

Introduction

the National Archives in London. However, frequent visits to various riparian places throughout the catchment, and discussions with local people who intimately understand the micro-scale environments in which they live and work, has enabled much deeper understanding in conjunction with the archival records of the very complex relationship between human work, life and play on the one hand and the river's power, agency and natural functions on the other.

Oral history has unique and specific benefits to environmental historians which are yet to be fully appreciated. Environmental history pushes historians, perhaps more so than those working in the other sub-categories of our discipline, to incorporate into our research absolutely every aspect of a particular environment, landscape or natural system. This leads us necessarily to consider all the senses, including sound, smell, taste and touch as well as sight. Unfortunately, the pages of seventeenth-century manuscripts and Victorian committee minute books do not feature scratch and sniff cards, but you can sit down and talk to someone who worked on the Tyne in the 1950s and ask them to describe their sensory experiences of the river, how it made them feel and when, how and why that changed over the course of their lives. Although it is limited to living memory, oral history has an enormous potential to reconstruct past environments, to answer questions that simply cannot be answered as a result of a long stint in the archives. Intimate anecdotes revealed in oral history interviews have illuminated the official histories I have tracked and they have imparted colour into the detailed framework of river legislation; the coming and going of local and national regulatory bodies and other organisations; world wars; and major engineering projects. In short, they bring the river's history to life and provide insightful and very deep meaning to the environmental development of the river. How else could I have learnt about the 'chiming' of hollow 'ice baubles' which hung one morning relatively recently on the overturned tips of grass blades as they swung gently over the water on the river banks between Fourstones and Haydon Bridge on the South Tyne? And how else could I have heard tales of children living in Hebburn on the south bank of the filthy Tyne estuary in the 1950s who called the river their 'playground' and spent entire days building rafts, sailing down the river and shooting at the ubiquitous rats with air rifles? Similarly revealing was a meaningful story from a woman who moved from Dundee in Scotland to North Shields specifically because the Tyne's riverscape reminded her of the Firth of Tay and her native home. The experiences of riparian industrial workers are central to understanding what we have done to the river and what the river has done to us. People who clocked on and off throughout their lives, working innumerable shifts around the river, who physically contributed to the enormous volumes of domestic and industrial waste which poured into the estuary via over 270 sewers. People who in more recent decades were able to use the much cleaner river for leisure, sport and for therapeutic reasons at the most difficult times of their lives. Such people carry very insightful stories in their heads which have not been committed to paper, but which can be recorded, analysed and used to illuminate environmental histories.

Even the process of recording an oral history interview encourages people to access distant memories and to clarify and consolidate their previously vague feelings and thoughts in relation to the river. For example, one interviewee appreciated the interview's capacity to channel her thoughts more explicitly: 'there's always a connection with the river and I didn't realise how deeply until we did this interview'.[68] It has been a wonderfully symbiotic process and very worthwhile in terms of the admittedly large amount of time invested in locating interviewees, organising interviews, finding appropriate locations in which to conduct them and then transcribing and analysing the recordings. The environmental historian cannot travel back in time to experience past landscapes and environments themselves, but she can talk to the people who did experience them and to people who witnessed gradual changes day by day over decades. If the right questions are asked, the interviewee can take the environmental historian to the heart of highly complex issues such as change over time, conflict and meaning as he or she perceived it.

The chapters have been deliberately overlapped chronologically as the different ambitions and perspectives of administrative, political and economic regulators and managers overlapped in reality, when multiple visions for the river clashed along administrative, territorial and cultural lines. While each chapter has a particular theme, some of those themes are administrative in focus (such as chapter three's focus on the TIC and chapter four's focus on the Tyne Salmon Conservancy), while others concern a particular time period (such as chapter one's focus on the early modern period, chapter six's focus on the 1950s and 1960s as the river's toxicity peaked and calls for a clean-up intensified and chapter eight's focus on the post-industrial clean-up era). Others focus on a particular issue (such as chapter two's focus on the long-term development of increasingly impatient calls for investment in making 'improvements' to the river's economic efficiency, chapter five's focus on scientific testing of river water

---

68. Interview with Pauline Stewart, born in Dundee, Scotland, 1968, staff nurse; recorded by Leona Skelton, at the Old Low Light Heritage Centre Café, 22 Jan. 2015, 12.30 pm.

Introduction

and fisheries and chapter seven's focus on the Kielder scheme). The chapters take us to the heart of particular visions for the river, and explain in depth the precise meanings behind particular idioms that were used to explain interactions between the river and humans. In particular, the word 'conservator' was used to convey very different conceptual meanings over the period under discussion, necessitating multiple explanations of the term according to the particular context of the era. Equally, 'river improvement' and 'waste' are also qualified with their historically specific contexts throughout the chapters. While the environmental river histories have been introduced in summary above, other relevant historiography with narrower themes as well as detailed case studies from the environmental river histories discussed above are considered in more depth in connection to the issues of particular chapters.

Chapter one explains the already heavily industrial nature of the pre-modern Tyne which required substantial environmental regulation well before the 1960s, underlining the urgent need for environmental historians to expand their chronologies back to well before 1800 and for many more early modernists to use environmental perspectives to understand their research topics in more depth. It tracks Newcastle Corporation's conservancy across three centuries, revealing the increasingly proactive regulation by the River Tyne Court (1613–1834) of actions which the River Jurors perceived as harmful. This regulation, it is argued, was inextricably linked to the relatively rudimentary technology available, which caused them to become paranoid about the river silting up and therefore to regulate stringently the deposition of solid material which could reduce the depth of their 'liquid highway'. It also explains how the corporation's prioritisation of amassing profits from their monopoly over shipping and ballast tolls led them to avoid strategically investing their income in making structural 'improvements' to the river which would not have directly boosted their income. As *Tyne after Tyne* pushes the story, and origins, of environmental stewardship back to the pre-Victorian era, and as it explores perceptions of harm and efforts to protect the river from perceived harm from 1529 right through to the present day, it will make an important, and urgently needed, addition to the currently nascent field of early modern environmental history, as well as to the worldwide field of environmental river histories written about the post-1800 era.

Taking a broad sweep from 1655 to 1855, chapter two dovetails and reconnects the Tyne's early modern and modern eras. It explains how the early modern conceptualisation of the river gave way increasingly, and over quite a long period from as early as 1655, to calls for wider democratisation of river management and a much more efficient programme of river 'improvements' to enhance navigability and maximise industrial riparian development. Firstly, focusing on Ralph Gardner's petition which he published as *England's Grievance Rediscovered* in 1655, the chapter explains the long-term rivalry between Newcastle and both North and South Shields over Newcastle Corporation's monopolistic insistence on bringing ships eight miles upriver from Shields to dock at Newcastle, where ships masters paid ballast and shipping tolls to the city's Mayor and alderman. It then analyses the impact of the Great Flood of 1771 and another very severe flood in 1815 on relationships with and conceptualisations of the Tyne and on attitudes towards river 'improvements'. It analyses the impact of the administrative change from the Tyne River Court to the River Committee, in 1834, and how the short-lived committee, still working under Newcastle Corporation as conservators, dealt with its last chance to implement efficiently a programme of river restructuring in the context of increasing calls to quicken their progress. Finally, the chapter analyses the Royal Commission of 1855 appointed to investigate the lack of progress hitherto on the river, including during the first five years of the TIC, explaining the consequences of the report's findings for the river and for the TIC.

Chapter three presents the TIC's particular vision for the river, their indefatigable drive, after the Royal Commission of 1855, to transform the angular, winding and shallow river into what they proudly called a 'grand and deep channel'. The chapter explains the creation of the TIC in 1850, the foundations of its jurisdiction and the administrative composition of its committees and management structure. It explains how the TIC's structure's design responded to increasingly heightened calls locally to include all riparian communities and industrial key players in the management of the river. And it explains how it was designed to enable it to secure central government funding in addition to its income from ferries, shipping and ballast tolls. Central government funding enabled it to restructure the river more quickly as new technologies became available, notably steam-powered dredging machines. It explains thematically how the TIC spent its income to transform the river between 1850 and 1968 in terms of the construction of docks and piers; dredging to improve navigation; dredging to extract resources from the river bed; straightening and canalising the channel; the drainage of untreated domestic and industrial waste into the estuary; and finally small steps towards regulation which minimally benefitted the river's environmental health. The chapter concludes that this period of the river's environmental story can and should be seen as a blip on the graph between a previously more equally matched compromise between Newcastle

Introduction

Corporation and the river's expression of its natural functions, albeit due to the limitations of relatively rudimentary technology, and a subsequent vision for the river in which the rights of wildlife and plant species to thrive in the riverscape are prioritised.

Covering the period from 1866 to 1950, chapter four focuses on the Tyne's fisheries. It explores the work of the Tyne Salmon Conservancy (TSC) which enforced the Salmon and Fisheries Acts across the catchment until 1950, when the Northumberland and Tyneside River Board took over its work. The chapter's chronology overlaps substantially with chapter three in order to emphasise that this vision for the river coexisted alongside the markedly different industrial vision driven forward simultaneously by the TIC. In this chapter, we learn about the TSC's work: to install fish passes on weirs and dams throughout the upper river valleys; to inspect industrial premises, domestic sewage infrastructure and agricultural activities such as sheep dipping; to restock the rivers with various fish species; and to regulate and issue net and rod licences. While the TSC rarely interfered in the tidal zone of the river and its tributaries, which was exempted from the legal category of 'streams' and therefore received no legislative protection from pollution, sometimes the bio-physical flows of the river water and its fish forced the TSC to engage with the TIC over particularly contentious pollution issues. Some of the deepest insights into the TSC's environmental attitudes can be gleaned from the times when they found themselves with no choice but to engage directly with the TIC in order to try to influence the latter's actions.

Chapter five focuses on the development of scientific understanding of the river's functions and of the impact of complex chemical and organic waste on the river water and its fisheries. It explains how the methodologies of river testing developed from the late nineteenth century and into the early twentieth century. Subsequently, it analyses the work of the Standing Committee on River Pollution's Tyne Sub-Committee (SCORP). This committee was appointed in 1921 to test the river water and its fish life in the tidal and non-tidal zones of the catchment area. Until its dissolution in 1939, it produced over 1,000 reports and summaries of the extensive experiments and investigations conducted at the Dove Marine Laboratory near the mouth of the river at Cullercoats. It provided objective information which local and national governors and the TSC desperately needed in order to substantiate and legitimise their political drive to acquire the necessary funds to overhaul Tyneside's sewage infrastructure so as to facilitate a major clean-up of the river. This body of extensive scientific research underpinned the development of quite a comprehensive yet ultimately unsuccessful Tyne sewerage plan known as the Humphreys and Watson Report (1936) under the direction of a Commissioner of Special Areas investigation. This report is also explained in detail.

Covering the period from 1950 to 1975, chapter six describes local governors' increasing frustration as the estuary's environmental health was further degraded by its reception of increasing amounts of sewage as the successful acquisition of funds from central government to support a Tyne sewage scheme was further delayed. The Tyneside Joint Sewerage Board was established in 1966, an astonishing thirty years after the Humphreys and Watson Report, which was unfortunately derailed in 1939 by World War Two. The chapter begins by discussing the new Northumberland and Tyneside River Board, which took over from the Tyne Salmon Conservancy in 1950, and its relatively minimal impact on the increasingly intense debate over the toxic estuary, which was biologically dead, whose water literally bubbled with toxic gases and which was described by many as an open sewer. It then discusses the Northumbrian Angling Federation and how and why the angling community effectively spearheaded the increasingly desperate calls for a clean-up throughout the 1950s and early 1960s. The chapter analyses the work of the Tyneside Joint Sewerage Board between 1966 and 1975, as it planned and constructed a major waste-water treatment works at Howdon and an extensive sewerage network to serve it. And it explains the establishment in 1965 of the Northumbrian River Authority, which was equipped with the legislative power to prevent future discharges of waste into the river estuary. Finally, it presents some oral histories of Tynesiders' relationships with the river before the clean-up, which demonstrates how local people were able to experience the heavily polluted river positively as well as negatively.

Chapter seven explains the enormous consequences for the river of damming the North Tyne valley just below the source of the North Tyne near Kielder in Northumberland. This created the UK's largest man-made lake, Kielder Reservoir, largely to satisfy the future water supply needs of Teesside's chemical industry, which was expected to expand further. The dam was constructed between 1975 and 1982 and had an enormous impact on the flow regimes of this powerful river, as well as eliminating substantial salmon spawning grounds. The chapter explores the Kielder scheme itself, which connected Kielder Reservoir to three rivers, the Tyne, Wear and Tees, via a subterranean aqueduct. During two public enquiries, in 1972 and 1973, the practicality and benefits of installing fish passes into the dams was debated intensely and the records of these debates reveal a great deal about different groups' relationships with the

Introduction

river and its fish life. They provide useful insights into important touch points between competing and incompatible visions of how the Tyne should be used.

Chapter eight discusses the regenerated Tyne and the relatively new prioritisation of environmental health, clean and unpolluted river water and the nurturing of wildlife and plant species so that they can thrive in a much more 'natural' riverscape. This chapter highlights that this vision for the river is no wider than that of either Newcastle Corporation in the early modern period or that of the TIC in the nineteenth and twentieth centuries, and that it also incorporates 'losers', notably the large numbers of unemployed and underemployed Tynesiders who are still reeling from deindustrialisation. This chapter analyses the lyrics of Jimmy Nail's song, 'Big River', to ask what is a 'big' or a 'good' river? It discusses recreation and tourism, the work of the Clean Tyne Project and the environmental charity Tyne Rivers Trust, the world of the kittiwakes as they utilise the Tyne as one of their key inland breeding sites and the return to the river of its salmon. It explores the very long-term legacies of industrialisation and explains what these mean for the river's future as the river bed continues to emit harmful chemicals into the water for the next several hundred years. It also considers artistic and creative meanings of the river, the music, plays and art inspired by the new and different clean Tyne, and it shares local people's experiences of the cleaner Tyne, gathered through oral history interviews.

Chapter 1

'HURTING THE RIVER OF TINE': PROTECTING A PRE-MODERN ESTUARY, 1529–1850

Introduction

Throughout the early modern period (1500–1800), rivers were strategically very important for trade and transport. For example, Christopher Smout observed how those living on Scotland's eastern coast in the seventeenth and eighteenth centuries preferred to import the abundant pine of Ryfylke and Sunnhordland from Norway, which was about three days' sail from the Firth of Forth, because it involved much lower transport costs than wood extracted from the Highlands.[1] Moreover, Adriaan de Kraker's research into urban Ice Accounts throughout the Little Ice Age (LIA) between 1330 and 1800 revealed that on Belgian and Dutch rivers and canals, where the transportation of people and goods between major towns was only practically possible on such water highways, local governors had little choice but to invest in the relatively expensive practice of ice-breaking as a matter of course.[2] De Kraker found that the region's pre-modern roads were so bad that during the Eighty Years War (1568–1648), 'no cavalry ventured in the area at all' and that water transport was so important during military campaigns that in some cases 'boats were even burnt in order to deprive possible use of barges by the enemy to transport troops and guns'.[3] During the LIA, ice jams and frozen canals and rivers challenged Belgian and Dutch local governors during harsh winters, and also during summertime droughts which reduced the amount of water in canals and rivers

---

1. Smout, *Nature Contested*, p. 49.
2. A. de Kraker, 'Ice and Water: The Removal of Ice on Waterways in the Low Countries, 1330–1800', *Water History* (2016), DOI 10.1007/s12685-016-1052-3 (open access with no page numbers). See also Lajos Rácz, 'The Danube Pontoon Bridge of Pest-Buda (1767–1849) as an Indicator and Victim of the Climate Change of the Little Ice Age', *Global Environment* 9 (2) (2016): 458–83.
3. Ibid.

Chapter 1. 'Hurting the River of Tine'

to very problematic levels. Nonetheless, they persevered because despite their practical problems, liquid highways were still infinitely preferable compared to roads.[4] At this time, carrying coal over land doubled the commodity's price for every two miles travelled, which meant that shipping was the easiest, cheapest and ultimately the most popular method of transport.[5]

In December 1529, the English Crown appointed the mayor and aldermen of Newcastle Corporation as official 'conservators' of the River Tyne, together with its tributaries which were known as 'creeks', from Tynemouth up to the river's tidal limit at Hedwin Streams near Wylam, by an Act of Parliament (21 Hen. VIII, c.18). In an age when land transport was inherently difficult and slow, their responsibility pertained largely to preventing the choking up of what was effectively a great liquid highway that was crucial to trade, notably the exportation of very large volumes of 'sea coal' shipped down the east coast to London and elsewhere in a flotilla of collier ships. Maintaining a navigable channel was crucial to securing the corporation's monopolistic and very substantial revenues from shipping and ballast tolls. Masters of ships paid tolls for docking, loading and unloading their ships at the Port of Newcastle, some eight miles inland from Tynemouth, and for unloading any ballast they had used to weigh their empty ships down on return journeys without cargo. Newcastle Corporation did not understand the deoxygenation caused by permitting urban sewers and riparian businesses such as brewers to discharge untreated liquid waste into the river water. However, they considered in breathtaking detail and depth the consequences of each and every application they received to make structural changes to the bed and channel of the river. From 1613, the corporation appointed a dedicated Tyne River Court with its own Water Bailiff to inspect the river and twelve River Jurors to enforce 21 Tyne-specific bylaws at a weekly court. They expressly forbade the deposition of any solid waste or ballast into the river water, either directly or indirectly, something which required substantial and sustained effort to regulate.

After examining in depth the state of the field of early modern environmental history, and making a case for more pre-modern environmental history research, the chapter discusses the need for legal river regulation in this period, the foundations and organisation of regulation and the manner and extent of regulation. It concludes that the Tyne's pre-modern conservators were in touch with their environment and its limitations and potential abuse, and that the

---

4. Ibid.
5. D. Levine and K. Wrightson, *The Making of an Industrial Society: Whickham, 1560–1765* (Oxford: Oxford University Press, 1991), p. 9.

Tyne River Court was an efficient system of environmental regulation. By far, the largest body of archival evidence delineating early modern environmental standards in relation to natural systems is national and local legislation and its associated court records, which explain in detail how such legislation was enforced, challenged and modified over time. This chapter draws primarily on the minutes of the River Tyne Court proceedings, extant from 1644 to 1834, as well as national court depositions, petitions, council minutes and financial records, to provide a meaningful insight into how the people who lived around the River Tyne's estuarine environment between 1529 and 1834 interacted with, damaged and sought to protect the natural system of their river estuary.

Early Modern Environmental Historiography

Environmental history has been largely preoccupied with industrial and post-industrial case studies, primarily as a result of the larger scale of environmental damage and overuse of natural resources after 1800, and even more so after 1880.[6] As John McNeill admitted, 'Pharaonic Egypt or Song China undeniably had policies toward the natural world, and disputes over the use of resources', but the 'systematic study of how states approached nature, how interest groups struggled over it, and how explicitly environmentalist organizations joined the fray is essentially confined to the era since 1880'.[7] But early modern, and indeed all pre-modern, societies can and should be analysed in much more depth by environmental historians in order to reveal more about the important drivers for change in environmental attitudes and values over long-term chronologies. Environmental historians can and should immerse themselves in the complexities of early modern historical development as much as, if not more than, their fellow economic, legal, political, social and cultural historians. They can reveal very usefully how socio-environmental interactions with soil, air, water, fire, trees and many other natural resources and systems shaped key issues including local and national governance, nationhood and identity, social interaction and riot and rebellion. As Sverker Sörlin and Paul Warde observe, 'there is a peculiar gap' between the 'relatively recent and limited discipline-based historiography and the omnipresence of nature and natural resources as fundamentals of human societies that goes back to the very roots of human

---

6. S. Mosley, *The Chimney of the World: A History of Smoke Pollution in Victorian and Edwardian Manchester* (Cambridge: The White Horse Press, 2001); A. Rome, 'Coming to Terms with Pollution: the Language of Environmental Reform, 1865–1915', *Environmental History* 1 (1996): pp. 6–28.

7. J. McNeill, 'Observations on the Nature and Culture of Environmental History', *History and Theory* **42** theme issue (2003): 5–43.

Chapter 1. 'Hurting the River of Time'

existence'.[8] Consequently, the relationships between pre-modern societies and their environments are currently misunderstood. As Martin Schmid highlights, 'we speak of "regulated" or "systematically trained" rivers from the early 19th century, but many rivers in Europe were by no means unregulated before that time'.[9] Despite the undeniable qualitative differences between 'the regulations of the 16th century and the work of a Tulla on the Rhine in the 19th century', Schmid elaborates, describing early modern European rivers as '"largely unregulated" or even "natural" rivers' is unjustified.[10] Although the scale of early modern industrial development should not be played down, as it has hitherto been, neither should the fact that its scale was significantly smaller be ignored or denied. Pierre-Claude Reynard encourages environmental historians to follow his lead in demonstrating that 'early modern concerns about industrial effluents were not marginal or nascent, haphazard or weak' but rather 'full-fledged and central to the preoccupations of those who thought about a liveable environment and acted to defend it'.[11] As a result of future research into early modern environmental regulation, in particular, Reynard believes that 'a solid core' of continuities will be revealed which connect pre-modern environmental attitudes with modern-day environmental impact assessments.[12]

In a similar vein, Sara Pritchard emphasises that environmentally progressive action was taken in particular historical circumstances well before the environmentalism of the 1960s, noting that

> late-eighteenth- and early-nineteenth-century [French] laws tended to promote continuity of use – a sort of ecological as well as economic status quo – over new development. In this respect, the early post-revolutionary state generally preserved a river's 'natural state'. Although all of these laws permitted property owners along a non-navigable river to continue using its waters, they also circumscribed 'private' rights.[13]

---

8. S. Sorlin and P. Warde, 'Making the Environment Historical: an Introduction', in S. Sorlin and P. Warde (eds), *Nature's End: History and the Environment* (Basingstoke: Palgrave Macmillan, 2009), pp. 1–19.
9. M. Schmid, 'The Environmental History of Rivers in the Early Modern Period', in M. Knoll and R. Reith (eds), *An Environmental History of the Early Modern Period: Experiments and Perspectives* (Berlin: Lit, 2014), pp. 19–26.
10. Ibid., pp. 19–26.
11. P. Reynard, 'Public Order and Privilege: Eighteenth-century French Roots of Environmental Regulation', *Technology and Culture* 43 (2002): 1–28.
12. Ibid., pp. 1–28.
13. Pritchard, *Confluence*, p. 33.

Pritchard demonstrates that, even while concentrating on a modern, twentieth-century case study, an appreciation of the long-term development of environmental attitudes, regulations and interactions can enhance our understanding of the multi-layered and long-established human interactions with the environment under study. Barca, too, emphasises the long-term historical foundation of nineteenth-century industrialism:

> Stemming from the political economy of the enlightenment project, the factory system in fact took place in a landscape that was the historical product of long-term interactions between social and natural forces. As in many other European valleys and rural communities, industrialisation was preceded by what historians call the pre-industrial system of production or proto-industry.[14]

In order to understand these important links, attention needs to be paid to the dovetailed and strong connections between medieval, early modern and modern attitudes and values in relation to the environment, rather than developing mutually exclusive, pigeon-holed research within respective epochs, as has been the pronounced pattern in the development of many other sub-disciplines of history. Indeed, as Martin Schmid comments, 'environmental historians should not take the epochal boundaries too seriously'.[15]

The task of investigating early modern environmental attitudes cannot be achieved by merely inspiring modern environmental historians to push their chronologies further back in time. There is a small, but growing, field of dedicated early modern environmental historians who are beginning to tackle environmental issues and topics with the benefit of crucial expertise in relation to the particular political, economic, religious, cultural, legal and social contexts of the period.[16] William Cavert, seeking to address the 'vast gulf' separating

---

14. Barca, *Enclosing Water*, p. 60.
15. Schmid, 'The Environmental History of Rivers'.
16. Smout, *Nature Contested*; B. Hanawalt and L. Kiser (eds), *Engaging with Nature: Essays on the Natural World in Medieval and Early Modern Europe* (Notre Dame, Indiana: University of Notre Dame Press, 2008); L. Skelton, *Sanitation in Urban Britain, 1560–1700* (London: Routledge, 2015); Knoll and Reith (eds), *An Environmental History of the Early Modern Period*; E. Newell, 'Atmospheric Pollution and the British Copper Industry, 1690–1920', *Technology and Culture* 38 (1997): 655–89; Reynard, 'Public Order and Privilege'; P. Reynard, 'Charting Environmental Concerns: the Reaction to Hydraulic Public Works in Eighteenth-century France', *Environment and History* 9 (2003): 251–273; A. Coney, 'Fish, Fowl and Fen: Landscape Economy in Seventeenth-century Martin Mere', *Landscape History* 14 (1992): 1–64; R. Oram, 'Waste Management and Peri-urban Agriculture in the Early Modern Scottish Burgh', *Agricultural History Review* 59 (1) (June 2011): 1–17; P. Warde, 'The Environmental History of Pre-industrial Agriculture in Europe', in Sorlin and Warde (eds), *Nature's End*; P. Warde, 'Imposition, Emulation and Adaptation: Regulatory Regimes in the Commons of Early Modern Germany', *Environment and History* 19 (2013): 313–337; P. Warde, 'The Idea of Improvement, c. 1520–1700', in R. Hoyle (ed.), *Custom, Improvement and Landscape in Early Modern Britain* (Farnham: Routledge,

Chapter 1. 'Hurting the River of Tine'

the pre-modern and modern worlds, has revealed that, between 1624 and 1640, Charles I deliberately excluded smoky industries from the area around his court in London to improve the quality of the air.[17] Cavert concludes that 'it is misleading to claim, as many environmental historians have done, that air pollution specifically, and the pollution of natural and built environments more generally, are intrinsically modern problems and concepts, meaningless before large-scale industrialization'.[18] John Morgan has researched understandings of, attitudes towards and efforts to mitigate flooding in early modern England, demonstrating that communities' environmental knowledge was far more sophisticated and deeply rooted than has been assumed.[19] Moreover, Daniel Curtis has analysed the environmental resilience of a very wide range of pre-industrial rural communities (late medieval and early modern Tuscany, the Dutch river area, Cambridgeshire, communities living on the North Sea coast and some regions in Apulia) to explain how institutional organisation, the distribution of landed property and individual and community rights were crucial factors shaping a community's unique potential to mitigate and respond to environmental crises effectively.[20] Recently, in 2014, Piet van Cruyningen ambitiously compared the complex negotiations over and resistance to top-down, large-scale drainage projects in England, the Dutch Republic and France throughout the sixteenth and seventeenth centuries. He found that such projects provoked greatest resistance in more centralised France and England than they did in the more decentralised Dutch Republic where 'Dutch politicians and entrepreneurs were more used to compromises, and solutions could be adapted to local circumstances'.[21]

A few published articles engage directly, and in some depth, with early modern rivers, in Venice, Holland and France, but the field lacks detailed

---

2011), pp. 127–148; P. Warde and T. Williamson, 'Fuel Supply and Agriculture in post-Medieval England', *Agricultural History Review* **62** (2014): 61–82; and Cavert, 'Coal Smoke', pp. 310–333; J. Morgan, 'Understanding Flooding in Early Modern England', *Journal of Historical Geography* **50** (2015): 37–50.

17. Cavert, 'Coal Smoke'.
18. Ibid.
19. Morgan, 'Understanding Flooding'.
20. D. Curtis, *Coping with Crisis: The Resilience and Vulnerability of Pre-Industrial Settlements* (Burlington, Vt: Ashgate Publishing Co., 2014).
21. P. van Cruyningen, 'Dealing with Drainage: State Regulation of Drainage Projects in the Dutch Republic, France, and England during the Sixteenth and Seventeenth Centuries', *Economic History Review* **67** (2014): 1–21.

monographs.[22] Understanding the evolving relationship between human societies and natural systems and resources, as well as how people understood and sought to mitigate environmental risk and environmental change over a longer period of time, well before 1800, is an urgent and potentially fruitful task. Perhaps this can be achieved most effectively and appropriately if experienced early modernists are inspired to adopt environmental methodologies rather than if environmental historians fully versed in the complex contexts of modern periods simply push their chronologies back into the pre-modern period.

It is important to analyse closely how the Victorian industrialists' ancestors perceived and protected the environment. As Robert MacFarlane explains, in his history of attitudes towards mountains, 'each of us is in fact heir to a complex and largely invisible dynasty of feelings: we see through the eyes of innumerable and anonymous predecessors'.[23] This, too, can be applied to attitudes towards the environment, conservation and sustainability, misconceived by many as a modern invention. In his impressive history of the early modern world, John Richards points out that 'as the term *early modern* suggests', the 'long-term trends that accelerated in this period deeply influenced massive and growing human-induced environmental change' after 1800.[24] And Ronald Zupko and Robert Laures warn that it is misleading to perceive 'environmental awareness' as a completely modern movement, 'arising out of the tumult of a half-century of war and depression like some Venus given birth in the crashing surf of a Mediterranean shore'.[25] Sixteenth-century concerns were, of course, born out of medieval concerns which had developed in similar veins. Richard Hoffmann 'seeks to encourage medievalists to think about the interactions between medieval society and its natural environment and to explore the ecological connections which shaped those changes', and he is keen to restore 'lost agency to natural systems which some, though not all, medievalists have tended

---

22. S. Ciriacono, *Building on Water: Venice, Holland and the Construction of the European Landscape in the Early Modern Times* (Oxford: Berghahn, 2006); K. Appuhn, 'Friend or Flood? The Dilemmas of Water Management in Early Modern Venice', in A. Isenberg (ed.), *The Nature of Cities: Culture, Landscape and Urban Space* (New York: University of Rochester Press, 2006), pp. 79–102.

23. R. MacFarlane, *Mountains of the Mind: A History of a Fascination* (London: Granta, 2003), p. 167. MacFarlane also highlights that contour lines were invented in the sixteenth century, well before the requisite technology was available to facilitate their effective use, p. 183. Similarly, the invention of the water closet by Sir John Harrington in 1596 preceded by centuries the requisite underground sewerage system needed to carry the augmented and problematically liquid waste produced by water closets and Joseph Bramah's patent of the water closet technology in 1778.

24. J. Richards, *The Unending Frontier: An Environmental History of the Early Modern World* (London: University of California Press, 2003), p. 2.

25. R. Zupko, and A. Laures, *Straws in the Wind: Medieval Urban Environmental Law – The Case of Northern Italy* (Oxford: Westview, 1996).

Chapter 1. 'Hurting the River of Tine'

to describe passively as objects of human action'.[26] Ellen Arnold has revealed how one medieval society, in the French Ardennes, exerted sophisticated control over water levels, highlighting the case study's important religious context.[27] One article squarely attributed the twentieth-century conservation crisis to medieval societies for having forged such deep anthropocentric religious beliefs, which led them to feel entitled to overuse natural resources.[28] As early as 1713, Hans Carl von Carlowitz, a tax accountant and mining administrator at the royal court of Freiberg, Saxony, criticised the rich for wasting wood, argued that mining was directly responsible for the reduction of forests across Europe and introduced the concept of 'sustainability'.[29] Indeed, as Christian Schagerl argues convincingly, 'it would be a mistake to idealize or unduly romanticize agricultural production of the past' when 'there were plenty of environmental problems from the overuse of woodland to dangerous erosion in the Mediterranean region'.[30]

It is important to remain mindful that early modern motivations to protect aspects of the environment were not explicitly or primarily environmental, in modern-day terms, but the basic spirit of environmentalism was certainly there well before 1800, albeit *avant la lettre*. Joel Kaye argued that, although between 1250 and 1350 the precise 'phrase and the concept' of a balance of nature was unknown, 'the sense conveyed by the phrase balance of nature was very much alive and active in scientific speculation'.[31] From the earliest pre-Socratic speculations right through to the present day, Kaye elaborates, 'where there is science one almost always finds at the least the assumption of a continuous

---

26. R. Hoffmann, 'Homo et Natura, home in Natura: Ecological Perspectives on the European Middle Ages', in Hanawalt and Kiser (eds), *Engaging with Nature*, p. 13. See also R. Hoffmann, 'Elemental Resources and Aquatic Ecosystems: Medieval Europeans and their Rivers', in T. Tvedt, and R. Coopey (eds), *A History of Water: Series II: Volume 2: Rivers and Society: from Early Civilizations to Modern Times* (London, 2010), pp. 165–202; R. Hoffmann and V. Winiwarter, 'Making Land and Water meet: Cycling of Nutrients between Fields and Ponds in Pre-Modern Europe', *Agricultural History* 84 (3) (2010): 352–380; I. Fay, *Health and the City: Disease, Environment and Government in Norwich, 1200–1575* (Woodbridge: Boydell and Brewer, 2015); C. Rawcliffe, *Urban Bodies: Communal Health in Late Medieval English Towns and Cities* (Woodbridge: Boydell and Brewer, 2013).
27. E. Arnold, 'Engineering Miracles: Water Control, Conversion, and the Creation of a Religious Landscape in the Medieval Ardennes," *Environment and History* 13 (4) (2007): 477–502.
28. L. White, 'The Historical Roots of Our Ecologic Crisis', *Science* 155 (1967): 1203–1207.
29. C. von Carlowitz, *Sylvicultura Oeconomica oder hauswirthliche Nachricht und Naturmassige Anweisung zur Wilden Baum*-Zucht, second edition reprint, Leipzig: heirs of the late Johann Friedrich Braun, 1732, (Remagen-Oberwinter: Verlag Kessel, 2009), as quoted in Schagerl, *Anthropocene*, p. 55.
30. Schagerl, *Anthropocene*, p. 95. See also J. Radkau, *Nature and Power: A Global History of the Environment* (Cambridge: Cambridge University Press, 2008).
31. J. Kaye, 'The (Re)balance of Nature, c.1250–1350', in Hanawalt and Kiser (eds), *Engaging with Nature*, p. 86.

and ordered (often cyclical) process of reciprocal interchange along with the recognition of an overarching conservation in the system of nature'.[32] Underlining Kaye's argument, Fiona Watson found 'little evidence' to suggest that contemporaries 'regarded timber as a resource to be plundered at will'.[33] While she warns historians to be 'very wary of transporting such [modern] values to the early modern world', she nevertheless emphasises that early modern people, confronted with having to 'stay and face the consequences of their inefficiency', were highly driven to work with, rather than to plunder, their environment.[34]

There are no specific nature essays written by the men who managed British rivers in the early modern period, describing explicitly their attitudes towards and valuation of river systems and regarding the risks, benefits and adverse effects of altering such systems in order to boost the efficiency of trade, industry and profit. As Barbara Hanawalt and Lisa Kiser observe, 'for many writing in these early periods, "nature" was arguably not even a discursive category; it simply went without saying'.[35] Perhaps Richard White's rejection of any separation between the human and the natural would raise few eyebrows in a seventeenth-century coffee house; he would merely be stating a widely acknowledged fact. Early modern contemporaries imagined a very clear separation between the spiritual world and the natural, physical world that they inhabited, but the latter's humans, animals and environments were completely entangled together. Our modern-day conceptualisation of a distinction between the natural and the human, therefore, is anachronistic in an early modern context. Nonetheless, early modern attitudes and values in relation to the environment can still be appreciated as part of the long-term process of developing the character of more recent attitudes. These societies created important political and legal frameworks within which they could and did purposely protect natural resources, systems and landscapes from perceived harm, before in-depth scientific experimentation confirmed exactly what could and could not damage natural systems in the long and short term. The popular ecology and environmental movement of the late 1960s and 1970s was unprecedented and it is rightly esteemed as an important landmark and turning point in British environmental history. However, it is equally important to listen to the pre-modern and early modern voices that survive intact in archival documents, explaining a different relationship with

---

32. Ibid., p. 88.
33. F. Watson, 'Rights and Responsibilities: Wood Management as seen through Baron Court Records', in C. Smout (ed.) *Scottish Woodland History* (Edinburgh: Scottish Cultural Press, 1997), p. 103.
34. Ibid., pp. 104, 106.
35. B. Hanawalt and L. Kiser, 'Introduction', in Hanawalt and Kiser (eds), *Engaging with Nature*, p. 2.

Chapter 1. 'Hurting the River of Tine'

the environment, in a very different context, on which current environmental attitudes are at least partly founded. Keith Thomas explained the developing relationship between human societies and the natural world between 1500 and 1800, concluding that there was a move from 'exploitation' increasingly towards 'stewardship'.[36] This chapter concludes that the Tyne case study strengthens his argument. In relation to the conservation of the Tyne estuary by Newcastle Corporation between 1529 and 1850, and by its Tyne River Court between 1613 and 1834, there was a discernible move away from exploitation towards much more careful and progressive stewardship.

Richard Grove, arguably the pioneer of research into early modern environmental attitudes, laments the 'absence of any attempt to deal with the history of environmental concern on a truly global basis' and argues that environmentally progressive attitudes substantially predate 1800.[37] He argues convincingly that 'the origins and early history of contemporary western environmental concern and concomitant attempts at conservationist intervention lie far back in time', but he attributes the development of these attitudes to the particular circumstances in which early colonists found themselves in the sixteenth, seventeenth and eighteenth centuries, when resources in the colonies were often scarce and therefore had to be used sparingly.[38] Grove is right to highlight that 'the ability of man to cause very marked ecological changes over wide areas of the globe and then to respond constructively to them has not been confined to the last three centuries'.[39] What the Tyne's early modern records show, however, is that serious environmental pressures occurred at home too, where environmentally progressive policies were consequently pursued out of necessity, or were motivated by very strong economic impulses. Perhaps experiences of real scarcity of resources in geographically isolated locations might have catalysed and sharpened the development of environmental awareness in England. But these attitudes were certainly not imported in the minds of colonists and disseminated throughout a completely environmentally ignorant homeland. Where Grove's argument excels is in its emphasis on resource scarcity as a catalyst for the development of environmentally sensitive attitudes. On the early modern Tyne, Newcastle Corporation's real fears that their economically crucial liquid highway would silt up are what really drove the development of

---

36. K. Thomas, *Religion and the Decline of Magic: Studies in Popular Beliefs in Sixteenth- and Seventeenth-Century England* (Harmondsworth: Penguin, 1973), pp. 58–59.
37. R. Grove, *Green Imperialism: Colonial Expansion, Tropical Island Edens and the Origins of Environmentalism, 1600–1800* (Cambridge: Cambridge University Press, 1995), pp. 1, 2.
38. Ibid., pp. 1, 2.
39. Ibid., p. 55.

Tyne-specific bylaws which happened to also deliver environmental benefits to the river.

Grove emphasises the very marked political changes which the experience of colonial expansion enabled at home in Europe, noting that 'the absolutist nature of colonial rule encouraged the introduction of interventionist forms of land management that, at the time, would have been very difficult to impose in Europe'.[40] He elaborates that, before colonial expansion, 'at the core of the developing economic system in metropolitan Europe, environmental anxieties were for a long time confined almost entirely to the prospect of a timber shortage – with the notable exception of the Venetian colonial state'.[41] Venetian governors were well ahead of their time in terms of understanding the interrelations of deforestation, water flow pathways and the movement of silt in rivers. During the 1450s, high rates of deforestation were perceived as having posed a significant threat to Venice's tidal lagoon because deforestation increased the amount of silt brought down in the neighbouring rivers; this led the Venetian Council of Ten to order the replanting of all felled woods at the edges of streams and rivers.[42] But, far from Grove's assertion that the Venetians' sharp environmental awareness was anomalous in the context of Old World environmental anxiety and concern, this chapter demonstrates that very similar anxieties were expressed by Newcastle Corporation in relation to the River Tyne. They, too, feared that the Tyne would silt up without stringent regulation and regular maintenance work to remove silt from the estuary bed. Indeed, Jenny Uglow compares the eighteenth-century Newcastle Corporation to the men of Venice, describing the pageantry surrounding the corporation's ceremonial, annual procession up and down the river aboard barges to confirm the tidal bounds of their jurisdiction as 'mimicking those of Venice'.[43] Perhaps, relatively isolated from London and from England's other large towns, the Tyne estuary provided precisely such a small, confined area, not dissimilar to a colonial island or to Venice's lagoon, where environmental concerns tended to develop out of necessity.

---

40. Ibid., pp. 7, 95.
41. Ibid., pp. 7, 95.
42. Ibid., p. 27.
43. J. Uglow, *Nature's Engraver: A Life of Thomas Bewick* (London: Faber and Faber, 2007), p. 57.

Chapter 1. 'Hurting the River of Tine'

The Need for Regulation

The relatively small scale of industrialisation during the early modern period has led to a widespread misconception that environmental damage was limited to negligible levels before industrialisation and gathered a much faster pace in the early nineteenth century. This implies that, while their relatively rudimentary technologies necessarily limited the amount of damage they were able to unleash, had technological developments occurred earlier, early modern societies would have damaged the environment on a much larger scale. However, close analysis of the methods, character and extent of early modern environmental regulations suggests that this would not necessarily have been the case. Rather, the character and stringency of their environmental regulations might well have been retained even had their scale expanded. In short, we should analyse the style, character and stringency of their river regulations in their own right and take more seriously the scale of environmental damage in the early modern period. We should also take very seriously Newcastle Corporation's and its River Jurors' clearly articulated perceived need to limit and control the impact of damage to the river's capacity to generate economic income. The misconception that early modern environmental damage was insignificant should be challenged more vociferously by early modern historians who are well aware of the already significantly large and increasing scale of industrialisation between 1500 and 1800 and the consequently necessary environmental regulation of the era.

Smout pushed the chronology of the human destruction of the Great Wood of Caledon back to well before the Romans' arrival, from about 1,700 BC, far earlier than is commonly believed.[44] Similarly, far from a 'natural', undamaged environment, protected by negligible trade and industry, the River Tyne's early modern estuary was increasingly a hive of commercial and life activities, especially below the Tyne Bridge between Newcastle and Gateshead which acted as an impenetrable barrier to large sailing ships.[45] The Tyne and its tributaries, known as 'creeks' or 'rivulets', were utilised strategically for their commercial benefits: as a source of fluvial power to turn water mill wheels in the upper valleys; as vast sinks for liquid waste drained from mills, glassworks, breweries, collieries, lead mines and tanneries; as a liquid highway for trade; and

---

44. C. Smout, 'Highland Land-use before 1800: Misconceptions, Evidence and Realities', in C. Smout (ed.), *Scottish Woodland History*, p. 6.
45. Wright, *Life on the Tyne*.

as profitable fisheries.[46] John Nef conjures up a well-informed, albeit imaginative, picture, that clearly demonstrates the need for environmental regulation:

> Picture the mouth of the muddy, narrow River Tyne, jammed with four or five hundred keels and two or three hundred ships … think of the hilly slopes to the north and south covered with hundreds of small carts and wagons, leaving behind them trails of black refuse on the green countryside; and then think of a time when this same countryside was at rest … when the only evidence of the coal industry was a few pits at the water's edge … In this comparison you have … a view of the change wrought around the town of Newcastle in the century following the accession of Elizabeth [i.e. 1558].[47]

The enthusiastic drive of local entrepreneurs to install infrastructure into the estuary's bed and channel, to facilitate more efficient loading of coal from the riverbanks into keels or colliers for export, had to be kept in check. In 1621, the largest Tyne Island near Elswick, King's Meadow, was a Crown possession 'demised by a custody lease' to Sir George Moore for forty years in 'some good hope that coals may be gained in the foresaid meadowe wherby a profit may be raised to the Crowne'.[48] In this context, Newcastle Corporation could, and sometimes did, order the demolition of constructions that they believed threatened the river. Between 1679 and 1680, Newcastle Corporation fought the south bank's owners, Durham's Dean and Chapter, which governed Durham as a County Palatinate, through Charles II's Exchequer Court to successfully prevent the construction of a large coal staith and ballast shore at Jarrow Slakes on land they believed was infirm.[49] According to one of the witnesses, Arthur Elliot, an 83-year-old Newcastle Waterman who could remember the river 'since infancy',

> severall of the river jury … were sent down by the mayor and burgesses to search view and try whether the ground … were firme ground and whether the same might be built without prejudice or damage to the river and to that purpose the said jury did take & carry with them … instruments wherewith to search the ground.[50]

---

46. E. Clavering and A. Rounding, 'Early Tyneside Industrialism: the Lower Derwent and Blaydon Burn Valleys 1550–1700', *Archaeologia Aeliana* fifth series, **23** (1995): 249–268.

47. J. Nef, *The Rise of the British Coal Industry*, 2 vols. (London: George Routledge & Sons Ltd, 1932), p. 32.

48. TNA, E 367/1444a: Exchequer Pipe Rolls, Crown Leases (23 May 1621).

49. TNA, E 134/31CHAS2/EAST18: Exchequer, Office of First Fruits and Tenths (Jan. 1679–Jan.1680).

50. Ibid.

Chapter 1. 'Hurting the River of Tine'

In 1695, Hugh Liddle, a Hebburn waterman of 62 years, gives us an idea of what such 'instruments' might have typically included. He recalled having 'tried the said place called Jarrow slake with a long poll of fower fathome length and the s[ai]d poll sunk in the s[ai]d ground called Jarrow slake soe deep that … [he] could not recover the same but lost the said poll in the Jarrow Slake'.[51] However simple such 'instruments' might seem in comparison to the powerful steam dredgers of the nineteenth century, or the complex testing equipment used by teams of scientists in the early twentieth century, they were a form of technology nevertheless. Their use by the River Jurors suggests that their understanding of the river, its characteristics and functions, was relatively sophisticated in the context of the period. Newcastle Corporation won the case against the Bishop of Durham; clearly, Jarrow Slake was unsuitable for development. The Tyne estuary needed to be regulated in order to protect such sites from inappropriate, fiscally-motivated and dangerous overdevelopment.

Despite the relatively rudimentary and limited nature of available technologies, motivation to alter the Tyne's channel and to construct projections into it, in order to facilitate and boost industry, trade and profit, remained high. In 1695, Hugh Liddle recalled how an angular rock projection, Bill Point, 'was cut at the charge of … [Newcastle Corporation] aboute fowerteene yeares agoe [i.e. 1681] and that the s[ai]d river was made more navigable and deeper in that place by that charge'.[52] Large-scale structural modifications were relatively rare, but they did occur. Several Newcastle salt-makers petitioned Parliament in 1655, complaining about the heavy expenditure they had incurred as they established their riparian facilities in the course of altering and preparing the channel for salt production and export. Subsequently, they spent £1,000 to replace their wharfs after their destruction by Royalists in the British Civil Wars:

> Considering the great charge, cost and pains bestowed and disbursed before that Manufacture [i.e. saltmaking] could be brought to perfection; as first, out of a waste and rockie piece of ground adjoyning upon the River of Tyne, in taking up the said rocks and stones, and in building wharfs and staiths along the said river, and after in placing salt pans thereupon; the removing of which rocks hath made the river thereabouts far better navigable than before, though with great charge to them.[53]

---

51. TNA, E 134/7WM3/EAST30: Exchequer, Office of First Fruits and Tenths (Feb. 1695–Feb. 1696).
52. Ibid.
53. Anon., *The Ancient Manufacture of White Saltmaking at South and Northshields, Sunderland and Blyth…* (1655).

Tyne after Tyne

Salt and coal production boomed along the Tyne estuary's riverbanks.[54] By 1652, Richard Hutchinson pleaded to the Court of Chancery that, unless he was granted the continued 'wayleave and liberty for leading of coles with waines waggons [and] horses of the carriages' to staiths on the river's north bank for export near Monkseaton and also to 'certaine salt pans at north sheles', that he would have to 'deprive many hundreds of people set on worke in digging sinking and trading of the said coles & in making of salt of there meanes of subsistance'.[55] The river's capacity for export underpinned substantial employment locally. The first glass works were founded by Admiral Sir Robert Mansell in 1619 at a site to the east of the north bank's Ouseburn tributary.[56] By 1736, there were six substantial glass works, developed by the Henzells and the Tyzacks, stretching from the Ouseburn to St Peter's downriver. They all utilised readily available ballast sand as well as significant quantities of mud from Jarrow Slakes on the south bank, which contained sand, limestone and salt in optimum proportions.[57] Soap works were also developed on the banks of the Tyne estuary from at least 1712, and potentially much earlier.[58] John Warburton established the first pottery in Pandon Dene around 1730, and many more were established over the course of the eighteenth century.[59]

Dams and weirs were installed at various locations to facilitate more effective fishing and water power for manufacture. In 1599, a 'weir or dam across the River of Tyne, commonly called Bywell Dam' increased the yields from fishing rights between Bywell and 'Hovingham [i.e. Ovingham] Burn'.[60] And, between 1583 and 1603, a 'p[ar]cel of a fishing in the water of Tyne' was leased in Queen Elizabeth I's manor of Tynemouth.[61] Moreover, the Crown leased a substantial salmon fishery to William Liddell at Newburn for £4 annually, which was described in 1649 as 'all that the Salmon fishing had gained … and caught by nett or otherwise out of … the River of Tyne … knowne by

---

54. J. Ellis, 'The Decline and Fall of the Tyneside Salt Industry, 1660–1790: a Re-examination', *Economic History Review* second series, **33** (1) (1980): 45–58.
55. TNA, C 10/15/83: Chancery Depositions (Michaelmas, 1652).
56. W. Campbell, *A Century of Chemistry on Tyneside, 1868–1968* (Newcastle: Society of Chemical Industry, 1969), p. 13.
57. Ibid., pp. 13, 15; U. Ridley, 'The History of Glass making on the Tyne and Wear', *Archaeologia Aeliana* fourth series, **40** (1962): 145–162.
58. Campbell, *A Century of Chemistry*, p. 17.
59. S. Linsley, 'Tyne industries', in D. Archer (ed.), *Tyne and Tide: A Celebration of the River Tyne* (Ovingham: Daryan Press, 2000), p. 195.
60. TNA, E 134/41Eliz/East34: Exchequer Depositions, Northumberland (1599).
61. TNA, C 2/ELIZ/F1/46: Chancery Depositions, (no exact date, but it refers to 1583 as a past date and it was recorded within Queen Elizabeth's reign).

Chapter 1. 'Hurting the River of Tine'

the name of Crooke fishing'.[62] Derwenthaugh Dam, situated above the tributary River Derwent's tidal limit, was constructed in the eighteenth century to power a brewery, paper mill and engineering workshops. Jeremiah Hunter was ordered by the river court in August 1702 to remove within one month the 'damme or sluce att Boggell hole' constructed recently which 'damnifies the river'.[63] In July 1723, Charles Montague, Esquire, was presented at the Tyne River Court because he

> had sunk some old keels and made a Rise and Stake hedge and casten great quantities of ballast into the hedge and on the sand there above the island called the [Dunston] Batts & seemed to be joyning the same to the King's Meadows [island] & thereby altered the course of the river which is a great nuzance and incroachment on the liberties of the river and may tend to the great prejudice not only of the river but to the creeks of the river.[64]

In the context of substantial and growing riparian industries, environmental regulation to protect the natural functions of the river estuary was essential.

By 1700, almost half of England's coal came from Northumberland and Durham.[65] In only three months of 1699, 250 ships exported coal from the Tyne and many others transported salt, lead, cinders, fish, corn, glass, iron, tallow, tobacco, nails, wool and stores.[66] Of the 268 ships that arrived in the Tyne during those three months, 232 were carrying only ballast.[67] Huge quantities of ballast, in the form of sand or gravel usually extracted from the Norfolk coast, Kings Lynn and the Wash, were used to weigh down and stabilise the plethora of coal-carrying colliers on their return journeys from London and the Baltic back to the Tyne. Stage masters of several official ballast shores unloaded ballast from ships in return for a fee payable to Newcastle Corporation. This motivated some ship masters to dump their ballast directly into the river. Maintaining a sufficiently deep and wide channel to facilitate the constant coming and going of large sail ships eight miles inland was a high priority with a huge economic value. As Watson observes, 'the care taken' in woodland management was 'very much dependent on the commercial value placed on the trees themselves'.[68] Similarly, motivations to regulate ballast disposal into the Tyne's estuary was

---

62. TNA, E 317/Northumberland /4: Exchequer, Office of First Fruits and Tenths (14 Dec.1649).
63. TWA, BC.RV/1/6: Tyne River Court Minute Book, 1695–1755 (31 Aug. 1702), f. 23.
64. TWA, BC.RV/1/6: Tyne River Court Minute Book, 1695–1755 (22 Jul.1723), f. 89.
65. Levine and Wrightson, *The Making of an Industrial Society*, p.3.
66. S. Linsley, 'The Port of Tyne', in Archer (ed.), *Tyne and Tide*, p. 174.
67. Linsley, 'Tyne Industries', p. 196.
68. Watson, 'Rights and Responsibilities', p. 101.

commensurate with its very high economic and commercial value. Stringent regulation of illicit ballast disposal into the channel directly underpinned income from shipping tolls. The eight-mile route upriver from Tynemouth to Newcastle was problematic, often requiring the services of a Newcastle Trinity House pilot to deliver ships safely through particular 'roadsteads' in the river. In return for a fee, the pilots manoeuvred ships past shoals, sunken and wrecked ships awaiting removal, sand bars and angular rock projections. In the nineteenth century, the invention of large steam ships spurred desires to maintain deeper navigable river channels, but sail ships required a wider channel. The masters and pilots of sail ships required greater room for error than their descendants who manoeuvred steam-powered vessels.

That technology was relatively rudimentary and engineers' comprehension of river systems was in its infancy explains precisely why regulation was essential. The corporation was only too aware that they could only reverse a severe reduction in the depth and width of the river very slowly and inefficiently, using shovels powered by the labour of keelmen. Therefore the Tyne's early modern conservators were perhaps significantly more motivated to protect the river from damage through solid waste disposal than their post-1800 descendants, who managed the river in the knowledge that they possessed the requisite technology, in the form of steam-powered dredgers, to reverse significant reductions in the river water's depth. Very similarly, medieval and early modern sanitation had to be regulated stringently because it was managed by respective householders whereas today far looser regulation of households is possible because waste-disposal is managed within centralised and heavily integrated systems that require relatively minimal householder compliance.[69] In relation to domestic waste disposal, it is much more important to appreciate how waste was processed, and the character in their own right of the systems practised, rather than merely the scale of the waste produced. The deeply entrenched and widely accepted stereotypical image of early modern urban inhabitants pouring all their waste into the river is grossly inaccurate. Before water closets had been installed in very large numbers in the later nineteenth century, most manure and human excrement was shovelled out of stables and dry privy pits and largely returned to the soil as a valuable arable fertiliser. Typically, it was heaped into middens or dunghills and either carted away to be sold to local farmers, collected from wharves and jetties and rowed away on keels or wherries to be dumped in the North Sea or loaded onto larger ships in the mouth of the river to be sold as arable fertiliser on a larger scale further afield. A small proportion of riparian

---

69. Skelton, *Sanitation*; Rawcliffe, *Urban Bodies*.

Chapter 1. 'Hurting the River of Tine'

domestic and industrial dunghills was washed into the river, either as a result of their wilful placement below the water mark or accidentally. However, early modern Tynesiders disposed of a far smaller proportion of their oxygen-hungry organic waste into the river compared to their descendants who, as late as the early 1970s, were still flushing untreated waste from their near-universal water closets directly into the estuary via over 270 sewers. Writing in 1948, Kempster highlighted the misguidedness of this method of waste disposal:

> Incidentally, the pumping of large quantities of liquid sewage after treatment into the estuaries of the sea tends to lower the underground level of water in the land area from which it is collected, and furthermore, it is open to doubt whether it is sound long-term agricultural policy to allow the solid content in the form of sludge to be removed decade after decade from the land and not returned to it as manure, as Nature intended.[70]

Early modern open sewers were designed to carry rainwater and small amounts of liquid waste to the river, and no solid waste. In this case, the scale of waste produced becomes far less relevant and indeed incomparable because the style and manner of the process itself was so different before and after 1800. The more environmentally sustainable, pre-1800 method of waste disposal could not have functioned without rigorous and effective environmental regulation and frequent inspections of the riverbanks.

The use of the estuary for water supply provides yet another significant motivating factor for rigorous environmental regulation of the estuary. As Smout highlights, in relation to northern England and Scotland, when river water was used to supply drinking water, before the construction of large-scale upland reservoirs provided preferable supplies, ensuring the cleanliness of river water, as far as technology and resources allowed, was a serious priority in local government.[71] Similarly stringent enforcement of local bylaws designed to protect the purity of river water supplies can be seen in the legal records of sixteenth- and seventeenth-century Inverness, Darlington, Berwick upon Tweed and Stirling.[72] As Smout elaborates, it was only after towns stopped relying on rivers for their water supplies that industries and municipalities 'felt free to pour greatly increased quantities of foul water into the rivers without giving the consequences much thought'.[73] By this time, he notes, the 'convenience' of

---

70. J. Kempster, *Our Rivers* (London: Oxford University Press, 1948), p. 56.
71. Smout, *Nature Contested*, p. 109.
72. Skelton, *Sanitation*.
73. Smout, *Nature Contested*, p. 109.

having 'a river in which to dump waste quickly outweighed complaints'.[74] This is true of the Tyne case study, where the disposal of liquid and solid untreated industrial and domestic waste into the estuary increased significantly after the Newcastle and Gateshead Water Company constructed several upland reservoirs from 1845 onwards.[75] From the late 1600s, and over the course of the eighteenth century, water was drawn directly from the River Tyne, using the Crowley Water works at Winlaton and the Gateshead Hawks works.[76] And, in 1680, Cuthbert Dykes installed an engine to draw Tyne water at Sandgate, Newcastle.[77] Protecting the river from unlimited corruption from solid domestic and industrial waste was a logical and obvious priority when water supplies were abstracted directly from the river. For many crucially important reasons, the motivation to regulate the environment of the River Tyne's estuary throughout the period 1529 to 1800 remained consistently high.

The Foundations of Regulation

In 1529, the English Crown confirmed the mayor and burgesses of Newcastle as conservators of the Tyne estuary by an Act of Parliament. This decision was made at the height of the Reformation, when King Henry VIII favoured town over clerical government, after Newcastle Corporation had fought the clerical Bishops of Durham for the conservatorship throughout the fifteenth century. This Act gave the corporation authority on behalf of the Crown to pull down all wears, gores and engines in the River Tyne, between Sparrow-Hawk and Hedwin Streams, which marked the Tyne's estuary. Subsequently, several successive Acts reconfirmed their conservancy. Newcastle's Trinity House was established in 1505 and it managed the weighing and retrieval of sunken ships, the provision of pilots to escort ships from Tynemouth to Newcastle, poor payments and hospitality for aged mariners and pilots and the maintenance of buoys and eventually leading lights to guide ships; but it did not regulate the river.[78] Though they worked closely with Newcastle Corporation on overlapping areas of river management, such as the production of river surveys, and

---

74. Ibid.
75. Rennison, *Water to Tyneside*, p. 61.
76. Ibid., p. xvii.
77. D. Archer, 'Kielder Water: White Elephant or White Knight?', in Archer (ed.), *Tyne and Tide*, p. 139.
78. G. McCombie, 'The Development of Trinity House and the Guildhall before 1700', in D. Newton and A. Pollard, *Newcastle and Gateshead before 1700* (Chichester: Phillimore and Co Ltd, 2009), pp. 172–173.

Chapter 1. 'Hurting the River of Tine'

its representatives sometimes reported encroachments which they noticed on the river, the members of Trinity House were not Tyne conservators.[79]

The sixteenth-century corporation used some of its income from shipping tolls to maintain the estuary. In October 1574, it paid 4d to the Bellman for his work 'goinge 2 times aboute the towne, for charging the commons to sende downe the rever for helping to git up the shippe that is sonke at Hawkes Nest'.[80] Similarly, a record was made in May 1591, when 8d was paid to John Belman for 'going aboute to warn the towne 2 times to helpe wey a ship which was over throwne'.[81] In January 1593, the corporation paid William Graie 2s 6d per week for inspecting the river, 'looking for casting ballist into the river or other rubbish eyther above the bridge or below or in Gateshide'.[82] Although William Graie was not a sworn and elected official, he was a paid civic employee responsible for reporting those who cast ballast into the river. From 1529 to 1613, Newcastle Corporation maintained and inspected the river using individuals employed on an *ad hoc* basis, seeking out those who threw rubbish or ballast into the river and presenting and fining them at the weekly Town Court. They also paid various watermen on an irregular basis to lift sand, gravel, rocks and rubbish from the river using shovels and keel boats. During the period 1529 to 1613, Newcastle Corporation's maintenance of the estuary was characterised by informality, irregularity and reactive efforts.

On 29 January 1613, a set of 21 Tyne-specific bylaws was passed in relation to river management at the Trinity House in London, to be enforced by Newcastle Corporation. Henceforth, the *ad hoc*, reactive system gave way to a much more proactive, centralised and regular system which enforced specific bylaws efficiently. Motivation and efforts to regulate the Tyne's estuary grew concomitantly with, and reflected, the increasing scale of industry and trade that threatened to damage it. The bylaws were surprisingly comprehensive, designed to regulate various aspects of industrial development and waste-disposal on the river and its banks. One of the bylaws forbade using ballast to dam and back wharfs and quays 'in all parts of the river', casting ballast on wharfs below high water mark or casting ballast at North or South Shields.[83] Another stipulated that riparian saltpan owners 'doe within six months build up their wharfs and

---

79. Ibid., pp. 172–173.
80. Anon., *Reprints of Rare Tracts and Imprints of Ancient Manuscripts Chiefly Illustrative of the History of the Northern Counties*, vol. 3 (London, 1847), pp. 18–19.
81. Ibid.
82. Ibid., p. 31.
83. Ibid., pp. 14–15.

keyes sufficiently above a full sea mark in height of the water' so that 'neither coals nor rubbish do fall into the river' and to 'carry away their pan rubbish every forty days'.[84] One bylaw instructed the corporation to inflict 'strict and severe punishment' upon masters of ships or keels who cast ballast into the river.[85] Waste disposal high above the river in Newcastle's streets was regulated too. One bylaw ordered 'that strangers shall be appointed every week to cleanse the streets in Newcastle of their ashes and other rubbish, to prevent the rain from washing the same into the river through Loadbourn', which demonstrates clear comprehension of the connected and consequential flows from private to main open sewers, to tributary rivers and eventually into the main river.[86] Another bylaw ensured 'that all the gates on the town key be locked up every night, except one or two to stand open for the masters and seamen to go too and fro to their shipps, which will prevent servants casting ashes and other rubbish into the river' and it stipulated that the gates should be watched throughout the night.[87] Extending the jurisdiction of Newcastle Corporation to the Tyne's tributary rivers too, they expressly forbade the construction of 'wyers, dams, or other stoppage, or casting of ballast in or near the said river or creeks', and the movement of ships during the 'night tyde' was banned outright.[88] One bylaw ordered that 'some trusty truly substantial men, burgesses of Newcastle, be appointed to view the river every week, and to make oath for the abuses and wrongs done unto the same'; they were to be truly objective men, possessing no coals, mines nor ballast shores.[89]

Every year from 1613, the corporation elected twelve River Jurors to present and fine at a weekly River Court individuals who contravened the river bylaws; and they appointed one dedicated, sworn officer, known as the Water Bailiff, to report offences done in the river. According to Arthur Elliot, a Newcastle Waterman of 83 years speaking in 1679, 'most of them ... [were] seamen'.[90] Ralph Tailor, a River Juror in various years after 1649, had trained as a Scrivener and by 1649 was a successful Notary Public; in such a capacity, he would have enjoyed the respect of Newcastle's inhabitants as a member of

---

84. Ibid.
85. Ibid.
86. Ibid.
87. Ibid.
88. Ibid.
89. Ibid., pp. 16–17.
90. TNA, E 134/31CHAS2/EAST18: Exchequer, Office of First Fruits and Tenths (Jan. 1679–Jan. 1680).

Chapter 1. 'Hurting the River of Tine'

the middling sort, but he never served on Newcastle Corporation.[91] The Tyne River Court convened each Monday morning from January 1613, but the court minutes are only extant from 1644 due to the violent and destructive sacking of Newcastle in October 1644, after a lengthy siege from February 1644 by the Scots Army led by General Leslie as part of the British Civil Wars. As 84- year-old Jane Roxby recalled in 1695, 'the place where the evidences and writings belonging to the mayor and burgesses of Newcastle were lodged was burnt … and … the ashes of the books and papers burnt in the s[ai]d fire lay in great heaps upon the sandhill in Newcastle as high as a mans waste'.[92] Throughout the seventeenth century, the annually elected Water Bailiff and River Jurors inspected the river and attended particular sites to assess applications and encroachments in depth. They enforced the river bylaws and presented and fined offenders at their weekly court. The River Jurors dealt with most applications to erect projections into the river, such as wharves, jetties and galleries or weirs, but Newcastle Corporation still dealt with some river applications. However, by the eighteenth century, the latter task had been delegated to the River Jurors in almost every case. A delegation or committee of between three and twelve jurors visited the site in each case and provided a detailed report to the next court, which ultimately decided whether or not to grant permission for the works to commence. In April 1701, they recorded that at Willington Shore, 'they have viewed & prickt the same with javelings & have found a good foundation about forty yards below the jettie and key formerly built', having reported that 'they find nothing but slake & sand to the height of a javelin about seaven foot' and it was ordered that 'speedy care be taken' in repairing the key.[93] The River Jurors were practical men who knew their river well; they were as actively involved in regulation on the river and riverbanks as inside their court room. The tripartite system of environmental regulation, river maintenance work and assessments of planning applications, continued until the mid-nineteenth century. The Tyne River Court continued to regulate the river estuary and crucially to 'conserve' its natural functions until the Municipal Corporations Act of 1835 forced major administrative changes and a River Committee took over the management of the river, still on behalf of Newcastle Corporation.

---

91. K. Wrightson, *Ralph Tailor's Summer: A Scrivener, his City and the Plague* (London: Yale University Press, 2011), p. 150.
92. TNA, E 134/7WM3/EAST30: Exchequer, Office of First Fruits and Tenths (Feb. 1695–Feb. 1696).
93. TWA, BC.RV/1/6: Tyne River Court Minute Book, 1695–1755 (14 Apr. 1701), f. 20.

The Character and Stringency of Regulation

The Tyne River Jurors protected the river estuary from overdevelopment, solid waste and impediments to its natural flow. Considering that the 1613 bylaws were designed by London's Trinity House, to be implemented top-down in relation to a provincial and distant river, they were remarkably in tune with Tyne issues. This suggests that communication between Newcastle and London in relation to river management was effective and strong, which is unsurprising given the extent to which London relied on a functioning Tyne through which to convey essential coal supplies. The Tyne's regulation was perhaps more urgent than that of neighbouring Sunderland's River Wear, where Commissioners were not appointed until 1717 by an Act of Parliament to hold their own regulatory court. The authors of the Tyne bylaws had a clear understanding of how river systems worked and of how to protect a river's natural functions from human damage. Time and again, the River Jurors record contraventions to their bylaws as having hurt, damaged or spoiled the river itself, rather than referring directly to Newcastle Corporation's income through tolls or to the interests of a particular private landowner. Whereas Paul Warde argues that pre-industrial regulators of agricultural practices 'did think that their neighbours' actions could affect their fortunes' and consequently agricultural 'by-laws and manorial records were preoccupied with neighbourly relations rather than ecological management' and should be considered as a '"social system"', the regulators of the Tyne estuary were concerned with the impact of human activities on the river itself.[94] This explains why the River Jurors always described the Tyne explicitly as the object, and indeed sufferer, of human actions which were perceived as damaging and even hurting it.

In February 1644, Anthony Davis was presented at the River Court because 'his key a great parte of it [is] ruinated & a dunghill made upon it the tide flowing amongst it to the hurt & damage of the river'; and in October 1647, Mr Martin Fenwicke of Denton was presented 'for having his manure which was cast upon Mr Lancelott Erringtons staith at Lemington so badly cast that part of it falls off into the river'.[95] These two presentments are typical of the many others recorded in the river court minute books. The contemporary method of waste disposal required frequent inspection and management in order to prevent significant volumes of waste from entering the river water. Although sewers in this period were supposed to be limited to liquid waste and rainwater,

---

94. Warde, 'Pre-industrial Agriculture', pp. 88, 90.
95. TWA, BC.RV/1/1: Tyne River Court Minute Book, 1644–1647 (20 Feb. 1644), f. 1; TWA, BC.RV/1/2: Tyne River Court Minute Book, 1647–1650, (15 Oct. 1647), f. 69.

Chapter 1. 'Hurting the River of Tine'

a minority of inhabitants did dispose of solid waste into these channels, which all ultimately drained into the Tyne. In November 1648, Nicholl Pickeringe, a Butcher of Newcastle, was presented because his servant 'swept the durt and filth of the street to the conduit and then opened the cocke of the conduit and let the water wash it downe the Banke into the river'.[96] Had he lived nearer to the river, in Sandgate, the Close or Gateshead, his servant would have been responsible for this offence. This presentment of someone living high above the river for damaging the Tyne demonstrates a clear understanding and an acute awareness of the connected flow pathways from private and main street sewers to the Tyne. In August 1647, Newcastle Corporation, which still decided some applications for riparian development, allowed Mr Harris and Mr Haynes to have joint interest in a 21-year lease of some glasshouses on the riverbank at Newcastle, on condition that 'they should cast no rubbish from their furnace forward but only backward'.[97] This clause was included specifically to protect the river from rubbish. It ordered that such rubbish had to be removed directly from the back of the property well away from the river frontage.

In October 1723, the River Jurors ordered that the 'wears and every thing done for diverting this ancient channel or course of the said river be forthwith removed and taken away so that the water may flow with its usual freedom into its natural receptacle'.[98] Clearly, they conceptualised the river primarily as a commercial system or facility, 'a great liquid highway', rather than as an element of nature to be admired and protected purely in its own right. However, the river itself is the focus of all of their presentments and regulations, rather than landowners; indeed, conversely, landowners were often punished for having offended or damaged the river. Moreover, the River Jurors were interested in educating rather than merely punishing contraveners. An 'antient custom in Newcastle' consisted of bringing ship masters who had been found guilty of having dumped ballast into the river, 'to the hurt of the said river', 'into the town chamber and there in the presence of the people had a knife put into his hand', the ship master was 'constrained to cut a purse with monies in it as who should say he had offended in as high a degree as if he cut a purse from the person of a man where by he might be so ashamed that he should never offend again therein'.[99] By comparing the disposal of ballast into the river to the act of cutting someone's purse strings, the corporation demonstrated

---

96. TWA, BC.RV/1/2: Tyne River Court Minute Book, 1647–1650 (11 Dec. 1648), f. 183.
97. TWA, MD.NC/2/1: Newcastle Common Council Order Book, 1645–1650 (18 Aug. 1647), f. 169.
98. TWA, BC.RV/1/6: Tyne River Court Minute Book, 1695–1755 (14 Oct. 1723), f. 92.
99. Anon. *Reprints*, pp. 16–17.

explicitly that offences against the river were serious, and that a natural river system could be hurt and damaged by such acts. This was proactively designed to achieve prevention rather than exclusively to exact retribution or to collect compensation for economic damage. One 1613 bylaw obliged all servants living in Gateshead, Sandgate and the Close to swear in court each year that they would not cast rubbish into the river.[100] Servants were typically responsible for waste disposal in most other towns too, but most of their counterparts, certainly servants living in contemporary Carlisle, Edinburgh, Berwick and York, were not presented in court for contravening waste-disposal bylaws; in these towns, at least, householders were presented and fined on their servants' behalves.[101] Yet in Newcastle and Gateshead, unusually, servants living around the Tyne estuary were made responsible for their own actions, which must surely have improved the efficacy of environmental regulation. Notably, households lacking servants were represented by either a widow or the householder's wife who swore the oath alongside her neighbouring servants.[102] This proactive bylaw, which maintained a regular system of preventative education, clearly demonstrates that protecting the river from rubbish was the priority and raising fines was merely a by-product of that regulation.

The eighteenth-century River Jurors introduced some imaginative innovations to boost the court's efficacy. They began to reward witnesses for reporting contraventions by paying to them part of the fine paid by the offender. In August 1767, the River Jurors received a complaint from John Turnbull, a keelman, against Richard Todd of Thistley House in the County of Durham, that he witnessed Richard casting 'a large quantity six cart loads and upwards of stones broken bricks, lime rubbish and dirt into the River Tyne to the great damage and prejudice of the same'.[103] And, in August 1780, Mr John Craister informed the court that he saw William Hatfield and John Hall, labourers, 'with rakes in their hands raking and putting the soils and mud of the said river from its place where the tide had left it … to the prejudice of the same'.[104] The words 'where the tide had left it' provide an insight into the direct way in which the River Jurors perceived the river as a living agent with its own capacity to move sediment. In this case, John Summers, who employed the labourers

---

100. Ibid.
101. L. Skelton, 'Beadles, Dunghills and Noisome Excrements: Regulating the Environment in Seventeenth-Century Carlisle', *International Journal of Regional and Local History* 9 (1) (May, 2014): 21–38; Skelton, *Sanitation*.
102. TWA, BC.RV/1/1-9: Tyne River Court Minute Books, 1644–1834.
103. TWA, BC.RV/1/7: River Tyne Court Minute Book, 1766–1772 (10 Aug. 1767), f. 47.
104. TWA, BC.RV/1/7: River Tyne Court Minute Book, 1766–1772 (27 Aug. 1770), f. 139.

Chapter 1. 'Hurting the River of Tine'

to do the work, was fined 1s and ordered to cease the activity immediately. Another case, submitted in June 1771, only seven months before a severe flood swept away most edifices in the river, was submitted by John Moses, esquire, of Hull, to build up his stone wear on King's Meadows, a Tyne island which he owned, as it had 'lately failed by means whereof the depth of water there hath been reduced and the fishery greatly prejudiced'.[105] The next month, after the Jurors had visited the island, they granted permission, having given very detailed consideration to the consequences of their decision. They recorded that the weir 'being composed of loose stones laid together is an improper one' because 'such stones for want of a proper fixture will be liable to be driven by the tides further into the said river', but a stronger weir 'would be of service to the river as well as to the fishery by giving such a check to the rapidity of the current there' and this would 'save some parts of the said island beneath from being washed into the river'.[106] Throughout the eighteenth century, fiscally motivated witnesses were potentially powerful, and indeed ubiquitous, arms of river bylaw enforcement. Similarly, Watson attributes the success of pre-modern Baron Courts to regulate Scottish woodland to 'the fact that the community as a whole was actively involved in it' as foresters and as '"sufficient witnesses" in any case requiring further investigation'.[107]

One obvious omission in the 1613 river bylaws was the impact of human activities on the river's wildlife, and on fish in particular, despite the operation of several substantial fisheries on the Tyne. However, the river court did sometimes regulate to protect fish even without a specifically relevant bylaw. In February 1786, Matthew Harrison swore that he witnessed Joseph Simpson, a fisherman of Ryton, on the southern bank of the Tyne, at a place called Pig's Hole 'take and kill two kipper or kidder salmons the same not being in season to the great destruction of the breed of salmons in the said river to the evil example of all others'.[108] This suggests that Smout's assertion that 'species preservation had no expression at all in the eighteenth century' is perhaps not completely accurate.[109] And Ralph Gardiner highlighted that in November 1649, when Captain Robert Wyard's ship was in the Tyne, 'one of his ships company … cast two or three straw mats out of one of his ships port holes'; during the case, it was assumed that this 'could do no harm to the river by reason its swim-

---

105. TWA, BC.RV/1/7: River Tyne Court Minute Book, 1766–1772 (17 June 1771), f. 166.
106. TWA, BC.RV/1/7: River Tyne Court Minute Book, 1766–1772 (1 Jul. 1771), f. 168.
107. Watson, 'Rights and Responsibilities', p. 110.
108. TWA, BC.RV/1/7: Tyne River Court Minute Book, 1772–1795 (6 Feb. 1786), ff. 32–33.
109. Smout, *Nature Contested*, p. 27.

ming to sea ... other than endanger the choaking of the fish'.[110] Although the potential damage to fish was played down, the fact that it is mentioned at all demonstrates that it was on the jurors' minds. As Thomas observes, 'long before the coming of pesticides and chemical fertilizers, pollution of the rivers killed the barbell, trout, bream, dace, gudgeon, flounders and other fish which had in Elizabethan times swum in the London Thames', noting 'since the thirteenth century there had been numerous attempts by statute, proclamation or forest law to prescribe a close season and to protect red and fallow deer, otters, hares, salmon, hawks and wild fowl during the breeding period'.[111] The lack of fishing regulations in the Tyne estuary contrasts sharply with the situation in the Firth of Forth in the same period, where fishing was tightly regulated.[112] Perhaps, for the most part, the Tyne River Jurors excluded wildlife from their conception of the estuary they had been appointed to protect.

Ballast heaps stored below the high water mark could be washed into the river very easily. Riparian residents and business owners were ordered to fence their properties to 'prevent the banks from falling and washing into the river, with the great floods, flashes and raines'.[113] In November 1646, Mrs Alnei's 'ballast shore was the worst & two heaps of ballast were washed off the said shore – one 19 yards long containing 100 tons of ballast above the water & the other 17 yards long containing 200 tons at least'.[114] But not all riparian ballast heaps were unstable. In 1698, Mr Rawling had been heaping ballast onto his holding area at Heworth Shore on the Tyne's south bank 'soe long unconveyed that the grass grows thereon'.[115] Rawling should have conveyed it more frequently, but he was clearly capable of heaping his ballast so stably that grass was able to take root and flourish from its relatively stationary structure. Contemporaries feared ballast falling into the river, warning in one bylaw that ballast quays must be kept in good order 'otherwise a hundred thousand tuns of ballast will fall into the river, to the destruction thereof'.[116] To counteract the inevitable silting up from fallen ballast, 'every winter season the poor keelmen and shewelmen' dug up and loaded into their keels large volumes of

---

110. R. Gardner, *England's Grievance Rediscovered* (London, 1655), p. 97.
111. K. Thomas, *Man and the Natural World: Changing Attitudes in England 1500–1800* (London: Penguin, 1984), pp. 275–276.
112. Smout and Stewart, *The Firth of Forth*, pp. 24–73.
113. Anon., *Reprints*, p. 17.
114. TWA, MD.NC/2/1: Newcastle Common Council Order Book, 1645–1650 (11 Nov. 1646), f. 74.
115. TWA, BC.RV/1/6: Tyne River Court Minute Book, 1695–1755 (11 Jul. 1698), f. 10.
116. Anon., *Reprints*, pp. 16–17.

Chapter 1. 'Hurting the River of Tine'

ballast and sand from the bed of the river.[117] This was a slow, laborious and expensive process, rendering essential rigorous environmental regulation that could reduce such work.

Conclusion

The renowned local eighteenth-century engraver Thomas Bewick was raised on the south bank of the Tyne at Cherryburn near Stocksfield and he spent most of his adult life in his workshop on The Side in Newcastle. Jenny Uglow, his biographer, believes that Bewick's attitudes towards river access rights and conservation more generally were well ahead of his time and that they developed as a direct result of walking along the Tyne frequently throughout his adult life between Newcastle and his childhood home at Cherryburn:

> In Bewick's suggestions we hear the voice of an early conservationist as well as a democrat – up to a point. Rivers should belong to the public, with access through a payment to the justice of the peace: a fishing licence, in effect. Commercial over-fishing should be stopped ... [and] something must be done about the 'filth from the manufactories', the sewage from the town and rubbish from the streets and the excess of lime and manure on the land, which sullied the waters.[118]

Uglow is right to highlight that these comments would be applauded today, and that Bewick was ahead of his time in terms of his attitudes towards the river and how it should and should not be used. She admits that Bewick's art was universal in its appeal, but she argues that it is also

> rooted in Northumberland and in the valley of the Tyne. All his life he walked the banks of the river and he knew it in all its moods, sleepy under early morning mist, driving on in flood, ruffled by wind. In woodcut after woodcut he had returned to the difficulty of crossing such waters ... The great river flowed through his art, and at the end it was waiting for him still.[119]

While it is not until the late-eighteenth century that we are able to hear such a personal, intimate and individual account of one man's relationship with the River Tyne and its natural resources, the Tyne River Court records nevertheless provide similarly deep insights into the management of the river and into the two-way socio-environmental relationship between its natural functions

---

117. Ibid.
118. Uglow, *Nature's Engraver*, p. 370.
119. Ibid., pp. 402–403.

and the people who sought to interact with its water, channel, bed and course throughout the early modern period.

Environmental regulation in the early modern Tyne estuary became increasingly regularised, more proactive and ultimately more efficient over the course of three centuries. Without the Water Bailiff, the River Jurors and their weekly River Court, the Tyne estuary would certainly have become much more problematically overdeveloped, Tyne water would have received more oxygen-hungry organic waste and much more complex webs of impediments to its flow would surely have been constructed, to the river's detriment. Despite the fact that the estuary's southern bank and the southern third of the river water and bed were owned nominally by the Bishop of Durham, Newcastle Corporation perceived themselves as the primary owners of the pre-modern Tyne's estuary. They certainly considered it to be a resource and a facility that they could rightfully utilise in order to generate profit and employment. Even when they used the words damage, destruction, hurt and spoil, they were referring to damage done to the river's efficiency to support trade, first and foremost. But their proactive regulation, and the time and effort they invested in controlling and ultimately limiting the adverse impacts of human activities on the river did have a positive effect on its environmental health. Newcastle's local governors clearly understood the river, how it functioned and the physical, if not the chemical and biological, impacts of waste disposal and ballast disposal on its flow speed and tide levels. Newcastle Corporation and Trinity House worked together to complete detailed surveys of the river and they were able to navigate ships from Shields to Newcastle and back because they understood every inch of the river's channel and bed. The River Jury regulated waste disposal relatively tightly at a weekly court. Contemporaries clearly feared 'damage' to the river, 'hurt' done to the river and 'spoiling' the river, which were all their own words. One might say that their systems were basic, that their technology was rudimentary and that their understanding of river systems was in its infancy. However, this is precisely why they acted with so much enthusiasm to protect the river's natural functions. They relied on it increasingly for trade, shipping and tolls and they feared harm done to the river because they were explicitly aware that they could only reverse such damage very slowly and inefficiently, using shovels powered by the labour of keelmen. Pollution was certainly substantially less serious in terms of scale between 1500 and 1850 than it became henceforth. But scale alone does not provide a satisfactory explanation as to why; the manner, extent and efficacy of environmental regulation, which laid

Chapter 1. 'Hurting the River of Tine'

the foundations of subsequent legislative frameworks and environmental attitudes, are as, if not more, important.

Although the river court could not possibly have prevented all contraventions of river bylaws, it was an effective legal facility, and became increasingly so over the course of the early modern period. Established in Newcastle in 1613, over a century before the Wear River Court was established in Sunderland, entrusted with increasing responsibilities to visit riparian sites, producing detailed site reports and making well-considered decisions, this court certainly cannot be described as unimportant, unnecessary or irrelevant. It represents a noteworthy development in environmental history, demonstrating a clear progression from the *ad hoc* and reactive management of the sixteenth century, to the regular and centralised regulation of the seventeenth century, to the imaginative and more inclusive innovations of the eighteenth century, which widened the community's participation in enforcing regulations. The importance and relevance of the extant, detailed Tyne River Court minute books within the context of environmental history cannot be exaggerated. The careful considerations and heartfelt concern of the Tyne River Court Jurors are heavily woven into the minute books they created, an important testament to their positive relationship with the River Tyne estuary of which they were so proud and on which they relied so heavily. Early modern people were not passive victims of nature, but nor were they active, wilful and irresponsible destroyers of it, as many of their nineteenth-century descendants arguably became. Interactions with natural systems were certainly perceived as a two-way process; the River Jurors knew what the river could do to them as well as, and sometimes because of, what they had done to the river. Records of early modern environmental regulation, of which there are many more under-researched examples, are no less important than seminal environmental texts from the age of environmentalism, such as *Silent Spring*.[120]

---

120. R. Carson, *Silent Spring* (London: Penguin, 2000), first published in the USA in 1962.

Chapter 2

'TINKERING' THE TYNE: INCREASING DEMAND FOR STRUCTURAL CHANGE, 1655–1855

Introduction

In the last chapter, we saw how fiercely Newcastle Corporation guarded their monopoly as conservators of the river. We learned about the efforts they made to regulate the impact on the river's natural functions of domestic and industrial waste, riparian building projects and other human activities. They did this to protect the liquid highway and navigable trading facility on which they relied so heavily. This chapter explores the long and complex process by which this oligarchy was undermined over two centuries, as Newcastle Corporation was accused of neglecting to invest the money it received from shipping and ballast tolls into funding structural improvements to the river's navigable channel. Consequently, its monopoly collapsed to make way in 1850 for the much more widely representative Tyne Improvement Commission, appointed by an Act of Parliament to manage and to improve the river's economic efficiency and navigability.

The chapter is split into five sections. It begins by analysing Ralph Gardner's ultimately unsuccessful petition arguing that North and South Shields should be permitted the right to receive ships at the mouth of the river, which he published in 1655 as *England's Grievance Rediscovered*. It then moves on to explain how the Great Flood of 1771 and the less devastating major flood of 1815 severely affected the relationship between people and the river and paved the way for subsequent attitudinal changes in relation to river improvements and trying to control the river more generally. Thirdly, it explores some serious letters of complaint concerning the lack of investment in river improvements in the early nineteenth century and Newcastle Corporation's last chance to cling onto their monopoly by creating a River Committee following the Municipal Corporations Act in 1835. The chapter then analyses the Royal Commission of

Chapter 2. 'Tinkering' the Tyne

1855, which was appointed five years after the Tyne Improvement Commission's establishment in 1850. By interviewing a large number of people with first-hand experience of managing the Tyne, it investigated Newcastle Corporation's historical lack of progress towards river improvements, and the TIC's lack of progress in its first five years.[1] The chapter is organised administratively and chronologically according to arguably artificial and anthropocentric chapters of the natural river's socio-economic and political management. However, each section focuses on the associated environmental consequences for the river's water, bed, channel and course and on what the important administrative and governance shifts reveal about the changing relationship between human society and this natural system over time. The chapter tracks administrative, political, legal and economic changes in order to understand how these new and different frameworks changed the language through which human society interacted with the natural river system. And it examines how different two-way socio-environmental interactions were encouraged or limited within different administrative, political, legal and economic parameters.[2]

Ralph Gardner's Petition, 1655

In the mid-seventeenth century, the people of North and South Shields on either side of the mouth of the Tyne had long appreciated that unnecessary and purely economically-motivated journeys eight miles upriver from Shields to the monopolistic port at Newcastle were causing many ships to sink. They were well aware that the establishment of ports at North and South Shields would obviate these unnecessary shipwrecks and improve the economic prosperity of North and South Shields. The people of Shields complained periodically over the centuries about the monopolistic and illogical arrangement and frequently approached national courts and the Crown to try to acquire the right to establish legal ports at the mouth of the river, but all these attempts were ultimately unsuccessful. Ralph Gardner, a Gentleman born in 1625 in Ponteland who became a brewer in North Shields at the age of 23, understood very clearly the injustice and consequences of Newcastle Corporation's oligarchic monopoly for people living at the mouth of the river. He challenged Newcastle Corporation vociferously in his petition, *England's Grievance Rediscovered*,

---

1. The establishment of the Tyne Improvement Commission is explained in more depth in chapter three.
2. Other environmental historians have analysed changing socio-environmental relationships within similar chronological and administrative frameworks, notably Cioc's *The Rhine* and Anfinson's *The River we have Wrought*.

published in 1655.[3] His arguments take us to the heart of the fiery politics that characterised the relationship between the people of Shields and of Newcastle. While Gardner largely omits environmental considerations from his argument, had he been successful the river's environmental health would have been improved. This case is an illuminating example of how natural systems' functions and environmental health can be constricted or liberated, sometimes unwittingly and unintentionally, by the political and economic decisions of local and national governors. Gardner's petition was ultimately unsuccessful in its aim to establish legal ports at North and South Shields, but by bringing together so many viewpoints on the issue, it provides a unique lens through which we can deepen our understanding of the grievances of the day. By 1655, this centuries-old issue was fuelling serious local conflict.

As we have seen, Newcastle Corporation exerted total control over the river and there was absolutely no chance that they would entertain removing the port to the mouth of the river at either North or South Shields. Such a change would, of course, have saved an awful lot of effort involved in navigating large sail ships up the river past problematic and periodically shifting sand shoals, unforgiving angular rock projections, unremoved sunken ships and sand bars, often requiring the use of skilled pilots provided for a fee by Newcastle Trinity House. Removing the port to Shields could even have saved lives too, because substantially fewer ships would have been sunk. Moreover, while riparian industries would still have continued on the banks of the estuary, moving the port to Shields would have prevented the dumping of large volumes of ballast into the river water and perhaps enabled the removal of large-scale infrastructure such as staiths which facilitated the loading of coal onto ships further up the estuary. But, most importantly for Newcastle Corporation, removing the port to Shields would have broken Newcastle's economic monopoly over very considerable shipping and ballast tolls. Understandably, Newcastle Corporation protected these fiercely.

The river was used and understood by everyone as an essential liquid highway, a regional asset with great economic value. But this liquid highway's practical benefits were distributed unevenly. The people of Shields had to watch market provisions sailing past them in large ships to be legally docked at Newcastle and then brought back down again on smaller boats to Shields. During very cold periods, which occurred frequently throughout the Little Ice Age (LIA) between 1330 and 1800, when the river typically froze over between Newcastle and Gateshead down as far as Bill Point, many boats were

---

3. Gardner, *Grievance*.

Chapter 2. 'Tinkering' the Tyne

effectively trapped at Newcastle, sometimes for months, unable to break out of the ice. River transport came to a standstill, which prevented the people of Shields from obtaining provisions as easily as they usually did, forcing them to use packhorses and carts on the perilously difficult and slow roads instead of using small boats to transport goods via the river. This only added to their frustration. Moreover, the provisions were often ingrossed or increased in price by the freemen of Newcastle, making them less affordable to the people of Shields when they travelled to buy provisions at Newcastle. This extract explains the nonsensical process of transporting all provisions upriver to Newcastle, where Gardner noted Newcastle Corporation 'do hinder a trade all the winter season by reason neither ships, nor boats, can pass up the river which is often frozen below the ballast shoars, called the Bill Point and half down the river it never freezeth lower'.[4] In his frustration, Gardner elaborated

> all provisions brought in by sea are compelled up to Newcastle and there ingrossed into the free mens hands; people often going to market have lost their lives, and many starved to death in the two counties w[h]ich cannot get to Newcastle market, in the winter season by reason of the great storms of snows, and the river frozen and no market allowed for the counties relief at Shields, where many thousand of passengers, sea men and inhabitants are being twelve miles from any market in the same county.[5]

To resolve this illogical and unfair situation, Gardner proposed that North Shields should be made into a market town so that the people there could 'be relieved with provisions during the time the river is frozen' without the 'loss of a daies labour and great charge to the poor in going by water in boat'.[6] This simple change, he argued, would also 'save the life of many a man and beast from falling into coal pits which lies open after the coals [have been] wrought out; being covered with snow'.[7] The passion behind Gardner's argument is evident in his description of Newcastle's mayor and aldermen as 'tyrants' who prioritised collecting their shipping and ballast tolls above all other considerations even as men were losing their lives in shipwrecks.

Adriaan de Kraker has researched the widespread practice of ice-breaking on Belgian and Dutch rivers and canals, which was conducted as a matter of course throughout the LIA between 1330 and 1800.[8] This represented a sub-

---

4. Ibid., p. 71.
5. Ibid., p. 109.
6. Ibid., p. 63.
7. Ibid., p. 63.
8. Kraker, 'Ice and Water'.

stantial investment of both man- and horse-power and financial investment in ice-breaking boats. Therefore the practice must have crucially underpinned social, economic and political life in these societies. De Kraker found, for example, that the boats were operated by twelve men and that they featured two strong ropes which connected a central mast to two respective teams of horses on each bank.[9] 'Totalling 40 horses', he elaborates, and 'pulling one big ice breaker through the ice', this required such a monumental effort of organic power that the commander of the boat had to use a 'primitive loudspeaker to command the horse drivers'.[10] In light of de Kraker's findings, it is surprising that there are no records from this period of ice breaking on the Tyne, which was further north than Belgium and Holland and which also facilitated economically important trade throughout the LIA. Perhaps in Belgium and Holland, where unfrozen rivers and canals were essential for the transportation of people as well goods between major towns, local governors were faced with little choice but to break the ice in order to enable society to function. As de Kraker notes, 'the barges of the sixteenth-early nineteenth century functioned like stage coaches did on land' and these barges even featured 'first and second class compartments where passengers were served food and drinks'.[11]

Gardner continued to undermine Newcastle Corporation's authority over what he clearly understood as a system ultimately beyond the control of man:

> If these men could command the wind, and seas, not to rage and swell but to be hushed into a calme and the river kept from friezing until they sent down help from Newcastle their reply might be admitted but since the wind, sea and ice are not controllable by their charter, what abominable tyranny what savage inhumanity is it to deny ships in distresses.[12]

In Gardner's mind, a mere charter did not enable Newcastle Corporation to control the weather in order to make safe the journeys they insisted upon from Tynemouth to Newcastle. If they could not improve the safety of journeys upriver, Gardner argued, it was unreasonable to force people to continue making them.

The document was written originally as a petition to be presented in Parliament to the Lord Protector, Oliver Cromwell. Gardner begins his petition stating:

---

9. Ibid.
10. Ibid.
11. Ibid.
12. Gardner, *Grievance*, p. 203.

Chapter 2. 'Tinkering' the Tyne

> For his highness, Oliver, Lord Protector of the Commonwealth of England, Scotland and Ireland
> May it please your highness,
> [I] do humbly present herein some collections of records taken out of most judicatures concerning the abuse of the coal trade, the burrough and the corporation of Newcastle upon Tine, its charters, evidences and depositions; proving thereby general wrongs and insupportable burdens.[13]

Gardner then goes on to call Newcastle Corporation 'destroyers of the famous river of Tine; forcing boats and ships to sink'.[14] He went into enormous detail, analysing several charters giving Newcastle Corporation the right to manage the river monopolistically, to enforce river bylaws and to collect shipping and ballast tolls. He complains that the bylaws written by London Trinity House in 1613 had not been effectively enforced, particularly in relation to preventing the deposition of ballast into the river water. Furthermore, he expressed his great fear that the river would silt up and have a detrimental effect on regional and national trade and economy. London relied heavily on Newcastle coal, known in London as sea coal as it was transported down England's east coast and came to Londoners from the sea. At a time when technology was relatively rudimentary and when there were no steam-powered dredgers to clear a choked up river, Gardner's genuine fear was not irrational. Indeed, as we learned in chapter one, this particular fear was shared wholeheartedly by his enemies, the members of Newcastle Corporation.

Gardner accused Newcastle Corporation of many things, from hoarding grain to push prices up during times of shortage to deliberately delaying the rescue of men from sinking ships in the estuary, but his main concern was the silting up of the river, which he cited as their main failure and for which he believed they should have been stripped of their river conservancy rights:

> That they have spoiled the river with their ballast shoars by ships sinking in sailing up the river and returning back their ballast shoars being so full and heavy and hilly that every shower of rain and storm of wind doth blow and wash down the ballast into the river besides the weight in pressing down the walls to the great prejudice of the commonwealth; by the obstruction of the river and endangering of shipping. That by the negligence of the commissioners for the river above three thousand tuns of ballast have fallen into the river in one nights time.[15]

---

13. Ibid., p. iv.
14. Ibid., p. iv.
15. Ibid., p. 70.

He also went on to point out that by his own estimate 'within this twenty years where twenty ships of a certain burden could have rid afloat in most road steads in the river at a low water mark now not above four ships can ride afloat'.[16] He complained that the people of Shields were prevented from building ballast shores at convenient places near the mouth of the river purely so that Newcastle Corporation did not lose income from their own ballast shores further upriver. These ballast shores, according to Gardner, were so full, hilly and inadequate that much of the ballast was being washed directly into the river, making the channel even more difficult to navigate.

Of course, Gardner's petition was unsuccessful since, the day before it was due to be heard in Parliament, in December 1653, Oliver Cromwell dissolved the Long Parliament. Perhaps as a result of this coincidental event, Newcastle Corporation was able to continue their conservancy of the river until 1850, when the Tyne Improvement Commission, which represented all of the riverside communities, took over by an Act of Parliament. Ralph Gardner was imprisoned and fined heavily as a result of his challenges to Newcastle Corporation, including his refusal to close down his brewery in North Shields which provisioned ships in contravention of Newcastle's monopoly on brewing. Gardner wrote his *Grievance Rediscovered* during one of his periods in prison, probably in 1653. Regardless of its ultimate failure, it is nevertheless a powerful and detailed account of the struggles between Shields and Newcastle and an articulate, passionate and well-considered attempt to apply some common sense to an economically driven oligarchic system of river management. This system was, in Gardner's opinion, not just economically unfair, but also dangerous, badly organised, immoral and nonsensical. While the monopoly delivered ever more profits into the hands of a small group of powerful oligarchs, it failed to serve the needs of everyone living and working on the River Tyne's banks. Ralph Gardner is still admired today as a 'faithful son of Father Tyne' and has had a high school and football ground named after him. A monument to him was unveiled in Chirton in 1882, engraved with a quote from Tennyson: 'who suffered countless ills, who battled for the true and just'. Perhaps, we can all learn something from Ralph Gardner's rant against a non-democratic form of local, national and river governance.

---

16. Ibid., p. 70.

Chapter 2. 'Tinkering' the Tyne

The Great Floods of 1771 and 1815

Mark Cioc reminded us in his *Eco-Biography* of the fact that floods are natural events. He highlights that '"flood" is a highly anthropocentric term, rooted in the human proclivity to think of a river as having a fixed length but no prescribed breadth, with the result that the floodplain is often used for farms and settlements as if it were not part of the river system'.[17] 'During high-water periods', Cioc elaborates very graphically, 'rivers absorb the extra water much like a python digests its prey: a bulge (or swell) appears as the water passes downstream'.[18] As Olivia Laing observes, building on floodplains will remain 'a risky venture – until, of course, we find a way to make it rain at will', and she highlights that 'a flood is not entirely a destructive event'.[19] The river's most serious floods were natural events, but they have become an important part of the region's story, shared experiences that physically and often forcibly connect those living in riparian communities to the river as well as to each other. Narratives of so-called great floods are passed anecdotally from generation to generation, explaining the awe, the terror, even the perceived violence that the river inflicts on its riverside communities as a self-conscious, guilty and criminal agent. Stories of floods are preserved, celebrated and have entered the collective memory of the region because they mark the most noteworthy and memorable points at which the river permeated the artificial line between the human and the natural. In reality, the human and the natural are fully merged. They are only separate domains in the human imagination. Floods re-emphasise the strong bonds that connect elements of the physical environment which some divide between the human and the natural. They correct the artificial gap, or buffer zone, which many people create imaginatively between their human world and powerful natural systems such as rivers. The ways in which people remember floods underline the extent to which they conceptualise the natural and the human as incompatible, even as mutually exclusive, certainly as inhabiting very separate spaces, rules and characteristics. In the early nineteenth century, a widespread aspiration to dredge the Tyne more extensively and to place its powerful flow increasingly under human control gathered pace. This attitudinal change undoubtedly resulted, at least partially and for some probably subconsciously, from two serious floods, the so-called Great Flood of 1771 and a less serious but still quite devastating flood in 1815. The genuinely frightening experiences of these floods changed the relationship between local people

---

17. Cioc, *The Rhine*, p. 33.
18. Ibid., p. 35.
19. O. Laing, *To the River* (London: Canongate, 2012), p. 178.

Figure 4. Flood Markers at the Boathouse Public House, Newburn (Photograph: Gordon Ball)

and the Tyne, perhaps irreversibly, especially around the population centres of Newcastle and Gateshead and up and down the industrialised estuary. The floods have embedded themselves very effectively into the local collective memory.

Floods are one of the most serious and threatening ways in which a river can impact directly on the people living and working on and around it. In 1772, Rev. Isaac Farrar, Curate of Egglestone, wrote a narrative of the Great Tyne Flood of November 1771. He called it 'the most dreadful inundation that ever befell that part of the country', resulting in 'a scene of horror and devastation, too dreadful for words to express, or Humanity to behold with-

Chapter 2. 'Tinkering' the Tyne

out shuddering'.[20] This flood resulted in the destruction of the old stone Tyne Bridge, on which many houses and shops had been constructed. That he also described destruction further up the river suggests that quite a close connection existed between riparian communities both above and below the tidal reach at Hedwin Streams near Wylam:

> But Newcastle did not alone suffer from the terrible violence of this flood: Hardly a village or cottage-house from [South] Tyne-head, in Alston-moor, to Shields, escaped its destructive fury: The bridges at Alston, Ridley Hall, Haydon, Chollerford, and Hexham, were all carried away; the wooden bridge at Allendale was swept away entire, and discovered the next day lying across a lane near Newbrough, as exactly as if fixed there by human means. It is impossible to ascertain the prodigious number of horses, black cattle, sheep and other animals, that have perished and of corn and hay stacks, hedges, fences, implements of husbandry, and whole acres of ground, which have been swept away by the impetuosity of the torrent, whereby families who have lived in affluence and plenty are now reduced to the most abject misery and want.[21]

The Rev. Farrar's perception of the placement of the Allendale wooden bridge further downstream 'as if by human means' emphasises his appreciation of the flood as a completely natural and explicitly non-human event. In his mind, human and natural means were very separate processes. He went on to describe how 'many people were taken out of their houses through the roofs', describing 'the shrieks of women and children, frantic with all the agonies of despair' and how 'dead bodies and coffins were torn out of church-yards, and the living and the dead promiscuously clashed in the torrent'.[22] Perhaps, the meeting of the living and the dead symbolised, in Farrar's mind, the similarly incompatible clash between the powerful, natural river and the human riparian settlements in which it had wrought havoc. The topography of the riverbed had been changed substantially by the flood: 'the bed of the river Tyne being entirely altered by the flood, the Master and Brethren of the Trinity-house ordered the pilots to make a survey of the new channel in order to qualify themselves to lay the buoys in the proper places, that ships may be conducted up and down with usual safety'.[23] The pilots of Newcastle Trinity House had a very intimate knowledge of the river bed between the river mouth and the port at Newcastle, and they

---

20. Anon., *Narrative of the Great Flood in the Rivers Tyne, Tease, Wear &c on the 16th and 17th of Nov 1771. Collected from the most authentic papers yet published* (Newcastle, 1772), no page numbers in the pamphlet.
21. Ibid.
22. Ibid.
23. Ibid.

guided ships using particular pathways, which were known as 'roadsteads'. The Tyne was able to render useless the pilots' detailed and accurate knowledge of its bed, together with their ability to use it without risking the loss of property or human life. Throughout its history, the Tyne has expressed itself naturally and continued to thwart our human endeavours to put it in its place.

Some 44 years subsequently, in December 1815, John Bell recorded 'severe and widespread injury occasioned by the overflowing of the river'.[24] He noted that, as a result of the overflowing water, whose 'appearance was particularly awful', the 'Quayside and lower part of the Close were overflowed and almost every cellar filled with water'.[25] 'Throughout the whole of Saturday', he went on, 'the fire engines were employed in pumping the water out of the several cellars'.[26] Damage to agriculture was also severe:

> Many horses and cows have been drowned, both in their pastures and stalls and the quantity of sheep which have been drowned and washed away is very great. The loss of the latter animal is particularly severe. … Very great injury has also been done to the crops of corn on all the low grounds near the river, the soil off many of the fields being entirely washed away, and others covered with sand &c.[27]

John Bell personified the river in no uncertain terms, recalling 'the sudden rise and fury of the torrent'.[28] And he noted, 'the inhabitants of many cottages situated near the banks of the river at Newburn and Scotswood had very fortunate escapes, the water having entered their houses whilst they were in bed and they were obliged to be taken out by boats through the roofs and windows'.[29] The Tyne Bridge stood firm. It had been rebuilt relatively recently after the flood of 1771. But the bridge over the Tyne at Haydon Bridge was damaged and 'Eals bridge across the South Tyne in the parish of Knaresdale was also carried away'.[30]

These floods necessarily shaped local perceptions of the river and its place within society and the landscape. The floods might well have paved the way in the long and short term, as we shall see later in the chapter, for interested local people to accuse the river's official conservators, Newcastle Corporation, of

---

24. J. Bell, *An Account of the Great Flood in the River Tyne on Dec 30 1815* (Newcastle: J. Bell, 1816), p. 3.
25. Ibid., p. 4.
26. Ibid., p. 4.
27. Ibid., p. 6.
28. Ibid., p. 7.
29. Ibid., p. 6.
30. Ibid., p. 6

Chapter 2. 'Tinkering' the Tyne

ineffectual, slow and inefficient efforts to improve the river's structural capacity for trade. By the early decades of the nineteenth century, by which point the new technology of steam-powered dredging machines were available, it had become very obvious to many interested local people that the river bed was not being dredged anywhere near as efficiently as it could have been. In recent years, significant volumes of ballast had been allowed to enter the river. Historically, the depths of the navigable channel had been problematically low. A chart of the estuary created in 1650 shows water depths at low tide of eighteen feet between North and South Shields, which reduced to twelve feet only one mile into the river and to between nine and eleven feet at Newcastle.[31] A subsequent chart produced between 1700 and 1750 features even lower depths of thirteen feet falling to eight feet at neap tides and zero depth in some places at low tide.[32] As Peter Wright observes, in the 'mid-eighteenth century the draught of a 100-foot long English "Cat", with a tonnage of between 150 and 200 tons, was about 15 feet' which meant that 'with care, the river was navigable to quite large ships'.[33] However, as Wright explains, navigation to Newcastle was 'possible in a single tide with a favourable wind, but with contrary winds and low tides it may have been necessary to anchor and await deeper water and better conditions, rather than face the risk of running aground and stranding'.[34] Dredging the river bed would provide safer and more economically efficient transit for ships from Tynemouth to Newcastle and it would also provide more room for the river's water during periods of high water, thus reducing the risk of flooding. In an increasing number of local and national minds, something had to be done to improve the extent of human control over and the navigability and economic efficiency of this nationally strategic port.

The River Committee and Public Impatience for River Improvement, 1832–1850

In January 1832, John MacGregor addressed the coal owners of the district. He summarised in a very long letter of over a hundred pages the discontent felt widely in the region about the unacceptably slow speed of structural improvements to the river and 'the accumulation of sand banks in the channel,

---

31. Wright, *Life on the Tyne*, pp. 26–27.
32. Ibid., p. 30.
33. Ibid., p. 30.
34. Ibid., p. 32.

which have for ages partially obstructed the navigation'.[35] He expressed his concerns about the Tyne's capacity to deal with expansion in its trade as the British Empire developed and steam power enlarged the scale of international trade. He complained that nothing had been done following the creation of detailed plans earlier in the century. In June 1816, Mr John Rennie the Elder, was commissioned by Newcastle Corporation for £2,000 to produce an engineering report on the state of the Tyne estuary and a schedule of suggested works of improvement, but it had been shelved since its completion. Rennie was renowned for his engineering skill, having designed the docks at Hull and Liverpool, London's East India and West India Docks and the docks at Leith, Portsmouth, Holyhead, Ramsgate and Chatham. Newcastle Corporation's decision to shelve a detailed schedule of works designed by a man of Rennie's esteem understandably infuriated some local people whose businesses relied on an economically efficient Tyne.

MacGregor's description of the natural functions of the river is noteworthy because it describes the river in great detail immediately before very large-scale structural engineering projects were initiated by the TIC after 1850.

> Flowing through an Alpine country, their beds are rocky and pebbly; and such, for the most part, are those of the main stream and its few tributaries in consequence of which the waters under normal circumstances arrive pretty clear in their neighbourhood of Newcastle. ... The paucity of river water is, however, amply compensated to commerce by the tides of the German ocean, which here ascent to the celebrated boundary of Hedwin Streams, or seven miles above Newcastle. The Tyne is subject to heavy floods after continued rain or snow, during which its waters are in some degree loaded with earthy and arenaceous matter, but owing to the increased velocity most of this burden together with much of what had accumulated in the interval from other causes, is then carried to sea, so that freshes are to be regarded as salutary operations of nature in cleaning the channel. But notwithstanding sand-banks of considerable magnitude do exist in that portion of the channel between the Bridge and the Bar and seriously incommode the navigation. The principal of these are Walker, Cock-Crow, Coxlodge, Jarrow, Droitwich, Coble Dean, Middle-ground and In Sands, amounting collectively to, perhaps, one hundred and thirty eight acres.[36]

The sand banks were an important feature of the river before they were obliterated by large-scale dredging operations later in the nineteenth century. Although they shifted substantially with tides and flood events, that they were given names

---

35. J. MacGregor, *Observations on The River Tyne, with a View to the Improvement of its Navigation; Address to the Coal Owners of the District* (Newcastle, Jan, 1832), p. iii.

36. Ibid., p. 22.

Chapter 2. 'Tinkering' the Tyne

confirms that they retained a lasting foothold in the riverscape. MacGregor gives three reasons for the deposition of so much sand in the estuary: the washing down of silt from the upper river; the dumping and spilling of sand and gravel ballast from ships in the estuary; and the introduction of marine sand by the tide. This demonstrates that MacGregor had quite a sophisticated level of understanding in relation to the river system's functions. It confirms that the increasing impatience of MacGregor and his contemporaries to improve the river by controlling its natural functions, by redesigning and restructuring its channel and bed, cannot be attributed simply to their ignorance of either the Tyne's natural complexities or its perceived beauty. Despite clear appreciation of the river's wonder, beauty and natural efficiency, MacGregor wished to transform it. Clearly, in MacGregor's mind, to restructure the river was to improve the river.

In his letter, MacGregor complained of the sand banks, calling them 'the embarrassments in the river' and he lamented that 'rivers are seldom straight in their course'.[37] He believed that everything in nature 'aims at equilibrium', and that this aim was responsible for the 'rambling of rivers', but sometimes, he explained, 'the general procedure of nature is inconsistent with our local purposes'.[38] In this clear statement, he conceptualised the force of nature, its 'general procedure', as an independent agent and he admitted that he was proposing to alter the river because its natural expressions were not conducive to 'our local purposes'. In this sense, the natural functions of the river were not to be completely dominated or absorbed fully into the human domain, the infrastructural facility of the river. Rather, they were forces to be circumvented and manipulated towards human purposes by a process of negotiation, albeit a very unfair negotiation in which the ability of the river to express itself would be substantially curtailed, but nonetheless a two-way engagement with an independent force of nature. He noted that the most considerable projections were Bill and Whitehill Points and Fryer's Ballast Hill, Hebburn Quay and Whitehill Staith, and he complained that steam dredgers were already in use on the Thames, at Hull, Bristol, Sunderland and the Caledonian Canal. His suggestion to undertake 'proper husbanding of the water', in order to improve its capacity for trade, reveals a perceived synonymy between agriculture and river management.[39]

---

37. Ibid., p. 44.
38. Ibid., p. 44.
39. Ibid., p. 115,

Tyne after Tyne

In October 1832, MacGregor wrote yet another letter to local coal owners, merchants and ship owners, discussing his thoughts on a manual dredging machine, which had appeared on the river six weeks after his first letter. His opinion of the manual dredger, capable of dredging 35 tons of material per day, is crystal clear:

> Now it is somewhat singular that the Corporation of Newcastle seated in the midst of mechanical art and of an extensive coal district and whose river is a great focus of shipment should offer a reward for a retrograde invention which can only do in a day what a steam dredger can accomplish in half an hour. In the present day we could look with patience at such a machine only in China or within the territory of an African prince.[40]

MacGregor conceptualised this relatively slow dredging machine as incongruous in the context of the industrialising British Empire. Using some of the same examples and arguments as Ralph Gardner had done two centuries earlier in his *England's Grievance Rediscovered*, MacGregor criticised the corporation for its historic mismanagement of ballast deposition. He described how 'it was cast on shore by the shovel directly from the ship itself, or from lighters, when the ship could not approach the wharf conveniently' and that 'during this operation, much [ballast] from carelessness and design dropped into the river, notwithstanding the seeming precaution of stretching a sail between the vessel and the shore'.[41] He noted, too, that 'it was customary also to cast ballast in former times into small creeks whence it was washed back into the river by the tides, rain and the small runnels which frequently discharge into them'.[42] MacGregor suggested that the conservatorship of the river should be placed into the hands of appointed commissioners representing the whole estuary who could approve plans for jetties, wharfs and other river improvements. He would wait a further eighteen years before his wish was granted.

Following the 1835 Municipal Corporations Act, Newcastle Corporation, sometimes called Newcastle Common Council, became Newcastle Council and it appointed a River Committee to take over the work previously conducted by the Tyne River Court, its Water Bailiff and River Jurors. This governing institution was no more competent in relation to river engineering and arguably no less oligarchic than its predecessor, because crucially it did not represent the wider riparian communities or the manufacturing and coal owners up and

---

40. J. MacGregor, A Letter to the Merchants, Coalowners, and Shipowners of Newcastle on the Present State of the Conservatorship of the Tyne (Newcastle, Oct, 1832), p. 2.
41. Ibid., p. 29.
42. Ibid., p. 29.

Chapter 2. 'Tinkering' the Tyne

down the whole estuary. However, it did provide an opportunity for a change in the style of Newcastle's river management. The minutes of its meetings suggest a distinct change in tone, attitude and administrative efficiency, but in fifteen short years of existence it was unable to catch up with such a colossal mountain of work to drive forward the scheduled river improvements before Parliament established the more representative Tyne Improvement Commission in 1850.

The Newcastle Council River Committee met weekly at one o'clock on Mondays for two hours.[43] The committee of sixteen men was appointed to 'enquire into the present state of the River', to find the best methods of 'improving that state' and to obtain evidence from 'persons of practical skill and experience and persons having a practical knowledge of the River Tyne and from persons accustomed to engineering enquiries'.[44] The committee was to utilise all former surveys and plans of the river and to 'make use of some suitable boat or barge' in the course of its investigations to ascertain the most 'eligible means of improvement' and had to find suitable ways of raising the funds necessary to carry out such improvements into 'efficient execution'.[45] The committee inherited an enormous backlog of river improvements, and from its inception its members came under a great deal of pressure to drive them forward. At a meeting in February 1836, the committee decided that printing an informative pamphlet would help allay public concern about the lack of progress in relation to river improvement. The pamphlet included Rennie's 1816 plan, the opinion of the River Jury, the estimated costs of the proposed works and the views of several local people. In the same year, clearly possessed with a newly sharpened zeal to get on with this important work, the River Committee decided to acquire an efficient dredging machine, with an engine of '10 horse power with an iron boat', as soon as possible.[46] They also agreed that improving the quays and dredging the river bed should be progressed simultaneously.[47] In May 1836, the River Committee found an appropriate dredging machine from 'Messrs Fenton Murray of Leeds', who offered 'to supply a steam engine of 10 horse power with machinery for dredging (inclusive of wood work) for £1260'.[48] They needed it to work in depths of between four and fifteen feet, but potentially in depths of eighteen feet in the future. The records of the com-

---

43. TWA, MD/NC/238: Borough of Newcastle Upon Tyne River Committee Minute Book, f. 1.
44. Ibid., f. 1.
45. Ibid., f. 1.
46. Ibid., f. 3.
47. Ibid., f. 3.
48. Ibid., f. 6

mittee suggest that this was the first dredging machine to be used on the Tyne, given that they sought the services of an experienced man to get them started. However, as we have seen, four years earlier, in 1832, MacGregor complained about Newcastle Corporation's disinclination to acquire a new steam dredger to replace their older, more basic manual dredger.[49] There is no mention of the previous dredger in the River Committee's minutes, and they discuss their new dredger as if it were the first to be used on the river, which suggests that they were perhaps trying to disassociate themselves from the failures and tardiness of the previous conservatorship.

The River Committee dealt with applications to construct quays and tried to maintain the integrity of the river line drawn by Rennie in 1816. Alongside this traditional regulatory work, they drove forward various river improvement projects in a substantially more efficient manner than their predecessors, the Tyne River Court. They arranged for the removal of part of Whitehill Point and the adoption of a quay there. They conducted views of the river shores on their own barge. They made a lithograph of Rennie's plan of quays and jetties and river line to ensure that the quays didn't encroach too far into the river channel. And they regulated encroachments and ensured that river walls, quays and jetties were constructed of appropriate materials and well maintained. In February 1836, a Mr William Greaves proposed to remove clay from Bill Point and to reduce the stone to high water mark, for which he would charge nothing so long as he could profit from the materials removed. His proposal was approved. In June 1836, the committee directed the Water Bailiff to ensure that the glass manufacturers Tyzack and Dobinson 'shall be required to proceed to rebuild their sea wall near the Low Lights' and that 'they be allowed a reasonable quantity of Chalk Rubbish to back the work'.[50] The committee was quick to intervene when companies and individuals threatened the river's capacity to do its work properly. In October 1836, for example, the committee ordered that the 'Tyne Iron Company must be required to desist from depositing Iron slag on the banks of the river and think it probable that a quay may be necessary in order to prevent the iron slag already deposited sliding into the river'.[51]

In November 1836, they advised Newcastle Council to employ the services of Mr Cubitt, a consulting engineer, to aid their conservatorship of the Tyne.[52] Mr Cubitt was duly employed and was sent copies of Rennie's 1816

---

49. MacGregor, *Observations* (Jan., 1832).
50. TWA, MD/NC/238: Borough of Newcastle Upon Tyne River Committee Minute Book, f. 7.
51. Ibid., f. 11.
52. Ibid., f. 12.

Chapter 2. 'Tinkering' the Tyne

plan and reports straight away. The committee wished to direct several projects towards Mr Cubitt for his deliberation: 1) an extension of Newcastle Quay; 2) the removal or partial removal of Friars Goose Point; 3) the removal of Bill Point; and 4) the construction of a quay between Howdon Pans and the Lime Kiln shore, including the removal of Whitehill Point. It is important to bear in mind that the River Committee's members were not engineering experts; in many respects, they were starting from scratch on the serious business of improving the river structurally using technically sophisticated methods.[53] Mr Cubitt first attended the River Committee in March 1837, advising that he thought they would need some experienced person 'to take the direction of the dredging machine'.[54] They appointed a Mr Edwards for one month to start the dredging operations and they employed James Smith of Sunderland to the charge of the dredging machine at weekly wages of 26s.[55] However, in December 1839, the committee discontinued the use of the dredging machine and advertised in the newspaper to let the machine to private individuals on a temporary basis. In September 1840, the dredger was reinstated on the south shore between Tyne Bridge and the Brandling Junction Staith and at Bill Point, but, despite the River Committee's initial zeal, progress had lapsed considerably as it became increasingly clear that they were not up to the enormous challenge of improving the Tyne's navigability.

The Royal Commission of 1855

Only two years after the establishment of the TIC, in 1852, Edward Calver Esq., Admiralty Surveyor, wrote to the new improvemnt commissioners. He had serious misgivings about the commissioners' initial plans, stating that in his eyes the commissioners planned to 'uphold a system of river improvements which I believe to be as erroneous in theory, as I know it to be destructive in practice'.[56] He was a marine engineering expert, having spent his career surveying many ports and rivers along the eastern seaboard, including the Tyne. He emphasised that river engineering was in its infancy, and that

> each projector has, as it were, groped in the dark, hit upon what he conceived to a remedy and carried it out in many instances to the injury of the places

---

53. Ibid., f. 14.
54. Ibid., f. 16.
55. Ibid., f. 23.
56. Edward Calver, *A Letter to the Tyne Improvement Commissioners by Edward K. Calver, Esq. R. N. Admiralty Surveyor* (Newcastle, 1852), pp. 3–4.

operated upon; and where measures of the sort have succeeded they can scarcely be termed more than fortunate guesses; – this, I believe, every honest engineer will allow to be the case.[57]

He completed a detailed survey of the Tyne between Newcastle and the Tynemouth in 1813, which was incorporated into Rennie's plan, and in 1849, he undertook another. The major changes between these years were:

1) A loss of thirty-four millions of cubic feet of tidal water, every common spring;

2) The berthage in North Shields Harbour for heavy ships, including that for Government vessels, and which would again be required in case of war, had been reduced in breadth and depth;

3) Whereas the first interruption to navigation in 1813 was twenty-eight thousand feet within the Narrows, in 1849 it had narrowed even further to only fifteen thousand feet;

4) An encroachment of ninety-five acres upon the high water surface of the river;

5) That the deep water track of the whole river was slightly longer in 1850 than it had been in 1813;

6) That it had decreased in depth eight inches throughout and was 'decidedly inferior for all navigable purposes'.[58]

Three years after Calver's letter, in 1855, an investigative Royal Commission was appointed to inquire into the 'present state of the Tyne'. It interviewed a large number of witnesses who had been directly involved in conducting, or whose work had been affected by, Newcastle Corporation's, the River Committee's and the new TIC's river management. The commission sat in Newcastle between 24 and 31 January 1855, and it heard further evidence subsequently in London. The report that the commission produced after the hearings was published and made publicly available later in 1855. It is historically important because it provided the basis for the TIC's schedule of major river engineering works, which was pursued right up until 1968, but also because it provides a highly detailed and directly relevant snapshot of the condition of the river's bed, channel and course during a pivotal transition in the Tyne's environmen-

---

57. Ibid., pp. 3–4.
58. Ibid., pp. 3–4.

Chapter 2. 'Tinkering' the Tyne

tal history.[59] And it contains the answers to quite serious questions about the lack of progress in improving its capacity to support the maximal expansion of trade and commerce, even in the five years since the establishment of the TIC in 1850. In short, the report of this commission is the birth certificate of a new and different relationship with the estuary, which guided interactions with the river's natural functions, prioritising industry, navigation and trade, until the mid-twentieth century.

The report opens with its main finding, that 'during the last two or three centuries all the evidence would lead to the conclusion that a very general similarity has been maintained in the state of the Tyne' and that the 'the navigable state of the river has not been much altered'.[60] Several river surveys provided the basis for the questioning during the inquiry. The report noted that the most recent survey, produced for the Admiralty in 1849 by Mr Calver, an engineer, was 'so valued a work that the Admiralty sent his chart of the Tyne to the British Exhibition in 1851'.[61] They concluded that they were 'disposed to conclude from the evidence laid before us that not only should every river, as observed by Mr Rendel, be treated according to its own peculiar character, but that strictly speaking each part of the same river may require different management'.[62] This marks a step change in the appreciation of the Tyne's complexities and it confirms their acceptance that there was no one-size-fits-all system for redesigning rivers. Rather, tailored plans had to be developed in the context of the particular characteristics of each section of a river. Clearly, then, rivers were not perceived in quite the same way as railways and there was some appreciation of their natural characteristics and important differences, not only between each other but also between particular sections. After in-depth consideration of the merits and disadvantages of half tide and full tide training walls, the commissioners decided that full tide walls were the most expedient. The canalisation of the river was set in motion at this Royal Commission. This is why today we see the Tyne flowing at Newcastle and Gateshead between thick, austere and vertically straight walls well above the water line (usually!), rather than lapping against a more natural foreshore.

At the very beginning of the inquiry, Mr Webster, one of the interviewers of the investigation, accused the TIC of progressing in their initial years a plan

---

59. *Report of the Commissioners Appointed to Inquire into the Present State of the River Tyne; together with the Minutes of Evidence and Appendix* (London: George Edward Eyre and William Spottiswoode, 1855), p. ix.
60. Ibid., p. v.
61. Ibid., p. vi.
62. Ibid., p. vii.

'wholly unadapted to the altered state of times'.[63] Clearly, the Tyne commissioners had failed to administer the marked attitudinal changes and the faster speed of river improvements that the central government had fully expected to develop when it appointed the TIC in 1850. To their predecessors, Newcastle Council, Webster said,

> though you the conservators had in 1816 Mr Rennie's Report which is a most elaborate report and a chart of the Tyne, all you did with it was to keep it in your corporation chest. You have gone on tinkering the river, so to speak without any plan, just as it suited the particular emergency or interest or wishes or objects of the moment.[64]

The expression 'tinkering the river' reveals the frustration felt by central government. The government rejected such 'tinkering' in no uncertain terms and exerted maximal pressure on the TIC to step up the pace. To be sure, the pressure to modify the river very dramatically, and to make it work much more productively as a piece of nationally useful infrastructure, flowed from the centre in London to Tyneside.

Throughout the report, the commissioners emphasised the national importance of the river as an export facility for coal, noting for example that, in 1847, some 3,466,527 tons of coal were exported in 20,713 vessels.[65] Mr Webster did not mince his words when describing the state of the river below Newcastle:

> You must have seen the state of dilapidation which exists in many portions of the sides of the river. You must, I think, have been struck with the contrast exhibited between the state of the river near Newcastle and the state of the river a very little way down. You have had your attention called to the recommendations about Bill Point. You may remember that was cut down to a certain extent so as to give a better view but that the rock below was left untouched so that as regards the sailing channel, things are no better or very little better than they were in Mr Rennie's time [i.e. 1816]. ... And matters have gone on in a way which certainly is very unbecoming in the conduct of a river like the Tyne.[66]

Webster clearly respected the Tyne, and could see its potential to promote national prosperity in concert with other powerful rivers like it, but he was frustrated by its previous conservators' lack of progress and the lack of intensity with which the TIC had performed their first five years of work. He understood

---

63. Ibid., p. 4.
64. Ibid., p. 4.
65. Ibid., p. 6.
66. Ibid., p. 33.

Chapter 2. 'Tinkering' the Tyne

the river as capable of expressing its own agency: as he explained 'it was throwing away money to dredge until the training walls and other matters of that kind had been executed so as to allow the channel to do its own work to the extent which it would do and which it is well known it will do, in all cases of this kind'.[67] The river's ability to 'do its own work' was one of its independent and natural expressions. While the TIC manipulated the river to do this particular work of deepening its own estuarine channel, the commissioners were never able to completely control its capacity to do this work. The river could perform the work the TIC wanted it to do in certain circumstances. But, crucially, the TIC had to work within those circumstances in order to reap the benefits of a hard-working Tyne. In this way, the Tyne set the parameters within which the TIC had to work in order to achieve their ambitions and it did not obey their orders without question. Rather, it negotiated its working conditions.

Joseph Straker, a TIC commissioner, was also a ship owner, merchant and coal owner and he had worked around the river for over fifty years. He criticised Newcastle Council for not having treated the river as a whole:

> I am of opinion that the river should have been treated as a whole, not to have been tinkered and patched up in the way that it has been, here and there and anywhere, but that should have been treated as one great whole measure which should have been commenced at the bar and worked upwards. That is my opinion.[68]

When Straker was asked 'how many winters has ice come down in any great body, so as to be injurious to shipping?', he replied

> Twice I remember its being completely fast below the bridge right across. On one of these occasions they used sledges upon it, and had booths upon it, and various things below bridge. When it broke up of course it was very dangerous to the ships down the river; but I only recollect two or three occasions in which it has occurred in 50 years.[69]

This battle against the river's climatic changes is reminiscent of the same old problems Ralph Gardner had complained about in 1655.

Straker explained that even the establishment of the TIC in 1850 had failed dramatically to alter the previous system of conservancy. While the TIC was nominally more widely representative than Newcastle Corporation, when asked 'has the management been substantially in the same hands?', he

---

67. Ibid., p. 36.
68. Ibid., p. 41.
69. Ibid., p. 54.

answered 'it has', elaborating that 'it results from a part of the commissioners being composed of members of the Newcastle Corporation who have always been able to carry a majority in the commission'.[70] Straker was asked if the improvement of the river had been 'much retarded' by the disputes between Newcastle and Shields, and he answered 'I think so'. This led the interviewer, Mr Webster, to ask

> are you aware that in consequence of the disputes which took place in the Mersey between Liverpool and Birkenhead, the Crown interfered and that a Conservator of the Mersey is now appointed who takes charge of the whole of that river without the interference of either Liverpool or Birkenhead?[71]

This was a subtle threat that if such counterproductive disputes continued between Newcastle and Shields, the Crown had the power to impose a similar system of conservancy on the Tyne. Clearly, the push for greater efficiency, speedy improvement and a much greater zeal for the transformation of the Tyne emanated largely from central government. The Tyne commissioners, after five years of progress that was deemed to have been nowhere near swift enough, were essentially being ordered in no uncertain terms to improve their performance or face exclusion from the management of the river. In this conceptualisation, the Tyne belonged to the whole nation and it must be made to work for the whole nation's prosperity, regardless of local and regional political conflict.

Commander William Purdo, another Tyne Commissioner, explained astonishingly simple practical problems that had contributed to Newcastle Council's poor conservatorship. When he was asked about the Corporation's use of river surveys, he replied

> I never saw them but once, when I went into the engineer's room and it is such a dark dog-hole that you cannot see them, and I wanted them very seriously ... to make my own marks upon them. ... The fact is there is no room to spread them out there; they cannot be dealt with.[72]

This 'dog-hole' was not a suitable nerve centre for the large-scale transformation that the Royal Commission was trying to initiate. Mr Matthew Popplewell, a Lloyds Shipping Surveyor of North Shields, also served as a commissioner and had worked on the river for 21 years. He brought the enquiry's attention to the marked changes which the Tyne made to the foreshore:

---

70. Ibid., p. 41.
71. Ibid., p. 52.
72. Ibid., p. 69.

Chapter 2. 'Tinkering' the Tyne

> The Narrows are much narrower than they were then [in 1825]. The sand shifts very much on the south side. One spring tide it is not the same breadth as the next tide. The sand is not left in the same position but will be altered every raging tide. On the north side it is further south and a hard foreshore is now formed; it was formerly very steep.[73]

The Tyne was able to move its sediment and bed according to its own needs and rhythms and this frustrated those who were trying to use it to support their work. This was a two-way interaction that continued, albeit to differing extents, throughout the whole period under discussion. Popplewell criticised previous operations 'in the time of the old corporation' when 'they actually employed a dredger to raise the sand up and to drop it down again that it should be carried away out of the river', which was largely unsuccessful as the material was reincorporated into the river bed.[74] He reassured the enquiry that 'we found the river in a certain state and it is our duty as commissioners to do the best we can to make the best highway'.[75] The enquiry's questions and scrutiny of the TIC's plans left the commissioners in no doubt at all about their responsibility to work this natural river system into the most efficient port, highway and infrastructural facility possible for the service of the region but of the country as whole.

Conclusion

Stefania Barca's research into the industrialisation of the Italian River Liri revealed that following the 1816 union of the Kingdom of Naples and the Kingdom of Sicily to form the Kingdom of the Two Sicilies, the governance of the river was liberated from the previous 'abuses of the feudal government', which had prioritised managing the water for the 'special interest' of grinding and fulling mills above the general interest.[76] She elaborates that widespread criticism of the previous management of the river under the Bourbon Monarchy, and during the political instabilities of the Napoleonic Wars, was not directed at the water or to the river itself, but rather towards the social government of the river as a 'social-natural hybrid'.[77] Therefore, Barca argues, 'nature was in no way a cause of decline and therefore the goal was not to dominate it but to restore a

---

73. Ibid., p. 71.
74. Ibid., p. 80.
75. Ibid., p. 76.
76. Barca, *Enclosing Water*, p. 25.
77. Ibid., p. 34.

lost harmonic co-habitation with it, akin to when southern Italians were free citizens and owners'.[78] This was not quite the case in relation the Tyne's early nineteenth-century governance, as the TIC certainly did not want to 'restore a lost harmonic co-habitation' with the Tyne, though there are commonalities between rivers' stories in terms of the criticism of the Liri's previous conservators and Newcastle Corporation. Those who criticised oligarchic Newcastle Corporation's lack of investment in river improvements were not attacking the fact that the river was governed, managed and dominated by human society. As Christopher Smout observes, this was the era of 'Improvement', by which time the desire to maximise the economic efficiency of rivers such as the Tyne had gathered enormous speed:

> The fruits of the Baconian and Newtonian revolutions were a resolve not to accept nature as an unalterable given, a fait accompli, but as an enormous unrealised opportunity for improvement if he were daring and knowledgeable enough. In Scotland, especially the phrase improver came to be associated with a whole new attitude to natural resources, one which was searching and critical, looking constantly for opportunities to change.[79]

Those who criticised Newcastle Corporation wanted to change the river's particular form of political and economic management. They wanted to appoint more widely representative conservators who considered the needs of all interested (human) parties. And the critics wanted the Tyne's conservators to drive forward river improvement projects much more quickly and efficiently in order to maximise the navigability and economic productivity of this nationally important river.

We can see this process as one of increasing social and political democratisation, as the outdated and dysfunctional, oligarchic and feudalistic governors of Newcastle Corporation were swept away to make way for a more modern and transparent representative organisation, the TIC. Although the new conservators were by no means perfectly democratic, they would nevertheless serve the wider needs of all interested (human) parties more fairly and more equally. However, because the main motivating factor driving this important change in the river's governance was to achieve even greater domination over the river's natural functions and expressions, this apparently progressive move from feudalism towards more widely representative river governance actually resulted in less liberty for the river itself. Ironically, therefore, the feudal and oligarchic early modern governors permitted the river more freedom, and worked with

---

78. Ibid., p. 34.
79. Smout, *Nature Contested*, p. 20.

Chapter 2. 'Tinkering' the Tyne

the river as a natural system in a far more environmentally sensitive manner as a result of a necessarily more evenly matched negotiation. Newcastle Corporation's ostensibly more democratic, modern and socio-politically reasonable successors had acquired powerful technologies that tipped the negotiations between their ambitions and the river's natural functions firmly in the TIC's favour. This underlines the necessity of environmental narratives of history that consider the treatment of natural systems, resources and environments and non-human objects and agents of historical change. By analysing such changes from the perspective of a river, we can see that seemingly progressive developments in human history can be diametrically different for a natural system. For example, the apparently progressive move to improve human public health and hygiene, by replacing dry privies (whose waste was returned to the soil as fertiliser) with water closets (which drained liquid organic waste directly into rivers), degraded the environmental health of many rivers by deoxygenating their water. Mid nineteenth-century 'improvements', therefore, in terms of both the TIC's wider geographical representation and in terms of better public health, marked the dawn of the Tyne's very worst period, when its conservators would deoxygenate its water, canalise its flow, excavate large-scale docks, dredge its bed to unprecedented levels and considerably restructure its banks.

Chapter 3

CREATING A GRAND AND DEEP RIVER: THE TYNE IMPROVEMENT COMMISSION, 1850–1968

Introduction

The TIC was a dedicated taskforce appointed by Parliament in 1850 to transform the Tyne into an economically efficient piece of infrastructure, a navigable port facility where industrial production and maritime trade could flourish maximally. The Tyne Commissioners worked very hard to progress this ambition until their disbandment in 1968. Commissioner Shotton expressed his feelings about the river at the meeting in February 1879, commenting,

> I believe we have the finest harbour of any commercial port in England and I will go further and I will say of the world. There is no place where there is such an amount of trade as is done on the Tyne where they have such facilities as here. The very fact of a steamer coming into this harbour on a dark night, without a pilot, drawing 18 feet of water, at low water, and with four or five feet of sea on the bar, is sufficient proof that such a harbour does not exist in any other part of the world. You may take London, Liverpool, Hull or any other port, either in England or on the continent and you will find nothing of the kind there.[1]

Shotton's words confirm that the TIC's members conceptualised their work as an all-encompassing mission, in which the commissioners believed very deeply, rather than merely as a task to be carried out at the behest of central government. In October 1881, the Marquis of Salisbury visited the Tyne, and the Tyne Commissioners were very proud to show him around the river on several barges, together with Sir Stafford Northcote and the Duke of Northumberland. After the ceremonial processions, the Marquis made a speech, in which he compared the scenes he witnessed on the river to those which had

---

1. *Proceedings of the Tyne Improvement Commission 1876–1968*, 92 vols. (Newcastle, 1876–1968), *Proceedings of the TIC 1878–1879*, p. 86.

Chapter 3. Creating a Grand and Deep River

greeted Mr Gladstone on his visit to the Tyne in 1862, a mere nineteen years earlier and six years before Gladstone became Prime Minister. He thanked the chairman of the TIC

> beyond all for the splendid sight which we have been enabled to witness in passing down this river. I am new to the country and I am no judge of the difficulties which have been overcome, or the opposition which has been mastered to make the Tyne the scene of such industry. I can well believe that there have been in the way of this, as all other good works, serious obstacles before success has been obtained; but I can see that take it as it stands, it is a splendid monument of engineering skill, of commercial forethought and of civic enterprise.[2]

In their industrial vision, the Tyne was admired and appreciated aesthetically as it emerged as a 'splendid monument of engineering skill'. Perhaps the Tyne's Victorians derived the same amount of wonder, enjoyment and pride as they gazed at the river's infrastructural modifications and its grand and deep channel as the Tyne's twenty-first-century conservationists draw today from its wildlife, plant species and clean water. By 1912, even an academic Geographer, A. Sargent, boasted that whereas 'the state of the channel was a burning question of local politics in the eighteenth and nineteenth centuries', now 'we have a deep-water canal, with a channel of some 30 feet to the Bridges' between Newcastle and Gateshead.[3]

Ceremonies and celebrations surrounding the development of the industrial riverscape played a crucial role in reaffirming, justifying and publicising the TIC's very particular industrial vision. In 1880, James Guthrie, who had served as the Secretary of the TIC, praised the commission's achievements in his book, *The River Tyne: Its History and Resources*, noting

> The whole of Tyneside, from Ryton to the sea, is covered with an active, industrious, and ever-increasing population, so much knit together as to form one whole community of half a million of people, all alike greatly dependent upon, and vitally interested in, the improvement and development of their common highway, the River Tyne.[4]

This 'common highway' was indeed the primary focus, the foundation and the lifeblood of Tyneside's industrial growth. It underpinned an enormous proportion of its capacity to trade, its shipbuilding and the disposal of its domestic and industrial waste. The Tyne Commissioners genuinely believed they were

---

2. *Proceedings of the TIC 1880–1881*, p. 9.
3. A. Sargent, 'The Tyne', *The Geographical Journal* 40 (5) (1912): 476–477.
4. J. Guthrie, *The River Tyne: Its History and Resources* (London: Longmans and Co., 1880), p. 36.

building a useful facility to sustain Tyneside in its very long-term future. The subsequent rapidity of deindustrialisation and the replacement of the TIC's vision with the very different vision for the river held by present conservators would, perhaps, have shocked and disappointed them profoundly. In order to fully comprehend the TIC's relationship with the river, it is important to consider it in its very particular historical context, in a climate of a perceived urgent need to maximise economic efficiency by expanding the river's capacity to boost trade and industry, as well as to minimise the shameful 'waste' of the river's power. The sharpness of the TIC's focus on the ambition to create 'a grand and deep channel' as quickly as possible, which bordered at times on obsession, cannot be exaggerated. This chapter explains their engineering projects in detail, but it is not an inventory of every minute impact their work had on the river – that would require at least ten 100,000-word volumes. Rather, the chapter makes sense of their vision, their relationship with the river and their fixation on economic efficiency.

Despite the enormous differences between the respective sizes of the Mississippi and the Tyne, John Anfinson's analysis of the major engineering projects that restructured the Upper Mississippi in the nineteenth and twentieth centuries under the direction of the ambitious US Army Corps of Engineers, on the orders of Congress, is a story that chimes considerably with the large-scale restructuring of the Tyne during the same period. Anfinson observed 'the Corps' challenge was to make the river like the railroad – less natural but more practical'.[5] His point that, as a result of the restructuring of its channel, the Mississippi 'no longer wasted its energy', would have made a great deal of sense to the members of the TIC.[6] As Porter highlights in relation to the Thames Embankment project, 'a public works project shows how technology mediates between cultural values, social groups, and institutions on the one hand, and the natural environment (as perceived and modified by humans) on the other'.[7] Mark Twain worked as a pilot on the Mississippi in the early nineteenth century as it was transformed increasingly from its natural condition, which he knew intimately and which he perceived as beautiful and romantic, to a more controllable and economically efficient river. Twain lamented how the 'national government has turned the Mississippi into a sort of two-thousand-mile torchlight procession' and that 'where the river, in the Vicksburg region, used to be corkscrewed, it is now comparatively straight – made so by cut-off;

---

5. Anfinson, *Mississippi*, pp. 100, 105.
6. Ibid.
7. Porter, *Thames Embankment*, p. 8.

Chapter 3. Creating a Grand and Deep River

a former distance of seventy miles is reduced to thirty-five'.[8] However, even Twain understood the economic sense of the river improvements, noting 'when a river in good condition can enable one to save 162,000 [dollars] and a whole summer's time, on a single cargo, the wisdom of taking measures to keep the river in good condition is made plain to even the uncommercial mind'.[9]

Elsewhere, the Rhine was also facilitating industrialisation and was consequently viewed by those who managed it exclusively in terms of its potential to contribute to industrial growth. As Cioc notes, 'out of nearly 700 blueprints and plans, treaties, agreements etc which passed before the Rhine commission between 1816 and 1916, not one concerned the water quality, the floodplain or biodiversity'.[10] While 'a dozen' addressed hazardous substances, Cioc emphasises that this was only in direct relation to the safety of people and property and unrelated to the river water itself, elaborating that 'the river that existed in the minds of Eurocrats had no biological life'.[11] This certainly also applies to the TIC. Smout highlights how major engineering works on many nineteenth-century rivers resulted in their reduced capacity to change their course independently, which led to the loss of many rivers' natural islands. He laments how 'rivers that engineers have tried to confine between banks and levees' previously 'meandered wildly', changing their courses often and creating oxbow lakes, islands and swamps.[12] Smout explains that whereas William Roy's military survey of Scotland in 1750 featured 21 islands on the River Tummel between Pitlochry and the Tay confluence, only four remain today.[13] This chapter describes how several of the Tyne's river islands were also removed purposely through dredging operations. Similarly, on the Rhine, the Tulla Engineering Project (1816–1876) removed an incredible 2,218 river islands between the Swiss and Hesse borders.[14] The Tyne's scale is substantially smaller than that of many other rivers. However, the TIC's attitudes towards restructuring the Tyne, by constructing a series of large-scale engineering projects to drive forward trade and industrialisation with maximal speed and efficiency, were remarkably similar to those of many other rivers' nineteenth-century conservators.

---

8. M. Twain, *Life on the Mississippi* (Ware, Hertfordshire: Wordsworth Editions, 2012), pp. 188, 247.
9. Ibid., p. 195.
10. Cioc, *The Rhine*, p. 45.
11. Ibid.
12. Smout, *Nature Contested*, p. 91.
13. Ibid.
14. Cioc, *The Rhine*, p. 53.

Tyne after Tyne

The TIC's Structure and Purpose

In January 1849, Newcastle Corporation appointed a special committee on the River Bills which oversaw the establishment of the TIC. The commission was a representative assembly of commissioners appointed by an Act of Parliament passed in 1850, drawn from the ranks of Gateshead, Newcastle, Tynemouth and South Shields town councils, local riparian business owners, shipowners and coalowners. In this sense, the commission's design was similar to that of the Metropolitan Board of Works which managed large-scale engineering projects such as the Thames Embankment, representing the City Corporation and all of the London borough councils.[15] The TIC's task was to progress, manage and control industrial development, efficient shipping, tolls from vessels, public river ferries and structural improvements to the channel of the river within the tidal range of the River Tyne up to Hedwin Streams and within the tidal ranges of all the Tyne's tributaries. It rarely intervened in matters relating to the upper river valley above the tidal ranges. The TIC was heavily bureaucratic, appointing various sub-committees (the finance committee, a dredging and river works committee, a piers committee, a docks committee, a harbour and ferry committee, a parliamentary committee and a collision committee). The committees all met separately, usually weekly, and then reported back to the main commission once every month except August. The public was not permitted access to the commissioners' meetings, though the subject of whether or not to allow them to watch TIC meetings was discussed at a meeting in July 1876, when the commissioners decided against such a change. The TIC set into motion the wheels of several major construction projects on the river: Tyne Dock; Edward Albert Dock (previously called Coble Dene Dock); Northumberland Dock; a very extensive dredging schedule, including the removal of the river islands west of Newcastle; the construction of the Tyne Piers; the creation of the Tyne Main turning circle which widened the river on its south bank to allow ships to turn; the removal of angular rock projections including Felling Point, Bill Point, Friar Goose Point and Whitehill Point; and the replacement of the stone arched Tyne Bridge with Armstrong's Swing Bridge to enable the industrialisation of the river west of Newcastle and Gateshead.

By the time the commission disbanded in 1968, and the Port of Tyne Authority moved into the TIC offices on Bewick Street in Newcastle to take over their responsibilities, the riverscape had been transformed. Alongside substantial engineering works, they had also managed shipping tolls, Tyne ferry

---

15. Porter, *Thames Embankment*, p. 4.

Chapter 3. Creating a Grand and Deep River

Figure 5. Tyne Improvement Offices, Bewick Street, Newcastle, opposite Central Station (Photograph: Gordon Ball)

services and many applications to protrude into the river or to discharge waste into it. While the TIC's work ticked along in a remarkably uniform manner, passing through the same committees and sub-committees and driving forward what was essentially one very long-term and comprehensive plan to maximise the economic efficiency of the river, some jurisdictional changes occurred. For example, the jurisdiction for harbour lights was transferred from the historic Trinity House to a new TIC Harbour Lights, Buoys and Beacons Committee on New Year's Day in 1883, marking the end of 378 years of the Trinity House's responsibilities in this area. In mid-1885, moreover, Jarrow Town Council asked to be represented on the TIC and their request was granted, furthering the commission's geographical representation.

In mid-1876, the commissioners raised a Tyne Improvement Bill in which they asked for increased funding from Parliament to continue their river works, but it was unsuccessful. Consequently, they were 'compelled' to 'suspend their great river and dock works which were progressing most satisfactorily'.[16] They suspended all work except that on the piers. The Tyne, therefore, was permitted a very short vacation from its dizzyingly rapid transformation, courtesy of Parliament, before the TIC tried again a year later. This time, they submitted a Tyne Improvement Bill to raise higher shipping tolls and this one passed through Parliament. All river improvement works suspended the previous year were resumed in earnest. The Tyne's short holiday was over. Between 1862 and 1877, the TIC had made startling progress. An astonishing £3.5 million

---

16. *Proceedings of the TIC 1875–1876*, p. 185.

had been invested into the engineering works, 62 million tonnes of sediment had been dredged from the river bed in the estuary, numerous sand banks had been removed and several angular rock protrusions had been blasted off using explosives. Moreover, the trade of the river had doubled and the tonnage of the vessels entering and leaving the Tyne was larger than that of the Thames and second only to that of the Mersey. Tyne tonnage equalled one sixth of all of England's river trade, four fifths of Scotland's river trade, more than that of the whole of Ireland and one ninth of that of the UK. The Tyne's coal shipments were larger than those of anywhere else in the world, at over eight million tonnes annually and the scale of its shipbuilding operations was second only to that of the Clyde. At the Jubilee Exhibition in Newcastle, in October 1886, the TIC proudly exhibited displays demonstrating their improvement works to the general public.[17]

The TIC dealt with recreational applications, such as boathouses for rowing clubs and changing rooms for swimming clubs, but they always insisted they were not responsible for recreation on and around the river. In August 1896, Mr Lucas complained that

> there is a great misconception in the minds of a large number of people as to the duties and responsibilities of the Tyne Commission. There are a large number of people who consider it part of our business to provide recreation for the public. The fact is we have nothing to do with that. We have to provide piers and improve the waterway for ships. We have nothing to do with the pleasures of the public.[18]

Perhaps the TIC's reluctance to encourage recreation in and around the river resulted from wider concerns about immorality and maintaining a strong work ethic in the population. Porter argues that there are no cafes or restaurants along the broad, tree-lined boulevard of the Thames Embankment, which was designed and managed by a body very similar to the TIC, the Metropolitan Board of Works, because 'Victorians associated such things with dissolute Paris society'.[19] In April 1889, the TIC received an application from the South Shields Model Yacht Club, requesting permission to erect a clubhouse on the TIC's ground opposite the South Park at South Shields.[20] The club had eighty members who owned about 150 yachts, varying in size from five to fifty tons. Their application emphasised that over two-thirds of the members were working men who

---

17. *Proceedings of the TIC 1885–1886*, p. 487.
18. *Proceedings of the TIC 1895–1896*, p. 430.
19. Porter, *Thames Embankment*, p. 10.
20. *Proceedings of the TIC 1888–1889*, p. 180.

Chapter 3. Creating a Grand and Deep River

had to carry their yachts at least a mile to the lake by which 'their pleasure is made a toil'.[21] Therefore, they argued, their members needed a place to store the yachts in order to 'maintain what is a useful and innocent recreation'.[22] The TIC engineer approved the application as a temporary structure, subject to immediate removal if required. The commission was not actively against such 'innocent' recreation, but it never promoted it and within the grand scheme, it was certainly no more than a marginal concern.

When the TIC's river works neared the widely cherished and beautiful Frenchman's Bay, the commissioners received a petition asking them not to destroy 'one of the most charming pieces of coast scenery on the north-east coast'.[23] The petition highlighted that the signatories were 'greatly interested in the preservation of the beauties of the neighbouring coast' and that the commissioners' work in the vicinity of the Frenchman's Bay 'seriously threatens to interfere with the picturesque character of that spot and the vicinity'.[24] The 232 signatories included the Mayor of Newcastle, Alderman Wilson, Mr John Hancock, the Rev. Dr. Bruce, and 'a great number of scientific and influential gentlemen in the district', though notably no ladies.[25] The petition was referred to the Piers Committee, but the work went ahead regardless. This petition followed the loss of the Lady's Bay, which had been filled with stone from the river works and had consequently become unsuitable for bathing. However, the Tyne Commissioners did make efforts to save a picturesque place on the coast called Fairy's Kettle, 'where the colours on the rocks were perfectly charming'.[26]

Docks and Piers

The first 'improvement' to be completed by the TIC was Tyne Dock, which was opened in 1859 at South Shields. In 1875, work began on the Coble Dene Dock at North Shields.[27] Constructing this dock involved the excavation of over 20,000 cubic yards of clay and earth in a typical month of construction. The majority of dredged material was taken to be dumped at sea, but some of it was used on the staith approach roads, tipped behind the masonry of the

---

21. Ibid.
22. Ibid.
23. *Proceedings of the TIC 1881–1882*, p. 129.
24. Ibid.
25. Ibid., p. 128.
26. Ibid., p. 130.
27. *Proceedings of the TIC 1875–1876*, p. 14.

dock entrances and on the earth dam in the dock. Helpfully, some people were only too happy to remove clay from the construction site. In November 1877, Henry Wilson of the Wallsend Cement Company made a successful application to the TIC to remove from the Coble Dene Dock Works 'a quantity of clay which can be excavated from a part of the ground near the river', promising to provide their own craft and to fund the full cost of excavating and loading the clay.[28] Each month, around 300 concrete blocks were prepared in the TIC yard at Howdon and installed to face the river walls of the dock, which required a substantial investment of labour. In August 1884, after only nine years of construction work, the Prince of Wales visited the river to open the Coble Dene Dock, which was named officially the Albert-Edward Dock. Lord William Armstrong entertained the royal party at his home at Cragside, near Rothbury in Northumberland, before processing to the dock from Newcastle on one of 25 ceremonial steamers. Armstrong, the so-called Water Wizard of the North, had generated the world's first hydro-electric power at Cragside in 1868. A large timber structure was erected at the Albert-Edward Dock for the opening ceremony, which seated 2,000 spectators and around 1,000 linear yards of fencing was erected to contain the public.[29] Many more applications were sanctioned to construct a great number of smaller docks up and down the estuary, but the completion of the two major docks, Tyne Dock on the south bank and the Albert-Edward Dock on the north bank, marked a significant milestone for the TIC.

The engineering challenge of constructing large-scale piers at the river mouth dragged on for decades as rough seas, ice, damage from ship collisions and financial problems continually impeded the project. The TIC engineer, Mr Walker, submitted plans for the Tyne Piers in 1853, but it was widely agreed that his proposed piers were inadequately small.[30] He submitted revised plans in 1861, for piers terminating at thirty feet at low water, which were put into execution later that year. The length of the North Pier was designed to be 2,470 feet with another 450 feet extending below water and the length of the South Pier was to be 4,205 feet with another 900 feet under water.[31] Concrete blocks were prepared by masons in advance before being deposited by barges to be installed into the 'superstructure of concrete and built stonework'. Because the lower and larger sections of the piers were installed 21 feet below low water,

---

28. *Proceedings of the TIC 1877–1878*, p. 3.
29. *Proceedings of the TIC 1884–1885*, p. 375.
30. *Proceedings of the TIC 1875–1876*, p. 183.
31. Ibid.

Chapter 3. Creating a Grand and Deep River

they were fixed by divers.[32] In April 1878, the commissioners debated whether to allow the public to use the piers as a promenade for a small fee.[33] Mr Milvain was motivated by the prospective income from tolls, but Mr Stephenson was concerned about keeping order and thought it would require the services of two policemen. Mr Cail thought it would be unfair on those who could not afford the toll.[34] Mr Shotton commented,

> the pier was a beautiful promenade and it would be a great pity and source of great regret if the commissioners entertained the idea of making people pay who went there. The rich could easily afford to pay, but poor people in many cases would be deprived of the pleasure of walking there. ... If a board was put up cautioning people against ill-behaviour and the police made periodical visits, they might secure the good behaviour of that class of young men who went to the pier not with any intention of doing anything wrong, but who generally on a Sunday night ran about in a foolish way.[35]

In November 1881, the issue was raised again and the commissioners agreed that the TIC had been 'appointed for the purpose of improving and deepening the channel and had nothing to do with making promenades upon the piers'.[36]

While the work on the piers continued, in 1883, the commissioners debated the wisdom of removing the rocks near Tynemouth known as the Black Middens, which would subsequently go on to be recognised in the late twentieth century as a hugely important ecological site and a Site of Special Scientific Interest (SSSI). Mr Walker, the engineer, advised not to remove the rocks until the South Pier was completed opining that 'there must be something for the sea waves to break upon and that the Black Middens must be left as a beaching ground for the sea'.[37] Clearly, the commissioners saw the Black Middens as part of their industrial facility; the rocks were welcome to stay as long as they were useful and did not impede progress. Mr Newall compared the mouth of the Tyne to Hell's Gate in New York, where a reef of rock had been undermined and blown up in the East River entrance to the harbour, explaining that he 'was glad he had not to go through [Hell's Gate] again' and that the 'commissioners would not desire to do that with the Black Middens for a long time yet' as they

---

32. Ibid.
33. *Proceedings of the TIC 1877–1878*, p. 101.
34. Ibid.
35. Ibid., p. 102.
36. *Proceedings of the TIC 1881–1882*, p. 29.
37. *Proceedings of the TIC 1882–1883*, p. 81.

Figure 6. The Mouth of the Tyne, showing the Black Middens in front of the north pier (Photograph: Gordon Ball)

'were of use at present'.[38] The sheer chance that they happened to be useful to the functioning of the port enabled this ecologically important site to dodge the 'improvement' bullets being fired all around them by the TIC.

By 1893, the bulk of the work on the piers had been completed, and Mr Cail announced

> we are getting somewhat closer to the end of this long business of the piers. There are now something like seven blocks to lay on one side and eleven on the other. ... But we are in the hands of Neptune, who may put an end to any calculations.[39]

The piers were completed by 1896, and, after some repairs were made to the north pier, they were opened to the public in the following year to be used as promenades. It had been a busy half century for the Docks Committee and the Piers Committee.

---

38. Ibid.
39. *Proceedings of the TIC 1892–1893*, p. 401.

Chapter 3. Creating a Grand and Deep River

Figure 7. The Black Midden Rocks in front of the north pier (Photograph: Gordon Ball)

Dredging for Industrial Progress

The Tyne Commissioners went full steam ahead with a large-scale plan for dredging as soon as their finances allowed, and notably with dramatically increased zeal following what must surely have been a humiliating Royal Commission into the state of the Tyne in 1855. In their very early years, however, in the early 1850s, economic expediency prevented the TIC from purchasing a fleet of steam-powered dredgers. In June 1851, when a dredger from the River Tweed became available either to buy or to hire, the TIC recorded 'in the present state of finances the commissioners do not deem it proper to purchase or hire the dredger in question'.[40] However, once the commission became established and started to amass some funds from ferries and shipping tolls, they were able to double their dredging capacity from a single dredger in 1850 to two, purchasing the second in 1853. By the late 1850s, they had started to deploy the dredgers in multiple locations around the river, both above and below the multi-arch stone Tyne Bridge, which prevented large ships from moving under it. In 1857, the TIC's own engineer, Mr Brooks, explained the necessity, in his eyes, of removing some problematic shoals above bridge at Blaydon,

---

40. TWA: IC/T/1/1: River Tyne Commission Minute Book, 1850–1855 (12 June 1851).

These shoals are of small extent but in their present condition divide the channel in the vicinity of Blaydon into a series of pools; the shoals themselves constitute so many separate bars preventing the discharge of the natural backwater and the ingress of the tidal water.[41]

The desire to dredge above the bridge increased following the opening in 1876 of William Armstrong's innovative swing bridge, which rotated 180 degrees to enable ships to pass on either side.

The TIC started to 'improve' the channel above bridge, at Lemington Point and Blaydon, but funding was tight and the Privy Council wrote to the TIC in July 1876 to ask why they were investing in works up river to the detriment of 'urgent harbour works'.[42] This extract from the minutes of a meeting held in January 1876 demonstrates the TIC's genuine fear that if they did not improve the channel above bridge, they might seriously regret it in the future.

> They all knew that a few years ago Newcastle was simply at the top of a creek. The river was not navigable up to Newcastle except for a class of small steamers and small vessels, which were now entirely going out of use. Now, these small steamers and small sloops which used to come up to Newcastle, were going out of use, none of them were replaced when they were lost or out of date. The whole of trade had gone into a larger class; and if the Tyne Commissioners had not deepened the river in the way they had done, we would have lost the whole of our trade. Newcastle now, instead of being at the top of a creek, was, as it were, in the centre of a large, deep, navigable river, which is equal to a dock.[43]

The words 'equal to a dock' provide a fantastically clear insight into how the commissioners conceptualised their work and the river itself. They were literally trying to convert the natural river system into a piece of fully controllable infrastructure such as a dock. The commissioners looked to the example of the improvements made in the past to justify their further plans to improve the estuary in the future. Consequently, the TIC steamed ahead with dredging the channel above bridge, resulting in increasing numbers of applications for newly viable industrial riparian development in that area. Companies such as the Pioneer Foundry at Blaydon and Newburn Steel Works wrote letters complaining about the slow speed of progress on 'up river' improvements. Newburn Steel Works advised the TIC that 'the only rational conclusion of the matter appears to us to be to push forward with the adopted plans', noting that 'even a day's delay may necessitate weeks of persistent effort in order to recover the loss so

---

41. TWA: IC.T/1/2: River Tyne Commission Minute Book, 1855–1859 (9 Apr.1857).
42. *Proceedings of the TIC 1875–1876*, p. 169.
43. Ibid., pp. 59–60.

Chapter 3. Creating a Grand and Deep River

sustained' and going so far as to say that 'it seems to us in fact to be suicidal in the extreme to pursue any other course'.[44] These letters were not needed, however, because the TIC secretary was instructed to reassure the respective companies that 'there is no present intention on the part of the commissioners to interfere with the progress of the works above bridge'.[45]

Dredging between Newburn and Ryton increased the power of the water force moving down a steeper course and this caused the tidal limit to move from Hedwin Streams upriver about a mile to Wylam. Hedwin Streams was designated as the tidal limit in 1292, so this marked quite a significant change in the river's hydrological regime. In the 1880s, Dutch engineers were invited to lead a scheme to alter and widen the course of the river between Lemington and Blaydon Haughs. A river island called Dent's Meadows was removed and the entrance to Lemington Loop was cut off and silted up, creating the Lemington Gut, although Canary Island at Lemington Point was not removed during these works. Work began in November 1881 to remove by dredging King's Meadows Island, the largest of several above bridge including Annie's Island, also known as 'the Queen Anne Island', and Bent's Island. King's Meadow was nearly a mile long and covered 35 acres. The islands officially belonged to the TIC. In July 1860, the commissioners leased the King's Meadow to William Armstrong's Elswick Ordnance Works for 35 years, for the purposes of proving their guns, providing that the TIC retained the right to end the lease with a year's notice if they required the island for river works.[46] Historically, the islands had been outside Newcastle Corporation's jurisdiction, and officially part of Northumberland, with the effect that this risqué place was able to be used somewhat outside of the law. King's Meadow was home to a pub called the Countess of Coventry and regular horse races were held there. It also provided pasture for many milk cows. William Armstrong pressured the TIC to remove the river islands to ease the logistics of exporting munitions and vessels from his works.[47] The TIC emphasised, at a meeting in March 1876, that they would make some compensation to the public for the loss of this important part of their river, as well as to themselves for having lost substantial land. As they were losing land in the middle of the river, they added more land to each

---

44. *Proceedings of the TIC 1898–1899*, pp. 133, 134.
45. Ibid., p. 135.
46. TWA: IC.T/1/3: River Tyne Commission Minute Book, 1859–1862 (12 Jul. 1860).
47. M. Chaplin et al., *Tyne View: A Walk around the Port of Tyne* (Newcastle: New Writing North, 2012), p. 155.

riverbank, but emphasised that there 'ought to be some of this land secured for public landing places and other public purposes'.[48]

Following Lord Armstrong's death in 1900, the commissioners confirmed the large influence of Armstrong and his works on their decision to dredge above Newcastle, including the removal of the Tyne islands:

> I do not know that the Commissioners would really have committed themselves to the important work of the dredging in the upper reaches of the river beyond [i.e. west of] the swing bridge but for the fact that those colossal works had been put there at Elswick [i.e. Vickers-Armstrong Works]. ... There is no doubt that the operations of the commission to which I have alluded were to our mutual satisfaction. It was a great advantage to him [i.e. Armstrong] and his important firm that they should have an open waterway to his quays and be able to take and launch vessels of the largest size and take them safely out to sea.[49]

Pressure to dredge the Tyne above Newcastle continued in earnest throughout the late nineteenth century. In January 1899, the TIC received a letter of complaint from Newburn Steel Works about the lack of progress and the latter's perception that the TIC purposely prioritised dredging the lower estuary. Dredging the Tyne near Newburn, they argued, was a work 'eminently essential to the best interests of the river throughout its whole course'.[50] They complained that they 'watched with some solicitude the fitful operations of the ladder dredger' when it was operated near their works and they accused the TIC of only putting the dredger to work above bridge 'when there was nothing else for it to do' in the lower estuary.[51] The TIC was conducting work that had an enormous potential to benefit riparian businesses. The local politics surrounding decisions to develop the river in some areas, to the detriment of others, were sometimes quite intense.

The TIC maintained their own dredgers, which they sometimes hired out for private use or leased on a long-term basis to various companies in Amsterdam and to the River Wear Commissioners. Robert Hunter, a Tugmaster, recalled rescuing one of the TIC dredgers at South Shields in 1930:

> Then there was the Tyne Improvement Commission dredger that had been working the North Channel in the harbour entrance. A gale sprang up from the north and the vessel was driven towards the rocks near the Groyne at South

---

48. *Proceedings of the TIC 1875–1876*, p. 127.
49. *Proceedings of the TIC 1900–1901*, p. 147.
50. *Proceedings of the TIC 1898–1899*, p. 133 (letter from Newburn Steel Works dated 24 Dec. 1898).
51. Ibid.

Chapter 3. Creating a Grand and Deep River

Shields. ... [We] saved the dredger which was safely moored at the Howdon Yard of the TIC. My tug had to go into dry dock for repairs to its bottom plates.[52]

If a private company requested the use of a TIC dredger to increase the depth of water near their yard or dock, it had to pay two-thirds of the cost of dredging and the TIC bore the cost of the other third. In some cases, the TIC paid all the costs of dredging private businesses' docks and berths if they had silted up as a direct result of TIC engineering works. Although coal dust is not actually very harmful to the river water or to its wildlife, significant volumes of it were inevitably deposited into the Tyne around large-scale coal staiths, which contributed to the silting up of staiths. At a meeting in July 1876, in response to a complaint from John Fenwick and Sons of the coal exchange in London that the coal staiths near Jarrow had silted up, the TIC recorded:

> The silting up of the berths referred to ... has been chiefly caused by the dust and waste consequent upon the manner of shipping the coals at the spouts. The coals are dropped from the spouts which are not arranged to meet the hatchways of the loading vessels. They have consequently to drop through a considerable space except at high water and the dust whenever there is any wind is blown from them into the river, gradually, in 14 or 15 years, causing the silting up now complained of.[53]

In this particular case, the staiths had to be dredged at the expense of the staith owners. Dredging created some unforeseen problems. It made some moorings unsafe at Shields harbour, for example. The Privy Council wrote to the TIC in July 1876 to tell them that if they wished to dredge deep, they needed to extend the piers to provide protection to moored boats. The Privy Council was concerned about this issue in the context of a potential maritime war with a foreign power. In a letter from Edward Lishman, a business owner at Mill Dam, South Shields, received in September 1877, the TIC was advised that the 'river should be at once dredged and restored as far as practicable to its former good condition', by which Edward meant to its former depth to allow larger vessels to dock there. Through modern-day eyes, 'former good condition' would be as close to the river's natural, pre-industrial state as possible, but through nineteenth-century eyes it meant its previously economically efficient good condition.[54] In February 1892, Mr Cowen complained that 'a very large amount of the material which has to be dredged comes from the neighbourhood of Corbridge', and while he understood 'our powers do not go so far

---

52. J. Proud, (ed.), *A Tug's Rescue Work: The Autobiography of a Retired Tugmaster* (2003), p. 18.
53. *Proceedings of the TIC 1875–1876*, p. 18.
54. *Proceedings of the TIC 1876–1877*, p. 189.

up the river', he proposed to construct a weir head at the west end of Ryton Willows to 'prevent a large portion of this material coming further down, and thus relieve our dredging operations'.[55] The chairman sanctioned the proposal, commenting 'I fully agree to the policy of treating our work as one continuous whole, and it is not economic to the lower part of the river to neglect the upper'.[56] This statement underlines the TIC's prioritisation of economic issues above all other considerations. They were not considering the river as a whole for environmental reasons, but only looking to reduce the amount of material they would have to dredge in the estuary. To use Richard White's words, the river was conceptualised as a whole 'organic machine'.[57]

The commissioners debated the impact of dredging to lower the infamous Tynemouth Bar (a sand bar), which extended between North and South Shields and presented a significant impediment to ships' passage. In 1878, TIC Engineer Messent reported that it

> allowed a much larger quantity of sea or tidal water to enter the river, but I think that the general advantage to the trade on the river produced by the improvements will more than compensate for the particular inconvenience that may be suffered by the Carville Chemical Co or other manufacturers similarly situated.[58]

The concern here was not that more seawater would enter the estuary, to dilute the freshwater from upstream, but rather that manufacturing businesses at the mouth of the river could suffer from stronger tides which would bring more silt to their docks. As Commissioner Shotton confirmed a few years later, in 1881, 'there was no doubt that there had been complaints of the very heavy seas rolling into the harbour in consequence of the great amount of dredging which had been done and the removal of the sand banks that had impeded the entrance of the river'.[59] One of these complaints, submitted in August 1881, from the owner of a public house near the river at Steel's Quay, North Shields, stated 'my tenant complains that the strong range of the sea, which now runs on to that river side shakes the building and does damage to the floor of the front room'.[60] Another complaint, in October 1882, explained how the dredging works near the Northern Rowing Club, whose boathouse was based at Elswick, had 'caused the soil of the foreshore (where we launch our boats)

---

55. *Proceedings of the TIC 1891–1892*, p. 94.
56. Ibid.
57. White, *Organic Machine*.
58. *Proceedings of the TIC 1878–1879*, p. 25.
59. *Proceedings of the TIC 1880–1881*, p. 38.
60. Ibid., p. 215.

Chapter 3. Creating a Grand and Deep River

to fall away and make it excessively deep and dangerous for us to arrive and depart at different times of the tide'.[61] The commissioners admitted having caused the damage and agreed to bear the cost of £10 to £15 of making a small wooden gangway. In July 1884, the TIC received a letter of complaint from John Clayton, of the Scotswood Suspension Bridge Company, regarding the undermining of the foundations of the Scotswood Suspension Bridge due to the dredging operations. The company had placed a large amount of slag on the north and south piers to protect them, but as the river had been deepened, the slag slid away and they felt that the bridge was in precarious danger of collapse.[62] The TIC's work did provoke some limited resistance, in the form of complaints like those above, but any negative impacts of the TIC's river works tended to be viewed very largely in terms of damage to people, property and businesses, by both the complainants and the Tyne Commissioners.

In their increasingly committed pursuit of a deeper river channel, the TIC used explosives on the bed of the river to complement their dredging operations. In June 1895, the TIC received a letter from their solicitors, advising them that the owners of Montagu Colliery were concerned that

> engineers are blasting with dynamite in the bed of the river Tyne at Bell's Close and that the depth of the Beaumont Seam which is worked out below the bed of the river is only from 90 to 100 feet and that they are seriously apprehensive that if any blasting takes place damage may be done to the rock which will allow water to get down through and in that event will have the effect of flooding all their mines.[63]

This concern was not for the long-term environmental health of the river itself, but rather to protect the owners of the colliery from losing property, assets and profit. But nonetheless, complaints such as this one demonstrate the limitations of the TIC's plans to convert the river into a functional facility 'like a dock'. The Tyne continued to express itself in contravention to their ambitions and plans and reminded the TIC on a regular basis that it was, first and foremost, a natural system.

In 1937, Durham and Northumberland Councils proposed a scheme, approved by the Minister of Transport in 1943, for three tunnels under the Tyne, comprising a cyclist, pedestrian and vehicular tunnel. Throughout the 1940s, discussions about the construction of the Tyne tunnels centred round the depth at which they were to be installed into the riverbed. Construction

---

61. *Proceedings of the TIC 1882–1883*, p. 30.
62. *Proceedings of the TIC 1883–1884*, p. 307.
63. *Proceedings of the TIC 1894–1895*, p. 314.

would limit for the very long-term future the maximum depth to which the TIC would be able to deepen the channel by dredging. As many highlighted, nobody knew how much bigger ships would become in the future and therefore the depth of water they would need to navigate their way to the ship repair yards situated to the west of the proposed tunnel, which would traverse the river bed between Howdon and Jarrow (seven miles downstream of Newcastle). The TIC objected to the Tyne Tunnel Bill of 1946 because it would have prevented them from dredging to fifty feet below the chart datum Low Waters of Spring Tides (LWST) and because it threatened their substantial income from river ferries.[64] Originally, the TIC wanted sixty feet for future dredging, but by 1946, they had reduced their requirement to fifty feet.[65] Although the TIC had been granted unlimited dredging powers by Parliament in 1908, the Director of Navigation at the Admiralty argued that 35 feet should be sufficient for the reception of future vessels.[66] As the commissioners explained

> The tunnel when built will determine the draught of water for practically all time and it would be deplorable if in the future our shipyards were precluded from building the largest class of vessel. No one can say that the present size of ships represents the limit and we must accordingly provide for some margin of safety against future development.[67]

The TIC sanctioned the amended plans in 1947 and construction work began that year. The cyclist and pedestrian tunnels were built thirty feet apart, some forty feet below the river bed and with external diameters of twelve feet (3.7 m) and eleven feet (3.4 m) respectively.[68] The new plans would enable the commissioners to dredge 'without liability' to fifty feet below LWST between the north and south edges of the dredged channel, sloping upwards to forty feet on each side of the river.[69] Britain's first purpose-built cyclist tunnel and a separate pedestrian tunnel were opened in 1951, contributing to the Festival of Britain, and in 1967 the much larger vehicular tunnel was opened to complete the trio.

The debate around the vehicular tunnel was less intense because the existing cyclist and pedestrian tunnels had already limited maximum future dredging. The escalators which enable pedestrians and cyclists to return to ground level at

---

64. *Proceedings of the TIC 1945–1946*, p. 208.
65. TNA, ADM 1/18389: RIVERS AND CANALS (68): Tyne Improvement Commission proposal for tunnel under the river Tyne: Admiralty statement of dredging requirements, 1945–46.
66. Ibid.
67. *Proceedings of the TIC 1945–1946*, p. 208.
68. Ibid., p. 416.
69. Ibid., p. 417.

Chapter 3. Creating a Grand and Deep River

each end of the tunnels were the UK's highest single rise escalators when they were constructed and they remain today the longest wooden escalators in the world. The vehicular Tyne tunnel proved very popular following its opening in 1967, and increasing volumes of traffic led to the construction of a second vehicular tunnel between 2008 and 2011. A colossal 400,000 cubic metres of sediment was dredged to make way for this new tunnel, and the material was piped to the nearby Port of Tyne's Tyne Dock where it was used to infill the disused dock. Tyne Dock had opened in 1859 as the TIC's very first major 'improvement'. The infilling of the dock reclaimed thirteen acres of land now used as an operational quay where, among other goods, substantial volumes of coal are unloaded from ships, making a mockery of the old idiom, 'it's like carrying coals to Newcastle'. The connections between past and present infrastructure and between the Port of Tyne and its predecessor, the TIC, could not have been made clearer than by this beautifully cyclical reuse of the river bed to renew the TIC's first major dock for the future.

Dredging for Resources

Useful resources such as gravel, stone and sand have been dredged from riverbanks and riverbeds for the purposes of construction since ancient times. But dedicated commercial dredging to extract such materials began to have an increasingly serious impact on the River Tyne and its tributaries from the late nineteenth century onwards.[70] Many companies were formed specifically to extract such materials, some of which were illegal and unofficial. Some companies created very deep holes in the channel in order to capture large volumes of gravel as the material descended, which deepened the channel even more rapidly.[71] All of these operations have left their mark on the riverbed, which is unlikely to recover from such large-scale extraction of gravel for several hundred years. Dredging was conducted primarily using one of two methods. Some dredged in the river channel using vessels fitted with machinery for working buckets which scooped up the ballast, gravel or sand from the bed of the river. Or, alternatively, materials could be dredged from the foreshore, dug manually and loaded into boats.

Between 1850 and the beginning of the twentieth century, the TIC granted permission to many private individuals and companies to extract materials from the river, such as clay, ballast and gravel. In September 1903, they outlined their

---

70. D. Archer, 'The Rape of the Tyne: Gravel Extraction', in Archer, (ed.), *Tyne and Tide*, p. 44.
71. Ibid., p. 52.

reasons for having done so, including their drive to remove as much material from the riverbed as possible to aid their own dredging operations:

> A considerable number of persons have for many years some with and some without the permission of the commissioners dredged gravel and ballast from the river bed and hitherto the commissioners have not objected to this being done because the doing of it really saved the commissioners having to carry out the dredging themselves. In other words it was necessary to remove a certain amount of ballast from the river bed for the purpose of improving navigation and whatever was done in the way of effecting such removal by outsiders lessened the work to be done by the commissioners.[72]

Clearly, the TIC was not explicitly aware, if at all, of the long-term consequences of such removal. For them, all of the riverbed's material was scheduled to be dredged at their expense anyway. However, following the turn of the twentieth century, their attitudes began to change in relation to the extraction of the river's resources, albeit not for ecological reasons. In May 1903, Henry Thompson applied to the TIC for permission to remove sand from the Herd Sands, near South Shields Pier, using a grab or sand pump. This application was referred to the engineer, who requested more detailed plans from Mr Thompson. After confirming that he planned to remove 35,000 tons of sand annually using a centrifugal pump, his application was denied on the grounds that 'it does not seem to be expedient that private persons or firms should be allowed to dredge in the position'.[73] Henry Thompson appealed to the Office of Woods at Whitehall, and the engineer had to write a further report explaining why he declined the application.[74] This report confirmed that, while the TIC had permitted the removal of such materials in the past, the practice had been stopped in December 1901.[75] Though it does not explain exactly why it was stopped, the report hints that the TIC had become concerned about conserving the riverbed's remaining materials to sustainably supply their own building projects in the long-term future.

Despite the fact that the TIC had stopped granting such licences, a lessee of the Duke of Northumberland's fisheries at Newburn, George Foster, had continued to allow extraction in return for payments.[76] Small-scale dredging operations were undertaken by several owners of wherries – including the Tyne

---

72. *Proceedings of the TIC 1902–1903*, p. 1246.
73. Ibid., pp. 745, 888, 1002.
74. Ibid., p. 1110.
75. Ibid., p. 1242.
76. Ibid., p. 1242.

Chapter 3. Creating a Grand and Deep River

Wherry Company, Kelly and Cockerburn, City Wherry Co. and an individual called John Armstrong – who removed 'ballast, gravel and sand from the bed or foreshore of the river at various points above low water', some paying a subsidy of 2s 6d per annum to the Duke of Northumberland and others 2s 3d to the Duke's lessee for each boatload of forty tons of material removed.[77] The TIC expressed disapproval, but the practice continued. In 1902, Mr John Ferguson of Newcastle paid George Foster £25 per annum for potential damage to his fisheries, and Mr John Lane of South Shields had paid him £7 10s per annum.[78] In the same year, the Duke of Northumberland's office wrote to the Tyne Wherry Company to offer to renew their licences for another year, until July 1903, upon payment of 2s 6d and also payment to His Grace's tenant, George Foster, of the Cromwell and Newburn Fisheries for damage caused by dredging.[79] George Foster made significant profits from this activity, but some people were able to extract materials without paying him. Mark Smith used his wherry to remove material from the riverbed at Newburn, but he told the TIC engineer that he 'had no permission from anyone to remove gravel from the foreshore nor did he pay anything to anyone for the privilege'.[80] Clearly, the full story of gravel extraction on the Tyne is irretrievable.

In light of these permissions granted by the Duke of Northumberland to dredge sand and gravel further upstream, the TIC subsequently reconsidered their rejection of Henry Thompson's application to remove sand near the South Pier on certain conditions. He could dredge for sand providing he did so at least 1,200 feet away from the foreshore, providing 'the sand be not lowered in any place more than 3 feet below the present level of the sand' and providing 'the dredging be not carried deeper than 25 feet below low water ordinary spring tides'.[81] In the early twentieth century, the TIC continued to grant some considered licences to extract materials at particular locations but they also rejected quite a few applications, granting licences to relatively fewer people who had to work according to much more complex conditions. In December 1901, the TIC granted permission to Mr John Lane of South Shields and to Mr John Ferguson of Newcastle 'to dredge sand, gravel &c by means of grab dredgers from the bed of the river in the vicinity of Newburn, this sand gravel &c being used principally for building purposes and in the construction of

---

77. Ibid.
78. Ibid., p. 1243.
79. Ibid., p. 1251.
80. Ibid., p. 1243.
81. Ibid., p. 1389.

Dry Docks &c'.[82] However, in 1904, the TIC rejected an application from the Newburn Hills Sand and Gravel Co. for permission to dredge for gravel and sand immediately above Newburn Bridge.[83] In July 1939, the Jarrow Dredging & Salvage Co Ltd applied to renew their application with a twenty per cent reduction in the rate they paid to the TIC, of 9d per ton, for gravel dredged from the River Tyne at Ryton. The licence had been issued in July 1925, but had expired in May 1939. The TIC granted permission for the company to continue to dredge and granted the twenty per cent rebate on their toll.[84] The licence was renewed again in March 1950, including the provision that the company must be responsible for the payment of rates and taxes on the gravel beds at Ryton.[85]

A typical company, the Tyne Washed Sand and Gravel Company Ltd, was established in 1913 and went into liquidation in 1948. It stated in its original articles of association that it would 'dig, sort, and deal in sand, gravel, stone and ballast of all kinds and to prepare the same for market or use at Wylam, Northumberland and elsewhere'.[86] In December 1915, Mr William Kirton applied to the Office of Woods for a formal lease to remove gravel from the river near Ryton and Wylam, within the jurisdiction of the TIC. He explained that he had

> carried on for over 12 years a business in which we dredged gravel from the Tyne and sold it in loads to all the important works on the Tyne and neighbouring ports. This material was obtained mainly from the Duke's [of Northumberland] boundary for which privilege we paid 4d per ton royalty. We also had the permission of the land owners west of the Duke's boundary to dredge from this area (now taken over by the Tyne [Improvement] Commissioners) for which we paid an annual sum. About 3 or 4 years ago the Tyne commissioners bought this land west of the Duke's boundary and would not allow us to take gravel from it, thus confining our operations solely to the Duke's area. The gravel in the Duke's area is nearly worked out and we can only depend on occasional floods bringing down small quantities. We have repeatedly tried to obtain the Tyne commissioners['] permission to dredge in their boundary and have offered to pay a similar royalty but they have refused to allow us this privilege. ... If your department can do anything in the matter we will feel greatly obliged as the

---

82. Ibid., p. 1242; *Proceedings of the TIC 1903–1904*, p. 745.
83. *Proceedings of the TIC 1903–1904*, p. 745.
84. *Proceedings of the TIC 1938–1939*, pp. 631, 634.
85. *Proceedings of the TIC 1949–1950*, p. 250.
86. TNA, BT 31/32163/131220: Tyne washed sand and gravel company Ltd.

Chapter 3. Creating a Grand and Deep River

gravel supply is now getting very small and we have big demands for various new government works apart from the usual river trade.[87]

The Duke of Northumberland granted a lease for dredging to Kirton in 1905, but he emphasised that certain areas belonging to the TIC must be left alone. The TIC refused to grant permission to Kirton to dredge because they needed to dredge materials from the river too, for their own river works, and they perceived him as a competitor. The TIC offered William Kirton the opportunity to buy gravel from them directly, but he declined.[88] In fact, the TIC was given permission to dredge in a nearby area owned by the Crown in return for a royalty of 4d per ton, which was formally agreed in October 1919.[89] By 1918, the TIC confirmed that they had dredged 12,313.5 tons of gravel in total, supplying it to only four companies: Palmers Shipbuilding and Iron Co.; Armstong, Whitworth and Co.; Smith's Dock Company; and the Newcastle on Tyne Electric Supply Company, supplying some 6,114 tons which amounted to almost half of the total dredged from Crown land in 1918.[90] The extraction of the Tyne's natural resources underpinned the expansion and development of Tyneside in the widest sense, including the expansion of the electricity supply network, the productivity of large-scale industrial workshops and the TIC's major river engineering projects.

In December 1915, the Office of Woods declined Kirton's request for permission to dredge and ordered him to cease dredging construction materials from the river. Nevertheless, Kirton continued to dredge for both gravel and sand within the TIC's property boundaries and in March 1916, the TIC wrote to the Office of Woods confirming Kirton's illegal activities on the south bank opposite Ryton Railway Station. Yet again, in December 1919, the Jarrow Dredging and Salvage Company, previously owned by William Kirton, was reported by the Office of Woods to have been dredging without permission at Ryton Willows opposite Newburn in an area known as 'The Spetchels', which belonged to the Ecclesiastical Commissions for England and Wales.[91] He used

---

87. TNA, CRES 37/999: Tyne River Removal of Gravel [letter from Matthew Kirton to Office of Woods, 16 Dec. 1915], pp. 1–2.
88. TNA, CRES 37/999: Tyne River Removal of Gravel [letter from TIC to Office of Woods, 17 Jan. 1916], pp. 1–2.
89. TNA, CRES 37/1026: Tyne River Removal of Gravel [letter from Office of Woods to TIC, 27 Oct. 1919].
90. TNA, CRES 37/1026: Tyne River Removal of Gravel [letter from TIC to Office of Woods, 14 Oct. 1919].
91. TNA, CRES 37/1026: Tyne River Removal of Gravel [letter from Office of Woods to Morton Evans, 17 Dec. 1919].

a grab dredger called 'The Badger', for which the company was ordered to pay to the Commissioner for Woods £3 15s for trespass.[92] In July 1925, Kirton's Jarrow Dredging and Salvage Company signed a fourteen-year contract with the TIC for permission to dredge the gravel beds belonging to the TIC at Ryton, as long as they paid a rebate of twenty per cent to the TIC and respected the Crown's adjacent property. Some years later, in 1939, the TIC renewed the contract for another fourteen years, and in April 1950, the TIC renewed it again, modifying it to include additional provision for the payment by the company of any rates leviable on the gravel beds.[93] The politics surrounding the extraction and sale of the Tyne's valuable natural resources were complex. The intense rivalry over rights to extract the materials did not emanate from their environmental significance as they functioned effectively within the bed of the river, acting as a natural brake to the river's flow or as essential spawning grounds for migratory fish. Rather, the economic, political and legal rivalry over the Tyne's gravel, sand and clay reflected the strong local demand for construction materials with which to underpin Tyneside's expansion, in demographic, industrial and infrastructural terms.

Further up the river, on the South Tyne, where the TIC had no jurisdiction, gravel extraction was also commercially viable. There, too, it became the subject of intense legal debate. Throughout the 1920s and 1930s, Greenwich Hospital, the official owners of the riverbanks of the River South Tyne at Haydon Bridge on behalf of the Lord High Admiral of the United Kingdom, leased the exclusive right to extract gravel and sand from the riverbank and riverbed on the south-east side of the bridge. In January 1936, Mr Norman Veitch continued the lease held previously by his father, Mr William Veitch, who in 1933 had taken over the lease from Mr Matthew Kirton of Newburn (whom we met earlier). In an ultimately unsuccessful attempt to reduce the rent for the lease, Norman emphasised the lack of demand for gravel locally as 'no building operations were going on in the neighbourhood'.[94] Consequently, their extractions in 1934 and 1935 had been only 32.5 tons and 55.5 tons, respectively. The volume of materials extracted ebbed and flowed with the peaks and troughs in local construction activity.

By 1950, concerns were raised about increased rates of erosion on the bend of the river South Tyne at Haydon Bridge, and an Admiralty report was

---

92. Ibid.
93. *Proceedings of the TIC 1949–1950*, pp. 251–252; *Proceedings of the TIC 1938–1939*, pp. 631, 634.
94. TNA, ADM 169/893: River South Tyne at Haydon Bridge: River bank erosion and encroachments, river bed ownership and extraction of sand and gravel, 1950.

Chapter 3. Creating a Grand and Deep River

duly written. The north bank of the river 'a little to the east of the bridge' had been seriously undermined by the current previously.[95] The Newcastle on Tyne and Carlisle Railway Company, to which a strip of land very close to this undermined riverbank had been conveyed by deed in December 1839, expressed deep concerns in relation to the potential impact on their railway line. A legal argument ensued about whether the Admiralty, which owned the narrow strip of land between the railway company's land and the river itself, was ultimately responsible for addressing the problem, and about who operated nearby weirs that might have contributed to the undermining of the riverbank. In this context, the commercial extraction of gravel from the expanding deposition bank on the south side of the river was perceived positively as a means of protecting the bank from erosion. The naturally expanding deposition bank was forcing the river to take a more northerly course and thereby to erode and undermine the northern bank. In 1948, and again in 1954, the Admiralty granted a lease to extract 'large quantities of gravel' from 'the middle and south side of the river bed' at Haydon Bridge to Messrs Kirsopp.[96] As a result of such extraction, it was noted, 'the river returned more or less to its original bed' and 'the erosion of the north bank at the threatened point has ceased at least for the time being'.[97]

Following an administrative change from the Northumberland Rivers Catchment Board to the Northumberland and Tyneside River Board, in 1950, work to protect riverbanks from erosion could not be undertaken by the official upriver conservators, as their new policies dictated that they could only undertake such work in exceptional circumstances, such as in order to protect a major public footpath on behalf of a riparian council. As the Admiralty was not liable for the safety of the riverbank, it was left to the railway company to take action, but the Admiralty report made a point of noting that the lessees, Messrs Kirsopp, 'should be encouraged to remove the gravel in the middle and towards the south bank of the river at the point in question, since this will tend to prevent further erosion of the north bank'.[98] By October 1955, according to a report written by the Greenwich Hospital Northern Estates Office, a company called Haydon Bridge Gravel & Mineral Products Ltd was operating the gravel extraction there and 'are likely to remove considerable quantities as they are putting in a plant'.[99] The landowners anticipated that the company would

---

95. Ibid.
96. Ibid.
97. Ibid.
98. Ibid.
99. Ibid.

'work this gravel extensively', thereby protecting the northern bank opposite their operations from erosion.[100]

The extraction of materials from the Tyne's bed and foreshore became such a hot topic in the early twentieth century because it crucially supported the development of infrastructure, industry and demographic expansion across the whole Tyne catchment. Legal, political and economic factors were paramount as several organisations and landowners fought intensely over these valuable materials which were in demand locally. This enormous volume of correspondence, minute books, reports, licences and orders features some references to economic damage to the fisheries. But it contains none in relation to the environmental health of the river or to the very long-term damaging legacies which large-scale, commercial extraction was causing. As ever, ignorance was bliss.

Straightening the Channel

In 1950, in their centenary publication, *A Century of Progress*, the commissioners explained how previously

> vessels had to round friars goose point, bill quay point and bill point, the latter a wedge of rock 72 feet high jutting into the stream like the bill of a bird – hence its name. During the course of their improvement, the commissioners removed these points and extended the river width by as much as 400 feet in places and opened the higher reaches of the river to modern shipping.[101]

In 1861, the TIC Engineer, John Ure, provided very extensive plans for structural improvement, including removing the following angular rock projections, known as points: Felling Copperas Point; Friars' Goose Point; Point above Stella; Bill Quay Point; and Whitehill Point. In 1876, in their Tyne Improvement Bill, which asked Parliament for extra funds to support their improvement works, the commissioners compared the current significantly improved channel to the 'old torturous channel through which it was difficult to navigate one vessel'.[102] After further central government funding had been secured in 1877, the TIC's work on point removal continued in earnest. By 1882, Bill Point had been removed using explosives, resulting in an extended width inshore of 140 feet.[103] Work to remove Whitehill Point involved giving the landlord of the nearby Percy Arms only one month's notice, in October 1892, of the intended takeover of

---

100. Ibid.
101. TNA, ZLIB 2/73: *A Century of Progress*, p. 30.
102. *Proceedings of the TIC 1876–1877*, p. 183 (Petition to Parliament quoted in TIC meeting minutes).
103. *Proceedings of the TIC 1881–1882*, p. 12.

Chapter 3. Creating a Grand and Deep River

the site.[104] By December 1895, the TIC noted, 'the boring and blasting of the rock down to 27 feet below low water has been recommenced' and reported that '190 lineal feet of bore holes have been bored and blasted and 292 lbs of Gelignite have been used'.[105] Removing the angular points was a serious undertaking and required relentless and expensive effort over decades. The work on removing Felling Point was not completed until the end of 1938.[106]

While the engineering works were certainly not rushed, they were progressed urgently in order to increase the TIC's income from tolls as soon as possible. Mr Lawson advised the commissioners at a meeting in March 1894, 'the way to reduce your expenditure is to complete your river improvement within the shortest possible time and then your work would be reduced to maintenance alone'.[107] He compared the somewhat slower progress of 1894 to busier times, when the public was impressed by the speed of the river improvements, 'when every dredger, every hopper and every machine they had was not only in use but working night and day, a looker on might have thought that the River Tyne was simply an instrument to help the commissioners to carry out their work'.[108] In these industrial times, the optimum situation was one in which the river was used to its full advantage as an 'instrument' to help the commissioners with their work. In 1900, only forty years after Mr Ure had produced a plan of river improvement works, the TIC began work on the final section, work 'No. 25'. This comprised 'the widening, improving, and training' of the river between the east end of Ryton Island and the boundary stone near Hedwin Streams.[109] It involved excavating soil, sand and gravel and 'the formation of a river wall and bank and the lifting and relaying of soil on the land to the north of the river wall'.[110] By February 1930, the TIC was discussing the prospect of diverting the River Don at Jarrow. Jarrow Corporation applied for permission to go ahead with the plan whereby 'about 1300 feet of the old river channel will be filled up'.[111] The plan was sanctioned.

Some of the TIC's projects to straighten the river channel backfired as the river continued to behave in unpredictable and natural ways. As a result of some

---

104. *Proceedings of the TIC 1891–1892*, p. 398.
105. *Proceedings of the TIC 1895–1896*, p. 63.
106. *Proceedings of the TIC 1937–1938*, p. 807.
107. *Proceedings of the TIC 1893–1894*, p. 168.
108. Ibid.
109. *Proceedings of the TIC 1900–1901*, p. 126.
110. Ibid.
111. *Proceedings of the TIC 1929–1930*, p. 159.

of the TIC's engineering works, riparian land came under the threat of being washed away by the tide. The TIC attempted to manage this process by either allowing the river bank to be washed away until it reached a particular line or intervening to protect the land by erecting weirs to slow down the process of erosion. In some cases, the TIC stood to lose their own valuable land on which they could potentially further their business activities. But even when someone else's land was at risk of being lost, the TIC was concerned because the eroded soil washed into the river and had to be dredged at their expense. The issue was discussed extensively at the TIC meeting in March 1881, as erosion was occurring in many locations along the river, including those above the tidal reaches outside their jurisdiction. One case of erosion was occurring at a 'very bad place near Corbridge where a large promontory ran into the river and it was diminishing every year by the water rushing past it'.[112] The language used by the TIC Chairman to conclude the discussion alludes to a certain amount of respect for the river, and almost charges it with having its own agency or control over its functions:

> The Chairman said the upper Tyne changed its bed. While in some parts land was washed away, they heard of other pieces of land growing up at other parts; and he did not think the Commissioners could undertake to control those changes in a rapid-flowing river in the upper part. This was a matter requiring their attention; but he did not agree with Mr Shotton that it involved the large expense in dredging that he indicated.[113]

Just as the Tyne was perceived as having had the power to 'change its bed', so Sara Pritchard highlights how the River Rhone was perceived as a 'furious bull', an active agent capable of shaping its own destiny.[114] In February 1939, the TIC's canalisation of the River Team was blamed for increasing the rate of flow and causing flooding between Lobley Hill Bridge and Dunston on the tributary River Team.[115] Several engineering works were proposed to reduce the risk of flooding in that area and the Commissioner for the Special Areas (England and Wales) pledged 72 per cent of the total cost of the work which amounted to £33,450.[116] The remainder had to be raised by the local authorities and other bodies interested in the river valley. The TIC refused to contribute to

---

112. *Proceedings of the TIC 1880–1881*, p. 116.
113. Ibid., p. 114.
114. Pritchard, *Confluence*, p. 63.
115. *Proceedings of the TIC 1938–1939*, pp. 246–247.
116. Ibid.

Chapter 3. Creating a Grand and Deep River

the scheme.[117] The TIC's 'good work' to create their grand and deep channel of which they were so proud did not go as smoothly as they hoped it would when they prepared their initial schedule of works in 1860. From start to finish, the restructuring of the river was a two-way negotiation between the engineers' designs and the independent flows of what remained throughout the whole process a naturally powerful river system.

Domestic and Industrial Wastes

One of the most harmful effects of Tyneside's rapid industrialisation on the Tyne's health was the deposition into the estuary of increasing volumes of largely untreated domestic and industrial waste. In addition to the obvious problems resulting from depositing highly complex, poisonous chemical wastes into the river water, oxygen-hungry organic matter from domestic waste pipes depleted the river water's oxygenation, which crucially supported its fish life. The TIC granted permission to construct so many sewers to flush liquid and solid waste directly into the river that, by 1968, over 270 sewers drained into the estuary alone. Elsewhere, the installation of so many flushing toilets in early nineteenth-century London drove increasingly more untreated liquid waste directly into the River Thames which caused the 'Great Stink' in the summer of 1858, and motivated the very urgent development of a large-scale underground sewerage network in the city. The Victorians have been admired immensely for their successful, tireless and monumental efforts to solve the urgent technological problem of how to dispose of the higher volume, increasingly liquid, human waste which had been both augmented and liquified by millions of gallons of flush water. This is understandable, given the positive implications for public health and hygiene. But historians rarely mention that their innovative underground sewerage networks were only necessary because they had installed so many water closets in the place of far more environmentally sustainable, albeit unhygienic, dry privy pits which enabled a large bulk of excrement to be applied to arable land as fertiliser. Once major urban centres, such as Newcastle, had come to rely very heavily on the extensive subterranean sewerage networks that served their increasing numbers of water closets by draining untreated waste away from homes and businesses and directly into rivers, the social and economic consequences of simply blocking the outfalls became matters of life and death. Blocking the outfalls, therefore, became unthinkable. As Leslie Rosenthal concluded in her detailed study of several legal cases relating

---

117. Ibid.

to the dilemma between prioritising efficient sanitary drainage or clean and non-offensive river water, 'peremptory closure of sewage networks or sewage outlets into rivers would have had serious social consequences in the affected towns'.[118] Rosenthal laments that 'nuisance law in the civil courts is, by its very nature, fundamentally and functionally ill-equipped to play the role of society's protector of the environment: even were this to be desired'.[119]

In addition to the ever-growing number of sewers that it sanctioned, the TIC operated a flotilla of barges, known as hoppers, to transport large volumes of rubbish, including material lifted from the river bed by their own dredgers, along the Tyne to be dumped into the North Sea. Other companies and councils also had their own waste-disposal hoppers which disposed of their rubbish in a similar manner. The TIC went to significant lengths to regulate how far from the mouth of the river such hoppers were able to dispose of their rubbish. This might sound like an environmentally progressive policy, but it was exclusively to prevent any solid material being washed back up the river and deposited on the river bed, from where it would have to be dredged at the TIC's expense. The rubbish was supposed to be discharged more than three miles out to sea from the pier head, but sometimes this rule was broken. In the Tyne Improvement Act of 1850, it was stipulated that waste must not be discharged in water lower than fifteen fathoms, anywhere between Saint Mary's Isle and Souter Point, but a maximum lineal distance from the mouth of the river was not cited. The construction of the piers also had an impact on how far out the hoppers would need to go to ensure that the rubbish was not swept back up by the tide. In October 1885, the TIC passed their own bylaw, which they were entitled to do by the Tyne Improvement Act of 1865, in order to set a minimum distance of three miles and to increase the minimum depth to twenty fathoms.[120]

In February 1892, the distance of three miles was adjusted from the heads of the newly constructed piers.[121] Engineer James Walker was asked in December 1898 to investigate and report on the benefits of building four more iron hoppers to ensure that the maximum weight of rubbish was 550 tons each.[122] In June 1900, the TIC emphasised

---

118. Rosenthal, *River Pollution Dilemma*, p. 227.
119. Ibid., p. 230.
120. *Proceedings of the TIC 1884–1885*, p. 12.
121. *Proceedings of the TIC 1891–1892*, p. 189.
122. *Proceedings of the TIC 1898–1899*, p. 38.

Chapter 3. Creating a Grand and Deep River

the subject is one of the utmost importance, bearing in mind the fact that during the last ten years the annual quantity of dredged material deposited at sea by the Tyne Improvement Commissioners has averaged no less than 1,812,980 tons, exclusive of material deposited by corporations, manufacturers and others.[123]

This was a substantial volume of 'material' to be dumping out at sea. They realised that 'the deposition of this large quantity of material must be slowly but surely raising the bed of the sea off the entrance to the Tyne' and decided that it should only continue 'under the best possible system of control and supervision'.[124] One incident at 5 a.m. on 5 January 1908, led to the deposition of a considerable volume of rubbish directly into the Tyne. A wooden hopper called 'The Dustman', belonging to the Tyne Hopper Company, sank at the Northumberland Dock wall, 'laden with 130 tons of rubbish'.[125] Although it was raised successfully by the commissioners' workmen two days later, the bulk of the rubbish had sunk into the river water.[126]

The issue reared its head again in September 1938, when the TIC received complaints from fishermen that rubbish had been deposited within the three-mile boundary. The fishermen, from Cullercoats, provided a statement to the Tyne Salmon Conservancy Board, which it relayed in a letter to the TIC:

> The information given by two of the Cullercoats fishermen is that on the morning of the 21st May last they had great difficulty in hauling their crab pots which they had set the previous day at a depth of 16 or 17 fathoms. When the pots were eventually lifted they were found to be covered with masses of refuse which could only have come from one of your hoppers discharging immediately above them. These particulars are confirmed by another two fishermen who were engaged in the vicinity and in the opinion of my board they appear to be convincing.[127]

The Harbour Master and various officers who were responsible for taking measurements of the distance out to sea when the hoppers discharged their waste provided records stating that only one hopper was out on the day mentioned in the fishermen's statement and they measured it out to sea three miles.[128] The case was closed, but it underlines the potential inadequacies of disposing of rubbish in such a rudimentary manner.

---

123. *Proceedings of the TIC 1899–1900*, p. 508.
124. Ibid., pp. 508–509.
125. *Proceedings of the TIC 1907–1908*, p. 114.
126. Ibid.
127. *Proceedings of the TIC 1937–1938*, p. 730.
128. Ibid., p. 731.

It would be unfair to assume that the TIC were completely ignorant of the benefits of pre-treating waste. They were well aware that the use of settling tanks could reduce the amount of material they had to dredge from the river bed. As early as in May 1879, for example, the Benwell Local Board was prepared to buy three acres of land on which to construct a settling bed, at the cost of £4,000.[129] By October 1904, the TIC engineer insisted that in order to be granted permission to construct an outfall at Low Team, Gateshead Corporation must

> construct near the outfall of the proposed sewer a settling chamber so as to prevent the solids contained in the sewage from washing into the river Team, that the sewage be treated with some efficient precipitant and effectually screened and that the solids and sludge be regularly and systematically removed from the settling chamber at least once a week or oftener if required.[130]

Quite a lot of sewers were fitted with flap valves, but there were very few centralised pre-treatment facilities. One sewer, being constructed near Willington Bridge in mid-1893, was constructed in such a way that it was 'tide locked', which meant that it only flushed at low tide, as described by the TIC's engineer, Mr Messent:

> The proposed sewer will be tide locked at every tide as the gradient is very flat and it will be flushed at low tide by three of Adam's automatic flushing tanks, one of which will be supplied with water from the Wallsend Burn and the other two at intermediate points by the Newcastle and Gateshead Water Company, these tanks being arranged so that they would only work at low tide.[131]

Another proposal from Mr Taylor, of the Newburn District Local Board, suggested a scheme for a settling tank because the proposed sewer was to discharge at a recessed point in which water stood still for between four and five hours per day.[132] A screening and settling tank was to be built a hundred feet westward of the discharge.[133] The tank, to be placed between a wide screen and a narrower screen, was to be

> about 18 feet long by 10 feet wide and contain eight buckets for the deposit of solid matters which may pass through the first screen and are intercepted

---

129. *Proceedings of the TIC 1878–1879*, p. 126.
130. *Proceedings of the TIC 1903–1904*, pp. 741, 742.
131. *Proceedings of the TIC 1892–1893*, p. 248.
132. *Proceedings of the TIC 1894–1895*, p. 241.
133. Ibid.

Chapter 3. Creating a Grand and Deep River

by the second screen. It is intended that the buckets shall be regularly and systematically emptied twice a week and the solids be deposited on the land.[134]

In October 1901, an application from Benwell and Fenham Urban District Council for permission to construct a new sewer included quite extensive facilities for screening the sewage before it was discharged into the river:

> The sewage will first pass through a large screen, the bars of which will be 1½ inches apart then through another screen with bars ½ inch apart, thus effectually screening all solids, paper, and other matter from the sewage. The screens will be raked by hand twice per 24 hours. The matter retained by the screens will be placed in covered moveable galvanised iron receptacles (similar to an ash bin for house refuse). The contents of these receptacles will be removed twice weekly and taken out to sea. The council remove the house refuse of the district twice a week from a jetty in the neighbourhood and barge it to sea, and the intention is for the matter removed by the screens to be taken along with it.[135]

This is a remarkably complex system for the period. In March 1903, moreover, the TIC approved an application from the Castle Ward Rural District Council to treat sewage on land at Heddon on the Wall before it entered the river.[136]

The TIC only insisted on such elaborate screening and settling tanks to prevent the silting up of the areas beneath the outfalls, which would then have to be dredged. They were not concerned about the toxicity of chemical waste or deoxygenation. Nevertheless, the commissioners' encouragement of installing pre-treatment facilities into sewer systems marked an important change in their attitudes towards waste disposal. Although most sewers were planned carefully, some were installed without the TIC's permission and became quite serious nuisances. In July 1900, one sewer at Jarrow Slakes was reported to have left 'a slimy deposit on the foreshore' covering a semicircle whose radius was about thirty feet from the outlet of the sewer and 'as the tides during the occurrence of neap tides never reach the outlet the sewage discharged accumulates on the foreshore and, decomposing in hot weather, creates a most offensive and pestiferous nuisance'.[137] It was ordered to be redesigned through the proper planning process and with the help of the TIC engineer to ensure that the nuisance was abated. By February 1901, Jarrow Council had agreed to pay for a new sewer, which would be completed within one month.[138]

---

134. Ibid.
135. *Proceedings of the TIC 1900–1901*, p. 911.
136. *Proceedings of the TIC 1902–1903*, pp. 604–606.
137. *Proceedings of the TIC 1899–1900*, p. 563.
138. *Proceedings of the TIC 1900–1901*, p. 385.

Tyne after Tyne

Sometimes, the TIC granted permission to abstract river water for washing purposes, after which the dirty water was discharged back into the river. In February 1902, the Harton Coal Company wanted to complete engineering works to improve the railway connecting their colliery to their wharf at South Shields. This involved using large volumes of gravel and sand from an old ballast heap at Willington. The material needed to be washed before use, so an application was made to the TIC 'to pump water from the Willington Gut to wash the sand and gravel' in a basic washing machine 'and afterwards to let the dirty water flow back into the same gut' after having passed through a settling tank.[139] The project was sanctioned, the work was completed by October 1902 and the machine was taken away.[140] Moreover, an application from the Greenside Sand and Gravel Company was received in December 1946 for permission not only to dredge a berth at Newburn for access to the company's jetty, but also to install a suction pipe there to extract water from the Tyne. The water would then pass 'through a gravel washing plant' and 'return to the river from a settling pond at the downriver end of the site by percolating through the bank'.[141] The application was sanctioned on condition that 'none of the washings from the settling pond be returned to the river'.[142] At least some restraint was exercised.

In the early twentieth century, seriously harmful effluents were discharged largely untreated into the river by factories producing increasingly complex chemical products. The Tyne was the first place in the world where petrol was produced from coal – at the Newcastle Benzol Works at Blaydon. In 1928, Derwenthaugh Coke works was set up near the dam, where for every ton of coke produced, there was a by-product of one kilo of cyanide, which was flushed into the river water. Together with the many steamers' combined smoke, the heavily polluted riverscape became an increasingly challenging environment in which to live and work. One street of houses in Lemington called Bell's Close was specifically designed without back windows because the river pollution was intolerable. In July 1910, the TIC became aware that a sewer leading from the North Eastern Railway Company's Forth Cattle Docks was bringing a substantial volume of saw dust down to the mouth of the culvert at the foot of Tyneside Road, caused by the washing out of cattle trucks, which were

> swept out and the refuse thus removed, placed in trucks and taken to spoil heaps. After being swept out the trucks are washed down and although men

---

139. *Proceedings of the TIC 1901–1902*, p. 274.
140. Ibid., p. 1130.
141. *Proceedings of the TIC 1946–1947*, p. 130.
142. Ibid.

Chapter 3. Creating a Grand and Deep River

are employed to prevent sawdust getting into the sewer a considerable quantity does pass into the river.[143]

The company was ordered to construct a suitable trap to prevent the sawdust from passing into the river.

The deposition of waste into the river not only increased the depth of the river bed and changed the chemical composition of the water, but also increased the river water temperature. Several companies drew water from the river using suction pipes, used the water in various cooling processes, and then discharged it directly back into the river, raising the local water temperature. In May 1910, for example, the TIC engineer granted permission to the Castner Kellner Alkali Company to abstract water through two five-inch suction pipes from the dock and to discharge the water through a nine-inch diameter pipe in front of the quay.[144]

From the moment of its establishment, the TIC continued to sanction the construction of one new sewer after another, albeit according to certain conditions regarding pre-treatment, right up until the Northumbrian River Authority was established in 1965 with unprecedented power to prevent new discharges into the river estuary. During this time, there were surprisingly few serious challenges to their actions. However, in September 1958, one of the commissioners, Mr Gompertz, who represented South Shields Council, made a particularly outspoken and vociferous objection to the TIC's continued support of the construction of more sewers. By 1958, the Tyne estuary was so seriously deoxygenated by the disposal of untreated waste that it had been classified as biologically dead and its toxic waters literally bubbled between Newcastle and Gateshead. At the TIC meeting which sanctioned a new sewer outfall for the Consett Iron Company Ltd at Derwenthaugh, Mr Gompertz explained to the chairman that while he did not want to 'tax you too much, … I would like to ask what the sewage works will do'.[145] He revealed that 'what it will discharge is what concerns me' because 'I feel certain that part of the duty of seeing that the Tyne is not polluted any further or worse … is the duty of this board'.[146] The chairman replied that 'it deals with sewage' and Gompertz said, 'oh well if it is filth, I am going to object to it'.[147] After the Chairman then confirmed that the TIC had no power to object to sewage being drained into the Tyne,

---

143. *Proceedings of the TIC 1909–1910*, p. 575.
144. Ibid., p. 434.
145. *Proceedings of the TIC 1957–1958*, p. 113.
146. Ibid., p. 113.
147. Ibid.

Gompertz suggested that 'surely it is high time we did take upon ourselves that part of our responsibility'.[148] This obviously ruffled the Chairman's feathers, as he retorted, 'we have no powers to deal with sewage and if you are going to make a motion asking for powers I am going to rule you clean out of order'.[149] Gompertz reminded the commissioners of their role as 'custodians' of the river and questioned how it was possible that they could regulate the river in 'every way', yet have no responsibility for the disposal of sewage into 'a magnificent waterway'.[150] It seemed to Gompertz 'very wrong indeed that we with all the powers that we have ... cannot control sewage into our own river'.[151] Obviously missing Gompertz's point, or deliberately avoiding it, the Chairman responded 'as you well know ... we are concerned with the structure of the sewers at the outfall end' and 'we are not concerned with what goes into the sewers', emphasising that 'we must have no concern about that', before ruling Gompertz as 'out of order' and passing the Consett Iron Company's application for a new sewer outlet at Derwenthaugh.[152]

Only one month later, in October 1958, yet another application was about to be passed to construct a sanitary drain into the Tyne at Low Walker, received from Swan Hunter and Wigham Richardson Ltd. This proved too much for Gompertz, who objected to the fact that the TIC 'find drastic methods necessary where it is a question of £ s d, but where it is a question of the health of Tyneside, the pollution of a great river, a vulgarity that it is almost now an accepted face we have it without a murmur or word'.[153] In response to Gompertz's controversial utterances, which were exceptional in TIC meetings, the chairman addressed the issue of river pollution in depth in order to 'make the commissioners' position clear' and to explain that the TIC's hands were tied in relation to protecting the river against sewers' discharges.[154] The chairman began, 'there is some uninformed criticism and to suggest that the Tyne Commissioners are in any way responsible for the present state of affairs [i.e. the heavily polluted river] or that it is their duty to remedy it is unjust'.[155] Citing two Acts of Parliament, the 1948 River Boards Act and the 1951 Riv-

---

148. Ibid., p. 114.
149. Ibid.
150. Ibid.
151. Ibid.
152. Ibid., p. 115.
153. Ibid., p. 158.
154. Ibid., p. 163.
155. Ibid.

Chapter 3. Creating a Grand and Deep River

ers Prevention of Pollution Act, he explained that River Boards, such as their local Northumberland and Tyneside River Board, were established to deal with pollution. His key point was that, while this legislation was intended to protect rivers from pollution, it only included tidal waters or parts of the sea which had been declared to be streams under the 1876 Rivers Prevention of Pollution Act or the subsequent 1951 version. The Tyne estuary had not been declared as a stream in either of the Acts and therefore had no legal protection from discharges into its waters. The Chairman highlighted that the Minister of Housing and Local Government could classify the Tyne as a stream at any time, making the discharge of polluting matter into the river a punishable offence. But, as the Chairman was undoubtedly aware, the Minister was highly unlikely to make such a change. The Chairman was using the law to justify the TIC's actions and took no personal responsibility for the polluted river. He was appointed to obey the law and obey the law he did, to the letter. He went on, in some detail:

> It is obvious to everyone that any scheme for cleaning the Tyne will be on a gigantic scale if it is to have a chance of success. I think the cost which will be enormous is beyond local resources and must be widely borne. As individuals and as a Body we are just as much horrified at the pollution of the river as any other person or Body on Tyneside or elsewhere. As a dock and harbour authority, however, the prevention of pollution is not our function. I would counsel you not to be misled by specious arguments outside this Board room into accepting or attempting to accept a heavy responsibility which the Law already contemplates as the proper duty of another Body [i.e. the local River Board].[156]

Commissioner Russell commented that the River Board is the correct authority to deal with river pollution and that they 'are doing all they can to clear the river up, but they have very little or no control of tidal waters'.[157] Commissioner Pumphrey interjected to say that 'what we want is sewage cleaned up and the River Tyne made a decent river' and that 'if the River Board are going to do it then we should use all our powers to put those powers into their hands'.[158] This pleased Gompertz, who welcomed someone to the debate who, in his opinion, 'possesses sense'.[159] The Chairman summarised that 'we are all anxious to do it [i.e. initiate a clean-up of the river] but the law contemplates another method

---

156. Ibid., pp. 163–164.
157. Ibid., p. 165.
158. Ibid.
159. Ibid.

of doing it and it is not our job'.[160] Gompertz responded with deep criticism, 'for an organisation with vast Parliamentary powers and enormous control, tremendous income and prestige to say it cannot do anything to prevent the river from being polluted in this shameful way is a point of view I cannot understand'.[161] The Chairman admitted that 'we as individuals can do what we can but not as commissioners'.[162]

Another two months later, in December 1958, as yet another application to construct a sewer draining into the river was about to be passed, this time from the Associated Lead Manufacturers, Mr Gompertz raised the issue again.[163] Gompertz explained that he was 'trying to draw the attention of the board again to the fact that sewage is poured into the river by all and sundry', when

> all they have to do is to make application and we get a statement from the Harbour Master and get a statement from the engineer that all is well and I thought we might get a little more information regarding the sewage as to what risks we are running in further pollution of the river.[164]

The Chairman concluded that the TIC had 'no powers on that matter at all' and duly sanctioned the new sewer application.[165] In March 1960, Mr Gompertz resigned from South Shields Council and from his post as a Tyne Improvement Commissioner. His protest was an unusually vocal one. Although a few other commissioners supported Gompertz, the majority remained silent and the chairman's almost robotic and very dogmatic justification of the TIC's actions within a legal framework provides a valuable insight into the perspectives of the TIC. It enables us to make sense of why they continued to sanction sewer, after sewer, after sewer, until the river was classified as biologically dead. In their minds, they were merely obeying the law and performing the duties of their organisation.

Testing and Attempts at Regulation

Although complex, scientific testing of the water and discharges being made into the River Tyne's water didn't begin in earnest until 1912, simpler tests were carried out before this date. Highly complex chemical waste was discharged

---

160. Ibid., p. 166.
161. Ibid.
162. Ibid.
163. Ibid., p. 232.
164. Ibid., p. 233.
165. Ibid.

Chapter 3. Creating a Grand and Deep River

into the river from the late nineteenth century. In September 1895, the TIC engineer, Mr Messent, reported on an application from Williamson and Corder to discharge waste liquids onto the foreshore in front of their chemical works at Low Walker. Messent agreed to sanction the application provided the iron sewerage pipe be laid at two feet below LWST.[166] The bulk of the liquid was river water which had been extracted for the purposes of condensing steam and was still at 80 degrees Fahr. when it was returned to the river. Moreover, some of the water had been used for boiling bones, some of which was mixed with a weak neutral solution of calcium chloride.[167] This prompted the TIC to appoint an analytical chemist to assess the composition of the water to be discharged and it postponed sanctioning the application until they received the results. This is the first reference in the TIC minutes to scientific chemistry and it marks an important step in their comprehension of the river water's chemical processes.

The TIC approached J. and H. Pattinson, analytical chemists, based at a laboratory at no. 75, The Side, in Newcastle. They visited the works, took samples and reported back to the TIC in October 1895, concluding that the waste water originated from four sources. The first source was from the process of evaporation 'in vacuo' of water that had been used for cooling purposes and returned to the river warmed up to about 80 degrees Fahr. The works released some 3,000 gallons of this water per hour when their apparatus was in use.[168] The second source came from the process of boiling bones and this liquid contained some organic matter and some fats extracted from the bones, which caused the water to appear white. The works released 600 gallons of this liquid during two one-hour releases each week at temperatures of between 130 and 180 degrees Fahr., but as it was mixed with the first source of water before entering the river, its temperature was substantially cooler when it entered the river.[169] The third source came from the process of washing with cold water the ossein or gelatinous part of bones, as a result of which 'finely divided parts are removed and floated into the river' which resulted in a white and turbid liquid which discoloured the river water 'considerably'.[170] The fourth source came from the filter presses 'used in filtering precipitated phosphate of lime', which produced 'a weak solution of calcium chloride similar to that discharged

---

166. *Proceedings of the TIC 1894–1895*, pp. 431–432.
167. Ibid., p. 485.
168. *Proceedings of the TIC 1895–1896*, pp. 525–52.
169. Ibid.
170. Ibid.

from most of the chemical works on the river'.[171] This liquid was discharged at a rate of 200 gallons per hour during the daytime and was usually mixed and further diluted with other water before entering the river.[172] The TIC forwarded a copy of this report to Williamson and Corder for their consideration and then granted formal permission to discharge the waste liquids in December 1895. Henceforth, similarly thorough scientific analysis of liquid wastes was performed infrequently by the TIC if and when its engineers raised concerns about the complexity of wastes being emitted by particular riparian works. However, in the early years, the tests conducted by the TIC seem to have been conducted exclusively to minimise the amount of material which had to be dredged from the river bed. None of them was motivated by environmental concerns.

While the TIC's focus and primary motivation was to improve the economic efficiency of their River Tyne, they did nevertheless make some quite bold attempts at regulating particularly harmful activities in ways which would have had a positive impact on the environment, albeit unintentionally. The river was inspected once a month by the TIC engineer for encroachments. Any company found to have been responsible for erecting an unauthorised encroachment into the river was asked to apply retrospectively for permission. If permission was not granted, they were ordered to remove it at their own expense. Ultimately, this sort of regulation was designed to retain tight control over the TIC's jurisdiction and to prevent uncontrolled and chaotic riparian development or protrusions which could have impeded the river's flow, but it was a form of environmental regulation in effect, if not in intention. Ironically, in September 1894, the engineer reported an encroachment by the Union *Cement* Company in two places near the west end of their river frontage at Wallsend, consisting of 'ashes and rubbish faced with broken bricks forming a wall about 10 feet high with a batter of 4 feet built *without mortar or cement* [emphasis added]'.[173] Surely, this cement company could have got their hands on some cement with which to strengthen their river frontage!

In January 1891, the Anglo-American Oil Company proposed to build stores for their oil at the Lawe, South Shields. Engineer Messent took considerable care to ensure that the storage would be safe, the main concerns being that it could catch fire, that vessels could discharge their bilge water into the river and that oil or petroleum could leak into the river water.[174] He

---

171. Ibid.
172. Ibid.
173. *Proceedings of the TIC 1893–1894*, pp. 492–493.
174. *Proceedings of the TIC 1890–1891*, p. 108.

Chapter 3. Creating a Grand and Deep River

completed his first inspection of the stores following their construction in July 1892 and found a hole under the front wall, through which petroleum or oil could easily have escaped directly into the river. The TIC wrote to the company asking them to make the hole safe immediately, which they did.[175] Crichton and Company, which also traded in oil at their premises at the Lawe, was also subject to monthly inspections. In September 1892, both establishments were ordered to use a safety trough underneath the supply pipe when discharging. Mr Messent even supervised during discharges, which occurred about four times annually. Moreover, the TIC insisted that they built a wall eight feet in height around the tanks, in case of overflow or leakage. In October 1898, following a further inspection of both sites at The Lawe, those of the Anglo-American Oil Company and Crichton and Co., engineer James Walker reported, rather alarmingly, 'there is a possibility if all three iron oil tanks were to break or burst about the same time of 636,750 gallons of oil overflowing the walls of the reservoir and running into the river'.[176] He therefore ordered both companies to 'remedy it as soon as possible, either by increasing the size of their safety reservoirs until they are large enough to contain the total quantities of oil held by the iron oil tanks or by some other method'.[177] Despite regulation, however, accidents inevitably occurred. In July 1900, the River Police reported to the TIC that 'nine boxes of cartridges filled with gunpowder intended for the US cruiser Albany lying at Jarrow Slake' had fallen into the river.[178] The horse and cart containing the explosives belonged to Armstrong, Whitworth & Co Ltd, and the horse 'backed over the quay into the river' while left unattended.[179] All but one of the boxes was recovered, but the horse drowned.

In January 1903, the TIC engineer sanctioned an application from Mawson, Clark and Company, to retain a grease trap at the grease works at Dunston, which was designed to prevent grease, oil and tar from entering the Tyne. The trap consisted of

> three brick walls built across the ditch or runner varying from about 6 feet 8 inches to 5 feet 10 inches in length with two spaces 15 inches wide between the walls the two outer walls being 14 inches thick and two feet high and the centre wall 18 inches thick and 4 ½ feet high'.[180]

---

175. *Proceedings of the TIC 1891–1892*, p. 303.
176. *Proceedings of the TIC 1897–1898*, p. 687.
177. Ibid.
178. *Proceedings of the TIC 1899–1900*, p. 541.
179. Ibid.
180. *Proceedings of the TIC 1902–1903*, p. 400.

The principle was 'that if any oily matter should in spite of our precautions have got into the water floating towards the Tyne', anything lighter than water would have floated and would not have been able to rise over the lower blocks.[181] Although it was sanctioned, special conditions applied. They ordered the applicants to 'periodically remove the floating or deposited matter from the ditch so as to prevent it from being washed into the River Tyne by floods' and stipulated 'that if the trap be found not efficient further means shall be adopted by the applicants to prevent the oil, tar &c from passing into the Tyne'.[182] A similar drain at Scotswood was sanctioned in January 1944, complete with a grease and oil trap leading from Vickers Armstrongs Ltd, which was to be used 'for emptying a wash out pit beneath a railway track'.[183] In March 1902, the Hedworth Barium Company, which deposited waste materials on the commissioners' land at Jarrow Slake, was ordered to prevent the deposited material from being washed into the tributary River Don by forming 'a pitched slope of slag stones or other approved material' at least two feet thick to the satisfaction of the commissioners' engineer.[184]

In 1916, the Admiralty's Transport Department took action to prevent the leakage of oil by oilers in dry docks in response to several complaints received at the beginning of the year. The Admiralty reported 'attention has been drawn to the fact that oiler transports occasionally clean their tanks out and discharge the residue in ports such as the Tyne', which they pointed out is 'in contravention of the order given to the masters that oil fuel compartments are not to be washed out nor water ballast containing any admixture of oil pumped out in any port of the United Kingdom'.[185] In order to prevent future leakages, they ordered that 'actual cleaning should be done in the river and the vessels proceed outside to pump out waste, when absolutely necessary to have all tanks cleaned' and where a 'vessel is only docking for cleaning and painting, the tanks can be steamed out and the residue all pumped into one tank for pumping out when vessel leaves the port'.[186] Throughout the twentieth century until their disbandment in 1968, the TIC made reasonable efforts to ensure that at least some potentially harmful and problematic substances such

---

181. Ibid.
182. Ibid.
183. *Proceedings of the TIC 1943–1944*, p. 131.
184. *Proceedings of the TIC 1901–1902*, p. 381.
185. TNA, MT 23/534/16, Pollution of River Tyne by Oilers in Dry-dock: Complaints and instructions regarding prevention (1916).
186. TNA, MT 23/534/16, Pollution of River Tyne by Oilers in Dry-dock: Complaints and instructions regarding prevention (1916).

Chapter 3. Creating a Grand and Deep River

as oil and chemical waste products did not enter the river water. They were motivated to protect their property rather than the environmental health of the Tyne in its own right, but their regulatory actions had small positive effects on the river's health, albeit in the context of much more severe negative effects from their other activities aimed at transforming the river into an economic and industrial facility.

The TIC's Intervention in Non-Tidal reaches

The TIC had no jurisdiction above the tidal limits of the river and its tributaries, but waste disposal up river did have an adverse impact on their dredging operations and efficient shipping. Their first record of discussing this issue appears in September 1876, after the previous session of Parliament had passed the Rivers Pollution Prevention Act, forbidding the deposition of solid materials into rivers, both tidal and non-tidal. Although the Tyne above its tidal limit was not in their jurisdiction, the TIC took action to deter business owners upriver from depositing waste material into the river. Following a report from the river constable, advising the commissioners that Fourstones Colliery's waste was being deposited into the river above Hexham, they wrote to the colliery owner, who replied, promising that 'no such deposit should in future be made to the injury or prejudice of the river'.[187] Several other police reports were received detailing how waste materials were piled near to the river, in order that the material would be washed away during high water. The TIC erected signs at several locations upriver stating that 'the placing of materials in positions liable to be washed into the river is an offence and that the parties guilty thereof incur penalties imposed by law'.[188] The hypocritical commissioners worked with the upper river's local police force, in an area outside their own tidal jurisdiction, to use a national law to reduce the cost of their dredging operations in the estuary. They did this, astonishingly, while they continued to sanction the discharge of ever more solid waste directly into the estuary.

In October 1876, the TIC received a police report that thousands of tons of waste had been carted to the river at Corbridge and placed where it would be washed away. The TIC appointed a sub-committee of four commissioners to visit the upper reaches of the river and inspect the extent to which rubbish was being deposited into the river. Tyne Commissioner Plummer made his own contribution to the report, recalling that, while waiting on the Fourstones

---

187. *Proceedings of the TIC 1875–1876*, p. 200.
188. Ibid.

railway platform, 'to his perfect astonishment he saw a tramway laid from the boiler house of a pumping engine direct to the river where there was a staith and all the ashes from the boiler were upset into the river'.[189] At the meeting in October 1877, concern about material being washed down from above the tidal limit into the estuary, where it had to be dredged at the expense of the TIC, prompted the appointment of a sub-committee of six commissioners 'to examine and report on the subject of material being washed into the stream of the Tyne above the tidal flow, from the collieries manufactories and other works – from material being placed in a position so to be washed in – and also from the wasting of the banks'.[190]

The TIC became very concerned about the Rivers Conservancy Bill, which was presented to Parliament in April 1879, because they feared that a local River Board would at best rival their jurisdiction and at worst completely overpower them. The appointment of local River Boards, it was hoped, would facilitate the enforcement of the 1876 Rivers Pollution Act and prevent flooding. The TIC sent a petition to Parliament in April 1879, arguing that no local board should be appointed because it would interfere with and impede their improvement works. This led to extensive debate among the commissioners at their next meeting in May 1879 over how far their jurisdiction should be expanded to prevent the appointment of a local River Board. Although James Guthrie, the TIC secretary, died suddenly in February 1880, his advice before his death in relation to the Rivers Conservancy Bill was to request that Parliament extend the TIC's jurisdiction to the upper reaches of the river. The minutes of the April 1881 meeting explain why:

> In many villages and large populations on the banks of the river it was a common practice to put rubbish of all sorts upon the banks of the river, within or near the water mark, so that when a flood such as there had been within the past few weeks came down the whole was swept into the river and had to be dredged out. It would be well if the commissioners could be appointed conservators of the whole river instead of the lower portion only and then they could deal with such evils as he had pointed out.[191]

Commissioner Hodgson went as far as to say 'the quantity of soil and rubbish washed down the river in times of flood was shameful', and blamed the Mickley Colliery Company, based at Stocksfield near Hexham, as the principal

---

189. Ibid., p. 214.
190. *Proceedings of the TIC 1876–1877*, p. 204.
191. *Proceedings of the TIC 1880–1881*, p. 149.

Chapter 3. Creating a Grand and Deep River

suspect.[192] The TIC sent river policemen to inspect as far as the source of the South Tyne near Alston and up the River Allen. It bears repeating that the TIC was entirely motivated by saving money on dredging in the estuary rather than any of today's conservation concerns.

The river police made several reports of the deposition of waste materials on the riverbanks at places such as Corbridge, but the TIC was powerless. At a meeting held in February 1876, the 'superintendent of Police reported the circumstances connected with the deposit of material at Corbridge, in a position liable to be washed into the river'.[193] However, the TIC was powerless to act against this transgression. The River and Ferry Committee sent a man up river once a month to inspect what was being done to prevent rubbish and other materials being washed into the river. The commissioners agreed that 'in very nearly all cases' proprietors had done what they could to prevent waste disposal into the river.[194] In June 1883, for example, the commissioners wrote to the Surveyor of the Hexham Local Board to ask him to ensure that no more rubbish was deposited on Mill Island. He replied to assure them that a new place for the purpose had been provided and that no more rubbish would be placed there.[195] The TIC, which used a rigid interpretation of the law to justify many of their operations, as well as to explain their abdication of responsibility in relation to the heavily polluted river water, were sending committees up river outside their jurisdiction to work with local business owners and councils, despite having no official capacity to do so. This disregard for the law was fuelled entirely by the desire to reduce the cost of dredging operations in the estuary.

Conclusion

The TIC was respected for its technical expertise. It was asked by Parliament in August 1884 to provide advice on several technical questions to be passed to the International Consultative Commission on the Suez Canal. The TIC employed an engineer, on quite a respectable salary (£1,500 in 1884) to report on all the applications they received to build on the riverbanks, to construct quays protruding into the channel or to discharge material directly into the river water. The engineer visited each site, completed an engineering assessment and recommended whether or not the TIC should grant permission. When an

---

192. Ibid.
193. *Proceedings of the TIC 1875–1876*, p. 73.
194. *Proceedings of the TIC 1886–1887*, p. 161.
195. *Proceedings of the TIC 1882–1883*, pp. 266–267.

application was sanctioned, the TIC allowed neighbouring parties one month during which they could voice concerns before the applicants could begin work. Despite all these policies and procedures, they nevertheless sanctioned nearly all the applications they received, and the ones they did reject were rejected because they threatened the TIC's economic interests on the river. They rejected no applications on the grounds of environmental concern. Though there is no evidence in the TIC minutes suggesting that larger businesses were favoured over smaller businesses when applications for riparian developments were considered, there was one special case: that of Lord William Armstrong. At a meeting in September 1877, the TIC discussed an application from Armstrong which had been delayed. Commissioner Dryden attempted to rush the application through, stating 'Sir William Armstrong is not a man to dally with a thing of this sort'.[196]

The TIC were concerned about waste-disposal, but only because they wanted to minimise their expenditure on dredging solid material from beneath the sewer outfalls. The usual conditions of permission to construct sewers nearly always included the removal of accumulations of solid material underneath the outlets at the expense of the applicant. Although the commissioners were oblivious to the harmful chemicals being discharged into the river through the sewers, and did little to regulate the disposal of domestic waste which deoxygenated the water, they were extra vigilant about very large volumes of solid material and rubbish being washed into or dropped directly into the river. Once an incident was reported to the TIC, its secretary wrote to the accused company urging them to take action and in most cases they did so immediately. In August 1885, the TIC ordered E. Richardson and Sons, paper manufacturers on the River Team, to stop casting mud accumulated at their works into the Mill Race which drained into the Tyne.[197] In April 1887, the TIC received a report from the river police that some workmen who cleaned out ash pits in Gateshead had been tipping seven cartloads of ashes directly into the Tyne. The Gateshead Magistrates Court fined the men, who were working under the management of Alexander Elliot, a contractor, the sum of 5s each.[198]

As we have seen, the TIC believed deeply in the benefits of their important work and they justified what they were and were not responsible for within the law. Sometimes, river works were justified because they alleviated the ravages of unemployment. At a meeting of the Social Democratic Federation, in December

---

196. *Proceedings of the TIC 1876–1877*, p. 193.
197. *Proceedings of the TIC 1884–1885*, p. 331.
198. *Proceedings of the TIC 1886–1887*, p. 206.

Chapter 3. Creating a Grand and Deep River

1887, the organisation resolved to ask the TIC to 'make use of the Act passed some years ago, empowering them to straighten and deepen the river west of Newburn as thereby a considerable advantage would accrue to those who are now destitute'.[199] In such cases, it is important to remember that humans are part of the natural world and they benefited, and perhaps even survived and were able to reproduce successfully, because of these engineering river works. The TIC were proud of their industrial river and its capacity to support such large-scale employment across Tyneside. The commissioners conceptualised their work as a battle to protect profit-making trade and shipping against the natural, harmful functions of the river. From time to time, natural forces interrupted their work. For example, in December 1882, the river improvement works west of Scotswood Bridge had to be stopped due to a large blockage of ice; they noted 'the tide, when flowing quickly, brought large blocks of ice up, and when the tide receded the ice was left behind, and it was impossible to get river craft down'.[200] In November 1880, the TIC described 'a storm of extraordinary and unprecedented violence', almost personifying the natural and uncontrolled river and deeming it in clear terms the enemy of industrial progress.[201] But they also congratulated themselves for having managed against the odds to create piers sufficiently strong to withstand such powerful natural forces, noting 'it may, I think, be considered a fair subject for congratulation that the piers works (temporary and permanent) have suffered so little'.[202] This encapsulates in essence how they conceptualised their work between 1850 and 1968. However quickly the TIC managed to progress river improvement projects, they could not overcome all the river's natural expressions.

---

199. *Proceedings of the TIC 1887–1888*, p. 23.
200. *Proceedings of the TIC 1882–1883*, p. 33.
201. *Proceedings of the TIC 1880–1881*, p. 24.
202. Ibid.

Chapter 4

FISH IN THE TYNE:
THE TYNE SALMON CONSERVANCY, 1866–1950

Introduction

While the riverscapes of the Tyne's upper reaches looked less industrial than those of the estuary, highly polluting industrial activities were conducted there too. In 1859, seven years before the Tyne Salmon Conservancy's (TSC's) establishment, Walter White toured Northumberland and the border, leaving a highly detailed account of the Tyne riverscape, which the TSC were soon to regulate. White studied the river's changing character intently as he travelled down the South Tyne from Alston all the way to Tynemouth, stopping at many places *en route*. At Alston, he described the South Tyne as 'a shallow mountain river, in a bed filled with big stones, received as it passed the Nent, a little stream that rushes down from the eastern hills'.[1] In the Nent valley, he witnessed the intensive work of the lead miners, where 'all the water of the washings before its final exit from the premises, is made to flow into "slime pits", where it remains for a time almost stagnant, until it has thrown down the light particles held in suspension'.[2] 'These particles', he went on, 'form thick beds of "slime" in which is contained a considerable quantity of lead'.[3] After two rollers and a web of canvas were moved 'uphill', the slime was dropped onto it from a trough as water fell down on it simultaneously in a 'brisk shower'.[4] The lead subsequently fell into a trough and 'the fine sand and mud' was washed away into the stream.[5] This water, sand and mud which was washed into the river system still contained very small particles of lead and other harmful metals such as zinc and cadmium. The legacy of this serious form of pollution is that today

---

1. White, *Northumberland and the Border*, p. 26 (chapter 4).
2. Ibid., p. 31 (chapter 5).
3. Ibid., p. 32 (chapter 5).
4. Ibid.
5. Ibid.

Chapter 4. Fish in the Tyne

lead particles are still suspended in the river bed and banks and even in the plant species growing along the South Tyne. The particles are highly unlikely to be washed away completely for several hundred years.

Walking along the South Tyne from Haydon Bridge towards Hexham, White described the main Tyne as

> a smiling vale beautified by cultivation and foliage; no longer the wild slopes of rock and heath as we saw at Alston. And the river itself, broader and deeper than in the hills, flows along its stony bed, rippling cheerfully in reply to the salutations of the leaves. Along this smiling vale runs the road to Hexham, now low among trees, now high over the shoulder of a hill, whence you get pleasing views of the river. The smoke of a lime-kiln and the chimney of a paper-mill on the farther bank seem to be ominous of a change; but happily we are more than a day's walk from the edge of the smoky region.[6]

White was explicitly aware of leaving one distinct region of the river and entering a new and different zone in the estuary, which he called the 'smoky region'. Between Hexham and Bywell, 'on nearing the river', he notes, 'my walk became delightful, between banks of ferns and flowers, overshadowed by beech and ash and elm', where 'whichever way you look the landscapes are sylvan and pastoral'.[7] At Bywell, he observed how

> the water tumbles with cheerful roar over a long dam, and a bit of cliff shoulders up overhung with bush, and the shore is broken by patches of rock and edges of green turf, and here and there a gravelly shoal rises from the ripple.[8]

Eventually, White reached the outskirts of Newcastle, at Newburn, where he discerned a distinctly different riverscape, 'a route that revealed to me a disagreeable variety of dirt and disorder … the great army of industry', where 'at times the river is visible, and we now look down upon keels, large flat boats laden with coal'.[9] By the time he reached Scotswood Suspension Bridge, 'we go on with a smoky view before, past King's Meadow Island, past the great engineering works at Elswick … into the busy streets of the Metropolis of Coal'.[10] As White travelled from St Anthony's lead works on the north bank east of Newcastle, towards the river mouth, he observed how

---

6. Ibid., p. 40 (chapter 6).
7. Ibid., p. 46 (chapter 6).
8. Ibid.
9. Ibid., p. 51 (chapter 6).
10. Ibid., p. 53 (chapter 6).

river and shore show more and more signs of trade and labour as we descend: half a dozen steamers on the stocks, rows of coke ovens all a-glow, troops of boiler-makers raising a deafening clatter, heaps, nay mountains, of slag and refuse ballast, more steamers on the stocks, cranes, sheds, chimneys, staithes, the big beam of a steam-engine rising and falling in the distance, piles of timber, inclines that resemble railway cuttings sloping down to the water's edge, while here and there a green field and hedgerow left amid the havoc and encroachment plead with silent eloquence for Nature.[11]

Figure 8. Looking downriver at the Tyne from St Anthony's, Walker, 2015 (Photograph: Gordon Ball)

White's experience of travelling down the river stimulated all his senses, and it is significant that he highlights the sounds and the smells as well as the sights. He personifies the hedgerows and green fields as incongruous, natural and silent features 'amid the havoc'.[12] From Northumberland Dock on the north bank, White walked along the river bank close to the water, on ground which he described as 'muddy, spongy, slimy, stony, and coaly, full of ins and outs and ups and downs, running under staithes and jetties, crossing yards

---

11. Ibid., p. 74 (chapter 9).
12. Ibid.

Chapter 4. Fish in the Tyne

pervaded by the smell of pitch and tar'.[13] I wonder, were White transported forward in time to the present day, if he would be impressed or disappointed?

It is surprising that the passing into law of the Public Health Act in 1875, which J. Kempster called 'the Magna Carta of Public Health', did relatively little for the Tyne's environmental health.[14] In fact, it encouraged the construction of even more water closets to improve public health and hygiene, and even more underground sewers that drained directly into the Tyne estuary. The Public Health Act of 1875, section 17, part III states

> Nothing in this act shall authorize any local authorities to use any sewer or outfall for the purpose of conveying sewage or filthy water into any natural stream or into any canal, lake or pond until such filthy water is freed from all excrementitious or other foul or noxious matter such as would affect or deteriorate the purity and quality of the water in such stream or watercourse, or in such canal, lake or pond.[15]

But the River Tyne's estuary was not legally designated as a stream. If it had been, and the provisions of the Public Health Act had been strictly enforced, a very large proportion of Tyneside's booming industrial production would have been shut down. As Kempster elaborates, 'it is astonishing to notice ... how timid the legislature has been where pollution is concerned, as if afraid to compel its citizens to cease injuring a national asset, i.e. pure river water'.[16]

As the TIC sanctioned the installation of a succession of sewers draining an increasingly toxic cocktail of domestic and industrial waste directly into the estuary, an organisation of other Victorians took action to protect the Tyne's fish life. The passing of the Salmon Fishery Act of 1861 followed substantial nationwide investigations into the condition of salmon fisheries in many rivers in the form of a Royal Commission Report on Salmon, conducted between 1855 and 1861. The Salmon Acts resulted from the government's multiple concerns over the long-term sustainability of inland fisheries to support the nation's food supply, anglers' concern about a reduction in the enjoyment of their sport due to declining numbers of salmon and also some stirrings of wider environmental concerns about water quality. Consequently, in 1866, the Tyne Salmon Conservancy was appointed to begin its work to protect salmon and other fish from physical impediments to upstream migration such as weirs

---

13. Ibid., p. 83 (chapter 9).
14. Kempster, *Our Rivers*, p. 61.
15. TNA Legislation Database, Public Health Act, 1875, online at: http://www.legislation.gov.uk/ukpga/Vict/38–39/55 [accessed 11 Jul. 2016].
16. Kempster, *Our Rivers*, p. 68.

and dams and from the harmful effects of waste disposal. Its official title was The Fishery Board for the Fishery District of the River Tyne and in the City of Newcastle. Its principal responsibility was to enforce the provisions of the Salmon Fishery Acts, but its minute books demonstrate that members' concern for fish and the riverscapes through which they swam was far more personal, far deeper, than their nominal and civic responsibilities might initially imply. This representative board of around twenty men met at the Moot Hall in Hexham, Northumberland, every three months. As we have seen with the TIC, Victorians thrived on sub-committees and bureaucracy, and the TSC was no exception. The board appointed several geographical sub-committees which conducted more focused meetings in relation to particular sections of the river: River Rede District; North Tyne and Tyne Proper District; South Tyne District; Lower Tyne District; and Coast. And it appointed a Finance Board and a Watch and Conservancy Board. The geographical boards raised income through the sale of rod licences for several pounds annually, some of which was invested into restocking the river with fish. For example, In December 1923, the board purchased 2,000 yearling trout from the Barrasford Hatchery, placing 1,500 in the Tyne between Wylam and Hexham and 500 in the Derwent tributary.[17]

This chapter explores the TSC's perspective, and their particular vision for the Tyne, situating it in the context of other different visions for the river. Just as Porter argues that there were multiple imaginative versions of the Thames Embankment, 'as many different "Embankments" as there were institutions, groups and individuals involved with it', there were also multiple 'Tynes' in the minds of different Tynesiders who represented different regulatory authorities, different industries and different socio-economic classes.[18] However, this chapter is not a story of the TSC versus the TIC, or to put it into Matthew Evenden's words, a story of 'fish versus power'.[19] For the most part, the two bodies continued their work in largely separate and co-existent domains. While the TSC had sub-committees to oversee the fisheries of the estuary, most of its work was conducted in the upper river valleys, in the non-tidal reaches. The chapter explains the TSC's work, the ways in which it regulated those responsible for polluting the river water and it discusses the TSC's important role as demands for a clean-up started to gather pace in the 1920s and 1930s.

---

17. NRO, 3451/A/1: Board of Conservators of the Fishery District of the River Tyne minute book, March 1915–December 1929, (20 Dec. 1923).
18. Porter, *Thames Embankment*, p. 10.
19. Evenden, *Fish versus Power*.

Chapter 4. Fish in the Tyne

The Tyne Salmon Conservancy's Work

On 15 December 1866, the Tyne Salmon Conservancy held its first quarterly meeting at the Moot Hall in Hexham and set up its offices in the same town. From the outset, discussions focused on enforcing the 1865 Salmon Fishery Act. The conservancy's seal proudly featured a salmon. They confirmed the boundaries of their jurisdiction with neighbouring conservancies, began issuing rod licences for fees and appointed several inspectors of fisheries including Mr Snowball. In October 1868, the TSC ordered the Warden Paper Mill's owner, Alexander Adam, to install 'a grating' across the mill race for 'preventing the descent of salmon or the young of salmon'.[20] Warden Paper Mill has produced paper since 1763 and still operates at its original site on the South Tyne under its new name of Fourstones Paper Mill. In relation to another paper mill, in October 1873, the TSC paid a large sum of £75 14s to Rev. Dixon Brown 'on account of the fish pass at South Tyne Paper Mill dam', presumably to fund the construction of the pass.[21] The board was beholden to various landowners for permission to install fish passes over mill dams, but landowners rarely refused permission. In June 1872, Thomas Ridley was asked if he would permit the installation of a fish pass 'at a price not exceeding £25' in his Chollerford Dam; Ridley granted his permission and the fish pass was installed at the expense of the TSC.[22] The TSC was undertaking remarkably proactive interventions to improve the health of the Tyne fisheries. For example, two months later, in December 1873, they took 'salmon ova from the waters of this district for purposes of artificial propagation'.[23] The men of the TSC were as passionate about the health of the Tyne's fisheries as those of the TIC were about dredging, shipping tolls, docks and piers.

For the most part, the TSC did not interfere in the business of the TIC, in the operations of the Newcastle and Gateshead Water Company or in the affairs of the riparian councils of the estuary. The board was well aware that the pollution of the estuary was as overwhelming and complex as it was integral to the regional economy, which perhaps explains their focus on the upper river valley primarily above Hexham and on both the North and South Tynes and their tributaries. But they did intervene in particularly severe pollution issues in the estuary, especially when relatively simple interventions could have a substantially positive impact on the health of the fisheries. In May 1888, for

---

20. NRO, 1454/2/3: Tyne Salmon Conservancy Minute Book, 1866–1894 (31 Oct. 1868).
21. NRO, 1454/2/3: Tyne Salmon Conservancy Minute Book, 1866–1894 (11 Oct. 1873).
22. NRO, 1454/2/3: Tyne Salmon Conservancy Minute Book, 1866–1894 (15 June 1872).
23. NRO, 1454/2/3: Tyne Salmon Conservancy Minute Book, 1866–1894 (10 Dec. 1868).

example, the board wrote to the Mayor of Newcastle requesting that Newcastle Corporation bid their surveyor and other relevant employees to abstain from using caustic soda as a disinfectant in the sewers of the city between May and June so that 'there may be no recurrence of the great destruction of fish which occurred last year after the application of this deadly substance as a disinfectant in the city sewers'.[24] Their concern was limited to only two months of the year when it would have the most adverse impact on fish, rather than seeking to eradicate the use of caustic soda throughout the year in order to improve the health of the whole river system in its own right. This confirms their preoccupation with the health of the fish rather than the wider environment of the river water itself. Their conceptualisation of the river environment and its many interconnected ecological networks was in its infancy, but the TSC had made a good start. The Tyne would have to wait another three quarters of a century for the game-changing publication of Rachel Carson's *Silent Spring* in 1962.[25]

Frequently, following reports from their own inspectors, the TSC intervened to protect the fisheries from quite serious pollution incidents above the estuary. In December 1869, for example, they discussed the disposal of Hexham's sewage into the Tyne and authorised 'the chairman to act in the name of the board and to take such steps and obtain such legal advice as he may deem necessary to put a stop to the pollution of the river'.[26] No further references to this particular pollution issue were entered into the minute book, though they communicated with the Newcastle and Gateshead Water Company frequently to offer their support to help to abate river pollution. In October 1874, they wrote to the company 'expressing the readiness of this board to co-operate in attempting to abate the pollution of the River Tyne'.[27] Two years later, in February 1876, they requested that the company 'put a grating on the race at Newburn to prevent the destruction of smolts', offering to stand the cost if the Newcastle and Gateshead Water Company declined to pay for it.[28] In February 1889, the board negotiated with the water company in relation to their large-scale water supply operations at Catcleugh Reservoir, agreeing

---

24. NRO, 1454/2/3: Tyne Salmon Conservancy Minute Book, 1866–1894 (3 May 1888).
25. R. Carson, *Silent Spring*.
26. NRO, 1454/2/3: Tyne Salmon Conservancy Minute Book, 1866–1894 (11 Dec. 1869).
27. NRO, 1454/2/3: Tyne Salmon Conservancy Minute Book, 1866–1894 (24 Oct. 1874 and 26 Feb. 1876).
28. NRO, 1454/2/3: Tyne Salmon Conservancy Minute Book, 1866–1894 (24 Oct. 1874 and 26 Feb. 1876).

Chapter 4. Fish in the Tyne

during the months of February, March and April when the water flowing down the River Rede into the dam or reservoir at Catcleugh is less than 4½ million gallons per day and at such times during the remainder of the year when such flow is less than 2 million gallons per day, the company will allow the whole of such flow to pass down the stream.[29]

This record demonstrates that the TSC had quite a sophisticated comprehension of flow regimes and their impact on the fish. In April 1870, the TSC tackled the serious issue of sheep bathing, recording 'many persons are accustomed to bathe sheep with preparations having poisonous ingredients therein', discharging the resultant liquid into the Tyne and its tributaries which 'destroys the young of salmon', by which they meant smolts, sometimes also referred to as parr.[30] They resolved to 'print a notice to be circulated by the officers of the board stating the above facts and giving notice of the penalty attached to the offence under Section 5 of the Act of 1865'.[31] The TSC worked very rigidly according to the Salmon and Fisheries Acts and their minute books reveal that without their legal foundation, power and legitimacy, their potential to protect the Tyne's fish life would have been minimal.

In February 1894, the question of constructing a dam across the river above Ryton was discussed and the commissioners asked their engineer to prepare a quotation for materials and labour.[32] The TIC was warned by a letter from their solicitors, Clayton and Gibson, in July 1894 that wild rumours were spreading of a seventy feet high dam, and that the TSC was planning to raise serious objections because it could adversely affect the passage of salmon up the river, which would reduce the yield of the several rod fisheries above the proposed dam and potentially increase the yield of the Duke of Northumberland's fishery at Ryton below the dam. The fisheries above the proposed dam expressed their desire for compensation if the dam went ahead. One suggestion was made for the commissioners to purchase the Duke's fishery and then ban extracting salmon from it to ensure that if there was a delay in salmon passing up, the entire stock could not be swept away.[33] The Duke of Northumberland wrote to the TIC in April 1899 to request compensation for the destruction to the Duke's fishery as a result of the deepening of the river from Leming-

---

29. NRO, 1454/2/3: Tyne Salmon Conservancy Minute Book, 1866–1894 (23 Feb. 1889).
30. NRO, 1454/2/3: Tyne Salmon Conservancy Minute Book, 1866–1894 (9 Apr. 1870).
31. Ibid.
32. *Proceedings of the TIC 1893–1894*, p. 110.
33. *Proceedings of the TIC 1893–1894*, p. 392.

ton to Newburn.[34] In October 1900, the question of damage to the Duke of Northumberland's fishery was raised again, this time relating to his Cromwell Fishery between Newburn Bridge and Blaydon Ferry, the damage having been

> caused by the fact there are at present some half dozen different persons removing sand and gravel from the river bed and it is quite impossible for His Grace to know which of them have been deputed by the Commissioners to perform the dredging which you state in your letter to be necessary for the carrying out of the commissioners authorised improvements.[35]

The Duke's solicitors asked for compensation and they wrote to the TIC in February 1901 to state formally the damage sustained at all of his fisheries, noting that his Tynemouth and Newburn fisheries had been 'practically destroyed' and his Cromwell fishery was being 'very seriously damaged'.[36] They demanded that the commissioners pay him some compensation and ensure that only people sanctioned by the TIC were allowed within the bounds of his fisheries, but the TIC managed to persuade him not to pursue them for compensation. Crucially, from the very early twentieth century onwards the TIC discontinued their practice of permitting all applicants to remove as much gravel, sand and ballast as they wished from the estuary.

The TSC inspectors were often able to prevent pollution only because they had the weight of the Salmon and Fisheries Acts behind them. The TSC was born out of the Salmon Acts and without them it would have been powerless. While, from a modern-day perspective, their focus on fish life might seem at times rather narrow, in the wider context of their era their actions were very progressive. First and foremost, they were working within the legislation available to protect several key aspects of the Tyne's environmental health from damage in order to encourage the salmon to thrive, but many of their actions created wider environmental benefits too. It is difficult to comprehend that the TSC's environmental sensitivity and its members' relatively deep ecological understanding co-existed with the attitudes of the TIC, whose commissioners gave minimal consideration to the environmental health of a river which they conceptualised very much as an economic facility. That such markedly different perspectives in relation to the environment developed and managed to co-exist in the same society reminds us of the complexity and multi-faceted nature of environmental attitudes, values and debates as the environmentalism of the 1960s developed in its long-term history.

---

34. *Proceedings of the TIC 1898–1899*, p. 457.
35. *Proceedings of the TIC 1899–1900*, p. 880.
36. *Proceedings of the TIC 1900–1901*, p. 289.

Chapter 4. Fish in the Tyne

The Consequences of Scientific Progress

The TSC was finding its way through an innovative form of environmental governance as ecological and scientific understanding was developing gradually. Over the decades of its operation, the TSC's policies were not totally consistent, reflecting changes in available knowledge and understanding of fisheries. They certainly prioritised the health of salmon above other fish species, but their support of other fish species fluctuated over time. In April 1874, they noted 'with regret' that their northern neighbouring conservancy of the River Coquet 'have abandoned their attempts to exterminate the bull trout in their district as it is much feared that if they are allowed to breed in the large quantities' and they worried that 'they will spread along the coast and find their way into the Tyne to the injury of the true salmon'.[37] Bull trout is a variety of brown trout which goes out to sea, *Salvelinus Confluentus*, a char of the family Salmonidae, native to north-west North America and commonly called the 'Dolly Varden'. It is common to south-east Scotland and north-east England. However, by October 1887, the TSC's policy on bull trout had changed. The board took action to encourage an increase in the numbers of bull trout in their own catchment, in the River Allen, a tributary of the South Tyne. The board noted that 'there is a want of bull trout in the River Allen which is caused by the shallowness of the water at its junction with the South Tyne' and they agreed to ask Lord Strathmore 'to cause two small weirs to be put up at the junction and so confine the water within a narrower channel and thus give the fish a good run up the Allen'.[38]

In December 1884, the board proudly granted permission to an agent of New Zealand's government to 'take salmon ova out of the north Tyne water for scientific purposes [and] be transferred to the New Zealand acclimatization society which is accredited by the government of New Zealand'.[39] By May 1890, the TSC were researching the methods for artificial breeding and considering establishing their own hatchery, noting their application 'to the Board of Trade for information as to the results of artificial breeding in some of the foreign governments such as the French and Norwegian rivers'.[40] The board was well connected globally and engaged with scientific methods of salmon conservancy that were very much at the cutting edge. As scientific methods of analysing pollutants' impact on river water and fisheries developed in their sophistication,

---

37. NRO, 1454/2/3: Tyne Salmon Conservancy Minute Book, 1866–1894 (25 Apr. 1874).
38. NRO, 1454/2/3: Tyne Salmon Conservancy Minute Book, 1866–1894 (6 Oct. 1887).
39. NRO, 1454/2/3: Tyne Salmon Conservancy Minute Book, 1866–1894 (4 Dec. 1884).
40. NRO, 1454/2/3: Tyne Salmon Conservancy Minute Book, 1866–1894 (2 May 1890).

the board began to read many analytical reports that identified various collieries and metal mines as the indisputable culprits in damage to fisheries across the catchment. In December 1915, they received a report from the chemical analysists, J. and H. Pattinson, confirming that the effluent from the coke ovens at another colliery, West Wylam Colliery, was injurious to fish.[41] Inspector Crawford visited the site and confirmed that the owners were taking steps to prevent pollution by pre-treating their waste before discharge. At a meeting in March 1915, the TSC discussed a letter received from the Board of Agriculture and Fisheries informing them that the grant they had applied for in 1909 to execute work on Warden Dam had been withheld due to the 'present national crisis' of World War One. The work had been completed and paid for in 1913, and claimed from the Board of Agriculture and Fisheries subsequently, so this left the TSC substantially out of pocket.[42] In May 1915, Haltwhistle Angling Association complained to the board about their failure to spend further sums on the dam at Warden. The TSC replied, explaining that a 'considerable sum' had already been spent and that they had assurances from the owners of the mines at Nenthead that they had taken action to 'considerably reduce the amount of deleterious effluent discharged into the river'.[43] They promised to write to the owners of Mickley Coal Company to ask what steps they were taking to prevent pollution at Wylam Colliery.[44] In March 1917, the TSC decided to prepare a report on sources of pollution in the Team, Nent and South Tyne for the Board of Agriculture and Fisheries.[45] A year later, in response to the emerging evidence of pollution, the TSC clerk wrote to various companies situated along the South Tyne, instructing them of specific measures, recommended by Inspector Crawford, which needed to be taken to prevent pollution in the river. They advised the Vielle Montagne Zinc Co. to adopt the use of more settling tanks, the Alston, Haydon Bridge and Haltwhistle Gas Works to remove gas lime from the river banks, the Settlingstones Bartyes Mine Co to provide more

---

41. NRO, 3451/A/1: Board of Conservators of the Fishery District of the River Tyne minute book, March 1915–December 1929 (9 Dec. 1915).
42. NRO, 3451/A/1: Board of Conservators of the Fishery District of the River Tyne minute book, March 1915–December 1929 (11 Mar. 1915).
43. NRO, 3451/A/1: Board of Conservators of the Fishery District of the River Tyne minute book, March 1915–December 1929 (15 May 1915).
44. Ibid.
45. NRO, 3451/A/1: Board of Conservators of the Fishery District of the River Tyne minute book, March 1915–December 1929 (8 Mar. 1917).

Chapter 4. Fish in the Tyne

settling tanks and the Warden Paper Mill to prevent spent liquid from finding its way to the river and to provide settling tanks.[46]

World War One made quite a splash in the fortunes of the fish, as the board's records confirm. Although access to fish in the river was usually strictly regulated, the board loosened regulations during World War One to facilitate the 'fullest possible facilities in the present national emergency to anglers desirous of capturing coarse fresh water fish in their district'.[47] That the TSC's regulation of river pollution entered a temporarily less stringent period during the war is obvious from an entry in March 1918, which suggested that 'immediately after the war the question of the pollution of the South Tyne and its tributaries be again reconsidered by this committee'.[48] Pollution incidents were particularly harmful when water levels were low. This was especially dangerous for smolts because it encouraged them to move downriver to the heavily polluted estuary. In May 1918, it was reported:

> that the Tyne has been very low for many weeks. A few inches of fresh water came down at the beginning of the week and unfortunately caused the smolts to descend into tidal water, which is much polluted at present and large numbers are dying. Children and gulls are picking them up on the foreshores at Gateshead and Newcastle and for a considerable distance down the river. I have never seen the river in a worse state of pollution than it is at present, in fact it is as bad as it is possible to be.[49]

The board sent some of the smolts to Professor Meek at the Ministry of Agriculture and Fisheries for analysis, but the board was tentative in its regulation of the companies discharging waste into the river. For example, it asked rather humbly for business owners' permission in advance before undertaking inspections. In March 1919, the TSC wrote to the Plashetts Coal and Coke Company (which operated on a site now underneath the Kielder Reservoir) to ascertain the cause of pollution into Plashetts Burn.[50] In October 1918, the board wrote to several companies asking if Inspector Crawford could inspect

---

46. NRO, 3451/A/1: Board of Conservators of the Fishery District of the River Tyne minute book, March 1915–December 1929 (14 Mar. 1918).
47. Ibid.
48. Ibid.
49. NRO, 3451/A/1: Board of Conservators of the Fishery District of the River Tyne minute book, March 1915–December 1929 (11 May 1918).
50. NRO, 3451/A/1: Board of Conservators of the Fishery District of the River Tyne minute book, March 1915–December 1929 (3 Mar. 1918).

their properties. Twenty agreed, three refused and three said they were too busy to see the inspector.[51]

Some companies that had been found guilty of causing damage to the Tyne fisheries were asked to contribute to the restocking of fish. They were not being fined officially, but rather asked to rectify some of the damage they had caused. In December 1918, the board asked the Mickley Coal Company to provide a contribution towards restocking the river with trout, and the company sent a cheque for £25.[52] The board matched the contribution and spent a total of £50 on 1,000 two-year old salmon fario trout from the Solway Fishery Company, in Dumfries, which were placed into the river at Wylam.[53] While it appeared aesthetically cleaner than the estuary, the upper valley suffered from serious pollution too. In September 1931, the South Tyne Committee submitted a report of Inspector Crawford's observations at Haltwhistle Gas Works which 'by the escape of a deadly liquor … all the fish in the [Haltwhistle] burn below the gas works were poisoned'.[54] The company admitted liability for allowing a tank containing a deadly liquor to overflow 'due to an oversight' and offered to pay compensation; the board accepted £30 for restocking the burn and the river and the case was closed.[55] In December 1935, moreover, the Barrasford Sanatorium was found to have polluted the Swinburn with oil, for which they had to pay £13 to the board to cover the cost of restocking the river with trout.[56] And in October 1944, the ICI chemical works at Prudhoe were charged £1,000 for restocking the river to compensate for fish killed by their disposal of harmful waste.[57] This underlines the narrow manner in which the TSC conceptualised their responsibilities, namely to ensure the fish stocks remained sustainably high rather than to protect the wider riverine environment for the benefit of all flora and fauna and for the water quality per se. Having said this, their work represented a very good start in the context of the pre-*Silent Spring* era and their understanding of the impact of pollution on

---

51. NRO, 3451/A/1: Board of Conservators of the Fishery District of the River Tyne minute book, March 1915–December 1929 (10 Oct. 1918).
52. NRO, 3451/A/1: Board of Conservators of the Fishery District of the River Tyne minute book, March 1915–December 1929 (12 Dec. 1918).
53. Ibid.
54. NRO, 3451/A/1a: Board of Conservators of the Fishery District of the River Tyne minute book, 1930–1950 (15 Oct. 1931).
55. Ibid.
56. NRO, 3451/A/1a: Board of Conservators of the Fishery District of the River Tyne minute book, 1930–1950 (19 Dec.1935 and 19 Mar. 1936).
57. NRO, 3451/A/1a: Board of Conservators of the Fishery District of the River Tyne minute book, 1930–1950 (19 Oct. 1944).

Chapter 4. Fish in the Tyne

fish life was actually very sophisticated. They were true trailblazers of ecology and conservation, well ahead of their time, fumbling in the dark as they discovered new and different ways of intervening to improve the Tyne's fisheries, and achieving a great deal in the process.

Tackling the Estuary's Pollution

Sometimes committees of the board went out to inspect multiple sites, as in March 1919, when they inspected the Dunston Paper Mills, the Team By-Product Company's works and the Gas Company's premises on the banks of the Team Gut. The worst report produced by the Lower Tyne Committee after their inspection was about the Team By-Product Company:

> The effluent which the Team By-Product Company are sending into the stream was found to be as black as ink and strongly smelt of pitch tar or creosote and appeared to be of such a crude and deadly character as to kill all fish life with which it came in contact. Thousands of gallons per hour of this effluent pass into the stream, polluting the Team Gut and rendering it black and filthy. As the stream is tidal here, the rising tide flows into the River Tyne, the effect of it is noticeable below the High Level Bridge all along the South Shore of the river. ... [We] have no doubt that the effluent from these works is the cause of the death of the thousands of smolts that have been found poisoned in the river when they reach the mouth of the Team. So far as your Committee could see, the By-Product Company's effluent is unfiltered and untreated in any way. An attempt had been made at some period, to provide a small filtering bed of cinders which has become congealed with tar, forming a sort of asphalt surface hard enough for anyone to walk upon. Connection with this filter bed is apparently now severed and the effluent seems to come direct from the Works to the Team through a pipe about 12 inches in diameter discharging into an open channel.[58]

The board requested an interview with the manager of the by-product company and it forwarded samples of the effluents to the Board of Agriculture and Fisheries and the Fishmongers Company for analysis.

In comparison to the TIC, the TSC had a much more intense interest in the impact of pollution on the environment, largely resulting, of course, from their need to protect the fish which needed clean, oxygenated water. But by protecting the fish, they also protected the river itself. As early as in December 1919, the TSC suggested that the way to clean up the Tyne was to form a River

---

58. NRO, 3451/A/1: Board of Conservators of the Fishery District of the River Tyne minute book, March 1915–December 1929 (3 Mar. 1919).

Board representing the conservancy, representatives of the various corporations and the town planning and sanitary committees.[59] This marked the first suggestion that a team comprising multiple partners should address the pollution on the Tyne in a comprehensive manner. In December 1920, Inspector Crawford reported that 'the sewage from North and South Wylam flows direct into the Tyne in a crude state and without treatment and that it was most objectionable when the river was low as it had been of late'.[60] Northumberland County Council's Medical Officer confirmed that he was dealing with the situation, but by May 1921, conditions for the smolts had not improved, as confirmed by Inspector Crawford's report. He recorded 'a large number of smolts have died in tidal water', describing 'large numbers ... floating on the top of the water in a sickly state from Lemington right through Newcastle'.[61] Crawford explained that the By Product and many other works were 'still idle' and that therefore residential sewage was capable of killing smolts. He highlighted that, although the Tyne was 'very low and foul', that nevertheless he had 'never known smolts to be overpowered by pollution so far up the river as Lemington and Scotswood'.[62]

As the scientific evidence mounted against dangerous domestic organic waste, the board got actively involved with sewer applications. They attended a Public Inquiry at Jarrow in December 1921 into the construction of a large sewer at Monckton, South Shields, and suggested treating the effluent by filtration beds or a sewerage farm to render it 'innocuous to fish and human life'.[63] This view was supported by the local inspector of the Ministry of Agriculture and Fisheries. Following the TSC's intervention in the proposed sewer construction at Jarrow, the Standing Committee on River Pollution's Tyne sub-committee (SCORP) found a stronger voice in the debate:

> Having in view the very unsatisfactory condition of the River Tyne as a salmon river, [we] strongly resent any scheme being sanctioned whereby additional

---

59. NRO, 3451/A/1: Board of Conservators of the Fishery District of the River Tyne minute book, March 1915–December 1929 (11 Dec. 1919).
60. NRO, 3451/A/1: Board of Conservators of the Fishery District of the River Tyne minute book, March 1915–December 1929 (9 Dec. 1920).
61. NRO, 3451/A/1: Board of Conservators of the Fishery District of the River Tyne minute book, March 1915–December 1929 (9 May 1921).
62. Ibid.
63. NRO, 3451/A/1: Board of Conservators of the Fishery District of the River Tyne minute book, March 1915–December 1929 (15 Dec. 1921).

Chapter 4. Fish in the Tyne

crude sewage could be diverted and discharged direct into the estuary of the River Tyne.[64]

The board was a firm supporter of the work of SCORP's Tyne Sub-Committee, the body appointed by Parliament in 1921 to conduct scientific analysis of the river water and fish species. In May 1932, March 1933 and March 1934, for example, the TSC made three respective grants of £25 each to the Dove Marine Laboratory, where SCORP conducted its work.[65]

In October 1939, the TSC tackled the perennial issue of sheep dipping in the headwaters of the South Tyne above Alston by asking the National Farmers' Union for assistance:

> The case of the serious mortality to trout in the South Tyne above Alston caused by sheep dip solution entering the river, a report of which was fully set out in the agenda, was given careful consideration resolved that in view of the seriousness of this form of pollution the clerk be instructed to get in touch with the National Farmers' Union (Northumberland branch) and ask for their co-operation in the matter.[66]

The board also took action to try to explain the dangers of sheep dipping in the river, agreeing 'that the press be requested to emphasize the matter ... and that if practicable a notice be inserted in the *Newcastle Journal* sometime in April stressing the danger of allowing sheep dip solution to enter the river'.[67] The TSC's annual report for 1939 included a description of their findings regarding sheep dipping.[68] That year, the board had called the attention of farmers in Northumberland, Durham and Cumberland 'to the serious effect caused to rivers and streams by pollution from the effluent from sheep dipping baths and troughs being permitted to run direct into burns and streams'.[69] They emphasised that this was especially harmful when it was allowed to drain directly into the river 'without the effluent being purified by being allowed to drain or

---

64. NRO, 3451/A/1: Board of Conservators of the Fishery District of the River Tyne minute book, March 1915–December 1929 (letter from SCORP to the TSC, Jan. 1922). For further information on SCORP, see chapter 5.
65. NRO, 3451/A/1a: Board of Conservators of the Fishery District of the River Tyne minute book, 1930–1950 (19 May 1932, 16 Mar. 1933 and 15 Mar. 1934).
66. NRO, 3451/A/1a: Board of Conservators of the Fishery District of the River Tyne minute book, 1930–1950 (19 Oct. 1939).
67. Ibid.
68. TWA, G/TFB/1/1: The Fishery Board for the Fishery District of the River Tyne. Annual Report for the year 1939 and Annual Report for the Year 1940.
69. Ibid.

filter over land or gravel'.[70] Sediments collecting in the bottom of sheep dipping troughs contained arsenic and sulphur, which were capable of killing trout and salmon. The TSC threatened a £50 fine and passed various rules and regulations to the local constables to ensure that no more harmful pollutants were discharged into the river through the processes associated with sheep dipping.

In late 1944, the TIC received a serious complaint from the TSC about oil pollution in the river estuary.[71] The harbour master and the police superintendent produced reports on the matter and sent them to the board, which declined to take the matter further. Though there is no specific reference to link them explicitly, it is highly likely that the TIC's increasingly rigorous regulation of oil tankers in the river towards the end of the conservancy was in response to the TSC's complaint. In October 1931, the board noticed an increase in the numbers of complaints about river fish affected by 'tar, creosote, oil or other effluents', which was surprising because 1931 had featured 'for several months in the summer constant rainfall and floods in the Tyne district'.[72] They believed that it might have resulted from 'the river bed which may for many years have been coated with the sediment from the tar and bye product works' and become 'stirred up by the heavy rainfall and floods and the water in the river'.[73] The chairman of the board, who had a 'lifetime experience of river fishing in the Tyne', confirmed that 'some of the fresh run river salmon have had a tarry flavour' and he elaborated that 'occasionally one is caught in the North Tyne at Chipchase Castle (about 25 miles from Newcastle) and the fish is usually a very fresh run one showing that the taste disappears after a few days in purer water'.[74] The board was explicitly aware that regardless of their efforts to install fish passes and to improve fish stocks and river water quality in the upper river and its tributaries, serious damage was caused to descending smolts when they entered the heavily polluted water of the river estuary. While they made substantial efforts towards the clean-up of the Tyne estuary, ultimately the pollution was too overwhelming for one small fishery board to resolve.

Section 8 of the 1923 Salmon and Freshwater Fisheries Act enabled the TSC to prosecute anyone who discharged any liquid or solid matter into water, causing it to be poisonous or injurious to fish, but the board agreed that the

---

70. Ibid.
71. *Proceedings of the TIC 1944–1945*, p. 36.
72. NRO, 3451/A/1a: Board of Conservators of the Fishery District of the River Tyne minute book, 1930–1950 (15 Oct. 1931).
73. Ibid.
74. Ibid.

Chapter 4. Fish in the Tyne

mixed nature of a large number of polluters in the estuary made the enforcement of this particular section of the Act largely impossible. Alternatively, Section 55 of the 1923 Act gave them the option to apply to the Ministry of Agriculture and Fisheries and to the Ministry of Health to hold a Public Inquiry before possibly classifying the Tyne estuary as a stream for the purposes of protecting fisheries. However this, as the board undoubtedly realised, would have meant closing down the bulk of the riparian industries and more than 270 sewers which drained largely untreated waste into the estuary, thereby causing very serious economic and public health challenges. Given the already high unemployment rates as the country suffered from the Great Depression, such action was unlikely to receive public support. The board continued to protect fish in the upper valley and did their utmost to inspire and support efforts towards a thorough clean-up of the estuary. In May 1932, the TSC seriously considered taking matters into their own hands by removing smolts from the upper river and transporting them safely to the estuary below the worst of the pollution, but their subsequent records are silent on this proposal.[75] In March 1939, the board resolved, rather pessimistically

> In view of the fact that the quantity of untreated sewage that is being discharged into the estuary has very largely increased and that the discharge is likely to be still further increased and also that the inflow of fresh water at the top of the estuary is about to be decreased especially during droughty periods the board views the future with grave misgivings.[76]

They worked hard to install fish passes, to restock fish when numbers declined, to manage the issuing of rod and net licences and to deal with the very serious incidents of pollution in the upper valley. The Acts at their disposal were not strong enough and economic dependence on the serious pollution in the estuary meant that tackling pollution was largely beyond their grasp. They did, however, play a substantial role in amassing the evidence necessary to mount a serious proposal to clean-up the Tyne estuary.

Conclusion

The TSC's particular vision for the river clashed considerably with that of the TIC, but the two organisations never confronted each other vociferously.

---

75. NRO, 3451/A/1a: Board of Conservators of the Fishery District of the River Tyne minute book, 1930–1950 (19 May 1932).

76. NRO, 3451/A/1a: Board of Conservators of the Fishery District of the River Tyne minute book, 1930–1950 (16 Mar. 1939).

Tyne after Tyne

Perhaps the TSC was ahead of its time, but its indefatigable actions to gather supporting evidence for a concerted effort to clean-up the Tyne in the future formed a substantive link in the long-term development of the plans to clean the Tyne. The successes of the Northumberland and Tyneside River Board, which succeeded the TSC, together with those of the Northumbrian River Authority, the Tyne Rivers Trust, Northumbrian Water Ltd and the Environment Agency, which continue to tackle serious environmental problems across the Tyne catchment, all stand on the shoulders of the Tyne Salmon Conservancy. It was not a grass-roots neighbourhood action group or a philanthropic charity, but nor was it a gentleman's club or an angling club. It was a serious conservancy born out of the Salmon Acts, which had been created specifically to enforce the Salmon and Fisheries legislation on behalf of central government. In many respects, they were pioneers in the very long-term historical development of the environmentalism of the 1960s. They had the weight of the law behind them, but the legislation proved inadequate in several important ways. The exemption of the Tyne estuary from the legal status of streams prevented the TSC from creating real improvements in the river's environmental and ecological health, but they did not abandon the estuary. Working within the law, they did what they could, by making close, strong and productive connections with the SCORP scientists in the 1920s and 30s and by getting involved with plans to construct sewage pre-treatment works. Scientific developments in the analysis of pollutants facilitated a huge leap forward in their work. As the evidence mounted, so too did their motivation to gather support for change and to substantiate their argument that making changes to facilitate a cleaner river was necessary and right.

Chapter 5

TESTING THE TROUBLED WATERS: SCORP'S TYNE SUB-COMMITTEE AND A SUCCESSION OF UNSUCCESSFUL REPORTS, 1921–1945

Introduction

In 1931, the Minister of Agriculture and Fisheries, Dr Christopher Addison, attempted to shock the Minister of Health, Arthur Greenwood, into supporting a major Tyne Sewerage Scheme funded by central government. He cited an observation of a dead dog floating up and down the Tyne estuary continuously for several days before it was eventually swept out to sea. The Tyne Sewerage Scheme would have diverted untreated industrial and domestic waste from the Tyne estuary via an interceptor sewer out into the North Sea, but the Ministry of Health argued that rejection of the scheme would not necessarily lead to serious health risks. As Addison explained, however, the scheme would

> get rid of conditions which must always be obnoxious, depressing and demoralising and at times I understand in the heat of the summer actually constitute a public nuisance. It has been suggested to me that as there is no evidence of epidemics of zymotic or other diseases being prevalent on Tyneside, there is no public health case to warrant expensive measures for the cleansing of the estuary. ... Public health properly conceived denotes something more than the avoidance of smells and epidemics. The condition of the estuary is undeniably foul, and it cannot be desirable to have an oscillating body of sewage at one's doors. ... [As reported by] one of our observers on the Tyne ... for days on end the body of the same dead dog was deposited at intervals on the same mud bank and carried away only to be brought back again.[1]

---

1. TNA, HLG 50/2051: Tyne Salmon Conservancy: Discharge of sewage into River Tyne (1930–51), Addison's memo for Parliament, item 18.

Tyne after Tyne

The image of the dead dog floating up and down the river was, perhaps, sufficiently dramatic to shock a Minister who focused exclusively on reducing serious risks to human health, albeit not quite enough to fund the scheme. How far this canine drama shocked the Tynesiders who witnessed the spectacle themselves, however, is questionable.

As chapter four explained, from the early twentieth century onwards, increasingly sophisticated methods of scientific analysis of river water and its pollutants created a mountain of evidence to substantiate the arguments of the growing number of people who wished for a cleaner Tyne. This chapter analyses many scientific reports produced between 1921 and 1939 by the Standing Committee on River Pollution's Tyne Sub-committee (SCORP). However, it does so with Pritchard's observations in mind:

> Environmental historians often rely on scientific and technical documents in order to historicize and assess environmental change. Although there is certainly variation in how environmental historians treat these records, they are frequently not scrutinized and contextualized in the same way as other historical records. For many environmental historians, the fact that these documents are 'scientific' or 'technical' grants them a privileged epistemological status.[2]

This chapter does not accord scientific reports a special status exclusively because of their scientific nature. It does, however, emphasise that regardless of these reports' shortcomings in terms of scientific sophistication, compared to modern-day scientific understanding, the act of conducting experiments on the river water is historically significant in its own right. The testing itself is evidence of interest and investment in monitoring the Tyne's health to understand the impact of pollution on its bio-physical processes. A wide range of scientific and technical reports produced by SCORP is utilised here to explain the severe damage that had been caused to the Tyne's environmental health and what the production of and responses to these reports can tell us about changing attitudes towards the Tyne's environment. The chapter then explains increasingly serious proposals to clean the Tyne throughout the 1930s, including the establishment of a Joint Committee to progress the plan for a Tyne sewerage scheme in 1931 and the creation of the robust Humphreys and Watson Plan in 1936, which was unfortunately derailed by the more pressing economic demands of World War Two.

---

2. Pritchard, *Confluence*, p. 15.

Chapter 5. Testing the Troubled Waters

A Thousand Reports

When the Ministry of Agriculture and Fisheries Standing Committee on Rivers Pollution was appointed in 1921 to investigate the extent of pollution in several rivers across the country, it appointed a Tyne Sub-Committee. A group of chemists and biologists worked for nearly two decades to collect samples of river water from many locations across the Tyne catchment and analyse them at the Dove Marine Laboratory in Cullercoats Bay, near the mouth of the Tyne in Northumberland. The team submitted approximately 1,000 reports between 1922 and 1939. The Water Pollution Research Board had carried out an intensive survey of the River Tees before 1921 and this may well have inspired the Standing Committee and its River Tyne Sub-Committee. The complex industrial waste in the Tees was comparatively more severe than that in the Tyne due to the dominance of its chemical industry.

Figure 9. Dove Marine Laboratory, Cullercoats Bay (Photograph: Leona Skelton)

In 1931, SCORPs Tyne sub-committee produced a summary report of all of their findings from 1922, prepared by a biologist, Dr H. Bull.[3] Their work covered seven areas: the water's oxygenation; industrial effluents; physiological experiments on live fish; various physical factors influencing fish life and other chemical factors; bacterial content of the water; sewage; and smolt mortality.

---

3. TNA, MAF 326/322: River Tyne Sub Committee: condition of tidal portion of River Tyne; summary of evidence, 1922–1931 (1932), report no. 374 (29 Jan. 1932).

Their main achievement was to have proved 'the existence of many miles of water between Wallsend and Blaydon with NO oxygen at or near the surface'.[4] At Newcastle, they discovered 'a January maximum of 80% of saturation and a July minimum of 26%'.[5] The results of their tests on the effluents from the Team By Product Company were particularly shocking:

> Teams By Product Co: total effluent stated in 1927 to be 120,000–130,000 gallons per hour, includes effluents from tar producer plants, naphthalene condenser water and coke washing water. 260 tons of water per hour are pumped from the river Team to quench coke and wash naphthalene.[6]

The combined effluent of another company, Blaydon By Product Works, on Blaydon Burn, had a serious deoxygenating effect on the water. On the River Derwent, Consett Iron Company's effluents from new coke oven works were discharged in volumes of up to 1,000 tons per hour.[7] The final words of the report expressed the scientists' hope 'that the local authorities being satisfied of the value and impartiality of the evidence already accumulated by the River Tyne Pollution sub-committee' would 'come to a definite conclusion upon the relative parts played by the various polluting agents' and 'bring pressure to bear for their reduction or removal'.[8] SCORP's impartiality was crucial to its perceived legitimacy in the eyes of local authorities and the economically valuable businesses that were being blamed for such serious pollution.

For one of Dr Bull's reports, in relation to the Tyne estuary during 1938, regular observations were recorded at certain times of day in April, May and June, 'recording the tide, the temperature of the water, the chlorine parts per 1,000, the dissolved oxygen, parts per 100,000 and % sat., cyanides parts per 100,000 and tar acids per 100,000'.[9] In addition, weekly observations were made at eighteen locations in the estuary. Although average oxygenation for the three months between April and June was considerably lower than that for any year since observations had been made, they also noted an improvement in the condition of the estuary 'as regards cyanides and tar acids'.[10] They attributed this partly to an improvement in the condition of the estuary near St. Anthony's

---

4. Ibid.
5. Ibid.
6. Ibid.
7. Ibid.
8. Ibid.
9. TNA, MAF 326/460: Observations upon pollution of River Tyne Estuary (1938), report no. 576 (9 Mar. 1939).
10. Ibid.

Chapter 5. Testing the Troubled Waters

Tar Works, presumably following 'their installation of a system of baffle plates through which their effluent now passes prior to its discharge into the river'.[11] Bull also noted 'certain firms have shown great willingness to try and reduce the amount of cyanides discharged into the river during the smolt descent'.[12] When comparing the results to those of the previous year, Dr Bull recorded:

> In 1937 I said that that year the death of smolts could not be attributed to the deficiency of oxygen. In 1938 it appears that during the period when smolts were known to be attempting the descent, conditions were almost continuously lethal from this standpoint alone.[13]

This demonstrates that the scientists were on a steep learning curve and sometimes had to correct their earlier findings when new knowledge came to light.

One report, on the fishing season of 1926, submitted in March 1927, was completed by T. Leach, the TSC's Inspector of Fisheries, and R. Gill, biochemist to the Tyne sub-committee. The TSC maintained a close professional relationship with SCORP during its years of operation, providing its Inspector of Fisheries to conduct some of its work. The report confirmed that the catch by all methods, rods and nets, was greater than in any year since 1914. Their explanation for the improved catch was the coal stoppage of May to November 1926, which had resulted in the closing down of all by product works, together with the lower water temperatures of the spring season. While industrial waste had been substantially reduced, domestic sewage had not. Crucially, however, they had still recorded low oxygen levels in the summer, thus revealing the relatively very serious impact of domestic sewage in its own right. In 1921, another stoppage had also temporarily closed down the By-Product Works, but adult salmon and their young (smolts) still died in large numbers. The authors of the report concluded that sewage rather than the chemical waste was the major factor:

> The coal stoppage did not materially affect the dissolved oxygen values in the estuary. The estuary of the Tyne continued to be overloaded with sewage. In intervals between the floods of the past summer, very low oxygen values were frequently recorded. Sewage is the chief polluting factor on the Tyne – in contrast with the Tees.[14]

---

11. Ibid.
12. Ibid.
13. Ibid.
14. TNA, MAF 326/134: Condition of River Tyne: 1926 Fishing season (March, 1927).

Another report, also submitted in 1927, explored the concentration of dissolved oxygen in the water at the Swing Bridge, based on weekly tests of the water from 1922 to 1926. The report, compiled by Dr E. Jee, technical adviser to the Standing Committee, concluded that 'an unsatisfactory condition of the tideway of the River Tyne synchronises with high water temperature and low supplies of fresh upland water' and that low values of dissolved oxygen were caused by 'the excessive amount of sewage which continually flows into the tideway especially in the Newcastle Gateshead area'.[15] Conversely, the report also highlighted how 'relatively satisfactory values of dissolved oxygen will be found as to synchronise with low water temperature and more particularly with heavy and sustained upland floods'.[16] This explained why dissolved oxygen levels were at their maximum in January, at eighty per cent, and their minimum in July, at only 26 per cent. The report confirmed that the Tyne at Newcastle is 'in an unsatisfactory condition of oxygenation' between April and October and it advised that 'remedial measures' needed to be taken to increase dissolved oxygen 'in the month of minimal oxygen to a value not less than 50% of saturation' to support migratory fish.[17]

Another test by the Standing Committee took place on the river at Felling from October 1923 to August 1926.[18] Marjorie Siddons White completed the tests, which were carried out weekly between St Anthony's and Felling, six metres below the surface from a boat in the middle of the river. The water collected was tested for salinity, free carbon dioxide and hydrogen concentration. They found that oxygenation rose up to 92 per cent in January and descended to zero in July and August.[19] She also noted that 'during dry periods a considerable time seems to be taken for the water in the river to be completely changed as objects have been seen floating in the river at Felling for many days'.[20] The oscillation of waste between Newcastle and the sea is explained fully:

> Assuming that the mean tidal current at Newcastle has a velocity of as little as 2 knots it follows that during a semi tidal period of 6 hours the slack water at Swing Bridge might be expected to reach a distance of 12 miles before the next slack tide. If such were the case it would follow that the zone of pollution

---

15. TNA, MAF 326/141: Condition of River Tyne based on concentration of dissolved oxygen at Swingbridge, Newcastle upon Tyne (1927).
16. Ibid.
17. Ibid.
18. TNA, MAF 326/100: River Tyne Sub Committee on the condition of the river at Felling, report number 131 (1926).
19. Ibid.
20. Ibid.

Chapter 5. Testing the Troubled Waters

would extend for about 12 miles. Such a result, however, would imply complete scouring of the river basin each tide, as Newcastle is less than 12 miles from the open sea, and this manifestly does not occur.[21]

Due to the Tyne's relatively long tidal stretch, waste deposited into the river can take up to ten days to reach the sea, as it can become trapped between the turning tides and oscillate up and down, as in the case of the dead dog cited above. This is, in fact, another example of the river's independent agency. However inadvertently, the river's physiognomy exacerbated its own predicament.

The volume of water passing under Wylam Bridge was measured by a gauge, 'fixed to the Bridge whose zero is stated to be 6.18 feet above the Tyne datum, whatever the latter may be'.[22] The water level was read twice daily at 8 a.m. and 4 p.m. by the toll collector, Mr Jones.[23]

Figure 10. Wylam Bridge, 2015 (Photograph: Gordon Ball)

The report concluded that, without frequent rainfall, 'so persistent is the influence of the polluting materials poured into the river about Newcastle … the amount of dissolved oxygen remains below a conservative value neces-

---

21. TNA, MAF 326/5: Pollution of the River Tyne at Swing Bridge, report number 32 (Dec. 1922).
22. Ibid.
23. Ibid.

sary for the passage of fish to and from the sea'.[24] Their findings could not have been clearer. They recommended 'a conciliatory attitude towards the manufacturing interests as lesser offenders' and to direct their efforts primarily towards the sanitary authorities responsible for the domestic waste which was a proportionately larger contributor to the deoxygenation of the river water.[25]

Testing was conducted in the upper reaches of the river, too, outside the TIC's jurisdiction. In July 1924, E. Jee produced a report 'on the condition of oxygenation of the upper river Tyne (non-tidal) between Corbridge and Wylam with special reference to local methods of sewage disposal'.[26] This particular report was instigated by the Ministry's District Inspector for the North East, Mr Paynter, who had pointed out that sewage disposal at places such as Corbridge and Wylam should be conducted through outfalls extending much further into the river 'so as to avoid objectionable back waters of decomposing sewage which he had observed at times of low water'.[27] Professor Hutchins suggested that such settlements might be remedied 'in certain cases by quick transfer of raw sewage to the river' in order to 'spread the sewage quickly through as big a volume of water as possible' before it had a chance to deoxygenate the water.[28] The report highlighted the typical results of extensive sewage pollution in this section of the Tyne, such as 'grey algal growths below the outfalls and deposition of sludge or faecal mud banks', which were 'foetid breeding grounds of germs'.[29] In the low water, they observed a concentrated solution of highly deleterious matter.[30] The authors of the report feared that the Ministry of Agriculture and Fisheries would see no urgent need to bring pressure on the local authorities to incur expenditure even for 'such rudimentary treatment as sedimentation'.[31] They understood that, unless the volume of water was large enough, significant volumes of sewage had the potential to reduce oxygenation to such a low level as to make fish life impossible. Although settling tanks would have allowed much of the solid waste to be removed, they were ambivalent about the benefits of this pre-treatment because they understood that 'stale or septic sewage is more damaging to a river than when fresh

---

24. Ibid.
25. Ibid.
26. TNA, MAF 326/33: Oxygenation of Upper River Tyne (1924).
27. Ibid.
28. Ibid.
29. Ibid.
30. Ibid.
31. Ibid.

Chapter 5. Testing the Troubled Waters

owing to the increased rate at which dissolved oxygen is used up'.[32] The report proposed the argument that, providing the sewage was disposed of into higher velocity water through outfalls further out into the river water, there was no need 'to sediment, screen or otherwise hinder the rapid passage of sewage into the river'.[33] An investigation in May 1924 confirmed that Corbridge, home to 2,920 people, and Wylam, home to 1,610, were both discharging their sewage into the river crude. An inspection of the outfalls at Wylam revealed 'no sewage fungus' but 'the stones were covered with dark slime, probably algal growth, which was devoid of insect life'.[34] They found that the water at Corbridge was less oxygenated than that at Wylam, which they perceived as 'self-purification' in the latter case. They found no evidence of unsatisfactory oxygenation, but they did advise Wylam Urban District Council to extend the outfalls further into the river, as suggested by Mr Paynter.

SCORP's research formed the backbone of supporting evidence in subsequent arguments to fund a major clean-up of the Tyne. Their impartiality was crucial to the legitimacy of the evidence they produced because their findings had large potential to threaten business interests around the estuary. The important work undertaken by these scientists confirmed that, while industrial wastes contributed complex and poisonous chemicals into the river water, in the grand scheme of things the overwhelming volume of domestic organic waste had such a phenomenal deoxygenating effect on the water that it was comparatively more harmful. Their evidence underpinned later efforts to secure central government funding for the subsequently proposed Tyne Sewerage Scheme, by supporting their argument to clean the Tyne, but also by informing and shaping the design of the scheme to tackle domestic as well as industrial waste. Moreover, the TSC were able to use the SCORP reports to deepen their own understanding of the impact of pollution on fish life and to support their efforts to improve the river's environmental health.

A Tyne Sewerage Scheme and the Joint Committee

Early in 1931, an attempt was made to get some plans off the ground to divert sewage from entering the Tyne, by means of a large trunk sewer out to sea. The project was estimated to cost £3,500,000, excluding facilities to process complex industrial waste. One of the main arguments in support of the plan

---

32. Ibid.
33. Ibid.
34. Ibid.

was that, by alleviating unemployment significantly, it would divert unemployment payments that were already being discharged and therefore represent a saving on the cost of the scheme's construction. Both the TSC and SCORP's Tyne Sub Committee had been considering an improvement plan for years. At the quarterly meeting of the TSC, in December 1930, the board made several resolutions which they forwarded to the Fisheries Secretary in London.[35] The TSC asked the Agriculture and Fisheries Minister to approach the Minister of Health and, with or without his help, to arrange

> an early meeting at Newcastle on Tyne of all the city borough and district councils and heads of industrial works on Tyneside, to consider the question of a comprehensive scheme to deal satisfactorily with the whole of the sewage and other industrial pollution on Tyneside.[36]

The board also requested the Agriculture and Fisheries Minister to ascertain whether or not a government grant out of the unemployment fund could be obtained for the scheme, to minimise costs locally. Together with several local councils, the TSC and SCORP's Tyne Sub Committee worked together to write a letter to the Unemployment Grants Committee to try to secure central-government funding for the scheme, but it was unsuccessful.[37]

A letter from the Ministry of Labour at Newcastle to the Ministry of Labour in London, in December 1930, confirmed that 20,151 Tyneside men were registered on the local unemployment exchanges and that, of this number, 18,800 were wholly unemployed, a total of 24 per cent locally.[38] The Ministry of Labour at Newcastle was disbursing £20,000 weekly to the unemployed.[39] It fully supported the TSC's case, noting 'my committee notes with concern the statement of the Tyne Fishery Board that especially under certain conditions the estuary is even now practically nothing more than an open sewer'.[40] The Newcastle Ministry of Labour emphasised the point that such a project could stem 'the otherwise inevitable demoralisation of the recipients of unemployment benefit' and confirmed that it had resolved unanimously at a special meeting held on 9 December 1930 to urge the government's Ministry of Labour 'to

---

35. TNA, HLG 50/2051: Tyne Salmon Conservancy: Discharge of sewage into River Tyne (1930–51), letter dated 18 Dec. 1930, item 7.
36. TNA, HLG 50/2051: Tyne Salmon Conservancy: Discharge of sewage into River Tyne (1930–51), resolutions of their meeting, item 8.
37. TNA, HLG 50/2051: Tyne Salmon Conservancy: Discharge of sewage into River Tyne (1930–51).
38. TNA, HLG 50/2051: Tyne Salmon Conservancy: Discharge of sewage into River Tyne (1930–51), letter from Newcastle Ministry of Labour to Ministry of Labour, London, 11 Dec. 1930, item 9.
39. Ibid.
40. Ibid.

Chapter 5. Testing the Troubled Waters

ensure that very serious consideration is given to this aspect of the question'.[41] They even suggested, ingeniously, that readily available unemployed miners would be highly suited to this sort of tunnel work, and that the plans could be produced to start work in as little as four to six months because a lot of the preparatory work had been completed. Even the Ministry of Agriculture and Fisheries secretary admitted, in a letter to the Minister of Health in February 1931, that the scheme was not being sought purely for the advancement of Tyne fisheries.[42]

Dr Christopher Addison, Minister of Agriculture, produced a memo for Parliament, arguing for the adoption of the Tyne Sewerage Scheme.[43] He argued that improving the salmon fisheries of the country would improve the employment of inshore fishermen, who were 'on the whole in a bad way'.[44] He explained that the necessary first step in improving the salmon fisheries was 'relief from pollution'.[45] If this argument regarding fisheries was not sufficiently persuasive, he deftly highlighted 'that as a self-respecting nation we ought not to be willing to let out rivers or any parts of them be reduced to the condition of open sewers'.[46] While the UK's salmon fisheries were still the most productive in Europe, their productivity was nevertheless declining and they were 'capable of very substantial improvement'.[47] In order to maximise salmon production, he argued, 'it is necessary that the river should be in a wholesome condition'.[48] He described the Tyne as 'potentially a first-class salmon river', and argued the case for diverting the sewage currently discharged directly into it, which he described aptly as a 'death trap':

> There is a great mass of sewage oscillating backwards and forwards in the estuary, because, owing to the length and narrowness of the estuary before the ebb tide had carried the foul waters out to sea, the flood meets it and carries it back again. As a result, there is over a length of some six miles, a great accumulation of sewage, sufficient during a great part of the year to take out of the water every

---

41. Ibid.
42. TNA, HLG 50/2051: Tyne Salmon Conservancy: Discharge of sewage into River Tyne (1930–51), letter from Secretary of Fisheries to Ministry of Health (16 Feb. 1931).
43. TNA, HLG 50/2051: Tyne Salmon Conservancy: Discharge of sewage into River Tyne (1930–51), Addison's memo for Parliament, item 18.
44. Ibid.
45. Ibid.
46. Ibid.
47. Ibid.
48. Ibid.

article of oxygen and thus to present a formidable barrier to salmon trying to enter the river and a death trap to smolts attempting to descend to the sea.[49]

The Minister of Agriculture also pointed out that a sewerage scheme would create substantial economic savings for the TIC, which would have far less solid material to dredge from the estuary's river bed.

The plan being proposed was to divert the Tyneside sewage into two trunk sewers, one on either side of the estuary, which would carry the waste down to a point near the mouth of the river for treatment before being discharged into the sea. It was estimated that it would take between three and four years to complete. To justify why the Tyne needed to be cleaned more urgently than the UK's other rivers, Addison argued that it had

> not yet been so far destroyed that is could not be rehabilitated, because the facts of the condition of the estuary and of what governs it are well established, because proposals for improving the situation have been advanced in the locality and because the Tyne is an unobstructed river and great part of it – that known as the north Tyne – is clean and healthy.[50]

The Minister of Agriculture was keen to emphasise that he wasn't arguing purely for the case of the fisheries, but for wider benefits too, 'not least of which', he argued, was the removal of 'what I think may safely be described as an offence against the public sense of decency'.[51]

In response to Addison's presentment to Parliament, many ministries, local bodies and boards lodged their doubts that the scheme should go ahead. There were many reasons for the doubt. There was some uncertainty that trade waste, to be excluded from the scheme, was less dangerous than sewage to fish life, despite SCORP's confirmation that domestic waste was more harmful overall. The local authorities were very short of money because unemployment was so high, at 25 per cent. The conditions were not perceived as sufficiently serious to warrant urgent action, especially as there was no evidence that the polluted Tyne endangered public health. And the cost of the scheme was not economically viable in the context of potential financial reward from more productive salmon fisheries. The Tyne salmon catch had declined in the long term, from 850,000 lbs in 1878, to 40,000 lbs in 1930, but compared to very recent years 40,000 lbs was perceived as a relatively good catch.[52] This did not

---

49. Ibid.
50. Ibid.
51. Ibid.
52. TNA, HLG 50/2051: Tyne Salmon Conservancy: Discharge of sewage into River Tyne (1930–51), item 62, letter from Rucker to Greenwood.

Chapter 5. Testing the Troubled Waters

help Addison's argument. Since 1918, other sewerage schemes in the UK had benefited from £52 million of funding from central government and £9 million had been spent in the financial year 1930–31 alone, yet the government chose not to fund the clean-up of the most heavily polluted salmon river in the country, the Tyne. The ministries in London declined the request to provide central funding for the scheme because there was no evidence of any serious discontent or danger of riot from any groups except those seeking to protect the fisheries. In March 1931, Greenwood, the Minister of Health, admitted to Addison that the scheme was far too expensive and that the government felt it would be more expedient to invest the money in health insurance.[53] Clearly, the government had decided that it was not going to pay for a cleaner Tyne unless it was absolutely forced to do so. As Smout and Stewart observe in relation to their Firth of Forth case study, 'above all it [i.e. the Firth of Forth's pollution problem] needed a refreshing mid twentieth-century belief in big government and a willingness to spend a lot of taxpayers' money for a lot of public good'.[54] The Tyne would not see the benefits of this 'refreshing' belief in big government until the early 1970s.

The TSC held a meeting in the Newcastle Moot Hall in June 1931 to discuss pollution in the Tyne. It was chaired by Mr Clive Cookson and attended by several members of SCORP's Tyne Sub Committee, including Professor Meek and Dr Jee, and representatives of several local councils.[55] The Town Clerk of Newcastle highlighted the expediency of going ahead with the scheme sooner than later. They all agreed that the TSC clerk would write to each of the local authorities, asking them to appoint a representative to join a committee to investigate the Tyne's pollution. At its first meeting, on 14 December 1931, it discussed the serious issue of cyanide content in the river water:

> Cyanides have been found in the effluents of coke-oven works to the extent of 8 parts per 100,000 and they are a usual constituent of the effluents from such works using the direct process. There is evidence that a concentration of only one-fortieth of this is fatal to fish in a few minutes. Two tablespoonfuls of such an effluent would have serious effects on human beings, and half a pint possibly cause death in a few minutes.[56]

---

53. TNA, HLG 50/2051: Tyne Salmon Conservancy: Discharge of sewage into River Tyne (1930–51), minutes of the meeting, p. 1, item 60 and p. 2, item 61.
54. Smout and Stewart, *The Firth of Forth*, p. 272.
55. TNA, HLG 50/2051: Tyne Salmon Conservancy: Discharge of sewage into River Tyne, (1930–51) items 86–88.
56. Ibid.

This first meeting marked a positive step, but the Joint Committee members had set themselves an incredibly difficult challenge to convince central government to pay for a cleaner Tyne in the context of a major economic depression, high unemployment and no clear evidence that the Tyne's pollution posed serious risks to public health. The battle continued.

Unsuccessful Reports

Throughout 1932, the Joint Committee (comprising representatives of the local authorities, the TSC and SCORP's Tyne Sub-Committee) compiled a report on the state of the Tyne estuary, written by Clive Cookson. His account of a visit with medical health officers to Blaydon in July 1932, explained that conditions there 'can only be described as nauseating and thoroughly objectionable' and that

> apart from ocular evidence of large quantities of faecal matter, a continuous succession of bubbles of gas was seen rising to the surface of the river: not only did this occur near the outfalls but in midstream and over a considerable area of the estuary, notably of hydrogen sulphide to the extent of 75% of its volume.[57]

The report explained how dredging the estuary to 25 feet had reduced the 'natural scour' of the river, resulting in waste moving to and fro within the estuary without being flushed out successfully.[58] Cookson described the deepened part of the estuary as 'virtually a septic tank' containing an 'oscillating barrage of polluted water'.[59] Their appeal to the government for funding could not have been clearer:

> After consideration of all the circumstances we feel that the saturation point when untreated sewage can be discharged into the estuary *with safety* [emphasis added] has been reached and passed and we feel that local authorities on both sides of the river should meet in conjunction with the representatives of the Ministry of Health and other government departments concerned to consider the situation as it now exists. We are definitely of the opinion that a scheme for the treatment of the whole or major portion of the sewage at present discharged into the estuary cannot be long postponed.[60]

---

57. TNA, HLG 50/2051: Tyne Salmon Conservancy: Discharge of sewage into River Tyne (1930–51), item 104, report of the Joint Committee: 'Pollution of the Tidal Waters of the River Tyne'.
58. Ibid.
59. Ibid.
60. Ibid.

Chapter 5. Testing the Troubled Waters

They declared that a Joint Sewage Committee should be appointed to replace their Joint Committee, representing not only the local authorities but also local and commercial interests.

The report was submitted to the Ministry of Health at the end of 1932. However, astonishingly, W. Ross, of the Ministry of Health, concluded that the report was biased, and written from the standpoint of the fisheries. He argued that because SCORP was involved in the production of the report, it is 'therefore not by any means clear to me that the report now under consideration is entirely unbiased'.[61] He explained that consequently, 'I am somewhat loath to accept the report entirely at its face value'.[62] He did admit, however,

> there are certain definite statements in the report as to the discharge of sewage, the continuous emission of gas as bubbles rising to the surface of the river from decomposing matter on the bed and the analysis of the gas so discharged which go to show that there is a very active septic action going on in the river below Blaydon.[63]

The Joint Committee continued to meet throughout 1933 and 1934 without achieving their ambition.

In mid-1935, the Joint Committee renamed itself as the Joint Sewage Committee and commissioned a medical report, which they hoped would confirm that the estuary posed a risk to public health. This was all frustratingly slow. In December 1935, the medical officer's report, written by G. Humphreys, John Robertson, John Beale and W. Jameson, confirmed that there was no direct danger to health posed by the admittedly foul state of the river and advised a partial amelioration scheme.[64] In January 1936, the Joint Sewage Committee reported their own findings in relation to health, including 'the frequent bubbling of gas to the surface' and 'the almost total absence of dwelling houses close to the river' with 'here and there the unsightly ruins of dismantled works whose broken down walls and heaps of debris remain to disfigure the banks'.[65] The Ministry of Health funded an engineering report on a possible Tyneside sewerage scheme, completed by Sir George Humphreys and Mr Watson and submitted in November 1936, detailing two plans, one of which was larger and

---

61. TNA, HLG 50/2051: Tyne Salmon Conservancy: Discharge of sewage into River Tyne (1930–51), item 99.
62. Ibid.
63. Ibid.
64. TNA, HLG 50/2051: Tyne Salmon Conservancy: Discharge of sewage into River Tyne (1930–51), letter from A. Jubb to Minister of Health, 03/12/1935, item 136.
65. Ibid.

more comprehensive, involving various pre-treatment works.[66] The solution, as they described it, was 'the construction of intercepting sewers linking together the various outfalls and conveying the sewage to a suitable site or sites for treatment and disposal'.[67] They recommended the adoption of Scheme Two, which was more expensive but cost less per head and served a larger population. Scheme Two would drain 53 square miles, and involve eleven local authorities, 25 miles of sewers and a population of 685,000. It featured sedimentation treatment at a site near Jarrow and the discharge of treated waste into the sea near Souter Point; it was to cost £2,250,000 with a maintenance cost of £155,000, or 5s 2d per head.[68] Scheme Two was recommended because it accommodated future population growth. Moreover, although it was more expensive, it involved a lower spend per capita. The TIC chief engineer agreed that Scheme Two was the most expedient 'in order to purify the tidal portion of the River Tyne'.[69] Although the plan was accepted and funded in principle, it was shelved in 1939 as a result of World War Two and its enormous financial cost.

Unsurprisingly, the TIC was in full support of the scheme, as it would have reduced their dredging requirements substantially, providing they were kept aware of and allowed to manage any negative impacts of the scheme on shipping and trade on the river. The local authorities were even more motivated to implement the scheme, however, because it was their obligation to maintain the health of their respective populations whereas the TIC was merely a port authority. The TIC did feel to a certain extent marginalised by the plans, which seemed largely out of their hands, stating at their meeting in June 1937, 'the report is not sent to the commissioners for their observations, it is sent to them for their information by the Special Areas Commissioner, that is the difference'.[70] In December 1939, the subject was raised again, when the TIC received a copy of the report by Dr H. Bull, Biologist to the River Tyne Pollution Sub-Committee.[71] The TIC was asked to produce a report to the biologist detailing the number of sewers currently discharging into the Tyne together with an estimate of the solid waste they discharged annually and also the cost to the TIC for dredging that solid material. The TIC engineer replied in January 1940, confirming that there were 251 sewers between Wylam and the sea,

66. TNA, HLG 50/2051: Tyne Salmon Conservancy: Discharge of sewage into River Tyne, (1930–51), Humphreys Watson report, items 175–186 (10 Nov. 1936).
67. Ibid.
68. Ibid.
69. *Proceedings of the TIC 1936–1937*, p. 478.
70. Ibid., p. 481.
71. *Proceedings of the TIC 1939–1940*, p. 83.

Chapter 5. Testing the Troubled Waters

including those discharging into the tidal portions of the tributary rivers (the River Don, Willington Gut, Ouse Burn, River Team and River Derwent).[72] He estimated that together they discharged around 26,000 tons of solid material per annum at the cost of around £1,300 for dredging.[73]

In July 1943, the Newcastle *Journal* newspaper published a leaderette and article, entitled 'Foul' which stated, 'nobody will pretend that 20th century standards of sanitation are satisfied by the daily discharge of 25,000,000 gallons of untreated sewage into a river lined by big communities'.[74] It pointed out the issue of national competition for central government funds, advising urgency because 'we shall not be alone in seeking state assistance in the execution of healthful projects' and 'other districts have similar problems, and they are not waiting for victory to begin preparing solutions'.[75] The article blamed the war, noting that

> it is the opinion of many that if the outbreak of war in 1939 had not put an end to the negotiations and arrangements in connection with the major scheme this work of clearing the whole of the Tyne from sewage and pollution would now have been well in hand.[76]

By 1944, no further progress had been made on the Tyne sewage scheme, the salmon catch was down to only 550 lbs and the TSC lamented in June that year how 'the subject was allowed to die' and that the forthcoming and inevitable post-war housing plans would exacerbate the already slim chances of acquiring funding.[77] Furthermore, the Newcastle and Gateshead Water Company's abstraction of around 5,000 million gallons of water annually from upriver locations such as Catcleugh Reservoir, Barrasford, Wylam and Prudhoe had reduced the amount of fresh water coming down into the estuary to flush the effluent out.[78] Abandoning any hope of exacting change themselves, the TSC looked to the future and hoped that the new Northumberland and Tyneside River Board, which was to take over their responsibilities in 1950, would revive the subject once again. It did not.

---

72. Ibid., p. 128.
73. Ibid.
74. 'Foul', *Newcastle Journal* (14 Jul. 1943).
75. Ibid.
76. Ibid.
77. TNA, HLG 50/2051: Tyne Salmon Conservancy: Discharge of sewage into River Tyne (1930–51), Tyne Salmon Conservancy misc papers, item 223.
78. 'Foul', *Newcastle Journal* (14 Jul. 1943).

Conclusion

At the end of World War Two, with no knowledge of where the Tyne's future would lead, those who had worked tirelessly throughout the 1920s and 1930s to instigate a major clean-up of the estuary must surely have felt very disappointed. They had very little to show for their efforts, as the Tyne received ever more waste and ever less fresh water and as its fish life suffocated in a troubled, toxic and bubbling flow. The TSC placed hope in the future Northumberland and Tyneside River Board and effectively abandoned their once passionate and indefatigable efforts to get the scheme moving. The story of the failure to obtain the necessary funding for a clean-up of the Tyne estuary, when studied in detail between 1921 and the early 1940s, reveals that, during a period which has been characterised as one of environmental ignorance, people were in fact working very hard indeed, with zeal and passion to improve the river's environmental health equivalent to that which would motivate their descendants in the 1960s, albeit with substantially less success. The river's condition, as this historical analysis has demonstrated, is not necessarily a fair and accurate representation of all of its people's actions. Throughout the 1920s and 1930s, central government held the keys to constructing the infrastructure needed to enable the river to begin to recover ecologically, in terms of its natural beauty and in terms of its social-environmental relationships with the people who lived and worked on its banks. Between 1921 and the early 1940s, these important two-way socio-environmental relationships had been strained to breaking point, caught up in a seemingly endless and increasingly complex economic and political impasse. This story tells us much about the balance of power in the early and mid-twentieth century between central and local government, certainly between central government and Tyneside. Other major cities, too, were forced to wait until the late twentieth century before central-government funding was delivered to construct urgently needed river purifying large-scale waste-water treatment works, including Edinburgh's Seafield treatment works near Leith (opened in 1978) and Liverpool's Sandon Dock treatment works (opened in 1991).[79]

---

79. Smout and Stewart, *The Firth of Forth*, pp. 165–166; J. Sharples, *Liverpool* (London: Yale University Press, 2004), p. 128.

Chapter 6

'A MEDIEVAL STREET OF SQUALOR': THE FINAL DEMAND FOR A CLEAN-UP, 1950–1975

Introduction

On 16 October 1959, Tyneside's *Evening Chronicle* contained an article entitled 'Boffins sail down the Tyne on sewage survey'.[1] The newspaper called the scheme 'Operation Sewage' and explained that the research work being undertaken by engineers and surveyors, 'with warnings and criticisms of the filthy state of the Tyne ringing in their ears', would be completed in several months.[2] But Tynesiders would have to wait until the early 1970s before their waste water treatment works were eventually constructed at Howdon to free the Tyne from untreated waste. Passionate arguments calling for the government to fund a clean-up gathered pace in the early 1960s, spearheaded by the Tyne's angling community. As Marshall observes, following a 1959 salmon rod return of nil, 'Tyne anglers were in despair'.[3] But local people did not get behind the anglers in any significant numbers. According to Kempster, writing in 1948, the close association with anglers, who were perceived as wealthy and preoccupied with the selfish pursuit of their sport, rather than with the wider social and environmental benefits of cleaner rivers, deterred the majority of the population from joining the fight for more stringent regulation and major clean-up operations.[4] Kempster suggested that inland fisheries have not received the attention they perhaps deserve in the river pollution debate because

> our pressing industrial and agricultural problems have been of such magnitude as to have overshadowed the importance to the nation of its freshwater streams, which in the popular mind are apt to be mainly associated with the recreation

---

1. 'Boffins sail down the Tyne on sewage survey', *Evening Chronicle* (16 Oct. 1959).
2. Ibid.
3. Marshall, *Tyne Waters*, p. 61.
4. Kempster, *Our Rivers*, p. 5.

they afford to a relatively small clique of anglers, and especially with the rich, or at any rate supposedly well-to-do, man's sport of salmon fishing.[5]

Yet I found no clear evidence in the many records analysed during the preparation of this book to suggest that local people's disinclination to fight for a clean-up resulted from negative perceptions across Tyneside of anglers as wealthy and selfish sportsmen who acted in their own interests rather than those of the wider community. Nevertheless, Kempster experienced such debates himself, and his point is convincing. Moreover, the Tyne anglers themselves certainly agreed with Kempster's interpretation, noting in 1960, 'why, many people will ask, should millions of pounds be spent to aid the sport of a comparatively few anglers?'[6] They admitted that this was 'undeniably logical from the view of the anti-clean-up brigade', but local people's disinclination frustrated them nevertheless.[7] However large this anti-clean-up 'brigade' was, it was not organised in any strategic way and it did not interfere specifically to impede the anglers' campaign. Their refusal to support the anglers was a potent weapon in its own right.

The Tyne joined a whole series of other British rivers that had also become very heavily polluted by the mid-twentieth century, including the Clyde, the Mersey, the Firth of Forth and the Trent. With the exception of the unusually well-preserved chalk streams of the Test and Itchen, most of Britain's major rivers were heavily polluted, and north-east England's Tyne, Tees and Wear were some of the most severely affected. Sara Pritchard has analysed how increasing environmentalism in the late 1960s led people to challenge industrial developments that were not in best interests of the River Rhone.[8] Many other western environmental river histories have also identified the 1960s as a pivotal period during which the balance between the perceived importance of using a river maximally for its economic benefits and protecting its environmental and ecological health tipped towards the latter. Changing attitudes towards rivers was merely one integral element of a much wider environmental movement that rose globally to challenge a plethora of environmental damage.[9]

---

5. Ibid.
6. Northumbrian Anglers' Association [hereafter NAA], *Handbook Handbook and Guide to North Country Angling* (1960), p. 65.
7. Ibid.
8. Pritchard, *Confluence*, p. 5.
9. Cioc, *The Rhine*; Barca, *Enclosing Waters*; Coates, *Six Rivers*; Evenden, *Fish versus Power*; Smout and Stewart, *The Firth of Forth*.

Chapter 6. 'A Medieval Street of Squalor'

Chapter five left the Tyne's toxic water bubbling, its fish struggling to breathe and its people in a political and economic impasse in their attempts to secure the necessary central government funding for the infrastructure to divert the untreated waste of over 270 sewers away from the estuary so that it could begin to recover. This chapter explains how the local governors' efforts were rewarded, eventually. The chapter explores the minimal impact of the new Northumberland and Tyneside River Board from 1950 in a decade of relative lack of progress towards a clean-up. It then explains the increasingly impatient demands for a clean-up, led by the Tyne's anglers. Finally, the chapter explains the establishment of the Northumbrian Rivers Authority in 1965, equipped with the power to prevent new discharges of untreated waste into the estuary, and the creation in 1966 of the Tyneside Joint Sewage Committee, which succeeded where its predecessors had failed. They managed to get some plans off the ground and secured funding to free the Tyne from the chronic pollution that had transformed its waters into an open sewer. In this climate of marked attitudinal change, and a fundamental reconceptualisation of how the river should and should not be used, the dogmatic TIC's days were numbered and it was disbanded in 1968.

The 1950s on Tyne

The River Boards were established following the River Boards Act, 1948, which applied to the whole of England and Wales, except the Thames and Lee catchments. Eight river boards were established early in 1950, and nine more during the summer of that year. They took over from existing authorities, such as the Tyne Salmon Conservancy Board.[10] The Northumberland Rivers Catchment Board operated alongside the TSC from 1942 until both boards were replaced by the Northumberland and Tyneside River Board, which held its first meeting in July 1950. Immediately, very much in the style of their Victorian grandparents, the board's members appointed a Fishery Committee and a Pollution Prevention Committee which both reported to one River Pollution and Fisheries Superintendent whose role was primarily inspectorial. The first issue the board discussed was pollution into Beamish Burn and its tributaries from the Stanley Urban District Council's sewage works and other sources. The case was referred to the Pollution Prevention Committee who worked with the council to improve the efficiency of their sewage works. From year to year, the board routinely managed the tasks previously overseen by the TSC, including

---

10. NRO, 3451/A/3: Northumberland and Tyneside River Board Minute Book, 1950–1951.

the issue of angling licences and the restocking of rivers with fish species which were struggling.[11] They also surveyed and approved urban and rural councils' applications for sewage infrastructural improvements in settlements throughout the non-tidal Tyne catchment area, but the TIC retained jurisdiction over applications to install even more sewers into the estuary until 1965, when the Northumbrian Rivers Authority arrived on the scene equipped with the power to prevent new discharges of untreated waste into the estuary.

The board purchased scientific testing equipment which they used in their laboratory to monitor the conditions of river water taken from a wide range of locations and to test fish that appeared to have been poisoned by pollutants in the river water. In January 1964, for example, they purchased a dissolved oxygen meter, a portable pH meter and a thermostatic water bath.[12] Local councils also submitted water from their sections of the river and its tributaries to the board's laboratory for testing. During the 1950s, the Northumberland and Tyneside River Board spent over £1,000,000 constructing sewage works in several locations in the non-tidal waters, but their hands were tied in terms of addressing the very severe problems in the estuary. The Rivers Prevention of Pollution Act 1951, which provided guidance on the river boards' responsibilities, excluded all tidal estuaries from the boards' jurisdictions. Above the tidal zone, however, they made some progress. In January 1964, the board discussed a pollution incident near Alston, noting,

> The Chief Pollution Officer reported that on the 2nd November 1963 approximately 100 dead brown trout had been collected by youths from the Coal Syke, a tributary of the Thinhope Burn (River South Tyne). The mortality had been reported to the board by the Alston Angling Association. Biological examination of the dead fish showed that death was due to penolic poisoning … it appeared that the mortality was caused by an escape of sheep dip from a communal dipper at Stone Hall Farm, near Slaggyford.[13]

The dipper in question, the officer noted, was owned by the Featherstone Estate. Previously, he had written to the agents 'drawing their attention to the mortality and asking them to take effective steps to prevent any future discharge of drainage from the dipper to the Coal Syke'.[14] The agents confirmed that 'they had instructed a local builder to construct an adequate soakaway to take the

---

11. Ibid., p. 21.
12. NRO, 3451/A/16: Northumberland and Tyneside River Board, Pollution Prevention Committee Minute Book, 1964–1965 (20 Jan. 1964), p. 2.
13. Ibid.
14. Ibid.

Chapter 6. 'A Medieval Street of Squalor'

drainage from the dipper and the work had now been completed'.[15] The case was closed.

Between 1951 and 1957, the Ministry of Agriculture, Fisheries and Food and the Government Chemist carried out chemical and temperature tests on the Tyne. They were primarily concerned about the impact on the river water of releases of heated water used for cooling the terrible twins, Stella North and South coal-fired power stations. Flanking both banks of the Tyne at Newburn, they were constructed from 1951 at a cost of £40,500,000 and became operational in several iterations between 1954 and 1957. The tests confirmed that the effluents were capable of producing a 3.2 degrees centigrade local increase in temperature.[16] They also confirmed that the river between Hebburn and Newburn 'was grossly polluted at all states of the tide and at times was completely devoid of oxygen', but found no 'significant change in the condition of the estuary as a whole, although river temperatures have been higher in the immediate vicinity of the outfall'.[17] Apart from the tests conducted to ensure that the new power station did not adversely affect the river water, the early to mid-1950s were quiet years in terms of central government's interest in a major clean-up of the river. No similar tests were completed on the impact of Dunston power station, which was constructed at the same time. Despite the presence of Stella North and South a short distance from her home in Newburn, Pat Rice, a retired shopworker born in 1938, can remember seals living there successfully, fifteen miles from Tynemouth in heavily polluted water. She recalled, 'when I was about 15 [i.e. 1953] up to about the power stations closing [i.e. from 1991], we had seals up the river so it was interesting to say, "have you seen the seal today?", they certainly came up as high as Newburn and just slightly further up'.[18] Pat's husband, retired glassworker Eric Rice, confirmed

> the reason the seal came up was the warmth from the cooling towers, the hot water coming out, well mussels grow around the outlets and that's what the seals were feeding on. Apart from the fish in the river they were feeding in the nice warm water, eating all the shellfish up.[19]

---

15. Ibid.
16. TNA, HLG 127/541: Proposed Tyneside Sewage Disposal Scheme, 05 Mar. 1960–16 Jan. 1961, note from Ministry of Agriculture and Fisheries.
17. Ibid.
18. Interview with Pat Rice, born in Newburn, 1938, retired shopworker; recorded by Leona Skelton at Pat's home in Throckley, 30 Jan. 2015, 10 a.m.
19. Interview with Eric Rice, born in East Denton, 1938, retired glassworker; recorded by Leona Skelton at Eric's home in Throckley, 20 Jan. 2015, 11 a.m.

Tyne after Tyne

This is an example of an environmental change, warmer river water, which had a surprisingly positive impact ecologically by providing the seals with a food source. Environmental changes, like government policies, often produce winners as well as losers. As Michael Chaplin noted walking around the modern-day Tyne estuary, which he calls 'a kind of Silicon Valley with dirt', a small corner of the functioning Paradise Works, in Scotswood, Newcastle, has been designated as a site of National Conservation Importance because the ballast on its old railway line makes an optimum habitat for four of Newcastle's five rare dingy skipper butterfly colonies.[20] While the wider regeneration efforts have undoubtedly improved the butterflies' ability to thrive, the butterflies are nevertheless winners from the river's industrialisation which brought the ballast there in the first place. Even on the River Nent, a tributary of the South Tyne that is heavily contaminated with lead, zinc and cadmium as a result of extensive metal mining, Calaminarian Grassland is flourishing because, unusually, it thrives on lead, zinc and cadmium.[21]

Smout and Stewart analysed the recovery of the Tyne's Scottish neighbour, the River Forth, as its waters became cleaner following deindustrialisation. Just as the Tyne's industrialisation created some ecological winners, they found ecological losers of regeneration. Instigating environmental changes perceived as conducive to positive impacts on ecology can sometimes cause damage, albeit unintentionally. As they note, by 1987

> it was clear that the Firth was a rapidly recovering ecosystem, and the process has continued ever since. But it did not benefit everything. For one group of ducks, which had adapted to feeding on the marine worms and organic residues from the distilleries and breweries, the recovery in water quality was an unmitigated disaster. The scaup is a marine duck that breeds in Iceland and Scandinavia and winters in the Baltic, the North Sea and Atlantic coasts of Britain. Even in quite small coastal communities, like Anstruther, the ending of raw sewage discharge has visibly changed what the birdwatcher is likely to see in winter on the coast: there is no chance of scaup now, and fewer goldeneye. Certain species of waders, like dunlin, turnstone and purple sandpipers have also become scarcer on the shore, and this effect, noticed elsewhere, has been related to cleaning up sewage effluent.[22]

---

20. Chaplin et al., *Tyne View*, p. 248.
21. Ibid., p. 202.
22. Smout and Stewart, *The Firth of Forth*, pp. 166–167.

Chapter 6. 'A Medieval Street of Squalor'

Similarly, Smout and Stewart explained how the removal of the mills upriver changed the Forth's flow, which reduced the numbers of dragonflies and frogs.[23]

Most of the TIC's members perceived their responsibilities as mutually exclusive from those of the TSC, and subsequently also from those of the Northumberland and Tyneside River Board which took over from its duties in 1950. While most commissioners of the TIC believed their sole responsibility was to maximise the economic efficiency of the river as a port and site of industrial manufacture, as we saw in chapter three, one exceptional Commissioner, Aaron Gompertz, who represented South Shields, held exceptional views.[24] He believed that sanctioning successive applications to dispose of yet more untreated waste directly into the river was 'very wrong indeed' and suggested that the TIC should use their power to decline new applications to prevent further damage.[25] The TIC, or at least most of its members, was able to continue to progress its own work in a robustly separate silo of commerce, navigation and industry without considering the wider environment, the river's fisheries or anything else that did not directly underpin their 'good work'. The law protected the TIC from having to consider social, environmental and recreational issues. But this situation, in which the TIC was able to remain indifferent to pollution, was unsustainable. Its days were numbered. The Tyne's anglers were the first people outside official, regulatory or governmental organisations to tackle vociferously the pollution of the estuary.

Final Demands for a Clean-Up

In 1960, the Northumbrian Anglers' Association printed their *Handbook and Guide to North Country Angling* and in it they included several letters of complaint about the condition of the Tyne that had been sent to the local *Journal* newspaper. One complainant, Harry, recalled how his Grandfather and friends used to fish and swim in the river near Jarrow in the 1880s, noting that he 'never spoke of pollution' and probably did not 'know the meaning of the word'.[26] Even in 1880, Harry admits, 'the insidious process had begun of converting quite deliberately an ordinary stretch of pure water into a noxious ditch, even,

---

23. Ibid., p. 174.
24. For more detailed information on Gompertz's argument, see chapter 3 (Domestic and Industrial Wastes).
25. *Proceedings of the TIC 1957–1958*, p. 113.
26. NAA, *Handbook*, p. 65.

to repeat the cliché which so exactly describes it now, an open sewer'.[27] His complaint was that if his Grandfather could return in 1960, he would find no fish and a swim would be rewarded with emerging from the water 'not only fouled and filthy, but in some danger of contracting one of those diseases like diphtheria, yellow fever, even some sort of plague'.[28] Surprisingly to many, perhaps, Harry did not blame the chemical factories' complex waste, but rather stated that 'the first really big river pollution factor' was the human waste that entered the river through the sewers after large numbers of houses started to be built with indoor bathrooms complete with water closets.[29] Harry called the Tyne 'a river which scythes the area in two like a mediaeval street of squalor'.[30] In 1960, Graham Cawthorne, Political Correspondent of the *Journal* newspaper, wrote quite a dramatic article comparing the Tyne to the ditches of Teheran.[31]

By 1960, every day the estuary's sewers disgorged approximately 35,000,000 gallons of untreated sewage into the river water.[32] Yet the anglers were the only people outside local governmental bodies who held 'meetings of protest', which resulted from their 'specialised interest in having a clean river'.[33] The anglers' *Guidebook* quoted Dr T. Coxon, Medical Officer of Health to the Tyne Port Health Authority, as having said that 'Tyne water in the industrial belt has practically none of the accepted characteristics and quality of normal river water'.[34] The anglers agreed, referring to the river as an 'almost static ditch of impurities'.[35] As we saw in chapter five, the clean-up had been derailed by World War Two and then delayed substantially after the war due to insufficient funds. In the context of very limited available central government funding, as the country recovered from the recent war, the challenge proved overwhelming. But the delay was also due to the local authorities' failure to demonstrate to central government, and in particular to the Ministry of Health, that the Tyne estuary posed a serious risk to health and was therefore an obvious and urgent national priority regardless of austerity. Mr Edward Short, Labour MP for

---

27. Ibid.
28. Ibid.
29. Ibid., p. 66.
30. Ibid., p. 67.
31. Ibid., p. 71.
32. Ibid., p. 67.
33. Ibid., p. 68.
34. Quoted in NAA, *Handbook*, p. 68.
35. NAA, *Handbook*, p. 68.

Chapter 6. 'A Medieval Street of Squalor'

Newcastle Central, mentioned the issue to Parliament three times, but received no favourable response towards his request for central funding.

The cost of a large-scale solution was rising by the day. By the time the plans to clean the Tyne were looked at again in the late 1950s, the total cost had risen to between £15 million and £20 million, whereas before World War Two, it would have cost only £3,500,000. The Tyne anglers knew that the key was to combine representatives of the multiple riparian local authorities in a joint committee. In October 1958, fifteen representatives of the Tyneside local authorities and two from the two county councils of Tynemouth and Northumberland met to form a Working Sub-Committee headed by Chairman Mr Renwick of Newcastle Council, described as 'an old man, but vigorous and interested'.[36] The committee also appointed Dr Cassey, head of Durham University's Engineering School, to create a survey and a hydrological report on the tides together with some chemical analyses.[37] They agreed to produce a report by 1960 containing a full evaluation of proposed schemes for improved sewage disposal in the context of the river's particular 'hydraulic, sediment and chemical' characteristics.[38] By October 1959, as the *Evening Chronicle* article cited above explained ('Boffins sail down the Tyne on sewage survey'), the Working Sub-Committee was making progress, compiling the evidence for their report. Mr Percy Parr, Newcastle's City Engineer, convened the committee as it tested the water and assessed the practicalities of installing the major sewerage treatment systems proposed. By this time the trunk sewer plans were out of date and pre-treatment works modelled on the successful example of the treatment works recently constructed at Felling at a cost of £250,000 seemed far more expedient. Some suggested turning solid waste into compost, but these ideas were not developed further.

At a meeting in London between representatives of central government and a few representatives of the Tyneside Working Sub-Committee, in July 1959, the urgency of the clean-up operation was discussed in direct connection to the river's potential dangers to public health.[39] The committee was well aware that 'migrant fish cannot make their way up the river, but there is no evidence that there is any danger to public health'.[40] The committee was also explicitly aware that industrial waste had to be tackled directly, in addition to domestic waste,

---

36. TNA, HLG 127/540, Tyne sewage scheme, 1958–1960.
37. Ibid.
38. Ibid.
39. Ibid.
40. Ibid.

if the river was to be cleaned up once and for all, noting, 'it is improbable that any marked improvement on the Tyne could be made by treating discharges of domestic sewage only'.[41] And it understood that the forthcoming Clean Rivers (estuaries and tidal waters) Bill, which eventually came into effect as an Act in September 1960, would apply only to new discharges, whereas the Tyne suffered from established discharges that would be exempt from the Act. In April 1960, the Working Sub-Committee hosted a parliamentary secretary, Sir Keith Joseph, MP for Leeds North East and secretary to the Ministry of Housing and Local Government, to review their work so far. After questions with Dr Cassie and other surveyors, engineers and representatives of local councils, the secretary was taken for lunch with Newcastle's Lord Mayor before boarding a boat for a river trip featuring tea on board and followed by a press conference.[42] During the visit, the Working Sub-Committee decided to put the pre-war proposals to one side due to the lack of a suitable and sufficiently large site and because the flotation tests off Souter Point had confirmed that if solid waste was disposed into the North Sea, substantial volumes would be washed back into the river.[43]

The Ministry for Housing and Local Government's own notes about the visit reveal that

> altogether one was left with the impression of 15 local authorities working smoothly together and anxious to see progress. There was a glancing reference during the meeting of the working committee to a possible defaulter but it seemed to be agreed that public opinion would be strong enough to take care of this. The boat trip down the river did not reveal much, the Tyne is obviously dirty but not dirtier than other large English rivers. There was only an occasional smell. Admittedly things are not at their worst at this time of the year.[44]

A few months later, in June 1960, the *Evening Chronicle* proclaimed optimistically 'The River Tyne will be a salmon river again in ten years'.[45] The article elaborated that Sir Keith Joseph, 'greatly interested by his recent visit to Tyneside', said that 'the money required to end river pollution in the Tyne is now forthcoming and that the only problem outstanding is one of hydraulics', concluding that 'not only anglers but all those who love the river and the wild life in and

---

41. Ibid.
42. TNA, HLG 127/541: Proposed Tyneside Sewage Disposal Scheme, 5 Mar. 1960–16 Jan. 1961.
43. TNA, HLG 127/541: Proposed Tyneside Sewage Disposal Scheme, 5 Mar. 1960–16 Jan. 1961, Parliamentary Secretary's Visit (29 Apr. 1960), ff. 19–20.
44. Ibid.
45. 'The River Tyne will be a Salmon River again in Ten Years', *Evening Chronicle* (11 June 1960).

Chapter 6. 'A Medieval Street of Squalor'

around it will be delighted'.[46] Good times for the Tyne and its salmon were just over the horizon.

The Tyneside Joint Sewage Committee and the Howdon Plan

The Working Sub-Committee submitted its report in December 1960. Its main findings were that a net movement upstream of the water near the bed of the river had an adverse effect on the passage of solid sewage out to sea, that the river's dilution did not justify the free discharge of untreated sewage into the river and that 'on the grounds of amenity alone' substantial benefits would be produced 'from the removal of objectionable matter from the river'.[47] The third finding focused on amenity in an attempt to compensate for the lack of evidence of danger to public health. The report also confirmed that during a tide cycle the volume of water entering the channel was 'at least 300 times' that of the sewage entering the river during the same period.[48] However, in reality, dilution was rather more complex than this suggests, due to stratification within the river water, meaning some layers could contain very high or very low levels of sewage. As the river, in the report's words, 'acts as a sedimentation tank, retains the settleable solids and moves them upstream', the report insisted that the minimum pre-treatment for sewage must be sedimentation.[49] The report's findings confirmed the urgency of appointing a Joint Sewerage Authority to progress the work of the Working Sub-Committee at a faster pace and more cohesively without any hindrance from the local councils' respective competing priorities. Shortly after the release of the report, in February 1961, R. Dyson, Chief Pollution Officer of the Tyneside and Northumberland River Board, and R. Porter, Chief Engineer of the TIC, were co-opted into the Working Sub-Committee to serve alongside the local authorities' representatives.

On 1 April 1965, under the terms of the Water Resources Act 1963, the previously separate Northumbrian and Tyneside River Board and the Wear and Tees River Board were amalgamated to form the Northumbrian River Authority with the power to decline new applications to discharge untreated waste into the estuary. This important administrative change strengthened the committee's plea for the government to fund a sewerage scheme. The new

---

46. 'The River Tyne will be a Salmon River again in Ten Years', *Evening Chronicle* (11 June 1960).
47. TNA, HLG 127/541: Proposed Tyneside Sewage Disposal Scheme, 05 Mar. 1960–16 Jan. 1961. Tyneside Sewage Disposal: Fifth Interim Report to the Working Committee by the Technical sub-committee (Dec. 1960), p. 3, item. 72.
48. Ibid.
49. Ibid.

argument that industry and business could no longer develop in the area until a sewage treatment works was constructed because the new Northumbrian River Authority was bound by law to prevent the further deterioration of the estuary was much more convincing. The Tyneside Joint Sewerage Committee was formed one year after the Northumbrian Rivers Authority, in 1966, after which they began to make real plans to develop a comprehensive sewerage system to serve Tyneside, which would divert untreated domestic and industrial waste, both liquid and solid, from the Tyne estuary. It is easy to understand why the TIC had to be disbanded, in 1968, following this immense tide of administrative and political changes that fundamentally reconceptualised how the river should be regulated.

In 1970, the Ministry of Housing and Local Government conducted an inquiry into proposals for reducing pollution in the Tyne estuary, and a report was compiled by N. Thomas.[50] The report's major proposal was a substantial treatment works at Howdon. It explained the lack of action in this important area since initial plans were proposed during the 1930s, noting 'little positive action concerning the serious nature of river pollution ensued until 1964', and the committee concluded 'that a co-ordinated system of sewage disposal, taking in all local authorities on Tyneside, should be considered as a priority need'.[51] The funding was put in place, the government passed the plans and the Tyneside Joint Sewerage Committee developed the Howdon Plan in more detail. The planning authority, Tynemouth County Council, sanctioned the plans for the Howdon scheme on the condition that 'all reasonable precautions' are taken 'to prevent the emission of offensive or obnoxious fumes or smells'.[52] In 1972, construction work began. Subsequently, 45 miles of interceptor sewers were installed along both riverbanks of the estuary and coastlines which carry the waste mainly by gravity. A tunnel was installed into the riverbed from Jarrow to connect the southern interceptor to the primary treatment plant at Howdon, which provided grit removal and primary sedimentation for the waste delivered from both interceptors. The Northumbrian Water Authority took over the partially constructed system in 1974 and oversaw the completion of the project, which cost £150 million. It took twenty years to construct the network of pipelines in its entirety.

---

50. NRO, 3451/A/40: Ministry of Housing and Local Government Inquiry into Proposals for Reducing Pollution of the River Tyne Estuary and adjacent Sea Beaches: proofs of evidence submitted by various interested bodies, (1970).
51. Ibid.
52. Ibid.

Chapter 6. 'A Medieval Street of Squalor'

The drive to clean the Tyne was spearheaded by the angling community, but was also driven in its later stages by the members of the Tyne Fishery District Riparian Owners and Occupiers Association, as demonstrated by their letter to the Ministry of Agriculture, Fisheries and Food in October 1974. This non-governmental group of private individuals wrote their letter as large parts of the Howdon scheme were still under construction and as a substantial scheme to dam the North Tyne valley near the source of the North Tyne at Kielder was awaiting confirmation. They argued that, although 'in recent years there have been some encouraging signs of recovery', they had received information that 'the anti-pollution operation of cleaning up the river Tyne was or is about to be curtailed in order to save money'.[53] They wished to make it clear that their association would 'view with concern any such steps', stressing the importance of continuing the work to clean up the river 'not only for the benefit of riparian owners but also for the whole of the salmon fishing industry'.[54] The anglers were no longer working alone in their efforts to maintain a strong momentum towards a successful clean-up, as people were increasingly persuaded of the expediency of creating a cleaner Tyne.

Stories from before the Clean-Up

The reports of local and central government and the opinions of scientists are detailed, accurate and very historically important. However, they do not take us to the heart of how the pre-clean up, dirty river made people feel, the people who interacted with the river as it flowed through their lives and livelihoods. By using oral history, we are able to gather partial reconstructions of a very different riverscape from the one we know today. Unlike the governmental reports of the 1950s and 1960s, and unlike the negative documents written by angry Tyne anglers who trying to persuade their readers that a clean-up was long overdue, oral histories enable us to see both the negative and the positive meanings people attached to the river as it bubbled with toxic gases and received the filth of the whole of Tyneside. Through oral history, we are able to understand those relationships from a more balanced perspective.

Jennifer Simpson, a retired schoolteacher, was born and brought up in Jesmond in Newcastle on Tyne, but has lived much further up the river for most of her life. She has fond memories of school boat trips in the 1940s to places

---

53. TNA, MAF 209/3042: Northumbrian Water Authority (Kielder Water) Order 1974: Fish Pass Facilities (1974–1977).
54. Ibid.

such as Ryton Willows and Tynemouth for picnics. Although she described the river water as 'not good, I wouldn't like to fall in the river water in those days', she also recalls how busy the river was, 'crowded with buildings and ships … at the river edge'.[55] An anonymous scientist and community worker who has lived near the mouth of the Tyne since birth in North Shields in 1976, describes the river while it was still industrial but on the cusp of dramatic change in the very early 1980s as

> dirtier than it is now, I can remember there being tanks on the other side of the river, yeah lots of fishing industry going on, my uncle used to be lock keeper up at the Albert-Edward Dock so I used to go there as well and that was all sort of decrepit and I used to like it.[56]

Despite the 'decrepit' nature of the riverscape during childhood, the interviewee still liked it and remembered the industrial scenes fondly. The interviewee described the water as 'murky', but 'can't remember it smelling'.[57]

Wendy Young, a full-time mother who now lives in North Shields but was born further up the Northumbrian coast at Amble in 1976, remembers the river during her childhood in the 1980s as she spent substantial time near her grandparents' house on the south shore at Hebburn. She remembers

> never being able to get actually down … it was all too sludgy and black and my Grandad would be wary about going over the edge because he would say that … you would die … if you swallowed the water, you know like if you fell in it wouldn't just be drowning it would be like getting seriously ill from swallowing the water … that's what they used to say anyway, it was like really dirty there you know.[58]

Yet, despite the industry on the river water and banks, she has positive memories of 'little ponds … by the river that we used to go looking for newts and stuff in and that kind of thing'.[59] No matter how toxic the river became, many Tynesiders found ways in which to value it, to engage with it positively and to have fun in its environment. Pearl Saddington, who manages the Old Low Light Heritage Centre at North Shields, was born in South Shields and has lived

---

55. Interview with Jennifer Simpson, born in Newcastle on Tyne, 1940, retired school teacher; recorded by Leona Skelton, at Tyne Rivers Trust Offices, Corbridge, 20 Jan. 2015, 2 p.m.
56. Interview with anonymous interviewee, born in North Shields, 1976, scientist and community worker; recorded by Leona Skelton, at the Old Low Light Heritage Centre Café, 22 Jan. 2015, 11 a.m.
57. Interview with anonymous interviewee, born in North Shields, 1976, scientist and community worker.
58. Interview with Wendy Young, born in Amble, Northumberland, 1976, full-time mother; recorded by Leona Skelton, at the Old Low Light Heritage Centre Café, 22 Jan. 2015, 11.30 a.m.
59. Interview with Wendy Young.

Chapter 6. 'A Medieval Street of Squalor'

there all her life. During childhood, she recalls, 'I remember just ships, ships, ships', the river water 'looking dark' and she describes how the soundscape has changed dramatically since her childhood, explaining that 'now when you go on the ferry, you hear the ferry, you hear the engine, but then you didn't hear the engine'.[60] This explains just how overwhelming the collective cacophony from the ships, the shipbuilding industries and the other riparian factories of heavy industry must have been for those living, working and growing up around the Tyne. As a child, Pearl made sense of and conceptualised her very strong bonds with the Tyne using a fictional story 'that my Mam was a mermaid and my Dad was a pirate and then they met and that's how I've got this massive affinity to the river'.[61] She remembers travelling from industrial South Shields as a child in the 1960s for day trips upriver near Hexham as

> a treat ... to go to Hexham to the clean river, you know cos you could see the bottom and you could actually paddle in it and you know look for fishes and stuff like that and it's different, the current's different and you can actually see it going over stones and everything, you can actually play in the river.[62]

Brian Pearson, who has lived all his life near the river in North Shields since 1941, recalls a very busy river estuary, explaining that it 'didn't matter where you looked there was shipyards, it wasn't very clean mind but yeah it was a very busy river'.[63] He laments the pollution of the river water and the malodours it produced, 'all the rubbish, all the offal and that went straight into the river, so you can imagine what it was, it smelt, you could smell it all over North Shields in the summer'.[64] Yet he recalls happy memories of using his 'old big wooden telescope and I would sit and watch the ships going past' and of hiring a rowing boat and fishing for the mackerel which followed the herring with his brother.[65]

Alan Fidler, who was born in North Shields in 1949, remembers how potentially dangerous the river water was to health:

> When I was a child it [the Tyne] was effectively dead, inert and ... if you fell in the river, you were taken to hospital to have yourself pumped out because

---

60. Interview with Pearl Saddington, born in South Shields, heritage centre manager; recorded by Leona Skelton, at the Old Low Light Heritage Centre, 22 Jan. 2015, 3 p.m.
61. Interview with Pearl Saddington.
62. Interview with Pearl Saddington.
63. Interview with Brian Pearson, born in Hexham [due to the wartime relocation of pregnant women during WW2], 1941, retired painter and decorator; recorded by Leona Skelton, at the Old Low Light Heritage Centre Café, 22 Jan. 2015, 3.30 p.m.
64. Interview with Brian Pearson.
65. Interview with Brian Pearson.

there were so many industrial pollutants in the water you had to more or less have your stomach pumped out to make sure you didn't ingest any really serious chemicals that were in the water.[66]

Matt Hall, born in Newcastle on Tyne in 1957, describes himself very proudly as 'a true and proper Geordie' and he remembers the river when 'it was just a big expanse of dirty, dark water'.[67] As a child, Matt felt that the river 'never had any real value, it never had anything exciting about it'.[68] Yet he does recall 'seeing the canoe races when I was a young lad, … the whole Tyne Bridge was packed with people and it was … the boat races, I can't remember the teams, but that used to be such a poignant time'.[69] Amid the dirty water, the booming industry and the suffocating salmon, it is important to appreciate that people still experienced positive interactions with the river.

Tony Henderson, a journalist born in 1947 who has lived in Tyneside his whole life, described:

> The water was black and it was full of raw sewage and it was just full of every type of rubbish you could think of that could float and it was, I remember you got sort of like multi-coloured patches, which was some sort of chemical or oil or other sort of pollutant and of course the smell from the river, the smell of the pollution could make your eyes water.[70]

However, even as his eyes watered, he was able to have fun playing by and even on the river as a child, despite the pollution:

> The riverbank used to be our playground and in those days kids would go off all day unsupervised and nobody seemed to be bothered about where they went. And so we would spend the whole day down on the riverbank and we would make rafts and go off into the river, amazing to think of it now, and you would watch all the detritus coming down the river. We used to play on unfenced chemical tips, from Reyrolles' huge factory in Hebburn and we used to sort of set things alight and bash things and throw them around and cook them and rub them down people's backs and so that's what we used to do and the river

---

66. Interview with Alan Fidler, born in North Shields, 1949, taxi driver; recorded by Leona Skelton, at the Old Low Light Heritage Centre Café, 22 Jan. 2015, 1 p.m.
67. Interview with Matt Hall, born in Newcastle on Tyne, 1957, Royal Mail processing operator; recorded by Leona Skelton at his home in West Denton, 23 Jan. 2015, 3.30 p.m.
68. Interview with Matt Hall.
69. Interview with Matt Hall.
70. Interview with Tony Henderson, born in Hebburn, 1947, journalist; recorded by Leona Skelton at his home in Cullercoats, 30 Jan. 2015, 2 p.m.

Chapter 6. 'A Medieval Street of Squalor'

then was alive with rats and we used to shoot them with air rifles and that was, that was our playground.[71]

It is remarkable how similar the descriptions of the river water are, all pointing to river water of a dark colour with lots of debris and sewage floating on the surface.

Dawn Tudge, who was born in Gateshead in 1974, was taken to the quayside market as a child and said 'I do recall the quayside being … in a pretty sorry state, you know it was before all the regeneration had started so it was kind of that period in between the industry going and the regeneration starting'.[72] Pat Rice, a retired shopworker who was born in Newburn in 1938, remembers a 'grey and dirty looking' Tyne, and noted that 'the further you got down the dirtier it got and the more debris that you saw', yet this was not incompatible with very happy Sundays spent during her youth near the river in the late 1940s and 1950s:

> We would leave bible class and head up the river and that was where we did our courting. So we would walk up the river and meet all your friends up the river. When we were, when I was about seven or eight we could get a ferry across the river at Newburn, just a small ferry, and it could take you across the river to Ryton Willows which had chuggy boats, roundabouts and Ryton Willows was the picnic area. The other thing we used to do was, there was a ferry came up from South Shields and we used to have a trip down at least once a year down the river, so that was … our holiday, a day down the river on the ferry that came up. … The view meant a lot, Ryton Tower from Millfield you could look right across and see Ryton tower and it [the Tyne] was always like a silver ribbon, out of that way industry and the other way this ribbon of silver greenery you know the green at either side.[73]

These recollections of the river before the clean-up and the major regeneration projects of the late-twentieth and early twenty-first centuries provide important information about the riverscape that simply do not exist in documentary archives. These interviews describe smell and sound as well as visual scenes of the river and they explain, often in poignant detail, how people felt about the river, what they did to the river and what the river did to them. One could be forgiven for assuming that people turned away from the river throughout the period during which it was so heavily polluted, when it carried potentially

---

71. Interview with Tony Henderson.
72. Interview with Dawn Tudge, born in Gateshead, 1974, PR administrator; recorded by Leona Skelton at her home in Ryton, 24 Jan. 2015, 1 p.m.
73. Interview with Pat Rice.

fatal chemicals. Newcastle Council's move in 1968 from their old Victorian Town Hall offices in the Bigg Market, relatively close to the river, to the new civic centre much further away, near the Haymarket, symbolises implied wider turning away from the river. But clearly people still engaged with the river in a number of important, pleasurable and positive ways during the period when it actually bubbled with toxic gases and contained so little oxygen that the estuary acted as an impenetrable barrier to salmon. It is only by talking to the people who played, lived and worked near the river during this period that these stories can be written into histories of the river alongside extensive scientific reports describing deoxygenated water, damning newspaper articles describing a bubbling Tyne that was a source of regional shame and council minutes describing the river as an open sewer.

Conclusion

This tale of two very different decades, of almost no progress at all during the 1950s followed by a flurry of action throughout the 1960s, can be attributed to the wider national economy and policies of austerity in the aftermath of World War Two. The passing of inadequate legislation that was not fit for purpose and which completely failed to protect the Tyne against untreated waste also played a major role. But the severe pollution of the mid twentieth-century Tyne has also to be attributed to ineffectual local politics. The local governors could not attract central government funding for a sewerage scheme because they failed to demonstrate that the Tyne's toxic water posed a serious public health threat. This is a clear example of local governance being forced to conform to the parameters set by central government, in this case a prioritisation of public health, in order to secure funding for crucial and very large-scale infrastructure which the locality was unable to fund independently. Perhaps the local governors might have had more success if they had made a more concerted effort to play to the government's tune by making more of the public health issue. This was not the first time central government had ridden roughshod over local politics. In 1850, the Tyne's local governance was fundamentally redesigned by Parliament, which sent the river's conservatorship down a very different track towards its vision of a 'grand and deep' industrial river with an increased navigational capacity. When it became clear that establishing the TIC had failed to speed river improvements sufficiently, the government appointed a Royal Commission in 1855 to hammer the message home.

Chapter 6. 'A Medieval Street of Squalor'

The common theme throughout the 1950s and 1960s was the labelling of the river as an open sewer. This particular metaphor reveals that, in this period, the river was conceptualised as a passive victim of human actions. The label confirms categorically that the human action to dispose of enormous volumes of organic and industrial waste into the Tyne's water was not the river's fault. Elsewhere, the Colorado River in California, USA, was referred to accusingly and pejoratively in the 1980s as a 'deficit river' when its flow proved insufficient to supply water to twenty million people inhabiting its basin, due to over-abstraction to supply water for agricultural irrigation and golf courses. Marc Reisner suggests that people's use of the term 'deficit river' suggests that they believed that the river was 'somehow at fault for its overuse'.[74] By contrast, in the case of pollution in the Tyne, the blame was placed squarely at the door of everyone who flushed their toilet into the estuary. Tynesiders accepted their guilt collectively. Whereas during several floods, in 1771, 1815 and 2005, the river has been conceptualised as a violent trespasser across that imaginary line between the human and the natural, encroaching onto and thereby destroying human territory, in this case the humans freely admitted that they were the encroachers, the trespassers, the morally wrong.

---

74. Reisner, *Cadillac Desert*, p. 121.

Chapter 7

DAMMING THE TYNE: THE CREATION AND IMPACT OF KIELDER RESERVOIR, 1975–2015

Introduction

In 1995, Richard White asked us to 'look for the natural in the dams and the unnatural in the salmon'.[1] Throughout the twentieth century, as ever more rivers across the world have been dammed to create reservoirs to supply water and to produce hydro-electric power, very large numbers of people have been unable to see 'the natural in dams'. In 1934, the Sunbeam Dam on the Salmon River (a tributary of the Snake River, which is in turn a tributary of the Columbia River, USA), was blown up illegally by activists who wished to free the fish.[2] The subsequent creation of eight federal dams between the Salmon River and the sea rendered this act of 'ecoterrorism' pointless.[3] Steven Hawley's research into this particular case revealed that unlike action to prevent other environmental interventions, such as logging, 'dam demolition seems to meet with a consensus much more easily in public opinion', suggesting that Sunbeam's 'construction may have been [perceived as] a greater crime than its destruction'.[4] In the UK, too, decisions to build dams for hydroelectricity and for water supply have been highly politicised and controversial, leading to narratives of dispossession among those who have lost their homes, communities and livelihoods under artificial lakes. Harriet Ritvo highlights that the nineteenth-century damming of Thirlmere, in England's Lake District, to supply water to the burgeoning industrial city of Manchester, aroused passions among those who wanted to

---

1. White, *The Organic Machine*, p. xi.
2. S. Hawley, *Recovering a Lost River: Removing Dams, Rewilding Salmon, Revitalizing Communities* (Boston, MA: Beacon Press, 2011), p. 2.
3. Ibid., p. 10.
4. Ibid., pp. 2, 6.

Chapter 7. Damming the Tyne

preserve the existing environment.⁵ In 1893, the Welsh Elan Valley's Afon Elan and Claerwen rivers were dammed to create a chain of man-made lakes to supply water to Birmingham and another Welsh river, the Vyrnwy, was dammed in the 1880s to supply water to Liverpool. The creation of Tryweryn Reservoir, in picturesque Snowdonia, Wales, in the 1950s, fuelled nationalistic outrage when the village of Capel Celyn (featuring a school, chapel, post office and twelve houses) was flooded to supply water to Liverpool, the closest city in England. Tryweryn Reservoir subsequently facilitated the development of a 500 kw hydro-electric power scheme, which triggered a far lower level of local resistance than the reservoir's original construction. Many reservoirs in the UK and around the world have been built, first and foremost, to supply water for domestic and industrial needs. While the production of hydro-electric power can have a detrimental impact on the landscape, producing local resistance in its own right, it is important to recognise the complex and subtle differences between perceptions of, feelings about and reactions to: 1) the construction of a dam; 2) the flooding of a valley to create a reservoir; and 3) the installation of plant to produce hydro-electric power, whether as part of the original design or subsequently. One person's strong objection to the proposed flooding of settlements to create a reservoir primarily to supply water might not necessarily develop into a subsequent objection to the generation of hydro-electric power as a by-product of an already-constructed dam and reservoir.

The first hydroelectric power station in the world, and the first house to be powered and lit by electricity generated by water power, was the home of Tyneside industrialist and inventor Lord William Armstrong who, as we have seen, played a crucial role in driving forward the industrialisation of the Tyne estuary by pressurising the TIC to dredge upriver from Newcastle to enable his Elswick munition works to expand maximally. Starting in 1868, he installed a hydro-electric plant at his house at Cragside in Northumberland, forty miles north-east of the much larger dam and power station opened near the source of the North Tyne at Kielder in 1982.⁶ This chapter explores and analyses the intense debate surrounding the creation of Kielder Reservoir, which is now the UK's largest man-made lake, and Kielder Hydro, England's largest hydro-electric power plant; and it explores the process of adaptation to the new and different riverscape it created by fish, humans and the river itself. By focusing in particular on the debate over aesthetics and local people's feelings in relation

---

5. Harriet Ritvo, *The Dawn of Green: Manchester, Thirlmere, and Modern Environmentalism* (Chicago: University of Chicago Press, 2009).
6. G. Irlam, 'Electricity Supply at Cragside', *Industrial Archaeology Review* 11 (2) (1989): 187–195.

to the visual impact of a new, artificial or 'enviro-technical' landscape, we can learn a great deal about how damming the North Tyne at Kielder fundamentally changed socio-environmental relationships between the river and the people who interacted with it, both in the North Tyne valley and further down the main Tyne where natural seasonal fluctuations in flow regimes were consigned to history and brought under human control.[7]

Writing in 1987, Beryl Charlton, noted that 'although the Upper North Tyne Valley was not unattractive, it was hardly an area of wholly unspoilt natural beauty, being dominated by the coniferous plantations of the Forestry Commission'.[8] But however far the massive swathes of England's largest commercial forest had already tainted the landscape of the upper North Tyne river valley before the creation of Kielder Reservoir, many believed at the time, and some still believe now, that its creation led to even further aesthetic degradation. Teesside's chemical industry, which the reservoir was originally designed to support, subsequently declined. Consequently, an intense debate continues today over whether Kielder Reservoir's capacity to generate hydro-electricity, to supply voluminous water and to be used as a recreational facility attracting around a quarter of a million tourists annually has outweighed environmental, emotional and ecological losses. Some people still feel anger and a real sense of loss whereas other local people have come to cherish this artificial landscape and even to perceive it as 'natural'. The chapter concludes that, while economics and politics are important factors within such debates, in relation to the debate over the Kielder scheme in the North Tyne riverscape, aesthetics played a larger role particularly for local people. Ultimately, their riverscape powerfully shaped daily experiences of life, work and play in their local environment and the Kielder scheme threatened to transform beyond recognition the place local people had come to cherish over the course of their lives.

Over the twentieth century, the natural flow of the North Tyne through this landscape was important to those who were descended from the long-established dispersed sheep-farming communities. It was also important to those whose families had moved to the villages of Falstone, Plashetts and Kielder in increasing numbers since 1925 to work in commercial forestry and coal-mining. Despite the forecasts predicting that a very substantial volume of water was necessary to meet the north-east region's projected future water shortfall, especially in terms of meeting demand from the then burgeoning chemical

---

7. Pritchard, *Confluence*, pp. 1, 15.
8. B. Charlton, *Upper North Tynedale: A Northumbrian Valley and its People* (Newcastle: Northumbrian Water, 1987), p. 152.

Chapter 7. Damming the Tyne

industry on Teesside, many people expressed serious objections to the scheme. They objected to: the dramatic aesthetic changes to the landscape; the flooding of communities, farms, houses and social facilities; potential environmental damage; and the cost of the scheme, which was estimated to be £23 million in 1969, but quickly rose to £85 million by 1974 and continued to rise to £167 million upon completion in 1982. The chapter explores the objections based on aesthetic changes to the landscape and potential environmental and ecological damage in order to highlight the useful insights that this outpouring of objections at the head of the North Tyne provide into people's relationships with their local river and the landscape through which it flowed. The chapter then discusses the intense debate, after the Kielder plans had been passed in June 1973, over whether and where to install fish passes.

The Kielder Scheme and its Local Enquiries, 1972–1973

In 1859, Walter White recorded that he had been told how Alston lead miners 'on the Tyne, not having enough water for their purposes, once cut a channel to feed their own stream with water from the Tees'.[9] Little more than a century later, the three rivers, Tyne, Wear and Tees, were connected by the Kielder Scheme in a much more technologically sophisticated and audacious manner, installing a large-scale dam near the source of the North Tyne at Kielder and connecting three rivers using a subterranean aqueduct. Following their initial idea to create Kielder Dam in 1965, the Northumbrian River Authority developed more detailed plans throughout the late 1960s and submitted an official proposal to the government in 1969. Kielder dam was a relative latecomer in the international context that included the Colorado's Hoover Dam, the Tennessee Valley Authority dams and the Columbia River dam schemes of the 1930s. However, the Glen Canyon dam was opened on the Colorado in Arizona in 1963. To consider objections to Kielder Dam, a Public Inquiry was held in Newcastle from 3 February until 15 March 1972. Inspections were carried out between 16 and 23 March and the plans were approved by the Secretary for the Environment in June 1973 following a brief re-opening of the Public Inquiry on 19 June 1973.[10] Construction work began in 1975 and the dam was opened by Queen Elizabeth II in 1982. The aqueduct linking the Tyne, Wear and the

---

9. White, *Northumberland*, p. 27 (chapter 4).
10. TNA, HLG 127/1286: Northumbrian River Authority, Kielder Water Reservoir Scheme: applications for licences in connection with impounding and abstracting water in connection with the Kielder Water Reservoir; TNA, AT 35/108: Procedural aspects of the post enquiry consideration of the Kielder Dam scheme, item 38, letter from the Department of the Environment, (14 May 1973).

Tees runs between a pumping station on the south bank of main River Tyne, just downstream of the weir at Riding Mill, southwards to connect to the River Wear and the River Tees. Diversions of water from Kielder can thereby nourish the flows of all three rivers rather than only the Tyne.

Kielder Water and the adjoining, smaller regulating Bakethin Reservoir (which is never allowed to dry out) have a combined capacity of 44,600 million gallons. Bakethin's capacity is 740 million gallons. The main impact of the dam was to artificially remove seasonal flow variations. Kielder's operating licence is based on a Minimum Maintained Flow (MMF), measured at a gauging station at Bywell on the south bank of the main Tyne, about halfway between Wylam and Hexham. The Kielder scheme was planned to be operated towards hydropower optimisation, within the parameters of minimum prescribed flows, requirements for abstraction and migration flow releases.[11] The 1971 Northumbrian River Authority's application for a licence from the government to impound and abstract water through the Kielder Scheme proposed to release water at a continuous rate into the North Tyne river, at least 12.5 million gallons per day between December and March and at least 25 million gallons per day between April and November.[12] The amount of water flowing past the Bywell gauging station would not be permitted to fall below eighty million gallons per day at any time and abstractions to the Wear and Tees using a pumping station at Riding Mill and a subterranean aqueduct would not take place unless a minimum of 200 million gallons per day were flowing past Bywell gauging station.[13] The licence the River Authority asked for would permit them to abstract a maximum of 50,000 million gallons per year, 200 million gallons per day and 8.5 million gallons per hour as long as the minimum flow rates were maintained at Bywell.[14] The rocks beneath the reservoir site are an alternating sequence of sandstones, shales and mudstones with several intercalated seams of coal. The sandstones were about forty feet thick and permeable whereas the mudstones and shales were impermeable, which meant that the movement of underground water could be controlled by injecting cement into the cracks in the impermeable rock. On top of the bedrock were superficial materials such as glacial boulder clay and alluvial gravels,

---

11. C. Gibbins et al., 'Developing ecologically acceptable river flow regimes: a case study of Kielder Reservoir and the Kielder water transfer system', *Fisheries Management and Ecology* 8 (2001): 463–485.

12. TNA, HLG 127/1285: Northumbrian River Authority, Kielder Water Reservoir Scheme: applications for licences in connection with impounding and abstracting water in connection with the Kielder Water Reservoir (12 May 1971).

13. Ibid.

14. Ibid.

Chapter 7. Damming the Tyne

sand and clay, less than twenty feet thick. The clay required for the rolled clay core and outer shoulders of the dam was to be excavated from the area of the reservoir basin without exposing the solid rocks. Sand and gravel were to be taken from the river alluvium upstream from the dam.[15]

In July 1971, the Tyne Fishery District Riparian Owners and Occupiers Association wrote to the Northumbrian River Authority to express their concern that the initial plans posed serious risks to both migratory and non-migratory fish. They advised them that the minimum flow rates at Bywell should be set at 'far in excess of 200 million gallons per day if migratory fish are to have a reasonable chance of survival in the lower reaches and tidal waters of the river'.[16] Riparian landowners abstracting water from the river for agricultural purposes were not liable to be charged by the water authority. The Water Resources Act 1963 stipulated that charges could only be levied 'in respect of services performed, facilities provided or rights made available by them'.[17] Northumberland County Council expressed their opinion in July 1971 that the abstractors of water on the Wear and Tees should have to compensate Northumberland County Council for 'the extra financial burden which the authority's proposals to transfer water to areas south of the Tyne would involve'.[18] The council also thought it was unfair that the Kielder Scheme did not make any provision for transferring water to the rivers Wansbeck and Blyth in Northumberland, which also underpinned quite extensive industries, while going to such lengths to supply water to the Wear and the Tees.[19] A day later, on 23 July 1971, the Northumberland Wildlife Trust expressed serious ecological concerns, as they foresaw

> a net loss of wildlife resources, thus aggravating a decline which is already serious elsewhere as a result of misuses of technology and a lack of ecological awareness. A wide variety of habitats would be lost since the reservoir would inundate the floor of the valley, which was spared to some extent when the forestry commission carried out large scale afforestation during the earlier years of this century.

---

15. Ibid.
16. TNA, HLG 127/1285: Northumbrian River Authority, Kielder Water Reservoir Scheme: applications for licences in connection with impounding and abstracting water in connection with the Kielder Water Reservoir, letter from the Tyne Fishery District Riparian Owners Association to the Northumbrian River Authority (13 Jul. 1971).
17. TNA, Legislation Database, Water Resources Act, 1963, online at: http://www.legislation.gov.uk/ukpga/1963/38/contents [webpage accessed 11 Jul. 2016].
18. TNA, HLG 127/1285: Northumbrian River Authority, Kielder Water Reservoir Scheme: applications for licences in connection with impounding and abstracting water in connection with the Kielder Water Reservoir, letter from Northumberland County Council to the Northumbrian River Authority (22 Jul. 1971).
19. Ibid.

These habitats include relict meadow grasslands, with unmown steep banksides, riverside alder woodlands, marshes and ponds, river shingle, scattered mixed deciduous woodlands, vegetated spoil heaps and railway embankments, valuable geological sections through Scremerston Coal Group as well as a number of scattered rock outcrops, and several derelict buildings. All of these support an extensive assemblage of flora and fauna which would be drastically reduced in this area if the reservoir was constructed.[20]

The key words are 'as a result of the misuses of technology and a lack of ecological awareness', which effectively accused the Northumbrian River Authority of ecological ignorance in relation to the potential consequences of their seriously unwise and irresponsible actions. The Trust was certainly confident for its time, lecturing and educating the government and the river authority about conservation and ecology. Mr A. Chown produced an engineering assessment in 1972, in which he mentioned that abstracting river water from the Tyne to flow down the Tyne-Tees connecting tunnel would reduce the water coming down to flush the estuary, worsening the very severe pollution in the Tyne estuary.[21] On the basis of these three initial objections, the Secretary for the Environment opened a Public Inquiry.

The scheme required approval by the Secretary of State for the Environment, unless the government could pass a private Bill through Parliament, as it was to flood 1,500 hectares (3,700 acres) of land which was vested in the Minister of Agriculture and managed by the Forestry Commission. In total, 69 houses (primarily forming the former coal mining community of Plashetts, whose mine was operational between 1850 and 1964), eight forestry workers' holdings, five farms, 720 hectares (1,800 acres) of mixed age plantations, a rugby clubhouse and a camp site were to be flooded, requiring total compensation of around £800,000.[22] The C200 road would also be flooded and require complete replacement. The final decision to go ahead with the Kielder Scheme was made in June 1973 by the Secretary of State for the Environment and MP for Hexham, Geoffrey Rippon. This decision followed a Public Inquiry held in the Moothall in Newcastle on Tyne from 3 February to 15 March 1972, which concluded that the scheme should go ahead. During this Inquiry, incidentally, the river smelt so bad that one of its meetings had to be stopped. The Public

---

20. TNA, HLG 127/1285: Northumbrian River Authority, Kielder Water Reservoir Scheme: applications for licences in connection with impounding and abstracting water in connection with the Kielder Water Reservoir, 1971, letter from Northumberland Wildlife Trust, (23 Jul. 1971).
21. TNA, MAF 135/775: Engineering Assessor's report, February and March 1972, item 23b, p. 44.
22. TNA, MAF 135/775: Northumbrian Water Authority (Kielder Water) Order 1974; includes Report of the Local Inquiry into the Kielder Water Scheme, item 48.

Chapter 7. Damming the Tyne

Inquiry was reopened on 19 June 1973 in order to hear more about seventeen proposed alternative sites, but again concluded that the scheme at Kielder should go ahead. The Order implementing the Kielder Water Scheme came into effect on 21 May 1974, preparatory work began that year and construction began on the site in 1975.

Unsurprisingly, many local people became very anxious about the potential aesthetic impact on their landscape of an earth dam measuring 3,750 feet in length with a maximum height of 168 feet. Some local people came together to form the North Tyne Preservation Society, and they formed a substantial element of the overall resistance to the scheme. However, not all organisations were wholly negative about the scheme. For example, the Northumbrian River Authority's report of the 1972 Public Inquiry noted that the Countryside Commission 'do not think the present landscape value of the site justifies an objection on their part' and that 'with the lake's intricate form and diversity of shapes and settings a thing of beauty could be created'.[23] Moreover, the Ramblers' Association said 'the natural scenery of the Kielder area, although originally pleasant and remote hill country, has no dramatic qualities and its value as walking country has been decreased by the coniferous afforestation'.[24] For most local residents, however, the landscape and its river North Tyne was something far more personal and ultimately possessed a far deeper meaning for them than it did to either the Countryside Commission or the Ramblers' Association. For example, Mr W. Charlton, a local resident, said

> There would also be a serious aesthetic loss. Until about 25 years ago the North Tyne was a quiet pastoral vale with scattered hill farms and cottages all the way up the valley. Much of this has now been lost to forest but that does not make what remains any less precious to the inhabitants of the valley. The reservoir would make the valley a less pleasant place to live in even if it were made more attractive to city dwellers for recreation'.[25]

In stark contrast to Charlton's intimate, personal and very warm words about a landscape which clearly meant a very great deal to him, is the description of the valley's landscape written by the Northumbrian River Authority in their report of the Public Inquiry in 1972:

> The reservoir site and its immediate surroundings form an irregular basin shaped area with the river winding along the floor with attractive farmland and de-

---

23. TNA, MAF 135/775: Northumbrian Water Authority (Kielder Water) Order 1974; includes Report of the Local Inquiry into the Kielder Water Scheme, item 23a.
24. Ibid.
25. Ibid.

ciduous trees along its banks. The forestry commission's coniferous plantations cover the surrounding hills and in places stretch down into the valley which they dominate. Kielder is a formal Forestry Commission village and Falstone an irregular settlement with attractive stone houses and a church.[26]

Overall, from over 200 objections, the grounds of objection were split into the following categories:

Grounds of Objection	No.
The reservoir would destroy a beautiful valley	69
The existence of more suitable sites for reservoirs	40
The loss of people's homes	39
The effects on communities of Kielder and Falstone	33
The loss of farmland	26

Figure 11. Grounds of Objection to Kielder Scheme submitted to Public Inquiry (1972)[27]

The category representing the largest number of objections was, unsurprisingly, that the reservoir would destroy a beautiful valley. This reflects the high esteem in which the Upper North Tyne valley was held by very many – albeit mainly local – people.

Susan Taylor, a resident of Castle Drive, Kielder village, wrote to the Public Inquiry explaining in depth her opinions about the landscape of the valley and its important differences from the mountainous scenery of the Lake District:

> It is overlooked (purposely?) that, unlike the North Tyne, the Lake District is a mountainous country which can tolerate huge expanses of water. A reservoir in the North Tyne would leave only the monotony of low spruce covered hills. Part of the attraction of the North Tyne is the contrast between the dark green hills and the bare moorland valley floor. I find it very difficult to believe that anyone can sincerely believe that a reservoir would improve our valley.[28]

Susan had a very clear view of her local landscape, what would fit into it and what would be aesthetically incongruous. A letter from Kielder Parish Council in July 1971 explained

---

26. Ibid.
27. Ibid.
28. TNA HLG 127/1280: Documents submitted to the Kielder inquiry, item 8, letter of objection from Miss Susan Taylor, 5 Castle Drive, Kielder (18 June 1971).

Chapter 7. Damming the Tyne

> That the beauty of the valley will be spoilt, when there is every reason to preserve what rural beauty remains to us. The character of the valley will be changed, to the loss of the inhabitants and visitors who enjoy its present beauty of quiet. The Parish Council is concerned about the appearance of the dams themselves, especially the main dam viewed from Falstone, and about the shore line which will leave a variable width of mud round the perimeter of the reservoir.[29]

In response to this letter, the River Authority made an important compromise to install a second smaller dam to create Bakethin Reservoir.

> It was realised that on drawing down the water level in the proposed Kielder Water reservoir there would be an area NW of Bakethin which could dry out during periods of prolonged water demand leaving an exposed surface devoid of vegetation which could be objectionable. To avoid this it is proposed to construct Work No 2 – the Bakethin Dam, whereby the water stored at the north western end of the reservoir will be retained at a high level when the main storage is drawn down.[30]

This regulatory, subsidiary dam would cut off the northern part of the reservoir (known as Bakethin) behind a dam measuring 600 feet in length and sixty feet in height.

In September 1974, the Forestry Commission in London submitted a report of the Kielder Scheme Public Inquiry to the Minister of Agriculture. In it they admitted that the reservoir would flood 'the most attractive part of the North Tyne valley', having 'an adverse effect on the landscape in the short term', but they emphasised that 'in the longer term it should add considerably to the visual attractions of the area', as well as providing 'facilities for a whole range of water sports and activities'.[31] They emphasised that 'the traditional character of the district may change, but the additional benefits from tourism and amenity services should justify this'.[32] The proposers of the scheme and the local and national governors who passed the plans conceptualised the impact of the scheme in terms of a simple exchange of some relatively small utilitarian assets for another much larger one, a view that seems to have left little room for the more imaginative and very long-established webs of meaning which

---

29. TNA HLG 127/1280: Documents submitted to the Kielder inquiry, item 91, letter from Kielder Parish Council, received 22 Jul. 1971 [not dated].
30. TNA, MAF 135/775: Northumbrian Water Authority (Kielder Water) Order 1974; includes Report of the Local Inquiry into the Kielder Water Scheme, item 23a.
31. TNA, MAF 135/775: Northumbrian Water Authority (Kielder Water) Order 1974; includes Report of the Local Inquiry into the Kielder Water Scheme, item 48.
32. TNA, MAF 135/775: Northumbrian Water Authority (Kielder Water) Order 1974; includes Report of the Local Inquiry into the Kielder Water Scheme, item 23a.

characterised local people's relationships with this landscape and riverscape. The Forestry Commission in London noted in their report to the Minister of Agriculture,

> This is a wild landscape and there is not a strong case for its preservation on these grounds. It has not been designated as an area of exceptional beauty and only a very small portion is included in a national park. The drowning of the valley would mean the loss of a varied and picturesque humanised landscape of considerable beauty and is to be regretted, although most people would find a lake such as this an exceptionally large expanse of water set in large scale scenes – more enjoyable.[33]

The report went on to discuss the architectural merits of the buildings that were to be drowned, going as far as to say that those buildings were 'beautifully related to their environment':

> Some seventy buildings would be lost. None is of outstanding architectural or historic importance and none is listed, however, most are of pleasant designs in the local vernacular beautifully related to their environment and their loss would be regrettable. With sensitive planting design it would only be a matter of time before the landscape looked completely natural.[34]

Their comment that the landscape would come to be perceived, eventually, as natural turns out to have been prescient because many visitors and some of the inhabitants who have moved to the area since the construction of the dam do refer to the landscape as 'natural'.[35] Funding was made available within the scheme to preserve the Victorian Kielder Viaduct, a listed monument in need of substantial repairs. Because Bakethin Reservoir was to flood the base of five of its arches, the engineers made efforts to protect them with concrete surrounds, which were grit-blasted for aesthetic reasons. When designing the main dam, the engineers and architects hoped that its pronounced curves would enable it to merge into the hills of the valley. The landscape architects ensured that the downstream face was finished in moorland topsoil and planted with indigenous grasses, but while the dam itself has been sheltered by deciduous trees quite effectively, the seven-mile long reservoir is very obvious indeed, and conjures a landscape that is incongruous in the UK and which arguably has more in

---

33. Ibid.
34. Ibid.
35. D. Moon and L. Skelton, 'Environmental Change: A Local Perspective on Global Processes', in P. Coates, D. Moon and P. Warde (eds), *Local Places, Global Processes: Histories of Environmental Change in Britain and Beyond* (Oxford: Oxbow Books, 2016), pp. 212–213.

Chapter 7. Damming the Tyne

Figure 12. Kielder Reservoir from Leaplish Waterside Park (Photograph: Gordon Ball)

common with the flat, forested landscapes of northern Scandinavia, Canada or the north-eastern states of the US.

The people who protested against the Kielder Scheme were not able to prevent it from changing the North Tyne valley irreversibly. However, the Public Inquiry's archives preserve the powerful feelings of loss, disempowerment and heartfelt pain expressed by an isolated, rural community who loved their landscape and their river in very complex terms, as a dramatic environmental change was inflicted on them. These socio-environmental relationships were incomprehensible to government officials who saw the riverscape in utilitarian terms, in much the same way as the recently disbanded TIC had viewed the Tyne estuary. They commented that the landscape was not particularly beautiful or unique and they used the fact that it was already partially down the road of degradation, due to the planting of massive dark swathes of forest, to justify their plans to degrade it even further. The land was purchased by force under the Water Resources Act 1963 and the Compulsory Purchase Act 1965. Particular focus was given throughout the Public Inquiry to recreation, to ensure that the public felt they were being compensated for their loss, which for some involved the enormous upheaval of having their homes purchased compulsorily. Following the unsuccessful attempts to prevent the Kielder scheme's construction,

Figure 13. Kielder Reservoir (Photograph: Gordon Ball)

the president of the North Tyne Valley Preservation Society, Sir Rupert Speir, a former MP for Hexham in Northumberland, said, 'we have put up a good fight' and 'naturally, we shall be watching all the development work like hawks to see that the damage to the environment is kept to the minimum'.[36] And so round two began: the fierce debates over whether or not to install fish passes.

The Fish Pass Issue

After the Kielder scheme plan was passed in June 1973, intense debate ensued over the question of fish passes. A valve shaft and fish pass was proposed as part of the early plans in both dams, but from the outset the Northumbrian River Authority were unenthusiastic about installing what they considered to be 'inordinately expensive fish passes'.[37] By the Salmon and Freshwater Fisheries Act 1923, passes had to be provided to facilitate the ascent of adult salmon from the estuary and the descent of smolts and kelts (salmon which has spawned). There were already fish passes at the weir at Riding Mill, and they had been planned at Kielder and Bakethin dams in the form of traditional pool type passes. The Agriculture, Fisheries and Food Ministry was unimpressed by the

---

36. 'Tyne Valley Flooding Approved', *The Times* (5 Oct. 1973).
37. TNA, MAF 209/3042: Northumbrian Water Authority (Kielder Water) Order 1974: fish pass facilities, 1974–1977, letter from I. Allan to Mr Small, Ministry of Agriculture, Fisheries and Food (19 Nov.1974).

Chapter 7. Damming the Tyne

River Authority's disinclination to fund the fish passes, stating:

> This recommendation attempts to put the onus on the water authority to use the Kielder scheme for what I regard as the best benefit to the River Tyne as a whole, both fishery wise and recreational wise and the implication is that if they do not do so we would regard the non-provision of fish passes as a retrograde step especially in view of the assistance which the minister has already given to the authority in its attempts to re-establish the river as a salmon fishery by preventing netting in the mouth of the river (as was being well practiced) and by regulating, additionally the inshore drift net fishery.[38]

In the Minister's mind, the 'best benefit' to the River Tyne 'as a whole' consisted of fisheries and recreational benefits for society. Perhaps, today, such a statement would include a whole range of other benefits, including many different wildlife and plant species, as well as hydrological and geological considerations. Nevertheless, the Minister was clearly in support of installing fish passes and definitely valued the Tyne's fish life.

If the water authority had installed the expensive fish passes into both dams, it would only have enabled spawning in about 3,000 square yards of ground upstream of the reservoirs. Gravel extraction over the centuries having taken a huge toll, spawning grounds were already limited. The water authority wanted to produce extensive supplies of salmon at a hatchery that would stock the feeder stream below Kielder dam. This alternative was approved by all who objected to the River Authority's refusal to install fish passes. As the Ministry of Agriculture, Fisheries and Food fully appreciated, in its letter to the River Authority,

> had all the original spawning grounds once available to fish before gravel extraction took place on these tributaries been still available, it would have been worthwhile to have enabled natural spawning to take place but there was no assurance from the water authority that the gravel extractions would stop.[39]

Consequently, the Minister concluded 'I have taken the line, therefore, that the authority should make the fullest possible use of the Kielder scheme for smolt rearing by the stocking of the two reservoirs [i.e. Bakethin and Kielder] and of the tributary streams coming into them', noting that the fisheries experts 'have already said that these streams can be considerably improved as salmon nurseries and I think that this ought to be done'.[40] The Ministry was reluctant

---

38. Ibid.
39. Ibid.
40. Ibid.

to clear the tributary streams of brown trout because this would have angered the large fishing community of 3,850 anglers who each paid £1.50 annually for their fishing licence from the local authority. The Ministry explained that the migratory salmon and trout would be 'hard put to survive let alone thrive' sharing the same waters and expressed its concern that salmon smolts would be subject to predation by the brown trout.[41] The spawning grounds in the feeder streams into the Kielder Reservoir were already being used for trout fishing, so these would have to be divested of trout before they could be used as salmon spawning grounds, which they feared would severely anger the trout fishermen.[42]

After continued debate over this controversial and complex ecological issue, detailed plans for stocking the rivers with migratory fish from a hatchery were prepared and the plans for fish passes were scrapped. The hatchery was constructed at a cost of £350,000 which was considerably less expensive than the proposed fish passes. Work began on the hatchery at Butteryhaugh, Kielder, in July 1977. This followed the Northumbrian River Authority's explanation to the Ministry of Agriculture, Fisheries and Food in January 1977 that commissioning of the hatchery had to be urgently scheduled for November 1977 as the 'progeny from spawning in that year will be denied a passage down river in 1979 by the plugging of the dam'.[43] The aim was to produce 100,000 under yearlings and around 60,000 yearlings annually.[44] The planners knew that the intake at Riding Mill would not suck in the fish providing the water velocity there was not above 1½ to 2 feet per second and they made provision for the expansion of the existing salmon hatchery to cater for the hatching of five million eggs. They planned to incorporate into the main dam the means of trapping adult salmon and sea trout to provide the eggs. They were confident that the transfers of water between the three rivers would not deter adult salmon from returning to their parent river, noting 'proposed transfers of waters would not have any material effect on the ecology of the receiving waters so far as fisheries are concerned'.[45] Seven out of 21 miles of spawning grounds were being drowned by the reservoir, but the planners still maintained that

---

41. TNA, MAF 209/3042: Northumbrian Water Authority (Kielder Water) Order 1974: fish pass facilities, 1974–1977, memo from D. Gilbert to Mr Small, Ministry of Agriculture, Fisheries and Food (4 Dec. 1974).

42. Ibid.

43. TNA, MAF 209/3042: Northumbrian Water Authority (Kielder Water) Order 1974: fish pass facilities, 1974–1977, letter from N. Ruffle, Director of Planning and Scientific Services, Northumbrian Water Authority, to Mr Small, Ministry of Agriculture, Fisheries and Food (24 Jan. 1977).

44. 'Fish hatchery on the Tyne', *Anglers' Mail* (20 Jul. 1977).

45. TNA, MAF 135/775: Northumbrian River Authority, 'Local Inquiry into Applications concerning the Kielder Water Scheme', Item 23a, pp. 41–42 (Apr. 1972).

Chapter 7. Damming the Tyne

if anything, the maintenance of satisfactory volumes of water would increase salmon survival. The River Authority also proposed provision for fish passes on present obstructions which would open three further miles of spawning gravel on the Warks Burn, Tarret Burn, Houxty Burn and about six miles on the West Allan, all feeding into the Tyne below the dams, which would have provided fifteen miles of spawning grounds, eight more than were functioning before the construction of the reservoirs. Neither the Northumbrian Rivers Authority nor the Ministry of Agriculture, Fisheries and Food can be accused of having completely sacrificed the North Tyne's fish life as the Kielder scheme's plans and construction developed. However, it is clear that the latter body, from its relatively powerful position within central government, expressed a greater inclination to safeguard the ecological needs of the fish than the Northumbrian Rivers Authority, which did not completely abandon the needs of the fish but nevertheless did prioritise economic considerations above these ecological needs. The Kielder salmon hatchery still functions successfully today. It still fulfils its statutory requirement to produce 160,000 salmon parr each year, which was the estimated loss to the salmon population of constructing the dam, but at its full capacity it can produce half a million salmon parr. Wild parr normally spend two years in the Tyne before they smolt and migrate out to the North Sea and north, usually to west Greenland before they come full circle, back to the Tyne to spawn and die.

Conclusion

As Christine McCulloch observes, 'no word expresses adequately the aesthetics of domination evoked by the spectacle of a large-scale landscape which has been radically and recently imposed by the ambition of a handful of politicians, engineers and scientists'.[46] Perhaps few events can force people to think more carefully about their relationship with their local river, its contribution to the wider landscape and ecosystem and the role it plays in their social, cultural and economic lives than the announcement of plans to dam its flow with an enormous concrete dam. As Richard White observed in relation to the political debates surrounding the planning of the Columbia River's Grand Coulee Dam in the 1930s, 'like Superman, it was always greater than its objects of comparison: larger than the Great Pyramid, higher than Niagara, more concrete

---

46. C. McCulloch, 'Kielder Water and Forest Park: The City in the Country', in Coates, Moon and Warde (eds), *Local Places, Global Processes*, p. 265.

than a transcontinental highway'.[47] In the North Tyne valley, an outpouring of objections explained local people's relationships with their River North Tyne in huge and very emotive detail. Some were only concerned about the loss of homes and community facilities. But many were concerned about the environmental impact of the dam, and some people still express those concerns. The debate is still unresolved. With the benefit of hindsight, Dr Ceri Gibson, who worked as an environmental scientist for Tyne Rivers Trust until 2015, would like to re-wild the river, which she defines as 'helping habitat to re-establish itself … where it's been altered', commenting 'I'd quite like to take Kielder Dam away and go back to how the river was'.[48] Alternatively, Martin Stark, an environmental consultant who has lived in Haltwhistle since 2011, said 'I love it [i.e. the Kielder Dam]' and he thinks 'it's a huge asset to the North Tyne'.[49] Forty years after the Kielder scheme was passed, the great bulk of the water that the dam was built to supply has never been needed. While it proved helpful in mitigating the effects of particularly severe droughts, it was not used to underpin the expansion, or even the maintenance, of the Teesside chemical industry. Moreover, in the decade following the opening of Kielder dam in 1982, the North Tyne angling community expressed complaints about the perceived lower oxygenation of water emanating from deep in Kielder Reservoir and about the different temperature of the water released from the reservoir.[50] Rather contrarily, some anglers have complained about the lack of heavy natural spate water while others are concerned that sudden and unexpected releases from the dam, used to produce hydro-electricity, cause problems for wading anglers.[51] However, as Marshall explains, the water's oxygenation increases as it 'tumbles' down the North Tyne valley and the temperature differences 'only affect the redds within a mile or two of the dam face'.[52] He also believed, writing in 1992, that the Kielder hatchery counteracts any losses.

Nonetheless, the dam created a new and different relationship with the river in the North Tyne valley, not only irreversibly so for local residents, but also for some 250,000 tourists who visit the area each year to enjoy a wide range of outdoor pursuits and for those who benefit from the hydro-electricity

---

47. White, *Organic Machine*, p. 58.
48. Interview with Ceri Gibson, born in Farnham, 1974, environmental scientist; recorded by Leona Skelton, at Tyne Rivers Trust Offices, Corbridge, 21 Jan. 2015, 11 a.m.
49. Interview with Martin Stark, born in the Wirral, 1956, fisheries and environmental consultant; recorded by Leona Skelton, at Tyne Rivers Trust Offices, Corbridge, 20 Jan. 2015, 11 a.m.
50. Marshall, *Tyne Waters*, pp. 134–135.
51. Ibid.
52. Ibid.

Chapter 7. Damming the Tyne

that the scheme produces, which is sufficient to power a small market town. Kielder Hydro is England's largest generator of hydro-electricity, but placing it into a global hierarchy of hydro-power production renders it almost insignificant. A water release from Kielder Reservoir of 1,300 million litres per day through the dam's two hydro-electricity turbines can produce enough power to light a town housing approximately 11,000 people whereas the Columbia River's Grand Coulee Dam, the USA's largest hydro-electricity producer (but only the sixth largest in the world!), generates enough electricity to supply 2.3 million households across several states.[53] Michael Marshall describes the flow of Kielder's released dam water: 'it rises high in the air as it leaves the face of the dam – twin jets of foaming white water'.[54] This is an awesome and powerful 'enviro-technical' spectacle, which epitomises and symbolises the totally blended, enmeshed and fused character of all of our socio-environmental relationships with the River Tyne's flows throughout its catchment over five centuries, but we must remain mindful of its relatively small scale within its global context.

Figure 14. The River North Tyne below Kielder Dam (Photograph: Gordon Ball)

---

53. US Department of the Interior, Bureau of Reclamation, 'Reclamation: Managing Water in the West', online at: https://www.usbr.gov/pn/grandcoulee/pubs/factsheet.pdf [accessed: 3 Jul. 2016].
54. Marshall, *Tyne Waters*, p. 134.

Chapter 8

'A BIG RIVER?'
REGENERATION, TOURISM AND THE CULTURAL MEANING OF THE TYNE, 1972–2015

Introduction

In 1893, a huge wooden jetty, Dunston Staiths, was opened on the Tyne's south bank to facilitate the export of ever-increasing volumes of coal out of the river. Less than a century later, in 1980, the *MV Lindo* was the last ship to receive coal from the staiths.[1] Since then, it has literally been left out for the birds, largely abandoned and unused by humans, except for its brief moment of fame in 1990 when it became the site of the Garden Festival. This was an attempt by the then Secretary of State Michael Heseltine to regenerate five deindustrialised cities across the UK (Liverpool, Stoke-on-Trent, Glasgow, Gateshead and Ebbw Vale). It is now a landmark Scheduled Monument, Grade II structure and Europe's largest wooden structure. As Tim Ingold highlights in relation to this bulky vestige of the Tyne's industrial heyday, the argument 'is no longer about the physical load it will bear, but about the weight of the past as it presses on the future'.[2] Recently, the renowned sculptor Wolfgang Weileder designed 'Cone', a temporary artistic edifice in the shape of the historically ubiquitous coal-fired Bottle Kiln (nine metres high and seven metres in diameter), which in 2014 was assembled on Dunston Staiths from eleven tonnes of slabs of a sustainable plastic material called Aquadyne and then dismantled to encourage us to understand buildings as temporary 'scaffolds for the life process that unfolds in them'.[3] The temporary nature of Weileder's 'Cone' reminds us of the vulnerability and often short-term existence of the structures installed into a riverscape, compared to the far longer-term endurance and awesome natural

---

1. S. Guy and A. Connelly, 'Placing Jetty', in S. Guy (ed.), *Catalyst: Art, Sustainability and Place in the Work of Wolfgang Weileder* (Berlin: Kerber Verlag, 2015), p. 35.
2. Tim Ingold, 'Foreword', in Guy, (ed.), *Catalyst*, p. 11.
3. Ibid., p. 13.

Chapter 8. 'A Big River?'

power of river systems. Cone's creator hoped to 'rescue' the term sustainability from 'the vacuous, rhetorical abstractions of environmental policy-speak, and to bring it down to earth in the vivid presence of materials, work and structure'.[4] In much the same way, this chapter attempts to articulate and explore the multiple and multi-layered meanings of the post-industrial Tyne, and the competing visions for its future, in a down-to-earth manner and using a framework which stretches beyond policy-makers' narrow definitions of ecological sustainability and environmental sensitivity. Just as the weight of the past presses on the future of Dunston Staiths, so too does the past weigh substantially on the River Tyne's future in both obvious and far more subtle ways.

The dramatically improved environmental health of the Tyne nowadays, signalled by the return of its prestigious title as England's greatest salmon river, is cherished across Tyneside, in north-east England and more widely throughout the UK, especially among anglers, conservationists and tourists who have visited the recently regenerated Newcastle-Gateshead quayside. The dramatic aesthetic changes to its riverscape, enabled by deindustrialisation and the subsequent clean-up of the river in the late twentieth century, have nurtured a relatively recent blossoming of interest in the Tyne's environmental health, its cultural heritage and its flora and fauna. By taking a step back and asking oneself what actually is a river, we can reaffirm the parameters of our definition and understand the Tyne as one particular and unique member of the wide range of different seaward flows that have been admitted to the club of rivers. For example, does a river have to move life-sustaining oxygenated water throughout its course or can its water be completely deoxygenated or full of toxic substances for some part of its course? Does it have to move water at all or can a dry channel that previously hosted a seaward flow of water still be called a river? Does a river have to provide a thriving habitat for flora and fauna? Does it have to support riparian industry and maritime trade? Are culverted rivers still real and 'natural' rivers? Charles Rangeley-Wilson draws attention to a remarkable example of a river in Slovenia, the Ljubljanica, which rises from and disappears into the earth to form seven seemingly separate streams with seven different names (the Trbuhovica, the Obrh, the Strzen, Rak, Pivka, Univa and Ljubljanica), and he ponders the controversy over whether or not this should be considered as one river, before the water was dyed and traced to confirm that the streams were indeed parts of a whole.[5] In the former lead-mining area of the Derbyshire Peak District, the upper reach of the River Lathkill mysteriously disappears during

---

4.   Ibid.
5.   Rangeley-Wilson, *Silt Road*, p. 123.

hot weather and periods of drought into subterranean drainage channels, known as soughs, which were constructed to drain local lead mines. While nobody would argue that the Tyne is not a river today, its status was questioned when it bubbled with toxic gases and was declared biologically dead in the 1960s, as many labelled it an open sewer. In the early nineteenth century, the main river estuary was disparagingly termed a 'creek' by those who wished to express their anger that Newcastle Corporation was failing to improve it structurally to its full capacity. Today, the Tyne's membership in the club of rivers seems fairly secure, but is it still a 'big river', if indeed it ever truly was, and what exactly does that mean? Are big rivers dimensionally large, clean, economically productive, heavily engineered, pure, natural, ecologically healthy or popular tourist attractions? Can they be all of these things, or only some? This issue is discussed throughout the chapter in relation to a plethora of different relationships between people and the river, in the past and present, and in relation to a diverse range of different visions for the river's future.

Iconography of the Newcastle-Gateshead Quayside

As a result of the regeneration project, overseen by the Tyne and Wear Development Corporation, One North East and several riparian councils, most notably Newcastle Council and Gateshead Council, today's riverscape of the Newcastle-Gateshead quayside is dramatically different from that of the 1980s.

On a summer's day, the industrial heritage of the river is difficult to find on the quayside among the bustling bars and restaurants, the river cruises and the hordes of tourists. The flagship regeneration project of the 1990s and 2000s was a strategic attempt by Newcastle Council and Gateshead Council to make a cultural investment of around £250 million in order to generate private economic investment in the area as it struggled to adapt to a deindustrialised regional economy. The BALTIC Contemporary Art Gallery was developed in a flour warehouse (originally constructed in 1949 and used as an animal food factory) at a cost of £46 million; the Sage Gateshead Music Centre was designed by Foster and Partners and cost £70 million; and the Gateshead Millennium Bridge cost £22 million (the world's first tilting bridge which won the RIBA Stirling Prize for architecture in 2002).[6] In recent years, 'Seaside at the Quayside', a mock seaside complete with beach huts, palm trees, sand and

---

6. S. Miles, '"Our Tyne": Iconic Regeneration and the Revitalisation of Identity in NewcastleGateshead', *Urban Studies* 42 (5–6) (2005): 917.

Chapter 8. 'A Big River?'

Figure 15. Newcastle-Gateshead Quayside, 1983 (Photograph: G. Melvin)

Figure 16. Newcastle-Gateshead Quayside from the Gateshead Millennium Bridge, 2015 (Photograph: Gordon Ball)

Figure 17. Newcastle-Gateshead Bridges (Photograph: Gordon Ball)

Figure 18. 'Seaside at the Quayside' (Photograph: Gordon Ball)

Chapter 8. 'A Big River?'

Figure 19. Gateshead Millennium Bridge (Photograph: Gordon Ball)

deck chairs, has been provided for the use of local people and tourists near the north side of the Gateshead Millennium Bridge.

Between 2008 and 2009, a small-scale barrage was installed near the mouth of the Ouseburn, a tributary of the Tyne in Newcastle, at a cost of £4.7 million. This relatively small construction was designed exclusively for aesthetic reasons, to prevent the tide going out to expose mud, silt, debris and malodours in this intended attractive waterside environment.

While the regeneration scheme has undoubtedly created a new and different riverscape, which appears to have made the very best of the vacuum left behind by deindustrialisation, it would be naive to describe this project as a total success. While the cultural facilities have attracted tourists, the employment opportunities created are largely casual, low-paid and seasonal. Arguably, this new vision for the river, for Newcastle and Gateshead and for the wider region, has been superimposed onto the local people's complex history, society and identity with very little forethought about the cultural fit and the real benefits of a modern art gallery or a classical music hall in a city that played such an enormous role in the UK's heavy industry. Many appreciate and celebrate these new additions and the complete re-conceptualisation of their quayside passionately, but some do not. As Steven Miles observes, 'there is undoubtedly a danger in assuming that cultural investment can provide some kind of an alternative future for all deindustrialised cities' and he highlights 'the social impacts of culture-led regeneration are not necessarily always positive'.[7] The new riverscape certainly makes an aesthetic impression, but it also tends to hide quite problematic industrial legacies that have not yet been addressed, such as relatively high unemployment and underemployment compared to the rest of the UK. As a sociologist, Alice Mah, noted, 'various sources, including interviews, newspaper articles and city council documents, indicate that there may be some residual contamination in parts of Walker from industrial activities'.[8] The shiny and new view as one gazes east from the Tyne Bridge hides quite effectively some serious flaws and local controversies in relation to the economic wisdom of this particular use of such a great and potentially economically productive river. And it diverts eyes away from the nearby abandoned and derelict industrial buildings and contaminated riparian sites both above and below the Tyne Bridge.

In a more positive vein, Miles highlights that investment in culture 'can reinvigorate the relationship between culture, place and personal identity and offer a permanent legacy', arguing that in the case of the Newcastle-Gateshead quayside the new iconography there 'offers a symbolic representation of a region that can succeed and a region that can begin to fight back from a period of industrial decline and neglect'.[9] The regeneration project has certainly recast the relationship between Tynesiders and the Tyne and disrupted people's ideas about what the river is for and how it should and should not be used. But the regeneration success story is no less biased and narrowly focused on its own unique combination of goals (cultural heritage, conservation, tourism and the environment), than the TIC's success story was focused on trade, navigation and commerce. Equally, the TIC's predecessors, Newcastle's Mayor and Aldermen, produced their vision for the river in an oligarchic bubble of property rights, economic monopoly and maximal profits from shipping and ballast tolls.

Stefania Barca analysed the process of regeneration on Italy's River Liri where, in a very similar vein to that of the Tyne's regeneration story, technocracy and deindustrialisation have led to one particular vision for the river's future, as a regenerated tourist attraction where industrial heritage can be celebrated but never resuscitated. The Liri's urban regeneration project at Isola Fluvial

---

7. Miles, '"Our Tyne"', p. 914.
8. A. Mah, *Industrial Ruination, Community and Place: Landscapes and Legacies of Urban Decline* (London: University of Toronto Press, 2012), p. 74.
9. Miles, '"Our Tyne"', pp. 921, 924.

Chapter 8. 'A Big River?'

Park, a joint public-private venture co-financed by the European Union, has restored many riparian factories, which have been reused as hotels, computer and telecommunication company offices and cultural and recreational facilities 'including a ticket office located in the old slaughterhouse'.[10] Barca notes, quite rightly, that such regeneration projects enable only

> one particular vision of the past, based on uncritical and celebratory views of the industrial era, as the time in which urban life was organised around industry and people adapted their bio rhythm to that of the textile and paper productions that gave prosperity to the town [which excludes] alternative visions for a different reconnection between local people and the river.[11]

The Tyne's regeneration has perhaps been just as narrow, but in a different way, by prioritising culture and conservation rather than industrial heritage. Barca asks 'will this collective memory include the trout, the otter and the other disappearing species of the Liri watershed and will they have a chance to find their way back to the river?'[12] Some ex-industrial workers around the Tyne, where industrial heritage is not quite as obvious and where the economic deprivation still endemic among some riparian communities is largely excluded from narratives of successful regeneration and the return of the salmon, might just as legitimately ask: does the collective memory of the Tyne include the ships, the dirt, the noise and the coal and will they have a chance to find their way back to the river?

Alice Mah, who in 2010 and 2011 studied the ex-shipbuilding community of Walker Riverside on the Tyne's north bank east of Newcastle, noted the city centres of Newcastle on Tyne and Niagra Falls, Ontario, are 'commonly seen as success stories, yet a closer look at particular old industrial communities within both cities reveals evidence of industrial and urban decline'.[13] Mah justified her choice of Newcastle as a case study to compare against Niagra Falls, Ontario, and Invanovo, Russia, above other UK post-industrial candidates, 'because some of its old industrial areas remained untouched by regeneration', because 'there was still a strong sense of local pride and collective memory based on shipbuilding' and because, she said, 'during my first visits to the city, I was struck by the juxtaposition between the regenerated quayside in the city centre and the abandoned shipyards to the east and west'.[14] Her analysis of

---

10. Barca, *Enclosing Water*, p. 143.
11. Ibid.
12. Ibid.
13. Mah, *Industrial Ruination*, p. 17.
14. Ibid, p. 25.

Walker Riverside revealed that 'the derivation is beneath the surface and that the perceived regeneration is largely superficial'.[15] From my own observations and first-hand experiences of the severe cultural misfits between the tourist attraction of the Newcastle-Gateshead quayside and the nearby ex-shipbuilding communities, I do not doubt that her conclusion hits the nail on the head.

Creativity on Tyne

The very dramatic environmental story of this once nationally strategic river and truly global port which sent its ships out to perform a range of important functions across the world, from ice-breaking to the transportation of oil to cruise lining, has inspired the creation of a wealth of books, plays and music. All these artistic expressions of socio-environmental entanglement are equally worthy of analysis from an environmental history perspective alongside the more obvious activities of heavily polluting riparian industry, salmon-fishing and the river's clean-up operation. *Tyne View: A Walk around the Port of Tyne* was written to share the experiences of a writer, a poet, a photographer and an artist, as they walked 42 miles around the River Tyne's estuary, via Wylam, over ten days in July 2011.[16] The author, Michael Chaplin, the novelist and screenwriter Sid Chaplin's son, focused on the relationship between the Tyne and Tynesiders, and this walk revealed a great deal more about the river's environmental history than could have been achieved during ten days' archival research. Readers can imagine wandering with the walkers, discovering the half-rotted, abandoned boats and rusty boilers on the mudflats. None of the senses are neglected and the environment is described objectively, in all of its unsavoury and gritty realism. *Tyne View* argues that the Tyne regeneration scheme was a success, as the walkers noticed redshank and curlew birds, green sandpipers and salmon. They also observed people growing tomatoes on tugboats and crab farms in the form of disused tyres, purposely laid along the edge of the river, into which the crabs are enticed.[17] They observed red kites, cormorants, nuthatch, treecreeper, pink-breasted bullfinch, kingfisher, brown trout, grayling, plant species such as buddleia, and butterflies such as tortoiseshells, red admirals and the rare dingy skipper, otters living on the mudflats and seals feasting on the salmon.[18] They walked through conservation areas full of wild

---

15. Ibid., p. 72.
16. Chaplin et al., *Tyne View*.
17. Ibid., p. 103.
18. Ibid., p. 133.

Chapter 8. 'A Big River?'

flowers and herbs and met representatives of community orchards and nature reserves instigated by local action groups. It is unsurprising that this book sold out in 2012 as it provides a framework within which people can make sense of the enormous environmental changes that have been played out on and around the Tyne from which some local people are still reeling. It celebrates the positive aspects of the abandoned vestiges of riparian industry and infrastructure, and enables local people to recalibrate their relationship with the new and different Tyne which flows through their lives.

'Tyne', a Live Theatre production in association with Newcastle's Theatre Royal, was performed at The Customs House, South Shields, and the Theatre Royal, Newcastle, in early 2014.[19] The production highlights the large extent to which the Tyne provided a focal point for the whole north-east English region and how greatly it was appreciated for facilitating the enormous development of industry and trade which provided livelihoods for so many. The storyline, of a recently bereaved brother and sister who read the bequeathed life story of their late father in an attempt to understand his working life around the river, before sending his ashes down the Tyne to the sea in a plastic boat-shaped container, conceptualises Tynesiders as 'sons and daughters' of the Tyne. In this framework, the Tyne is given the ultimate respect and gratitude as Tynesiders' collective mother, a provider of life and a powerful, regional, unifying and protective force. In the production, the river is referred to frequently as 'she' and as the story progresses through the ages, with the majority of the details and anecdotes taken from the twentieth century, it successfully develops a profoundly positive, and extensively personified, eponymous character of 'Tyne'.

In 2013, after a decade of creative inactivity caused by writer's block, the local musician Sting released an album entitled 'The Last Ship', which was shaped heavily by his direct experiences with the industrial River Tyne during his youth in the shipbuilding community of Wallsend on the north bank east of Newcastle. The music focuses on the hurly burly social interaction in the riparian shipyards and Sting's lament for the Tyne's historical shipbuilding success is very clear. Sting developed the album into a musical, which he performed in Chicago before adapting it to incorporate another local singer and actor, Jimmy Nail, and transferring it to the Neil Simon Theatre on New York's Broadway in 2014. The musical had to be shut down in January 2015 due to poor ticket sales, but its initial success is a testament to the appeal of the Tyne's globally significant industrial story. In the song 'Big River', which was released

---

19. Webpage at: http://www.live.org.uk/about-us/news/tyne-live-theatre%E2%80%99s-play-celebrating-the-river-returns-to-both-north-and-south-of [accessed 26 June 2016].

as a single in 1995, Jimmy Nail tried to provide hope and comfort to his fellow Tynesiders as they attempted to recover from the monumental and seemingly irreversible decline of their riparian industries that began in the 1980s. The song's lyrics chimed very poignantly with many local people who mourned the loss of their local river's significant contribution to the UK's national wealth, which was a huge source of regional pride. They also mourned the strong sense of community spirit that had thrived previously, binding together the families whose husbands, fathers, sons and brothers worked in the heavy industries.[20]

Nail's lyrics promise that 'the river will rise again', by which he meant that it will become great once again in terms of manufacturing productivity, navigation and trade.[21] Nail admitted that 'all the capstans and stevedores are gone', but emphasised that nevertheless Tynesiders' 'memories just like the seas live on'.[22] His words 'cos that was when coal was king, the river was a living thing' confirm his lament for the industrial river and that, despite the regeneration scheme which was well underway by 1995, he no longer saw the river as a 'living thing'.[23] In Nail's conceptualisation of how Tynesiders should interact with the Tyne, the river lived only so long as it underpinned economic productivity, a thriving regional economy and an identity of which Tynesiders could be proud. In some of the most poignant lyrics of the song, Nail advises that if we 'believe that there's a bond between our future and our past, then try to hold onto what we had, we built them strong, we build to last', which compares the region's ability to build strong ships which last to its similarly strong and resilient ability to cling onto not only their industrial skills and abilities, but also to their hope that the river 'will rise again' against the odds.[24] Perhaps for young Tynesiders today, the river has become 'big' once again, but in a very different way than Jimmy Nail and so many of his generation once hoped.[25]

For the generation that can remember the industrial river estuary, the people who were proud of its economic productivity, the creation and dissemination of cultural celebrations of the Tyne's industrial heritage can provide comfort in ways that the glitzy new tourist attraction of the Newcastle-Gateshead

---

20. For a more detailed account of the social and economic consequences of industrial decline in Walker Riverside, see Mah, *Industrial Ruination*.

21. J. Nail, 'Big River' (1995).

22. Ibid.

23. Ibid.

24. Ibid.

25. P. Coates, 'From One Big River to Another: Local Musicians Muse on Life, Death and Rebirth (?) on the Tees and Tyne', (Nov. 2014), online at: http://powerwaterproject.net/?p=504 [accessed: 11 Jul. 2016].

Chapter 8. 'A Big River?'

quayside, which glosses over and sweeps aside that industrial heritage, cannot. For those who do not possess first-hand memories of the pre-clean-up era, this author included, as well as for many if not all of those who do carry such pre-clean-up memories, the shiny and new quayside can be celebrated as exciting, as aesthetically attractive and as something to be proud of in a national, perhaps even an international, context. For others, however, the new riverscape with its BALTIC Centre for Contemporary Art, Sage Gateshead concert venue, river cruises and plethora of bustling gastro pubs and restaurants, is a deeply painful reminder of what our new and different relationship with the river has left behind. Some people paint nostalgic and romantic scenes of the industrial river in their minds while others have moved on. Younger Tynesiders are unable to imagine such a dramatically different, industrial riverscape, but they respect those who can remember it. By smoothing over the trauma of deindustrialisation, which many Tynesiders experienced as a very tumultuous, difficult and emotionally painful process, the regeneration success story and the celebration of the river's renewed environmental health have fundamentally altered, betrayed and excluded at least some people's complex relationship with the river. In reality, the changing relationship between Tynesiders and the Tyne during and after deindustrialisation has been, and still is, much more complex and far more emotionally traumatic for some than most people watching Sting's 'The Last Ship' on New York's Broadway or wandering around the BALTIC art gallery between a river cruise and a cream tea might realise.

River Recreation

It is important to appreciate that people have been enjoying the Tyne for centuries. Even as early as in the 1760s, Jenny Uglow reminds us that Thomas Bewick's childhood featured some quite exhilarating interactions with the Tyne near his home at Eltringham on its south side and his nearby school across the river at Ovingham. Uglow notes that as 'leader of the gang', Thomas 'persuaded his friends to crowd on to a huge piece of ice, which they steered downstream opposite the Parsonage garden, enjoying the sight of the Revd Gregson raising his hands in despair'.[26] Over two centuries later, in 1990, the Garden Festival, held on Dunston Staiths, marked an important turning point in the relationship between the Tyne and its human inhabitants as it publicly portrayed and celebrated a new and different, non-industrial vision for the river going forwards. The Tall Ships Race, which visited the Tyne in 1986, 1993 and

---

26. Uglow, *Nature's Engraver*, p. 15.

Tyne after Tyne

2005, also provided public opportunities at various stages of the regeneration project to express and reaffirm new connections to and meanings of the river. The popular long-distance Hadrian's Wall Path walk extends from Bowness on Solway in the West to Wallsend on Tyne in the east, following the north bank of the River Tyne for much of its 84-mile route. Many local people and tourists have sought and found pleasure on the river by embracing a wide range of river recreations, including angling, canoeing, sailing, windsurfing, riverside cycling and swimming. Some local people believe more could be done to encourage even more extensive river recreation and enjoyment of the river more generally. As David Fraser, who was born in Tynemouth and who has lived in Tyneside throughout his life, commented,

> looking at some video … [from] when we were in Bangkok and we were staying in a hotel on the Chao Phraya River there … and there wasn't an inch of the television screen which wasn't filled with crafts, and not only innumerable ferries, floating restaurants, travelling restaurants, tugs drawing barges, ships afloat, the river was heaving from side to side. And then I went to Hong Kong and … in the bay, to cross from Kowloon to the main island you've to run a gauntlet of hundreds of ships crossing in front of you. And then where my daughter lives in Singapore, you cannot see from her window out to the sea, it's anchored as far as the eye can see with ships waiting in the river. … I don't understand why we haven't got power boats racing up and down [the Tyne] and why there's not other forms of sport, there's innumerable things that can be going on. They don't go on the River Tyne, it's very underexploited in terms of its use from a water sports perspective that can draw an enormous crowd from an international basis and I'm not talking about just the Tall Ships coming once in a blue moon, but I mean an annual event, a small amount of cargo near the Tyne Bridge isn't quite the thing I'm talking about. … The river should be massed with people rowing boats and jet skis and all sorts of things, but for some reason it's empty and it's sad to see it as just a wasted water resource.[27]

For David, today's management of the Tyne wastes a potentially very large source of pleasure for local people and for tourists. But humans are not the only beneficiaries of today's ecological management of the river. A profusion of flora and fauna has been helped to flourish and supporting the diverse, and sometimes incompatible, needs of fish and seals and canoeists and anglers can be a challenging juggling act.

Aidan Pollard, a Fisheries Consultant who was born in Blaydon in 1945 and worked in the steel and coal industries, developed a very close relationship

---

27. Interview with David Fraser, born in Tynemouth, 1946, retired telecommunications engineer; recorded by Leona Skelton, at David's home, 30 Jan. 2015, 5 p.m.

Chapter 8. 'A Big River?'

with the river from a young age, evolving with his passion for angling. His grammar school 'had an angling club organised by two teachers and we travelled the Tyne catchment fishing, not always with permission, but most of the time'.[28] After being made redundant from the steel works, Aidan explained how he was able to use the river to develop a new career in relation to the fisheries of a Tyne tributary, the lower River Derwent, which involved working as the manager of a small fish hatchery there. He appreciates being able to fish in a much cleaner river compared to the Tyne of the 1950s:

> When I fished in the 50s, I was told by my Aunt to clean, I was given some fly fishing equipment, and I had to wash the line when I came home because raw sewage was discharged into the river in those days and was visible. So my Aunt made me meticulously clean, I had to wash myself and my fishing kit in the 50s. ... I can remember the sorry state of the Derwent in my youth, its huge pollutions, and very damaging pollution in the 80s and the recovery of that. I have very fond memories of the Derwent recovering from its very intensive industrial past to what is now quite a good fishing amenity river.[29]

One of Aidan's special experiences while fishing on the river took place one 'wonderful day in late April', when

> a huge fall of swallows ... were on bushes, I've never seen it before or since, hundreds, hundreds, more maybe and all the branches on willow bushes had birds on and that was probably migratory birds *en masse* and they'd spotted a huge hatch of fly off the river.[30]

Another memorable experience took place in the 1960s, when he can 'remember standing on Hexham Bridge' in the summer when 'the river was low and looking upstream and seeing the mass shoals of dace, in their thousands, very clear in the shallows above the bridge at Hexham', which he described as 'an amazing sight and it's never left me'.[31] Aidan explained that the high numbers of dace resulted from the 'excessive nutrient' available at the time.[32]

Barbara Wardle, who was born in 1947 and has lived in Haydon Bridge for nearly all her life, described a local beauty spot about a mile west of Haydon Bridge on the South Tyne where a large limestone rock rises out of the river channel. It attracted local people for picnics and swimming before severe pollu-

---

28. Interview with Aidan Pollard, born in Blaydon, 1945, Fisheries Consultant; recorded by Leona Skelton, at Tyne Rivers Trust Office, Corbridge, 19 Jan. 2015, 3 p.m.
29. Interview with Aidan Pollard.
30. Interview with Aidan Pollard.
31. Interview with Aidan Pollard.
32. Interview with Aidan Pollard.

tion deterred people from visiting the spot from the mid-1960s. She recalls that 'when we were kids, it was like Blackpool on a good day, everybody was there with their picnic and you could hardly find a place to sit' and she explained how the river was used as a 'natural swimming pool'.[33] Very few people use the beauty spot today, despite the cleaner water, because, Barbara suggests, 'I think the period when it wasn't as clean as it might have been made a shift' because 'traditionally parents had taken their children and older children had taken their brothers and sisters'; therefore the period of pollution broke a link in this intergenerational chain of place.[34]

River recreation is perhaps one of the most obvious ways in which humans can benefit directly from the clean-up and regeneration project. But human enjoyment of the new and different, cleaner riverscape is now managed carefully, and in some cases severely limited, in the context of the river's non-human inhabitants and its wider environmental health.

Ecological Responsibility

In 1989, the Clean Tyne Project was established. Managed and funded by the Port of Tyne and four riparian councils (Gateshead, Newcastle, North Tyneside and South Tyneside), it is a non-profit making environmental partnership which aims to improve the appearance and water quality of the River Tyne estuary by removing debris from the river water and banks using a barge, the 'Clearwater', which houses a crane. In recent years, the Port of Tyne sponsored the Clean Tyne Project to develop an education resource pack for local primary school teachers, featuring lesson plans linked to key stages one and two of the science, geography and history national curriculum, mind maps linking the river and its environment to other subject areas and frameworks for activities including a 'bird spotting challenge' and another entitled 'If you were walking along the River Tyne in the past, how would it be different?'[35] The pack explains:

> Because of its industrial history, the river was an easy place to dispose of waste products. Never mind what it looked like, how much damage it caused, or what the implications to wildlife were, the river was misused. But times have changed and we now know better than to use the river as a dumping ground.[36]

---

33. Interview with Barbara Wardle, born in Corbridge 1947, retired retail manager; recorded by Leona Skelton, at Tyne Rivers Trust Offices, Corbridge, 21 Jan. 2015, 2 p.m.
34. Interview with Barbara Wardle.
35. Clean Tyne Project, *Education Resource Pack* (2013).
36. Ibid.

Chapter 8. 'A Big River?'

In another section, entitled 'If the River Could Talk', the pack personifies the river to encourage the children to respect its agency and sensitivity to pollution, noting 'the river saw a great many new innovations' and 'the river helped to lead the way during the industrial revolution'.[37] Only a century ago, local schoolchildren's relationships with the Tyne were shaped by a very different set of ideals as they were exposed to maps of the British Empire and images of commerce and industry.

Since 2009, 98 per cent of the materials which the Clean Tyne Project has collected have been recycled. A substantial proportion of the debris removed is wood from the upper river valley, but other large objects such as shopping trolleys and bikes are removed too. In November 2013, the Tyne burst its banks and nearly swept away months of collected debris that was stacked up and awaiting collection for recycling at the Clean Tyne Project's riparian depot. The Tyne continues to interact with and undermine our efforts to interfere with its natural processes, even when such action has a positive impact on its environmental health. In February 2014, the Clean Tyne Project produced a River Cleanliness Index Survey by visually assessing 106 locations around the Tyne estuary for cleanliness between the river mouth and Wylam. The survey was undertaken to provide performance indicator figures to evaluate the success of the clean-up project overall and to identify 'hotspots' where large amounts of debris accumulate so that more attention could be directed towards them in the future. Using a grading system of A–E, A being excellent, 72 of the 106 locations were graded A (67.9 per cent), 22 were graded B (20.8 per cent), ten were graded C (9.4 per cent) and two were not surveyed.[38] During the survey, 69.9 per cent of the debris recorded was wood, 26.4 per cent was plastic, polysterene or rubber, 3.1 per cent was metal and 0.2 per cent was classified as miscellaneous.[39] The great bulk of the material that the Clearwater collects, therefore, is a natural product of the river. Dr Ceri Gibson, an environmental scientist who worked for Tyne Rivers Trust until 2015, explained that the Clean Tyne Project's work focuses on the estuary and on large and physical objects of pollution rather than on chemical pollution:

> I think it's cleaned up the tidal end … of the river, [but] it hasn't addressed … more dissolved pollution issues. … It's only talking about … the physical

---

37. Ibid.
38. Clean Tyne Project and the Port of Tyne, 'Clean Tyne Project River Cleanliness Index Survey Results Report' (26 Feb. 2014).
39. Ibid.

things that we find. But I think ... that monitoring work is brilliant because it's spreading the awareness more widely.[40]

The less visible, chemical pollution of the estuary is not so well publicised, but several agencies monitor and improve its chemical condition. The Port of Tyne tests the river bed's sediment in the estuary on a regular basis and Northumbrian Water Ltd and the local riparian councils have invested in a wide range of river restoration and redevelopment projects up and down the river banks.

In 2004, a small environmental charity, Tyne Rivers Trust, was established at Hexham to encourage the recovery of the Tyne's and its tributaries' environmental health across the whole catchment. It was born out of local concerns that the second vehicular Tyne Tunnel would adversely affect the Tyne's salmon runs. But it joined the UK's much wider River Trust Movement and grew beyond its origins as a small mitigation group to tackle increasingly complex catchment-wide issues. It has now established itself as the Tyne's environmental guardian for the long-term future. Its missions are: to improve and protect the river's water quality; to encourage native wildlife and plant species to thrive; to promote and develop more environmentally sensitive and responsible attitudes among local people by organising and overseeing community conservation events and activities; and to promote harmonious enjoyment of the river by respective recreational groups whose different uses of the river can lead to mutual frustration. As well as offering expert advice and a consultancy service that recommends conservation and management actions for river channels, river banks, in-river structures and the wider catchment, the Trust works to mitigate erosion and siltation, to install fish passes and other forms of 'green engineering' to assist migratory fish, to monitor water quality and temperature and to reduce the prevalence of invasive species. It has a full volunteer programme to tackle the practical tasks that keep the river in good health, from removing invasive species to restoring riverbanks and planting trees to reduce the risk of flooding. The Trust maintains a fruitful River Fly Partnership with the Environment Agency by training and supporting a large group of volunteers spread across the catchment to monitor the fly life of the river. This is not only creating a long-term entomological record of the species present but also highlights pollution events, which can then be reported to the Environment Agency which mitigates the pollution. Ceri Gibson, the environmental scientist who managed the Trust's voluntary River Watch initiative until 2015, is motivated by a strong desire to protect the river's independent agency against human activities, commenting 'I dislike where ... we see erosion

---

40. Interview with Ceri Gibson.

Chapter 8. 'A Big River?'

and control by man, which is not necessarily what the river is wanting'.[41] Her conceptualisation of the river's independent agency could not be clearer. Ceri found her River Watch work highly rewarding, as she recalled 'getting very wet on summer's evenings, but thoroughly enjoying it and just having those little nuggets of realisation fed back to me, I think that's great'.[42] As Christopher Smout notes, 'the rise of nature conservation as a powerful force in the twentieth century owes everything to the twinning of science and voluntary effort'.[43]

Barbara Wardle, a volunteer of the Haydon Bridge River Watch Team, explained that the Riverwatchers simply 'do what we can to help the river'.[44] Barbara is motivated to improve the river by very positive memories of the river's flora during her childhood in the 1950s:

> The flowers were just absolutely wonderful … the done thing then, you used to pick flowers and take them home, I wouldn't dream of picking them now. And the flowers were absolutely wonderful. … There certainly isn't as many now as there used to be. Things like thrift we don't get any more. There are some harebells but not many. … All the riverbanks were covered with flowers. I suppose now the ones near pastures that have been chemically treated and that kind of thing, you don't get anything like the quantity of flowers that you used to, which is a bit sad really.[45]

When Barbara recalled the river water itself, she emphasised its 'pristine' quality of the 1950s compared to the 1960s:

> It was absolutely pristine clear, the stones of a stony bed. If you walked in, your feet were in contact with stones, not slush, sand or slurry, which is what happened later on. Right through until the early to mid-60s, it was fairly well clean, you went in swimming and your feet touched rock underneath your feet or pebbles, but from about the mid-60s onwards it began to get to the point where if you plodged [i.e. stepped] into the water, you were plodging in gunk lying on top of the pebbles and that kind of thing. It's improved lately, it's certainly cleaner than it was but during the late 60s and the 70s it put you off going into the river really to swim. It definitely was not pleasant to put your feet in the stuff.[46]

The river's water quality is improving gradually, but it is by no means pristine. Nowadays, Barbara walks along the river banks every day with 'binoculars

---

41. Interview with Ceri Gibson.
42. Interview with Ceri Gibson.
43. Smout, *Nature Contested*, p. 30.
44. Interview with Barbara Wardle.
45. Interview with Barbara Wardle.
46. Interview with Barbara Wardle.

around my neck, with a litter picker in my hand and a plastic bag in my other hand'.[47] She has a very strong bond with the river, which has developed over several decades, and she devotes quite a lot of time to caring for the river and protecting it from activities that she perceives as harmful to it, such as the deposition of litter and the spread of invasive plant species. Her comparison of the Tyne and the Trent is particularly revealing, as a recent trip to visit a friend in Newark sharpened her appreciation of the Tyne. She explained what she likes about the Tyne, highlighting 'I like the fact that it's always on the move, it's not still like some other water places that you go to, you go and look at the Trent for instance ... it's a big river, but it was still and flat, you know, and didn't have the bubble and the interest that the Tyne has'.[48] Quite simply, she explained, 'water makes a place'.[49] Martin Stark, a Tyne Rivers Trust Riverwatcher in the Haltwhistle Burn catchment area who describes the Tyne as 'awesome', also appreciates the diverse range of different riverscapes within the catchment, explaining 'it has lots of different shapes, it has islands, it has fast flowing bits, slow flowing bits, deep water pools, it's got a variety of different forms and that provides that variety'.[50]

While the *Tyne Catchment Plan* (2012), funded and delivered by Defra's Tyne Catchment Partnership, proposed a comprehensive plan of action to improve the environmental health of the catchment as a whole, Tyne Rivers Trust inevitably focuses on certain issues, recreational groups, wildlife species and riparian places more than others. For example, it focused in depth between 2012 and 2015 on the Haltwhistle Burn Catchment Restoration project in collaboration with Newcastle University. This involved installing 'green engineering' at several sites within the tributary's catchment to 'create habitat, "slow the flow" allowing silt and sediment to drop out onto the floodplain, protect river banks from erosion and create access [for fish] to the Haltwhistle Burn from the South Tyne'.[51] The Trust has taken action to protect the Tyne's endangered freshwater mussels, one of only two viable populations in England, with a mean age of between fifty and eighty years.[52] Recently, Tyne Rivers Trust secured Heritage Lottery Funding to implement their Water Voles Heritage Project in the North

---

47. Interview with Barbara Wardle.
48. Interview with Barbara Wardle.
49. Interview with Barbara Wardle.
50. Interview with Martin Stark.
51. M. Newson and C. Gibson (eds), *Haltwhistle Burn: A Comprehensive Catchment approach to Headwater Runoff and Pollution. Technical Report of the 2012–2015 Catchment Restoration Fund Project* (Corbridge: Tyne Rivers Trust, 2015), p. 21.
52. Tyne Rivers Trust, Newsletter, issue 16 (Spring/Summer 2014).

Chapter 8. 'A Big River?'

Tyne Valley. This involved interviewing local people and encouraging them to share their memories of water voles in the North Tyne valley before the 1980s, when predatory American mink escaped from local mink farms and the water voles also lost their essential riverbank habitats. These factors coincided to reduce water vole populations very considerably. This project complemented the Forestry Commission's efforts to increase the provision of the water vole's habitat of grassy streamside vegetation by replanting trees further back from streams after felling.

Mary Wilson is a retired doctor who lives at Allerwash near a South Tyne tributary, Newbrough Burn, some 34 miles from Tynemouth. She walks her dogs along the South Tyne riverbanks twice every day and has become deeply familiar with her local stretch of the river, its wildlife and the soundscape of the flowing water and the riverbanks. She spoke enthusiastically, recalling

> Oh sometimes there's a sort of tinkling, sometimes it's just a gentle swoosh and other times when it's in full flood it's very exciting, it's covered in ice and the blocks of ice were crashing against each other. Another time I walked along the side and where the reeds and the rushes are growing at the side of long grasses at the side of the water, they'd obviously been dipping into the water and then there had been a severe frost, so on the end of all these bits of grass there was like a glass bauble and there was a breeze and they were chiming, … chinking against each other so it was a real tinkling noise you know walking along and that's just one … that would be gone the next day, but unless you're there, you don't see it and the same with the time I'd seen an otter, I'd seen otter paw prints before, I'd seen otter spraint, I'd always looked out for otters and then one day I just saw one just going into the water.[53]

Since 2010, Mary has worked as a Riverwatch volunteer for Tyne Rivers Trust. Each day, she records the temperature of the river water in Newbrough Burn, she samples the water quality once monthly and she also conducts monthly surveys of the invertebrates, commenting that 'I just feel so excited to be part of it'.[54] Mary has worked closely with Tyne Rivers Trust to inspire local school children in relation to her voluntary work. She describes the river between Newcastle and Gateshead as 'big and wonderful', but her intimacy with the tributary stream near her home in Allerwash clearly means far more to her:

> The bit that I live near is very important to me at the moment … I just love seeing the river, I like the wildlife along the river. I see quite a few different

---

53. Interview with Mary Wilson, born in Nottingham, 1948, retired doctor; recorded by Leona Skelton, at Tyne Rivers Trust Offices, Corbridge, 20 Jan. 2015, 11 a.m.
54. Interview with Mary Wilson.

birds there, I've seen otters on our bit of the river and it's never the same, it's just a wonderful place to walk and then to imagine a hundred years ago when there was all the industry and the mining and the lime kilns and just how noisy it must have been in those days.[55]

Mary's intimate experience of her local one-and-a-half mile stretch of the South Tyne leads her to conceptualise the river as 'almost a living entity'.[56] Jennifer Simpson also personified the river, noting 'at low tide it looks sad because it's all mud banks and so on'.[57]

Appreciation and deep understanding of a micro-scale environment is only possible when one communes with it very regularly, year after year and even decade after decade, which is usually only possible when someone lives very close to it. For example, Nan Shepherd's *A Living Mountain* leaves the reader in no doubt that she visited the Cairngorms a great number of times over the course of her life.[58] Similarly, John Lewis-Stempel's *The Private Life of an English Field: Meadowland*, which describes the micro-scale processes and interactions between a farmer, his family and the flora and fauna in one meadow in Herefordshire over the course of one year, confirms the author's exceptionally intimate relationship with a very small-scale environment.[59] A relatively early and important example of one particularly intimate relationship with the flora and fauna of a local area, Gilbert White's *Natural History and Antiquities of Selborne* (1789), was based on an incredible 43 years of nature and weather diaries detailing fastidiously the minutiae of the area around his parsonage in Hampshire.[60] Mary's experiences of volunteering to collect scientific data or to survey particular aspects of her local environment are not unusual nationally or globally. The early twenty-first century has seen a profusion of citizen science and there are many examples of transforming people's environmental awareness through involvement in various projects. One collaborative citizen agency project on the Salmon River, California, USA, has installed rain tanks to improve water security for rural residents and to increase late summer stream flow for salmon.[61] Cleo Woelfe-Erskine found that 'residents who participate in

---

55. Interview with Mary Wilson.
56. Interview with Mary Wilson.
57. Interview with Jennifer Simpson.
58. N. Shepherd, *The Living Mountain*, 2nd ed. (Edinburgh: Canongate Books, 2011).
59. J. Lewis-Stempel, *The Private Life of an English Field: Meadowland* (London: Black Swan, 2014).
60. G. White, *The Natural History and Antiquities of Selborne* (1789).
61. Cleo Woelfe-Erskine, 'Rain Tanks, Springs and Broken Pipes as Emerging Water Commons along the Salmon River', *Acme* 4 (1) (2015): 735–750

Chapter 8. 'A Big River?'

monitoring salmon populations, water quality and their own springs and rain tanks report that these activities have increased their sense of interdependence with other human and non-human neighbours who rely on the watershed's limited water sources'.[62] She elaborates that the project enabled people to conceptualise water as 'an interspecies commons' which is 'not just a non-living fluid, but rather an animate substance that connects humans to other species'.[63]

While it is an Area of Outstanding Natural Beauty, the long-term legacy of environmental damage caused by lead mining processes in the South Tyne continues to challenge the river's current conservators. A restoration project in the River Nent valley, a tributary of the South Tyne near Alston, is being conducted by a partnership comprising the Environment Agency, the Coal Authority (UK), Tyne Rivers Trust and the North Pennines Area of Outstanding Natural Beauty. Funded by Defra, the project addresses England's second most seriously damaged catchment by pollution from mine water.[64] Drainage channels, such as the seven-mile long Nent Force Channel, carry water from the Nenthead mines and discharge it directly into the River Nent. The catchment, which was a site of intensive metal mining until the 1920s, failed the EU Water Framework Directive's objective of 'good potential' with concentrations of lead, zinc and cadmium at 57 times the levels permissible within the EU Environmental Quality Standards.[65] While the restoration project is unlikely to reduce concentrations of harmful minerals in the River Nent itself, it aims to improve substantially the concentrations of lead, zinc and cadmium in the South Tyne. Tyne Rivers Trust makes considerable efforts to protect riverbanks from erosion and to restore those that have been eroded substantially, because when riverbanks are eroded or they collapse, the minerals they contain are disseminated into the river water. Both the Tyne Rivers Trust and the Victorian Tyne Improvement Commission have attempted to limit and control the Tyne's natural power and agency, but for very different motivating reasons.

The world's furthest inland colony of kittiwakes is one of the new cleaner Tyne's natural spectacles. The Tyne breeding population boasts around 1,000 pairs. Kittiwakes spend most of their time at sea feeding on sand eels and travelling as far as Canada, but each March they return to the Tyne estuary to breed on its bridges and buildings until August, whereupon they live out at

---

62. Ibid., p. 735.
63. Ibid., pp. 736, 744.
64. Restoring Europe's Rivers, 'Case Study: River Nent: Abandoned Metal Mines', online at: https://restorerivers.eu/wiki/index.php?title=Case_study%3ARiver_Nent%3A_Abandoned_Metal_Mines [website accessed 26 June 2016].
65. Ibid.

Figure 20. Remains of Kittiwake Nests, Baltic Centre for Contemporary Art, Gateshead (Photograph: Gordon Ball)

sea until the following spring. Seven-hundred pairs of kittiwakes breed in the Newcastle-Gateshead quayside area alone. The mess from their excrement and their nests, built from mud and vegetation taken from the river at low tide, sustains intense debate between local people who own quayside businesses and environmentalists who defend the birds' interests. Although the kittiwakes make their nests in the city centre of Newcastle, they still travel far out into the North Sea (up to 100 miles) to catch fish which they regurgitate to their young. In 1998, during the redevelopment of the Baltic grain warehouse into an art gallery, a Kittiwake Tower was built nearby as an alternative nesting site and it is now a nature reserve. The Tyne Kittiwakes Partnership currently safeguards the kittiwake population. It comprises the Natural History Society of Northumbria, the RSPB, Northumberland and Durham Wildlife Trusts, Newcastle, Gateshead, South Tyneside and North Tyneside Councils, Newcastle University, Northumberland and Tyneside Bird Club and several independent researchers and ornithologists.[66] In 1995, dredging operations ceased above Newcastle. Subsequently, the River Tyne Tidal Mudflat and the River Team Saltmarsh around the Dunston Staiths have expanded naturally, creating a ha-

---

66. For more information, see the Tyne Kittiwakes Partnership webpage at: http://www.nhsn.ncl.ac.uk/news/cms/tynekittiwakes/ [accessed 26 June 2016].

Chapter 8. 'A Big River?'

ven for rare wading birds, including the Golden Plover and Lapwing. Some of these birds roost in the staiths and feed on the mudflats, which feature several rare plant species, including saltmarsh grass, wild carrot, wild celery and sea aster.[67] Combined with even cleaner river water, otters may well use the site in the very near future. The concrete river walls have been colonised by teasels, buckthorn, gorse and alder. When the Derwenthaugh Coke works was closed down in 1986, Gateshead Council and the Environment Agency joined forces to fund a £350,000 scheme to install fish passes at Derwenthaugh Dam, one for salmon and one for eels and lampreys. We are still interfering with the river, still trying to alter its natural processes and systems with our engineered and unnatural installations. Such ecological interventions are very different from those with which the Tyne Improvement Commission attempted to transform the river into an efficient trade facility, but we continue nonetheless to manipulate and to exert influence over the natural course of events in the river's water.

The Tyne's Indomitable Natural Independence

As we saw in chapter two, the Tyne's serious floods have engraved themselves permanently into Tynesiders' memories and are even passed through successive generations. They fundamentally change our relationships with the river, and at times have encouraged us to seek to achieve control over its natural functions more effectively. For many, a river flood is the most terrifying and violent expression a river can inflict on human society. Kathryn Williams recalled her experience of the 2005 Tyne flood two years later, in 2007:

> It had been a sweet, romantic river. A Place to contemplate, to see electric blue kingfishers fly over, the sound of it bubbling and cooling on a summer's day, but now it had taken up arms. It was lifting itself higher and drinking the rain faster, gaining energy. Its volume intimidated. What had been a whimsy stream was now a torrent. Virulent. Creeping with fingertips towards rock, patio and bricks. Feeling its way into long for forgotten cracks, seeping into porous walls. The river has burst its banks like it was crying at a funeral. Heaving. Lapping a breath and heaving again. Water is like a ghost. You turn around and it has come closer. This river wanted to be a sea. It didn't feel like our garden. It smelt like the river. It had taken our home and like the unease after a burglary, we knew it was possible again.[68]

---

67. See Jetty Project Website online at http://jetty-project.info/context/environment/ [accessed 26 June 2016].
68. K. Williams, 'The Ouse Burn', in R. Deakin et al. (eds), *Caught by the River: A Collection of Words on Water* (London: Cassell, 2009), pp. 218–220.

Here, she described a metamorphosis of the river, from a 'sweet romantic river' to a completely personified thief that 'took up arms' and crept into her human territory, 'our garden' and 'our house'. Many recollections of floods talk about territory and the perceived encroachment of the water onto private property. The rivers are conceptualised as literally trespassing over the imaginary line many people continue to draw between the human and the natural. In this sense, humans can be hypocritical, as they rarely realise when they have overstepped the mark with the river and are in fact encroaching on its 'natural' space. In reality, of course, there is no such separation between the human and the natural, and the river can encroach into our lives, homes and settlements just as we can restructure the river, pour waste into it, suffocate its fish life and extract its gravel.

When the Tyne burst its banks in the city centre of Newcastle in November 2013, many local people blamed the lack of dredging, which had no longer been necessary since deindustrialisation substantially devalued the previously urgent priority of maintaining a deep channel capable of receiving and dispatching a plethora of large ships. Understanding how, when and why the river's bed, channel, course and water were changed as a result of the unique blend of political, social, economic and cultural circumstances which characterised particular time periods is a prerequisite to balanced modern-day debates between the environmental and governmental organisations designing the river's future policies. Environmental, economic, political and cultural priorities have to be balanced and decisions are far from easily made in relation to projects such as dredging activity by the Port of Tyne, river restoration schemes by environmental charities such as Tyne Rivers Trust and sewerage infrastructure improvements by Northumbrian Water Ltd.[69]

In September 2012, one of the Tyne's tributaries, the Newburn, which was culverted in the early twentieth century, collapsed spectacularly. A storm downpour washed away the foundations of a block of flats and then the rubble and floodwater entered the culverted channel further downhill and blocked it, causing the exit of the culvert to become blocked. The pressure built up until the roof of the culvert channel burst, which caused the sediment and flood water to move down into the settlement even further down the hill, near the river. The sediment eventually settled down in the river, creating a new projection or spit into the river, and it is still there now, complete with a navigational light. The river was able to redesign its riverbank and to move a large quantity of sediment, rubble and water downhill despite the engineered culvert that had

---

69. Williams, 'The Ouse Burn', pp. 217–218, 220.

Chapter 8. 'A Big River?'

been installed to direct its flow underneath housing and businesses. Events in Newburn in 2012 serve as a warning that we will always be in two-way negotiations with the Tyne about how and where it flows to the sea.

Stories from after the Clean-Up

Through oral history we are able to understand more diverse reactions to the new, regenerated river than we find in the almost exclusively celebratory and positive official and governmental records that have understandably cast the era between 1980 and 2015 as a regional success story.[70] There are, of course, many positive relationships with the new regenerated river. Many people deeply appreciate the cleaner River Tyne, which enables them to engage with wildlife, plant species and an aesthetically pleasing riverscape that stimulates all of their senses. However, the decline in heavy industry, which employed a skilled and well-paid workforce, and the concomitant development of poorly paid call centre and tourism jobs in venues such as the iconic concert venue, Sage Gateshead, and the BALTIC Centre for Contemporary Art have created deep controversies in some areas across Tyneside. The clean-up is not universally celebrated by all those living on the Tyne's banks. Some Tynesiders appreciate that the Tyne is there and that it is an important part of their identity as Geordies, but choose not to engage with it as a recreational facility. The anonymous scientist born in North Shields in 1976 'liked that it's been there', but 'I don't know whether I would say it's been important … I'm kind of indifferent to it … I don't really use it … just to look at it really, I've crossed it to get to South Shields occasionally but that's about it'.[71] This disinclination to engage with the Tyne is also important and we should not assume that a river, even one which scythes a heavily populated urban area in two, will necessarily develop strong relationships with everyone who lives near its flow. For some, it might not be any more significant in their lives than a road or a railway. The anonymous scientist hadn't looked for wildlife purposefully, but was pleasantly surprised by encountering it inadvertently, noting that during 'the great North Run opening ceremony so while that was going on there was actually big salmon jumping under the bridge, I was like oh, didn't expect that'.[72]

---

70. For oral histories of relationships with the Tyne before the clean-up, see chapter six, Stories from before the Clean-Up.
71. Interview with anonymous interviewee, born in North Shields, 1976, scientist and community worker.
72. Interview with anonymous interviewee, born in North Shields, 1976, scientist and community worker.

Tyne after Tyne

Before the construction of the vehicular Tyne Tunnel in 1967, people living downriver from Newcastle and Gateshead (where several bridges enable cars to cross the river easily), regularly queued to board the river ferries that crossed the water between several strategic points along the lower estuary. As Jimmy Nail reminded us in his song 'Big River', his father 'had to cross the river every day'.[73] The unavoidable pragmatic necessity of boarding a river ferry to reach the opposite bank for work, to go shopping or to meet friends and family facilitated a closer, physical and much more tangible, connection with the river itself. Down near the water close enough to smell it, being swayed by the movement of the tides and with the knowledge that falling into the river water would pose an immediate potentially fatal risk forged a necessarily closer connection with the river than one can possibly derive from zipping high over it on a metro train or driving under its bed through a tunnel. In the 1960s and 1970s, David Fraser used to look forward to riding the longer riverside railway line, which served riparian workers along the shipyards of the north bank towards the coast, each Saturday lunchtime after his working week as a telecommunications engineer:

> Rather than taking the normal electric train which was an express that ran directly to the coast, I would choose ... the train which chose to travel down the riverside, which was I think to connect workers, and as a result it would give me a spectacular view of the river because normally you cannot get directly close to the river on much of the north bank because of the vast amount of industries whereas this railway line used to penetrate all of those and give you a grandstand view of the slipways and the various ships and that was my sort of Saturday treat. And for many years I did that until that line closed, to passengers that is. It remained open for freight some time and I lost that opportunity.[74]

David appreciated and valued his 'grandstand view' of the slipways of the heavily industrialised river, and he clearly forged a special relationship with this engineered riverscape. He preferred to use a transportation system that enabled him to get very close to the river and facilitated the development of a closer relationship. At the same time as David was spending his Saturday lunchtimes appreciating the spectacular views from the Riverside Line, he also found the arduous practicalities of crossing the river in the 1960s before the construction of the vehicular Tyne Tunnel in 1967 frustrating, noting

> And of course you had the ferries at various points, there were three or so ferries I think at various points, passenger and car ferries crossing the river because

---

73. J. Nail, 'Big River' (1995).
74. Interview with David Fraser.

Chapter 8. 'A Big River?'

we had at that time no Tyne Tunnel for vehicular use, so you had two choices and it was a race to get to the ferry landing and count the number of cars in the hope that you were the last car that you might actually get on. But if not, then you were faced with waiting for the next ferry or alternatively you would then take the tortuous drive up to Newcastle to cross either the Swing Bridge of the Tyne Bridge and drive down the opposite side of the river.[75]

The physical barrier that the river presented to transportation before the opening of the vehicular Tyne Tunnel forced people to engage with the Tyne, albeit in ways that could be frustrating and inconvenient. Dawn Tudge, who lives in Ryton but works in Newcastle city centre, explained that 'for the past few years I've started just in the summer cycling into work along the riverside paths and I think it's only really when you get close to the river like that that you do notice these things cos there's so much that I noticed, particularly smells, as well, that you just never see or smell or hear from the bus or the car'.[76] In particular, Dawn enjoys 'just being able to smell grass and flowers on the bushes and what have you and [...] you know the tide's on the change, you know it's nice to smell a bit of a seasidey smell as well'.[77] While some people maintain closer links with the river by cycling and walking along its banks, improvements in transport infrastructure have reduced people's engagement with the Tyne. Ironically, improved connection has produced deeper disconnection.

Wendy Young, a full-time mother living in North Shields, appreciates the therapeutic benefits of the river water itself, explaining how,

> If I'm feeling sad, ... I'll have a little wander down to the end of the pier and stuff and you just kind of feel better after looking at the water for a while somehow do you know what I mean, it's strange but you do, I think you can really think, I think looking at big bodies of water really helps me think ... I think it puts things into perspective, because it's so big, it's a bit like looking at the stars or the mountains or something like that, do you know what I mean. It sort of just puts things in perspective for you a little bit.[78]

Even those who do not engage with river recreations such as canoeing or angling can benefit from the river's capacity to provide solace, calm and a sense of mental space. The Tyne's constancy and accessibility draws many people to its banks at times of confusion, crisis and sadness, but also to facilitate relaxation more generally as part of a normal routine. Brian Pearson, who was born

---

75. Interview with David Fraser.
76. Interview with Dawn Tudge.
77. Interview with Dawn Tudge.
78. Interview with Wendy Young.

in 1941, said 'I've always looked at the river as a friend'; he says it makes him feel 'happy' and he appreciates the fact that 'it's somewhere you can go and it's free'.[79] Whereas Newcastle Corporation and the TIC wanted to maximise their profits by using the river as a facility for trade, Brian is grateful that he can go there and enjoy being near it without having to pay a fee. Economics continue to shape how we interact with rivers. Sally Southern, a textile artist born in Easington in County Durham in 1973, can 'lose hours just sitting down watching the river', noting that 'you never get bored watching it, the flow of it, there's something relaxing about it and especially where it meets the sea'; she believes 'it's good for your soul being near water'.[80] Dawn Tudge said 'I always get a kind of peaceful feeling being next to water'.[81] And for Pauline Stewart, a staff nurse who moved to North Shields in 2001 from Dundee, in Scotland, the Tyne enables her to feel closer to her native home as the wide river mouth is reminiscent of Dundee's similarly wide River Tay. When asked how being near the river makes her feel, she responded, 'kind of at home in a way cos it reminds me of Scotland beside the River Tay, it's got connections for me that way'.[82] She recalled her first memory of seeing the Tyne when she moved to her new home in North Shields:

> My father in law took us down the back of the house and I just could not believe what was on our doorstep, it was the Tyne lit up at night and it was like something out of a fairytale. It was all the lights and in the distance I could see all the activity of the shipyards and just the winding nature of the Tyne lit up by moonlight and that stays with me, it's a beautiful river.[83]

Pauline also notes her appreciation of the riverscape at night: 'I love seeing it at night time, it's a like a glass flowing mirror' and she conceptualises the river as a powerful and positive force not only for her personally but for the local community as a whole: 'it flows through us, it's just like a life force energy and it's just part of the community'.[84] Matt Hall feels very positively about the regenerated and clean Tyne, the tourism and the wildlife which call it home. He feels 'very lucky, because I can come out of my house and within ten minutes be

---

79. Interview with Brian Pearson.
80. Interview with Sally Southern, born in Easington, County Durham, 1973, textile artist; recorded by Leona Skelton, at the Old Low Light Heritage Centre Café, 22 Jan. 2015, 9.45 a.m.
81. Interview with Dawn Tudge.
82. Interview with Pauline Stewart.
83. Interview with Pauline Stewart.
84. Interview with Pauline Stewart.

Chapter 8. 'A Big River?'

at the ... river whether it be in Newburn, Scotswood or a little bit longer down by the quayside so to me ... I'll give it all 10 out of 10 because I love it all'.[85]

Ruth Chittenden is a student who has only lived in Newcastle since 2013, having been born in Newcastle under Lyme in 1983. She likes 'the fact that it's a bit of nature in the middle of ... a big urban centre'.[86] Kate Eccles, a designer working in the arts and theatre industry who was born in Hexham in 1985, describes the Tyne valley near Hexham quite simply as 'green', elaborating 'I love the greenery, I genuinely love the Tyne valley and going along the river, I think it's got loads to offer, ... it's the heart and soul of this area'.[87] Pearl Saddington perceives the river as 'the life blood of the north east, it's like a big vein really ... it's really responsible for our Englishness'.[88] The Venerable Bede, known as the Father of English History, wrote the first history of the English nation, *The Ecclesiastical History of the English People*, in 731 AD on the southern shore of the Tyne at Jarrow. The Tyne has certainly shaped regional and national identity, and it has contributed significantly to economic prosperity and to many of the technological developments which made national industrialisation possible.

But for some, the clean Tyne is not perfect. Some see it as a lamentable shadow of its former industrial self. Although Brian Pearson enjoys walking along the cleaner river and hasn't seen any pollution in the water since 'the old days', he also expressed regret in relation to the lack of industrial production on the river. He said 'the river's dead, ... every couple of year[s] or so, we get a ferry [and] it goes up the river and every year there's less and less to see, there's just a rig yard, and there's one shipyard on the Tyne now'.[89] Jennifer Simpson is well aware that 'the coal trade was what brought the Tyne its fame really and its iron industries and so on so it developed because of the industries' and she clearly laments the absence of those industries, commenting 'now it's such a shadow really of itself industrialwise'.[90]

Dawn Tudge was not affected directly by deindustrialisation, but she still expressed quite strong feelings in relation to this issue:

---

85. Interview with Matt Hall.
86. Interview with Ruth Chittenden, born in Newcastle under Lyme, 1983, student; recorded by Leona Skelton, at the Old Low Light Heritage Centre Café, 22 Jan. 2015, 2 p.m.
87. Interview with Kate Eccles, born in Hexham, 1985, designer in the arts and theatre industry; recorded by Leona Skelton, at the Old Low Light Heritage Centre Café, 22 Jan. 2015, 9.30 a.m.
88. Interview with Pearl Saddington.
89. Interview with Brian Pearson.
90. Interview with Jennifer Simpson.

> I think the shipyards for instance supported massive communities and they've never recovered, you know places like Walker, Wallsend, have never bounced back. Even like this side of Newcastle you know places like Scotswood. You see old photos and you think alright there was like crushing levels of poverty quite often but the sense of community must have been really strong in those days and I don't think there is much of a community around the River Tyne anymore. I think, I'd hazard a guess that most people in Newcastle and Gateshead do have fond feelings for the river, I'd guess, but even so I don't think there's a riverside community.[91]

Pat Rice also feels strongly about the decline in heavy industries along and on the Tyne, explaining,

> I think that the decline in industry was a decline of the north-east and I think the industry in the north-east is negligible now and no matter what they say, call centres and things like that just do not come back and bring us back to the level we had before and we've got to do something about bringing manufacturing back onto the river.[92]

Nellie Faulks, a retired school teacher who was born in Tynemouth in 1948, went as far as to say that 'I really do think that the river should be working for its living'.[93] David Fraser asserted a similar opinion, commenting 'one thing that's not for the better is denuding [the river] of all the industries which supplied the river with its greatness, they've virtually all gone'.[94] Although he carries a plethora of historical memories of the industrial, busy river of the 1950s and 1960s, and David speaks positively of the Tyne as 'a sinuous river which is steeped in history and industry, driven principally by industry', he also said 'I'd possibly have to suggest now that it's a decaying river to be truthful'.[95] He explained his sadness as he introduced his grandchildren to the post-industrial river and the lack of interaction between himself and the Tyne nowadays:

> I don't require anything from the river, and unfortunately in some respects I don't give anything to the river. I've sailed up and down it on pleasure cruises, quite often in fact at least twice per annum if not more, and we'll do so simply because it's a wonderful vehicle for my children and grandchildren that is to actually see the river. But it does sadden me as we travel up and down so much

---

91. Interview with Dawn Tudge.
92. Interview with Pat Rice.
93. Interview with Nellie Faulks, born in Tynemouth, 1948, retired school teacher; recorded by Leona Skelton at the Tyne Rivers Trust offices at Corbridge, 19 Jan. 2015, 10 a.m.
94. Interview with David Fraser.
95. Interview with David Fraser.

Chapter 8. 'A Big River?'

partial dereliction or the remains of the industries which I was familiar with in the past which have now disappeared so it's a bit of a sorrowful trip for me. But at the same time I'm able to explain things and ... now and again you'll get a really exciting ship on the river or possibly even an oil platform coming in for repair or even the construction of some new parts of the oil platforms which is the only growth industry we can see. I believe wind turbines are now coming into the Tyne from abroad or being part assembled here as well so there are newnesses there, but as we move up towards the city Newcastle which was a tremendous hub of industry on the river, it's now social really, either side of the river it's either hotels, apartments or night life, you know radical change in the centre of town.[96]

David preferred the busy, industrial river, and he misses the strong local and regional pride that the economically productive Tyne underpinned and instilled in him in his youth, but he has not given up hope that the river could be economically productive again in the future. He said 'I still feel that it's a resource which could be exploited', and although

we've seen that fabulous industry move to ... the Far East or elsewhere ... I'd have really loved to have seen those things resurrected and there's a national pride in the area which if a large company was to want to develop on the river and there was a land mass available for them to be sort of anchored there, [if] the local authorities would support [it] and there was money available, I think industry could take off again.[97]

Whereas, 'in reality' he admitted 'I don't think that would actually happen', he emphasised nevertheless 'that's my ideal, if I could say, to reinstate the industry'.[98] For the people who lament deindustrialisation, from which many are still suffering even now, it is difficult to celebrate the clean Tyne, the regenerated quayside between Newcastle and Gateshead, the tourism it attracts and the major environmental improvements that enable wildlife and plant species to thrive. Only by conducting oral histories does the true complexity of local feelings in relation to the clean-up become apparent. Some people, such as Dawn Tudge, expressed ambivalence by speaking very positively about the sensory experience of cycling to work, but very negatively about the decline in industry. The post-clean-up era, of course, is far from complete and further improvements are continually being made to enable wildlife and plant species to thrive, to restore the riverbanks and to improve the river water quality.

---

96. Interview with David Fraser.
97. Interview with David Fraser.
98. Interview with David Fraser.

Perhaps in two or three decades' time, attitudes will have changed again as a new generation establishes its own multiple relationships and engagements with their River Tyne. Over the last five centuries, attitudes towards the Tyne have changed very swiftly from one generation to another. This underlines the urgent need to harvest the stories of local people as a matter of course when studying an environmental change as dramatic as the clean-up of the Tyne.

Conclusion

Sara Pritchard has observed that the prioritisation of environmental concerns above others such as economic productivity is far less likely to occur when a country is in crisis and far more likely to occur when its national needs are met.[99] She elaborates, therefore, that 'river history is limited by human history because it relies on human resources or lack of human need to harness the river's resources for its condition', noting that 'even when agencies and organisations seem to be putting the river first, they are often using the river to further their own reputation, political agenda or other objectives'.[100] It is important to remain mindful that the opportunity to put the environment first was created by deindustrialisation. Productive industry was not closed down strategically by angry anglers, conservationists or local and national governors to make way for a cleaner river as part of a grand master plan. As R. and D. Stradling remind us, 'if people were relying on paychecks from polluting businesses, they would not have been able to support environmental concerns that sought to close down such businesses, or at least to make them less profitable, thereby endangering jobs'.[101] In the case study of Cleveland, Ohio, 140,000 manufacturing jobs were lost between 1920 and 1990, which was a crucial prerequisite for the development of environmentalism.[102] The current vision for the Tyne, in which the river's environmental health and the needs of its flora and fauna are prioritised, was born out of the economic, political and cultural identity crisis that characterised post-industrial Tyneside.

All of the above ecological, environmental and recreational successes resulted from deindustrialisation and the regeneration efforts that stepped in to fill the resultant void that had characterised Tynesiders' socio-environmental relationships with the river in the 1980s and 1990s, as they came to terms with the loss of their industrial river. The late twentieth century saw the successful

---

99. Pritchard, *Confluence*, p. 3.
100. Ibid.
101. Stradling and Stradling, 'Perceptions of the Burning River', p. 521.
102. Ibid., p. 529.

Chapter 8. 'A Big River?'

diversion of untreated domestic and industrial waste from the river by means of Northumbrian Water Ltd's waste water treatment works at Howdon and the network of pipelines which serves it. Building on this crucial foundation, in the early twenty-first century, as the Environment Agency and Northumbrian Water Ltd have worked towards the ambitious environmental goals of the EU Water Framework Directive (2000), we have seen a profusion of ecologically responsible conservation efforts to boost the river's biodiversity. These efforts have created a cleaner and safer riverscape in which a diverse range of people can engage in river recreation. But while it might not seem obvious at first glance, especially in the aesthetically pleasing AONB of the upper South Tyne valley, there is still an inordinate amount of work to be done before the Tyne will be given a clean bill of health. First, it must be enabled and encouraged to recover from the serious legacies of its industrialisation: from gravel extraction, to riparian land contamination, to the incorporation of harmful minerals into its bed and banks.

Many histories have been written explaining what has been done to the Tyne – the extensive engineering works of the nineteenth century that turned it into a large-scale, grand and deep channel, the waste that was poured into the river's estuary via over 270 sewers, the piers that made its mouth safe for shipping and the iconic bridges that connected its banks. However, comparatively little has been written about what the river has done to us, how it shaped life experiences, how it made and makes people feel and how and why the organisations responsible for its management have started to work much more sensitively with the river as a natural system rather than as a profit-maximisation facility. Oral history can explain in detail, and without simplifying the true complexities of the issues, what the river has done to us and it should be used much more alongside documentary evidence to understand human relationships with rivers and how and why they have changed so dramatically over time. Sensory experiences, fond memories, stories of fear and joy, personal and intimate details of touchpoints between people's lives and the river that flows through their daily lives, livelihoods and communities are all there in the minds of people, people who are as much a part of the river's history as the river is part of theirs. Oral history is uniquely useful as a means of illuminating the two-way processes between the River Tyne and the people who have played, lived and worked near its flowing water.

CONCLUSION

Over five centuries, people have created a wide variety of new and different River Tynes both in their minds and physically on the ground. This study has revealed that many people carry personally precious bygone Tynes in their memories and they envision imaginative new and different Tynes of the future. Even the material Tyne, the river that is making its way powerfully to the North Sea today, is not perceived and experienced uniformly. For some it stirs lament, disappointment and sadness while for others it evokes hope, pride and wonder. Some, as we have seen, choose not to engage with it directly at all, while others spend time next to it daily. The Tyne has woven its way into and forged innumerable, unique and diverse socio-environmental relationships with the people who have chosen to engage with it as part of life, work and play. By taking the river and our changing interactions with it as a central focus, we can understand a great deal more about ourselves, about the limitations and value of our governmental structures and, perhaps most importantly, about our own place in the long-term history of interactions with the Tyne. By analysing the past conservatorships of a river, we can objectify ourselves through our descendants' eyes and reconnect ourselves not only to our past, but also to our future. Zooming out to study and make sense of our interactions with the Tyne over centuries rather than decades can sharpen our appreciation of the potentially temporary nature and vulnerability of our own conservatorship.

The changing meanings over time of the term conservator provide a revealing summary of the main temporal phases of socio-environmental entanglement with the Tyne: 1529 to 1855; 1855 to 1972; and 1972 to the present day. During the first phase, conservatorship meant the responsibility to prevent the liquid highway from silting up so as to ensure the continuity of substantial income from shipping and ballast tolls. This early modern concept of conservatorship was eroded in the mid-nineteenth century as the term came increasingly to mean very fast, maximal and large-scale 'improvement' of the river estuary's capacity for navigation, industry and trade. The investigative Commission into the State of the Tyne in 1855 confirmed and sealed the transi-

Conclusion

tion to this new conceptualisation of what conserving a river involved. If you ask a modern day representative of any of the agencies that contribute to the Tyne's current management how they understand 'conserving the river', they will probably tell you that it means protecting the river from previous and new pollution in order to encourage its native biodiversity and wider environmental health to thrive. However, if you look a little deeper into each of these three heavily simplified temporal phases, there has always been a minority of people who have imagined and desired conceptual Tynes that have contradicted and challenged the political status quo. Some, including Ralph Gardner, wanted to develop the Tyne's shipping infrastructure and riparian industries far more dramatically and in relatively undeveloped riparian places such as North and South Shields, whereas Newcastle Corporation wanted to maintain the oligarchic monopoly and the status quo which kept their coffers full. From 1866, the Tyne Salmon Conservancy's vision for the river as a fruitful habitat for thriving Tyne fisheries co-existed somewhat problematically with the very different industrial vision of the Tyne Improvement Commission, in which the Tyne was developed to its maximal potential to support industry, navigation and trade. In the early and mid-twentieth century, local governors wanted a clean Tyne, central governors were largely indifferent to the continuance of a dirty Tyne unless it threatened public health and SCORP scientists saw the river increasingly as an interconnected system which was sensitive to pollution. Even today, while the river's conservators pursue noble and progressive policies that prioritise the Tyne's flora, fauna and clean water, others are still dreaming of an industrial Tyne which once again works for its living and supports regional economic prosperity and pride.

Throughout the twentieth century, in the USA, the term conservation had widely divergent simultaneous meanings in the eastern and western states. As Marc Reisner observes, 'to easterners, "conservation" of water usually means protecting rivers from development; in the West, it means building dams'.[1] In the particular case of river management, as in every other aspect of society, politics, culture, economy and environmental interaction, humans will continue to disagree about what a river is for and about where exactly to draw the legal, political and economic lines that limit and guide our interaction with these powerful forces of water. 'Improvement' is an idiom and in the nineteenth century, it became an ideology designed consciously to instil a deep belief in the wisdom of changing the river in a particular way to prioritise industry, commerce and navigation. Today, another ideology of environmental and

---

1. Reisner, *Cadillac Desert*, p. 12.

ecological responsibility is attempting to herd Tynesiders towards its vision of a biodiverse, clean and natural river. But, as with any ideology, some people will always stray from the flock and develop different visions, some compatible and some incompatible, whether in their minds or on the ground.

While 500 years seems like a long-term chronology for a river history, any geologist will confirm that this captures merely a snapshot in the context of the river's total history. Yet it was during the last half millennium that the river's experiences became entangled and fused most dramatically with those of the humans living, working and playing on its banks. During this time the Tyne has seen numerous generations of Tynesiders come and go. The river of 1960, with its bubbling and toxic, discoloured water flowing within concrete and straight walls amid a cacophony of factories, metal-bashing industry and busy river traffic, might well have been unrecognisable to those who knew it before 1500, and perhaps even to those who knew the river before 1855, when it still featured substantial river islands, a sand bar between North and South Shields, the angular rock projections which punctuated its estuarine journey to the North Sea and the salmon that leapt towards their spawning grounds upriver. Would someone who last saw the Tyne estuary in 1960 recognise the riverscape today, with its river cruises, art gallery, music hall and clean water? The changes have been tumultuous, to put it mildly. How we make sense of those changes has enormous consequences for the future of the river and for the future of its people and their region. Authorities such as the Environment Agency, the Port of Tyne, Northumbrian Water Ltd, the Clean Tyne Project, local councils and the Tyne Rivers Trust, consider in depth proposals to change the river's future, as did all of their predecessors. By studying five centuries of Tyne conservatorship, regulation and management, we can see that the period between 1855 and 1972 was a blip on the graph of environmental concern, preceded and followed by more sustainable engagement with the river as a whole and natural system. Even during this blip, however, many people expressed environmental concern and organisations such as the TSC, SCORP, a plethora of local governors and Tyne anglers tried in historically important ways to protect the river's environmental health from harm, as they perceived it.

Where does the Tyne's environmental story fit in relation to White's 'organic machine', Pritchard's 'envirotechnical landscape', and Barca's 'industrial riverscape'? What this study has highlighted unmistakably is the multitude of different Tynes over time, space and in the minds of different Tynesiders. We have taken a tour of the main imaginative and actual Tynes that have been created, adapted and swept away, and a few personal and intimate Tynes too. But

Conclusion

we must appreciate that the overwhelmingly rich multitude of relationships between Tynesiders and the Tyne is far more complex than any study could capture in full. The framework provided in this study is just that, a framework. Onto this framework, hundreds of thousands of oral history interviews of people's relationships with the Tyne could be applied to create a very complex and realistic representation of the multifarious two-way interactions the river has forged with its people even within living memory. If we could reconstruct the true complexity of socio-environmental entanglements with the Tyne, even over the last 500 years, we would truly be dazzled by the multitude of meanings, feelings, visions and relationships that people have forged with just one river. This study was envisaged as a starting point and it is hoped that many more historians will contribute more detailed research to particular themes and shorter chronologies of its framework. For example, the relationship between Lord William Armstrong and the Tyne could easily fill a volume. So, too, could an environmental history of brewing and its impact on the river, of Tynemouth Rowing Club or of a particular Tyne tributary such as Haltwhistle Burn or Jarrow's River Don. In short, while we will never write the full history of our entanglements with the Tyne – or with any other river, for that matter – we should never stop trying to understand them and their importance to many crucial elements of our lives, livelihoods and futures.

Environmental historians already pay close attention to the two-way interactions between the human and the natural, but they must also attend to the complex historical development of administrative, religious, political, cultural, legal, economic, social and, perhaps most importantly, attitudinal change. Such changes over time set the parameters of socio-environmental engagement, fuelled different motivations to alter the environment and inspired and sometimes even forced people to reassess their environmental engagement over time. This study has argued that administrative changes have had the most profound impact on the changing parameters of socio-environmental entanglement with the Tyne. Institutions are merely sets or systems of rules, and as such they provide an excellent floor plan within which we can articulate and make sense of the dramatic changes that have remodelled our intercourse with the river, time after time. However, other factors played crucial contributory roles too, most notably economic, legal and political changes. As we have seen in every chapter, such important changes in human society can transform, and sometimes revolutionise, the whole framework within which a natural system can function independently. By imprisoning a sentient human being in a locked cell, you cannot necessarily kill their independent ability to move, to think, to feel and to perform biological functions. While a prison cell would limit some of the prisoner's natural expressions, by placing them between narrower parameters, the prisoner would continue to perform many of them regardless. Very similarly, the industrial Tyne continued to express itself independently within its new and different, but substantially narrower, parameters. The Tyne never died, even in the 1960s when its salmon suffocated in its toxic water. Over 500 years, the Tyne was never brought fully under human domination and never lost its capacity to behave in unpredictable, powerful and natural ways.

There were advantages and disadvantages for people, the river and its wildlife both before and after the clean-up that began in the early 1970s. The cleaner river was a central part of a new and different environment rather than a necessarily better environment. It is important to appreciate that local people have *both* positive memories of the industrial, busy and economically productive Tyne and negative memories of the more recent clean Tyne. Understandably, the clean-up of the Tyne has been celebrated by local councils, environmentalists, the local press, anglers, canoeists, cyclists, tourists and large numbers of the public. But while very few people would be happy to see 270 sewers draining domestic and industrial waste directly into the river estuary again, some people who can remember the busy, bustling and economically productive Tyne, do lament particular aspects of the 'dirty' environment in which they played as children and which provided employment for large numbers of Tynesiders working in heavy industries, most notably shipbuilding. Oral history interviews revealed the large, and perhaps surprising, extent to which more than a few people speak positively about the pre-clean up era and that happy and fond memories of direct engagement with the river coexist in some people's minds alongside heavily polluted water, malodorous air and a noisy soundscape. A biologically dead and deoxygenated river, it seems, was not incompatible with pleasurable engagement.

Throughout all the phases of development, the river's conservators have made their decisions according to the technologies available at the time. Before the arrival of steam dredgers, Newcastle Corporation was paranoid about the river silting up because they knew that such an economically damaging situation could only have been reversed very slowly by the labour of keelmen and their shovels. In this sense, while Newcastle's Mayor and aldermen worked with the river far more as a natural system and respected its capabilities to silt up, we should remain mindful that they were forced to do so by limited technology. The TIC was able to dominate the river far more assertively. Although even the Tyne commissioners did not control the river's natural functions com-

Conclusion

pletely, their technologically sophisticated toolkit enabled them to feel relatively complacent compared to their predecessors. This fuelled the commissioners' increasing confidence to make the river work as a facility, as a piece of infrastructure and as a powerful machine which, once constructed, could be relied on to do quite a lot of its own work as long as it was maintained efficiently. The current work to improve the river's environmental health is underpinned by a different sort of expertise, that of ecological science, but it is also only possible because economic dependence on the river was reduced very substantially by global economic shifts that resulted in late twentieth-century Tyneside's rapid deindustrialisation.

Less than a month before this study went to press, the UK voted to leave the European Union on 23 June 2016, with potentially enormous consequences for the Tyne's environmental health, notably in terms of the robust and ambitious protection it receives from the EU Water Framework Directive (2000). The River Tyne did not vote in the Referendum, yet its results could potentially impact on the river's health very significantly. Across continental Europe, several large and small rivers are necessarily international and communal. In 1986, for example, a fire in a Swiss riparian chemical factory at Sandoz on the River Rhine caused widespread damage to fish, as it ignited over a thousand metric tons of insecticides, herbicides, fungicides and fertilisers, but it also necessitated shutting down some Dutch water-supply intakes hundreds of miles downriver.[2] The potential for long-distance water damage means that many European continental countries must work together to share their rivers responsibly forever. In the UK, while the Tyne's source is below the Anglo-Scottish border, England shares several other rivers with Scotland. If the Scots decide to leave the UK in the coming months, and to remain in the EU, England will face a similarly unavoidable need to regulate rivers with a foreign neighbour whose regulatory framework and values in relation to rivers and to the wider environment are unlikely to be identical. Only time will tell what a future chapter nine of this book would have looked like. Had it been written in 2035, it would have had to make sense of the Tyne's post-EU era and how the UK's historic decision to leave the EU shaped a new and different relationship with a Tyne in the possession of fewer environmental rights. On a positive note, there are several robust safety nets that will in all likelihood ensure that the Tyne will continue to be protected from both historical and new harmful pollutants, limitations and damage. The Tyne Rivers Trust, the Environment

---

2. D. Kinnersley, *Troubled Water: Rivers, Politics and Pollution* (London: Hilary Shipman, 1988), p. 3; Cioc, *The Rhine*, p. 109.

Figure 21. Looking Upriver on the Main Tyne at Newburn (Photograph: Gordon Ball)

Figure 22. Looking Upriver to Newcastle from St Anthony's (Photograph: Gordon Ball)

Conclusion

Agency, the Port of Tyne, the Clean Tyne Project and Northumbrian Water Ltd are populated by people who respect the river as an ecologically complex, natural and whole system. They are well aware that this river system was taken to the brink by urbanisation and industrialisation and their work is organised within political, legal and administrative systems designed specifically to nurse the river back to health. Without an EU Water Framework Directive, will they continue to protect the river from pollution? I sincerely believe that they will and that Tyneside's oldest Geordie will continue to thrive and flourish as a natural, powerful and dramatic natural system. One thing is for sure, whatever political direction Tynesiders and the wider UK moves in next, the Tyne will come with us, as it has done in the past. For the most part, it will go with the flow.

In answer to the central guiding questions posed in the introduction, 'what have we done to the river and what has the river done to us?', this study has emphasised the large extent to which this is a symbiotic and dyadic process. Even the TIC, which tried more than any other organisation in the last five centuries to bring the river fully under their control, ultimately failed. While the TIC undoubtedly shaped and changed the river more than any of the other humans involved in its history, so too did the river shape the TIC, often forcing it to modify its own administrative and economic parameters. Many human cultures advocate the value of respecting and learning from one's elders. If the Tyne is indeed the oldest Geordie, like a village elder for Newcastle-Gateshead and perhaps for the whole Tyne catchment, then maybe it is fitting that our new and different socio-environmental parameters of river management encourage the Tyne to teach us as much as it possibly can about its biodiversity, its natural rhythms and our place within its fluid environment as it journeys from its sources to the North Sea. Undoubtedly, as the Tyne continues to flow into, through and out of successive future generations of Tynesiders, each will forge new and different visions with the river in their minds, reimagining new and different Tynes and engaging with them in diverse, sustainable and sometimes reckless and irresponsible ways, Tyne and Tyne again.

BIBLIOGRAPHY

Manuscript Primary

Northumberland Record Office, Woodhorn, Northumberland

1454/2/3: Tyne Salmon Conservancy Minute Book, 1866–1894.

3451/A/1: Board of Conservators of the Fishery District of the River Tyne Minute book, March 1915 to December 1929.

3451/A/1a: Board of Conservators of the Fishery District of the River Tyne Minute book, 1930–1950.

3451/A/3: Northumberland and Tyneside River Board Minute Book, 1950–1951.

3451/A/16: Northumberland and Tyneside River Board, Pollution Prevention Committee Minute Book, 1964–1965.

3451/A/40: Ministry of Housing and Local Government Inquiry into Proposals for Reducing Pollution of the River Tyne Estuary and adjacent Sea Beaches: proofs of evidence submitted by various interested bodies, (1970).

The National Archives, Kew, London

BT 31/32163/131220: Tyne Washed Sand and Gravel Company Ltd.

ADM 1/18389: RIVERS AND CANALS (68): Tyne Improvement Commission proposal for tunnel under the river Tyne: Admiralty statement of dredging requirements, (1945–46).

ADM 169/893: River South Tyne at Haydon Bridge: River bank erosion and encroachments, river bed ownership and extraction of sand and gravel, (1950).

AT 35/108: Procedural aspects of the post enquiry consideration of the Kielder Dam scheme, item 38, letter from the Department of the Environment, (1973).

C 10/15/83: Chancery Depositions.

C 2/ELIZ/F1/46: Chancery Depositions.

CRES 37/999: Tyne River Removal of Gravel (1915).

CRES 37/1026: Tyne River Removal of Gravel (1919).

E 367/1444a: Exchequer Pipe Rolls, Crown Leases.

E 134/31CHAS2/EAST18: Exchequer, Office of First Fruits and Tenths.

E 134/7WM3/EAST30: Exchequer, Office of First Fruits and Tenths.

E 134/41Eliz/East34: Exchequer Depositions, Northumberland.

Bibliography

E 317/Northumberland /4: Exchequer, Office of First Fruits and Tenths.

G/TFB/1/1: The Fishery Board for the Fishery District of the River Tyne. Annual Report for the year 1939 and Annual Report for the Year 1940.

HLG 50/2051: Tyne Salmon Conservancy: Discharge of sewage into River Tyne, (1930–51).

HLG 127/541: Proposed Tyneside Sewage Disposal Scheme, 5 March 1960–16 January 1961.

HLG 127/540, Tyne Sewage Scheme, 1958–1960.

HLG 127/1286: Northumbrian River Authority, Kielder Water Reservoir Scheme: applications for licences in connection with impounding and abstracting water in connection with the Kielder Water Reservoir.

HLG 127/1285: Northumbrian River Authority, Kielder Water Reservoir Scheme: applications for licences in connection with impounding and abstracting water in connection with the Kielder Water Reservoir (1971).

HLG 127/1280: Documents submitted to the Kielder inquiry.

MAF 326/322: River Tyne Sub-Committee: Condition of tidal portion of River Tyne; summary of evidence, 1922–1931 (1932), report no. 374.

MAF 326/460: Observations upon pollution of River Tyne Estuary (1938), report no. 576.

MAF 326/134: Condition of River Tyne: 1926 Fishing season, (March, 1927).

MAF 326/141: Condition of River Tyne based on concentration of dissolved oxygen at Swingbridge, Newcastle upon Tyne, (1927).

MAF 326/100: River Tyne Sub-Committee on the condition of the river at Felling, report number 131, (1926).

MAF 326/5: Pollution of the River Tyne at Swing Bridge, report no. 32, (December 1922).

MAF 326/33: Oxygenation of Upper River Tyne, (1924).

MAF 209/3042: Northumbrian Water Authority (Kielder Water) Order 1974: Fish Pass Facilities, (1974–1977).

MAF 135/775: Engineering Assessor's report, (February and March 1972, item 23b.

MAF 209/3042: Northumbrian Water Authority (Kielder Water) Order 1974: fish pass Facilities, (1974–1977).

MT 23/534/16, Pollution of River Tyne by Oilers in Dry-dock: Complaints and instructions regarding prevention (1916).

ZLIB 2/73: *Tyne Improvement Commission Centenary, 1850–1950: A Century of Progress* (1951).

Tyne and Wear Archives, Newcastle on Tyne

BC.RV/1/1–9: Tyne River Court Minute Books, 1644–1834.

MD.NC/2/1: Newcastle Common Council Order Book, 1645–1650.

MD.NC/238: Borough of Newcastle Upon Tyne River Committee Minute Book.

IC.T/1/1: River Tyne Commission Minute Book, 1850–1855.

IC.T/1/2: River Tyne Commission Minute Book, 1855–1859.

IC.T/1/3: River Tyne Commission Minute Book, 1859–1862.

Bibliography

Oral History Interviews

Anon., born in North Shields, 1976, scientist and community worker; recorded by Leona Skelton, at the Old Low Light Heritage Centre Café, 22 January 2015, 11 a.m.

Chittenden, Ruth, born in Newcastle under Lyme, 1983, student; recorded by Leona Skelton, at the Old Low Light Heritage Centre Café, 22 January 2015, 2 p.m.

Eccles, Kate, born in Hexham, 1985, designer in the arts and theatre industry; recorded by Leona Skelton, at the Old Low Light Heritage Centre Café, 22 January 2015, 9.30 a.m.

Faulks, Nellie, born in Tynemouth, 1948, retired school teacher; recorded by Leona Skelton at the Tyne Rivers Trust offices at Corbridge, 19 January 2015, 10 a.m.

Fidler, Alan, born in North Shields, 1949, taxi driver; recorded by Leona Skelton, at the Old Low Light Heritage Centre Café, 22 January 2015, 1 p.m.

Fraser, David, born in Tynemouth, 1946, retired telecommunications engineer; recorded by Leona Skelton, at David's home, 30 January 2015, 5 p.m.

Gibson, Ceri, born in Farnham, 1974, environmental scientist; recorded by Leona Skelton, at Tyne Rivers Trust Offices, Corbridge, 21 January 2015, 11 a.m.

Hall, Matt, born in Newcastle on Tyne, 1957, Royal Mail processing operator; recorded by Leona Skelton at his home in West Denton, 23 January 2015, 3.30 p.m.

Henderson, Tony, born in Hebburn, 1947, journalist; recorded by Leona Skelton at his home in Cullercoats, 30 January 2015, 2 p.m.

Pearson, Brian, born in Hexham [due to the wartime relocation of pregnant women during WW2], 1941, retired painter and decorator; recorded by Leona Skelton, at the Old Low Light Heritage Centre Café, 22 January 2015, 3.30 p.m.

Pollard, Aidan, born in Blaydon, 1945, Fisheries Consultant; recorded by Leona Skelton, at Tyne Rivers Trust Office, Corbridge, 19 January 2015, 3 p.m.

Rice, Eric, born in East Denton, 1938, retired glassworker; recorded by Leona Skelton at Eric's home in Throckley, 20 January 2015, 11 a.m.

Rice, Pat, born in Newburn, 1938, retired shopworker; recorded by Leona Skelton at Pat's home in Throckley, 30 January 2015, 10 a.m.

Saddington, Pearl, born in South Shields, heritage centre manager; recorded by Leona Skelton, at the Old Low Light Heritage Centre, 22 January 2015, 3 p.m.

Simpson, Jennifer, born in Newcastle on Tyne, 1940, retired school teacher; recorded by Leona Skelton, at Tyne Rivers Trust Offices, Corbridge, 20 January 2015, 2 p.m.

Southern, Sally, born in Easington, County Durham, 1973, textile artist; recorded by Leona Skelton, at the Old Low Light Heritage Centre Café, 22 January 2015, 9.45 a.m.

Stark, Martin, born in the Wirral, 1956, fisheries and environmental consultant; recorded by Leona Skelton, at Tyne Rivers Trust Offices, Corbridge, 20 January 2015, 11 a.m.

Stewart, Pauline, born in Dundee, Scotland, 1968, staff nurse; recorded by Leona Skelton, at the Old Low Light Heritage Centre Café, 22 January 2015, 12.30 p.m.

Tudge, Dawn, born in Gateshead, 1974, PR administrator; recorded by Leona Skelton at her home in Ryton, 24 January 2015, 1 p.m.

Bibliography

Wardle, Barbara, born in Corbridge 1947, retired retail manager; recorded by Leona Skelton, at Tyne Rivers Trust Offices, Corbridge, 21 January 2015, 2 p.m.

Wilson, Mary, born in Nottingham, 1948, retired doctor; recorded by Leona Skelton, at Tyne Rivers Trust Offices, Corbridge, 20 January 2015, 11 a.m.

Young, Wendy, born in Amble, Northumberland, 1976, full-time mother; recorded by Leona Skelton, at the Old Low Light Heritage Centre Café, 22 January 2015, 11.30 a.m.

Printed Primary

Anon., *The Ancient Manufacture of White Saltmaking at South and Northshields, Sunderland and Blyth...* (1655).

Anon., *Reprints of Rare Tracts and Imprints of Ancient Manuscripts Chiefly Illustrative of the History of the Northern Counties*, vol. 3 (1847).

Anon., *Narrative of the Great Flood in the Rivers Tyne, Tease, Wear &c on the 16th and 17th of Nov 1771. Collected from the most authentic papers yet published* (Newcastle, 1772).

Armstrong, W., *Observations on the Improvement of the Navigation of the Tyne* (Newcastle, 1836).

Bell, J., *An Account of the Great Flood in the River Tyne on Dec 30 1815* (1816).

Calver, E., *A Letter to the Tyne Improvement Commissioners by Edward K. Calver, Esq. R.N. Admiralty Surveyor* (Newcastle, 1852).

Clean Tyne Project, *Education Resource Pack* (Gateshead: Port of Tyne, 2013).

Dodd, P., *The Salmon of the Tyne and of the Dams* (1856).

Ellis, W., *News from Newcastle* (London, 1651).

Gardner, R., *England's Grievance Rediscovered* (London, 1655).

Guthrie, J., *The River Tyne: Its History and Resources* (London: Longmans and Co., 1880).

Johnson, R., *The Making of the Tyne: A Record of Fifty Years' Progress, with Numerous Views and Portraits of those Concerned in the Development of the River* (1895).

MacGregor, J., *Observations on The River Tyne, with a View to the Improvement of its Navigation; Address to the Coal Owners of the District* (Newcastle, Jan., 1832).

MacGregor, J., *A Letter to the Merchants, Coalowners, and Shipowners of Newcastle on the Present State of the Conservatorship of the Tyne* (Newcastle, Oct., 1832).

Newson, M., and Gibson, C. (eds), *Haltwhistle Burn: A Comprehensive Catchment Approach to Headwater Runoff and Pollution. Technical Report of the 2012–2015 Catchment Restoration Fund Project* (Corbridge: Tyne Rivers Trust, 2015).

Northumbrian Anglers' Association, *Handbook and Guide to North Country Angling* (1960).

Palmer, J., *The Tyne and its Tributaries* (London, 1882).

Proceedings of the Tyne Improvement Commission 1876–1968, 92 vols. (Newcastle, 1876–1968).

Proud, J. (ed.), *A Tug's Rescue Work: The Autobiography of a Retired Tugmaster* (2003).

Bibliography

Report of the Commissioners Appointed to Inquire into the Present State of the River Tyne; together with the Minutes of Evidence and Appendix (London: George Edward Eyre and William Spottiswoode, 1855).

Richardson, M. (ed.), *The Conservatorship of the River Tyne* (Newcastle, 1849).

Tyne Rivers Trust, Newsletter, issue 16 (Spring/Summer 2014).

White, G., *The Natural History and Antiquities of Selborne* (1789).

Watson, A., *The Tyne* (1889).

White, W., *Northumberland and the Border* (1859).

Newspapers

Graham, H., 'Winter Storms leave River Tyne flowing at Record-Breaking Rates', *Chronicle Live* (15 January 2016).

'Foul', *Newcastle Journal* (14 July 1943).

'Boffins sail down the Tyne on sewage survey', *Evening Chronicle* (16 October 1959).

'The River Tyne will be a Salmon River again in Ten Years', *Evening Chronicle* (11 June 1960).

'Tyne Valley Flooding Approved', *The Times* (5 October 1973).

'Fish hatchery on the Tyne', *Anglers' Mail* (20 July 1977).

Secondary Works

Ackroyd, P., *Thames: Sacred River* (London: Vintage, 2008).

Anfinson, J., *The River we have Wrought: A History of the Upper Mississippi* (Minneapolis: University of Minnesota Press, 2003).

Anon., *The Mid-Tyne Villages of Northumberland: a History in Photographs of Ovingham, Ovington, Stocksfield* (Morpeth: Northumberland County Library, 1993).

Appuhn, K., 'Friend or Flood? The Dilemmas of Water Management in Early Modern Venice', in A. Isenberg (ed.), *The Nature of Cities: Culture, Landscape and Urban Space* (New York: University of Rochester Press, 2006), pp. 79–102.

Archer, D., 'Kielder Water: White Elephant or White Knight?', in D. Archer (ed.), *Tyne and Tide: A Celebration of the River Tyne* (Ovingham: Daryan Press, 2000), pp. 138–156.

Archer, D., 'The Rape of the Tyne: Gravel Extraction', in D. Archer (ed.), *Tyne and Tide: A Celebration of the River Tyne* (Ovingham: Daryan Press, 2000), pp. 44–58.

Arnold, E. 'Engineering Miracles: Water Control, Conversion, and the Creation of a Religious Landscape in the Medieval Ardennes," *Environment and History* **13** (4) (2007): 477–502.

Barca, S., *Enclosing Water: Nature and Political Economy in a Mediterranean Valley, 1796–1916* (Cambridge: The White Horse Press, 2010).

Blakey, H., *Newcastle Potters and the Export of Earthernware from Newcastle on Tyne 1739 to 1796* (Stoke on Trent, 2001).

Bibliography

Breeze, L., *The British Experience with River Pollution, 1865–1876* (New York: Peter Lang, 1993).

Campbell, W., *A Century of Chemistry on Tyneside, 1868–1968* (Newcastle: Society of Chemical Industry, 1968)

Cadzow, A., D. Byrne and H. Goodall, with S. Wearing, *Waterborne: Vietnamese Australians and Sydney's Georges River Parks and Green Spaces* (Sydney: UTS ePress, 2011).

Cavert, W., 'The Environmental Policy of Charles I: Coal Smoke and the English Monarchy, 1624–40', *Journal of British Studies* 53 (2) (2014): 310–33.

Cavert, W., *The Smoke of London: Energy and Environment in the Early Modern City* (Cambridge: Cambridge University Press, 2016).

Chaplin, M., et al., *Tyne View: A Walk around the Port of Tyne* (Newcastle: New Writing North, 2012).

Charlton, B., *Upper North Tynedale: A Northumbrian Valley and its People* (Newcastle: Northumbrian Water, 1987).

Cioc, M., *The Rhine: An Eco-Biography, 1815–2000* (Seattle, Washington, USA: University of Washington Press, 2002).

Ciriacono, S., *Building on Water: Venice, Holland and the Construction of the European Landscape in the Early Modern Times* (Oxford: Berghahn, 2006).

Clavering, E., and Rounding, A., 'Early Tyneside Industrialism: The Lower Derwent and Blaydon Burn Valleys 1550–1700', *Archaeologia Aeliana*, fifth series, 23 (1995): 249–268.

Coates, P., *A Story of Six Rivers: History, Culture and Ecology* (London: Reaktion, 2013).

Coney, A., 'Fish, Fowl and Fen: Landscape Economy in Seventeenth-Century Martin Mere', *Landscape History* 14 (1992): 1–64.

Cruyningen, P., van, 'Dealing with Drainage: State Regulation of Drainage Projects in the Dutch Republic, France, and England during the Sixteenth and Seventeenth Centuries, *Economic History Review* (2014): 1–21.

Curtis, D., *Coping with Crisis: The Resilience and Vulnerability of Pre-Industrial Settlements* (Burlington, Vt: Ashgate Publishing Co., 2014).

Daniels, S., *Fields of Vision: Landscape Imagery and National Identity in England the United States* (Cambridge: Polity Press, 1994).

Deakin, R., *Waterlog: A Swimmer's Journey through Britain* (London: Vintage, 2000).

Dillon, P., *The Tyne Oarsmen: Harry Clasper, Robert Chambers, James Renforth* (Jesmond: Keepdate Publishing, 1993).

Dobson, H., *Exploring the Tyne Valley* (Morpeth: Henry Dobson, 2007).

Ellis, J., 'The Decline and Fall of the Tyneside Salt Industry, 1660–1790: A Re-Examination', *Economic History Review*, Second Series 33 (1) (1980): 45–58.

Evenden, M., *Fish versus Power: An Environmental History of the Fraser River* (Cambridge: Cambridge University Press, 2004).

Fay, I., *Health and the City: Disease, Environment and Government in Norwich, 1200–1575* (Woodbridge: Boydell and Brewer, 2015).

Bibliography

Foster, S. and C. Smout, (eds), *The History of Soils and Field Systems* (Aberdeen: Scottish Cultural Press, 1994).

French, R. and K. Smith, *Lost Shipyards of the Tyne* (Newcastle: Tyne Bridge Publishing, 2004).

Gibbins, C., et al., 'Developing Ecologically Acceptable River Flow Regimes: a Case Study of Kielder Reservoir and the Kielder Water Transfer System', *Fisheries Management and Ecology* 8 (2001): 463–485.

Gilvear, D. and S. Winterbottom, 'Changes in Channel Morphology, Floodplain Land Use and Flood Damage on the Rivers Tay and Tummell Over the Last 250 years: Implications for Floodplain Management', in R. Bailey, P. Jose and B. Sherwood (eds), *United Kingdom Floodplains* (London: Westbury, 1998), pp. 92–115.

Goodall, H., D. Byrne and A. Cadzoe, with S. Wearing, *Waters of Belonging: Arabic Australians and the Georges River Parklands* (Sydney: UTS ePress, 2012).

Graham, F., *Bellingham and the North Tyne: A Short History and Guide* (Newcastle: F. Graham, 1972).

Groundwater, K., *Maritime Heritage: Newcastle and the River Tyne* (Newcastle: Silverlink Publishing, 1990).

Grove, R., *Green Imperialism: Colonial Expansion, Tropical Island Edens and the Origins of Environmentalism, 1600–1800* (Cambridge: Cambridge University Press, 1995).

Guy, S. and A. Connelly, 'Placing Jetty', in S. Guy (ed.), *Catalyst: Art, Sustainability and Place in the Work of Wolfgang Weileder* (Berlin: Kerber Verlag, 2015), pp. 35–46.

Hanawalt, B., and L. Kiser (eds), *Engaging with Nature: Essays on the Natural World in Medieval and Early Modern Europe* (Notre Dame, Indiana: University of Notre Dame Press, 2008).

Hawley, S., *Recovering a Lost River: Removing Dams, Rewilding Salmon, Revitalizing Communities* (Boston, MA: Beacon Press, 2011).

Histon, V., *Unlocking the Quayside: Newcastle Gateshead's Historic Waterfront Explored* (Newcastle: Tyne Bridge Publishing, 2006).

Hoffmann, R., 'Homo et Natura, Home in Natura: Ecological Perspectives on the European Middle Ages', in B. Hanawalt and L. Kiser (eds), *Engaging with Nature: Essays on the Natural World in Medieval and Early Modern Europe* (Notre Dame, Indiana: University of Notre Dame Press, 2008), pp. 11–38.

Hoffmann, R., 'Elemental Resources and Aquatic Ecosystems: Medieval Europeans and their Rivers', in T. Tvedt and R. Coopey (eds), *A History of Water: Series II: Volume 2: Rivers and Society: from Early Civilizations to Modern Times* (London: I. B. Tauris, 2010), pp. 165–202.

Hoffmann, R., and V. Winiwarter, 'Making Land and Water Meet: Cycling of Nutrients between Fields and Ponds in Pre-Modern Europe', *Agricultural History* 84 (3) (2010): 352–380.

Ingold, T., 'Foreword', in S. Guy (ed.), *Catalyst: Art, Sustainability and Place in the Work of Wolfgang Weileder* (Berlin: Kerber Verlag, 2015), pp. 11–20.

Irlam, G., 'Electricity Supply at Cragside', *Industrial Archaeology Review* 11 (2) (1989), pp. 187–195.

Bibliography

Jonas, J., *Walking the Tyne: Twenty-five Walks from Mouth to Source* (Newcastle: Ramblers' Association, 2001).

Kaye, J., 'The (Re)Balance of Nature, c.1250–1350', in B. Hanawalt L. Kiser (eds), *Engaging with Nature: Essays on the Natural World in Medieval and Early Modern Europe* (Notre Dame, Indiana: University of Notre Dame Press, 2008), pp. 85–114.

Kempster, J., *Our Rivers* (London: Oxford University Press, 1948).

Keys, R., and K. Smith, *Tall Ships on the Tyne* (Newcastle: Tyne Bridge Publishing, 2005).

Keys, D., and K. Smith, *Tales from the Tyne* (Newcastle: Tyne Bridge Publishing, 2006).

Knoll, M., and R. Reith (eds), *An Environmental History of the Early Modern Period: Experiments and Perspectives* (Berlin: Lit, 2014).

Kraker, A. de, 'Ice and Water: The Removal of Ice on Waterways in the Low Countries, 1330–1800', *Water History* (2016), DOI 10.1007/s12685-016-1052-3 (open access with no page numbers).

Laing, O., *To the River* (London: Canongate, 2012).

Levine, D., and K. Wrightson, *The Making of an Industrial Society: Whickham, 1560–1765* (Oxford: Oxford University Press, 1991).

Lewis-Stempel, J., *The Private Life of an English Field: Meadowland* (London: Black Swan, 2014).

Linsley, S., 'Tyne Industries', in D. Archer (ed.), *Tyne and Tide: A Celebration of the River Tyne* (Ovingham: Daryan Press, 2000), pp. 190–206.

Linsley, S., 'The Port of Tyne', in D. Archer (ed.), *Tyne and Tide: A Celebration of the River Tyne* (Ovingham: Daryan Press, 2000), pp. 172–189.

Luckin, B., *Pollution and Control: A Social History of the Thames in the Nineteenth Century* (Boca Raton, Florida, USA: CRC Press, 1986).

MacFarlane, R., *Mountains of the Mind: A History of a Fascination* (London: Granta, 2003).

Mah, A., *Industrial Ruination, Community and Place: Landscapes and Legacies of Urban Decline* (London: University of Toronto Press, 2012).

Manders, F., and R. Potts, *Crossing the Tyne* (Newcastle: Tyne Bride Publishing, 2001)

Marshall, M., *Tyne Waters: A River and its Salmon* (London: H. and G. Witherby, 1992).

Marshall, M., *Turning Tides: A History of the Tyne and the Wear* (Newcastle: Keepdate Publishing, 1997).

McCombie, G., 'The Development of Trinity House and the Guildhall before 1700', in D. Newton and A. Pollard, *Newcastle and Gateshead before 1700* (Chichester: Phillimore and Co Ltd, 2009), pp. 63–81.

McCulloch, C., 'Kielder Water and Forest Park: The City in the Country', in P. Coates, D. Moon, and P. Warde (eds), *Local Places, Global Processes: Histories of Environmental Change in Britain and Beyond* (Oxford: Oxbow Books, 2016), pp. 258–267.

McNeill, J., 'Observations on the Nature and Culture of Environmental History', *History and Theory* 42 theme issue (2003): 5–43.

Miles, S., '"Our Tyne": Iconic Regeneration and the Revitalisation of Identity in Newcastle-Gateshead', *Urban Studies* 42 (5–6) (2005): 917.

Bibliography

Moon, D., and L. Skelton, 'Environmental Change: A Local Perspective on Global Processes', in P. Coates, D. Moon and P. Warde (eds), *Local Places, Global Processes: Histories of Environmental Change in Britain and Beyond* (Oxford: Oxbow Books, 2016), pp. 206–223.

Morgan, J., 'Understanding Flooding in Early Modern England', *Journal of Historical Geography* **50** (2015): 37–50.

Mosley, S., *The Chimney of the World: A History of Smoke Pollution in Victorian and Edwardian Manchester* (Cambridge: The White Horse Press, 2001).

Nef, J., *The Rise of the British Coal Industry*, 2 vols. (London: Routledge, 1932).

Newell, E., 'Atmospheric Pollution and the British Copper Industry, 1690–1920', *Technology and Culture* **38** (1997): 655–89.

Oliver, S., 'Liquid Materialities in the Landscape of the Thames: Mills and Weirs from the eighth to the nineteenth century', *Area* **45** (2) (2013): 223–229.

Oram, R., 'Waste Management and Peri-Urban Agriculture in the Early Modern Scottish Burgh', *Agricultural History Review* **59** (1) (June, 2011): 1–17.

Porter, D., *The Thames Embankment: Environment, Society and Technology in Victorian London* (Akron, Ohio, USA: The University of Akron Press, 1998).

Pritchard, S., *Confluence: The Nature of Technology and the Remaking of the Rhone* (London: Harvard University Press, 2011).

Rácz, L., 'The Danube Pontoon Bridge of Pest-Buda (1767–1849) as an Indicator and Victim of the Climate Change of the Little Ice Age', *Global Environment* **9** (2) (2016): 458–83.

Radkau, J., *Nature and Power: A Global History of the Environment* (Cambridge: Cambridge University Press, 2008).

Rae, I., and K. Smith, *Swan Hunter: The Pride and the Tears* (Newcastle: Tyne Bridge Publishing, 2001).

Rangeley-Wilson, C., *Silt Road: The Story of a Lost River* (London: Vintage, 2014).

Rawcliffe, C., *Urban Bodies: Communal Health in Late Medieval English Towns and Cities* (Woodbridge: Boydell and Brewer, 2013).

Reisner, M., *Cadillac Desert: The American West and its Disappearing Water* (New York: Penguin, 1993).

Rennison, R., *Water to Tyneside: A History of the Newcastle & Gateshead Water Company* (Newcastle: Northumberland Press, 1979).

Reynard, P., 'Public Order and Privilege: Eighteenth-Century French Roots of Environmental Regulation', *Technology and Culture* **43** (2002): 1–28.

Reynard, P., 'Charting Environmental Concerns: The Reaction to Hydraulic Public Works in Eighteenth-Century France', *Environment and History* **9** (2003): 251–273.

Richards, J., *The Unending Frontier: An Environmental History of the Early Modern World* (London: University of California Press, 2003).

Ridley, U., 'The History of Glass Making on the Tyne and Wear', *Archaeologia Aeliana*, fourth series, **40** (1962): 145–162.

Ritvo, H., *The Dawn of Green: Manchester, Thirlmere, and Modern Environmentalism* (Chicago: University of Chicago Press, 2009).

Rome, A., 'Coming to Terms with Pollution: The Language of Environmental Reform, 1865–1915', *Environmental History* 1 (1996): 6–28.

Rosenthal, L., *The River Pollution Dilemma in Victorian England: Nuisance Law Versus Economic Efficiency* (Farnham: Ashgate, 2014).

Rowland, T., *Waters of Tyne* (Warkworth: Sandhill Press, 1991).

Rowland, T., and J. Thompson, *Waters of Tyne: A River Journey through History* (Wardworth: Sandhill Press, 1994).

Sargent, A., 'The Tyne', *The Geographical Journal* 40 (5) (1912): 469–482.

Schmid, M., 'The Environmental History of Rivers in the Early Modern Period', in M. Knoll and R. Reith (eds), *An Environmental History of the Early Modern Period: Experiments and Perspectives* (Berlin: Lit, 2014), pp. 19–26.

Schneer, J., *The Thames: England's River* (London: Abacus, 2005).

Schwagerl, C., *The Anthropocene: The Human Era and how it shapes our planet* (London: Synergetic Press, 2014).

Sharples, J., *Liverpool* (London: Yale University Press, 2004).

Sheail, J., *An Environmental History of Twentieth-Century Britain* (Basingstoke: Palgrave, 2002).

Shepherd, N., *The Living Mountain*, 2nd ed. (Edinburgh: Canongate Books, 2011).

Shotton, J., *First, Famous and Forgotten Ships of the Tyne* (Newcastle: Summerhill Books, 2012).

Skelton, L., 'Beadles, Dunghills and Noisome Excrements: Regulating the Environment in Seventeenth-Century Carlisle', *International Journal of Regional and Local History* 9 (1) (May, 2014): 21–38.

Skelton, L., *Sanitation in Urban Britain, 1560–1700* (London: Routledge, 2015).

Smith, K., *Queens of the Tyne: The River's Great Liners, 1888–1973* (Newcastle: Tyne Bridge Publishing, 2007).

Smith, K., and T. Yellowley, *The Story of the Tyne: and the Hidden Rivers of Newcastle* (Newcastle: Tyne Bridge Publishing, 2015).

Smout, C., (ed.), *Scottish Woodland History* (Dalkeith: Scottish Cultural Press, 1997).

Smout, C., 'Highland Land-use before 1800: Misconceptions, Evidence and Realities', in C. Smout (ed.), *Scottish Woodland History* (Dalkeith: Scottish Cultural Press, 1997), pp. 5–22.

Smout, C., *Nature Contested: Environmental History in Scotland and Northern England since 1600* (Edinburgh: Edinburgh University Press, 2000).

Smout, C., and M. Stewart, *The Firth of Forth: An Environmental History* (Edinburgh: Birlinn, 2012).

Sörlin, S., and P. Warde, 'Making the Environment Historical: An Introduction', in S. Sörlin, and P. Warde (eds), *Nature's End: History and the Environment* (Basingstoke: Palgrave Macmillan, 2009), pp. 1–19.

Stradling, D., and R. Stradling, 'Perceptions of the Burning River: Deindustrialization and Cleveland's Cuyahoga River', *Environmental History* 13 (3) (July 2008): 515–535.

Bibliography

Summers, G., *Consuming Nature: Environmentalism in the Fox River Valley, 1850–1950* (Lawrence, Kansas, USA: University of Kansas Press, 2006).

Taylor, V., 'Local History and the Environmental History of the River Thames, 1960–2010', *Transactions of the London and Middlesex Archaeological Society* **64** (2014): 79–92.

Taylor, V., 'Whose River?: London and the Thames Estuary, 1960–2014', *London Journal*, **40** (3) (2015): 244–271.

Taylor, W., 'Misplaced Identities: Cultural and Environmental Sources of Heritage for the "Settler Society" along the Swan River, Perth, Australia', *National Identities* **9** (2) (2007): 143–161.

Thomas, K., *Religion and the Decline of Magic: Studies in Popular Beliefs in Sixteenth- and Seventeenth-Century England* (London: Penguin, 1973).

Thomas, K., *Man and the Natural World: Changing Attitudes in England 1500–1800* (London: Penguin, 1984).

Thornton, R., *The River Tyne from Sea to Source* (Newcastle: Zymurgy Publishing, 2002).

Twain, M., *Life on the Mississippi* (Ware, Hertfordshire: Wordsworth Editions, 2012).

Uglow, J., *Nature's Engraver: A Life of Thomas Bewick* (London: Faber and Faber, 2007).

Warde, P., 'The Environmental History of Pre-Industrial Agriculture in Europe', in Sorlin, S. and P. Warde (eds), *Nature's End: History and the Environment* (Basingstoke: Palgrave Macmillan, 2009), pp. 70–92.

Warde, P., 'The Idea of Improvement, c. 1520–1700', in R. Hoyle (ed.), *Custom, Improvement and Landscape in Early Modern Britain* (Farnham: Routledge, 2011), pp. 127–148.

Warde, P., 'Imposition, Emulation and Adaptation: Regulatory Regimes in the Commons of Early Modern Germany', *Environment and History* **19** (2013): 313–337.

Warde, P. and T. Williamson, 'Fuel Supply and Agriculture in Post-Medieval England', *Agricultural History Review* **62** (2014): 61–82.

Watson, F., 'Rights and Responsibilities: Wood Management as seen through Baron Court Records', in C. Smout (ed.) *Scottish Woodland History* (Edinburgh: Scottish Cultural Press, 1997), pp. 100–113.

White, L., 'The Historical Roots of our Ecologic Crisis', *Science* **155** (1967): 1203–1207.

White, R., *The Organic Machine: The Remaking of the Columbia River* (New York: Hill and Wang, 1995).

Williams, K., 'The Ouse Burn', in R. Deakin et al. (eds), *Caught by the River: A Collection of Words on Water* (London: Cassell, 2009), pp. 214–221.

Woelfe-Erskine, C., 'Rain Tanks, Springs and Broken Pipes as Emerging Water Commons along the Salmon River', *Acme* **14** (1) (2015): 735–750.

Wright, P., *Life on the Tyne: Water Trades on the Lower River Tyne in the Seventeenth and Eighteenth Centuries, a Reappraisal* (Farnham: Ashgate, 2014).

Wrightson, K., *Ralph Tailor's Summer: A Scrivener, his City and the Plague* (London: Yale University Press, 2011).

Zupko, R. and A. Laures, *Straws in the Wind: Medieval Urban Environmental Law – The Case of Northern Italy* (Oxford: Westview, 1996).

Bibliography

Websites

TNA, Legislation Database, Water Resources Act, 1963, online at: http://www.legislation.gov.uk/ukpga/1963/38/contents [webpage accessed 11 July 2016].

TNA Legislation Database, Public Health Act, 1875, online at: http://www.legislation.gov.uk/ukpga/Vict/38–39/55 [webpage accessed 11 July 2016].

Restoring Europe's Rivers, 'Case Study: River Nent: Abandoned Metal Mines', online at: https://restorerivers.eu/wiki/index.php?title=Case_study%3ARiver_Nent%3A_Abandoned_Metal_Mines [website accessed 26 June 2016].

Tyne Kittiwakes Partnership webpage at: http://www.nhsn.ncl.ac.uk/news/cms/tynekittiwakes/ [website accessed 26 June 2016].

See Jetty Project Website at http://jetty-project.info/context/environment/ [website accessed 26 June 2016].

Tyne Live Theatre webpage at: http://www.live.org.uk/about-us/news/tyne-live-theatre%E2%80%99s-play-celebrating-the-river-returns-to-both-north-and-south-of [website accessed 26 June 2016].

INDEX

A

Act of Parliament xvii, 35, 52, 56, 64, 70, 94
Addison, Christopher 157, 167–9
administration xii, 18, 22–3, 28, 30, 55, 65, 79, 84, 115, 185, 186, 249, 253
aesthetic xi, 6, 23, 91, 150, 195–7, 201, 202, 204, 209, 213, 217, 218, 223, 237, 245
agency (of River Tyne) 6, 9, 14, 15, 19, 27, 58, 71, 77, 85, 89, 118, 163, 227, 228–9, 233
agriculture xvi, 24, 31, 41, 51, 56, 74, 77, 175, 193, 199
Albert-Edward Dock 98, 188
aldermen 3, 30, 35, 67, 97, 218, 250
Allendale 73
Alston 5, 6, 73, 135, 138, 139, 148, 153, 178, 197, 233
Anfinson, John 22, 25, 92
angler; angling xvi, 6, 11, 26, 32, 141, 148, 149, 156, 175–8, 181–4, 187, 208, 210, 213, 224–5, 239, 244, 248, 250
aqueduct 32, 197, 198
Archer, David 13
Area of Outstanding National Beauty (AONB) xvi, 233, 245
Armstrong, William, Lord 98, 102–04, 136, 195, 249
Arnold, Ellen 41
art; artist 1, 11, 19, 21, 25, 33, 61, 212, 217, 220, 223, 234, 237, 240, 241, 248

B

Bakethin Reservoir 198, 203, 204, 206, 207
Ball, Gordon xiii, xiv
ballast 35, 46, 48–50, 53–4, 57, 60–2, 66, 67, 69–70, 75, 77–8, 109–12, 124, 132, 140, 146, 180
  toll 3, 29, 30, 35, 64, 66, 67, 69, 218, 246
BALTIC gallery 214, 223, 234, 237
Baltic Sea 1, 49, 180
Barca, Stefania 23, 38, 87, 218–19, 248
barge 34, 44, 68, 79, 80, 98, 120, 224, 226
bed (of river) 6, 13, 14, 19, 24, 30, 33, 35, 44, 46, 61, 62, 65, 73, 74, 75, 76, 77, 79, 82, 87, 89, 96, 107–11, 114–16, 118, 120, 121, 122, 125, 130, 138, 139, 146, 154, 168, 171, 185, 186, 228, 236, 238, 245
Belgium 34, 67, 68
Bewick, Thomas 61, 223
Berwick upon Tweed 2, 51, 58
bio-physical flows 16, 31, 158
bird 180, 212, 220, 225, 232, 234–5
Black Middens xvii, 99–100
Blaydon 101–03, 124, 146, 160, 170, 171, 224
Board of Agriculture and Fisheries *see also* Ministry of Agriculture and Fisheries 148, 151
boat *see also* keel 1, 21, 34, 53, 66–7, 68, 69, 74, 79, 106, 109, 139, 162, 184, 187, 189, 190, 191, 220, 224
boundary
  conceptual 25, 38
  property 112, 113, 121, 143
Breeze, Lawrence 16

Index

bridge 4, 11, 24, 53, 73, 74, 76, 85, 91, 102–04, 114, 115, 233, 237, 238, 245
  Allendale 73
  Gateshead Millenium 214, 217
  Haywood 139, 148
  Hexham 73, 225
  High Level 151
  Lobley Hill 118
  Newburn 112, 146
  Scotswood 107, 137, 139
  Swing 94, 162, 239
  Tyne 4, 11, 45, 73, 81, 94, 101, 190, 218, 224, 239
  Willington 122
  Wylam 163
Bull H. 159–61, 172
butterfly 180, 220
bylaw 35, 44, 51, 53–60, 63, 69, 120
Bywell 48, 139, 198–9

C

cadmium 6, 138, 180, 233
Calvert, Jayne xii
canalising 30, 83, 89, 118
Carmichael, James Wilson 1
Carson, Rachel *see also Silent Spring* 144
catchment xvi, xvii, 4–5, 6, 10, 14, 26, 27, 31, 116, 147, 148, 156, 159, 177, 178, 211, 225, 228, 230, 233, 253
Catcleugh Reservoir 144–5, 173
Cavert, William 38–9
Chaplin, Michael 180, 220
chemical 6, 31, 32, 33, 60, 62, 119, 123–5, 128–30, 133, 136, 159, 161, 165, 179, 182–3, 190, 192, 196, 210, 227–8, 251
chemist 129, 148, 159, 161, 179
child; childhood 27, 61, 73, 149, 188–90, 223, 226–7, 229, 231, 242, 250
Cioc, Mark 23, 71, 93

cleanliness (of the river) 3, 4, 18, 21, 28, 33, 51, 76, 91, 120, 127, 150, 151, 157, 158, 165, 168, 170, 180, 182, 189, 214, 225, 226–7, 229, 233, 235, 240, 241, 243–5, 247, 248, 250
clean-up (of the river) 3, 22, 28, 31, 32, 127, 142, 151, 154–6, 165, 169, 174, 175–93, 213, 220, 223, 226, 227, 237, 243, 244, 250
Clean Tyne Project xii, 4, 26, 33, 226–7, 248, 253
Clyde, R. 2, 15, 19, 96, 176
coal 1, 2, 14, 16, 35, 46, 48–9, 54, 56, 66, 67, 69, 75, 78, 84, 85, 94, 96, 105, 109, 124, 139, 140, 148–50, 161, 179, 196, 198, 200, 212, 219, 222, 224, 241
Coates, Peter x, xvi, 17, 18
collier ship 1, 35, 46, 49
colliery *see also* coal 45, 107, 124, 133–4, 148
colonialism 43–4
Colorado River 193, 197
Columbia River 14, 20, 22, 194, 197, 209, 211
commerce; commercial *see also* trade 1, 26, 45, 49, 50, 57, 61, 76, 83, 90, 91, 109, 114–16, 171, 181, 196, 218, 227, 247
community 17, 18, 26, 30, 32, 38, 39, 59, 63, 70, 71, 73, 78, 91, 173, 175, 176, 180, 187, 188, 194, 196, 197, 200, 202, 205, 208, 210, 219–22, 228, 240, 242, 245
concern, environmental / ecological 10, 37, 40, 13, 44, 56, 63, 107, 123, 130, 134, 135–6, 141, 142, 179, 199, 203, 208, 210, 228, 244, 248
confluence 5, 9, 93
Connelly, Angela xii
conservation; conservationist 3, 4, 6, 7, 10, 22, 24, 40, 41, 42, 43, 61, 91, 135, 151, 180, 200, 213, 218, 219, 220, 228, 229, 244, 245, 247

Index

conservator; conservatorship xi, 3, 4, 10, 19, 24, 25, 29, 30, 35, 50, 52, 53, 64, 74, 78, 80, 84, 86, 88–9, 92, 93, 115, 134, 192, 233, 246, 247, 248, 250
consumerism 21, 22
cooling, industrial 125, 129, 179
Corbridge 105, 118, 133, 135, 164, 165,
Corps of Engineers, US 22, 23, 92
Countryside Commission 201
Cragside 98, 195
Cromwell, Oliver 68, 70
Crown 35, 46, 48, 52, 65, 86, 113, 114
Cruyningen, Piet van 39
Cullercoats xvii, 31, 121, 159
culvert 9, 124, 213, 236
Curtis, Daniel 39
cyanide 124, 160–1, 169

D

dam 22, 23, 31, 32, 48–9, 53, 54, 98, 105, 124, 139, 142, 143, 145, 148, 187, 194–211, 235, 247
Daniels, Stephen 15
Deadwater Fell 5, 12,
Deakin, Roger 8
deforestation 44
deindustrialisation 33, 92, 180, 212, 213, 214, 217, 218, 223, 236, 241, 243–4, 251
Denham, Lucy xii
deoxygenation *see also* oxygen 35, 89, 123. 125, 136, 160, 164, 165, 192, 213, 250
depression, economic 155, 170
Derwent, R. 49, 160, 173, 225
Derwenthaugh 49, 124–6, 235
discharge (of waste into river) 18, 32, 35, 95, 120, 121–36, 145, 148–9, 151, 153–5, 160–1, 165–73, 177–8, 180, 184–5, 225, 233
dock; docking 1, 30, 35, 66, 76, 89, 94–102, 105–07, 109, 121, 124, 125, 127, 132, 140, 143, 174, 188
Don, R. 117, 132, 173 249
Dove Marine Laboratory xvii, 31, 153, 159

dredging; dredger 30, 47, 50, 69, 71, 75–81, 85, 87, 89, 93, 94, 96, 97, 101–24, 130, 133, 134–6, 143, 146, 168, 170, 172, 173, 195, 234, 236, 250
drinking water 51
drought 34, 155, 210, 214
Dudley, Marianna xi
Dunston 118, 131, 151, 179
Dunston Staiths xiii, 212, 213, 223, 234
Durham 46, 49, 58, 107, 153, 240
    Bishop of 47, 52, 62

E

ecology; ecological 4, 11, 17, 37, 40, 42, 43, 56, 99, 100, 110, 144, 146, 147, 151, 156, 174, 176, 180, 196, 197, 199, 200, 208, 209, 213, 214, 224, 226, 235, 244, 245, 248, 251, 253
economy; economic 1, 2, 3, 6, 8, 11–15, 18, 19, 22, 23, 24, 28, 36, 37, 38, 43, 44, 45, 49, 50, 58, 64–6, 68–70, 75, 76, 88, 90, 92, 93, 95, 101, 105, 106, 114, 116, 119, 130, 133, 136, 143, 146, 155, 158, 160, 168, 170, 174, 176, 177, 181, 192, 196, 209, 214, 218, 219, 222, 236, 240, 241, 243, 244, 247, 249, 250, 251, 253
ecosystem 19, 180, 209
effluent *see also* discharge; waste 37, 124, 148, 151–4, 159–61, 169, 173, 179, 180
Ellis, William 16
Empire; imperialism 15, 76, 78, 227
employment *see also* unemployment 48, 62, 137, 167, 217, 250
encroachment
    by river 193, 236
    onto river 53, 55, 80, 82, 130, 236
energy x, 15, 17, 25, 92, 235, 240
    renewable x, xi

Index

engineer; engineering *see also* Corps of Engineers 2, 3, 9, 12, 13, 18, 22, 27, 49, 50, 76, 78, 79–82, 86, 91–4, 96, 97–9, 101, 103, 105, 107, 110, 111, 113, 117–19, 122–5, 128, 129, 130–2, 135, 137, 139, 145, 171, 172, 175, 183, 184, 185, 200, 204, 209, 214, 235, 236, 238, 245
'green' 228, 230
Enlightenment 24, 38
Environment Agency xii, 4, 11, 25, 26, 156, 228, 233, 235, 245, 248
environmentalism; environmentalist 7, 36, 37, 41, 63, 146, 156, 176, 234, 244, 250
estuary, Tyne xvii, 3, 4, 14, 18, 27, 28, 30, 32, 34, 36, 43–9, 51–3, 55, 56, 58, 60, 62, 63, 66, 69, 72–9, 83, 85, 96, 98, 102, 104, 106, 119, 125, 127, 133–5, 138, 139, 141–4, 146, 149–56, 157, 160–1, 165–8, 170–1, 173–4, 177, 178–82, 185–6, 189, 192 193, 195, 200, 205, 206, 214, 220, 222, 226–8, 233, 238, 245, 246, 248, 250
European Union 219, 251
EU Water Framework Directive 233, 245, 251, 253
Evenden, Matthew 22, 142
excrement *see also* manure 50, 119, 141, 234

F

Falstone 196, 202, 203
fauna *see also* wildlife xiii, 3, 150, 200, 213, 224, 232, 244, 247
ferry 94, 189, 191, 238, 239, 241
feudalism 87–8
fish 59–60, 114, 119, 138–56, 159, 162, 164, 165, 167–71, 174, 177–9, 182–3, 189, 194, 195, 199, 207, 209, 224, 228, 230, 234, 236, 251
fish pass 143, 154, 155, 197, 206–09, 228, 235
fisherman *see also* angler 59, 121, 167, 208

fishery; fishing 59, 61, 110, 111, 116, 141–8, 150, 151, 154–5, 161, 167–9, 171, 174, 176, 181, 187, 188, 207, 208, 220, 225, 247
flood *see also* Great Flood 23, 30, 39, 59, 60, 61, 64, 71–6, 107, 112, 118, 132, 134, 154, 161, 162, 167, 193, 195, 197, 200, 203, 204, 228, 235–6
flood plain 9, 19, 71, 93, 230
flora *see also* flower xiii, 3, 150, 200, 213, 224, 229, 232, 244, 247
flow 4–6, 8, 9, 10, 12, 16, 17, 19, 31, 32, 44, 54, 56, 57, 62, 71, 89, 114, 118, 119, 130, 134, 145, 174, 181, 193, 196, 198–9, 209, 211, 213, 232, 237
flower *see also* flora 139, 221, 229, 239
forestry 196
Forestry Commission 196, 199, 200, 202–04, 231
Forth, R. 16, 17, 180–1
  Firth of 34, 60, 169, 176
Fox River 21
France 15, 24, 37, 39, 41, 147
Fraser, David xiii, 224, 238, 242
Fraser River 22
Frenchman's Bay 97

G

Garden Festival 212, 223
Gardner, Ralph 30, 64–70, 78, 85, 247
Gateshead *see also* Newcastle-Gateshead Quayside xii, 4, 26, 45, 52, 57, 58, 66, 72, 83, 91, 94, 122, 125, 136, 149, 162, 191, 212, 214, 223, 226, 231, 234, 235, 238, 242, 243
Gateshead Millennium Bridge *see* bridge
Gibson, Ceri xi, 210, 227, 228
Glasgow 2, 15, 212
glass making 45, 48, 80
Gompertz, Aaron 125–8, 181
Grand Coulee Dam 209, 211
gravel 6, 49, 53, 77, 117, 124, 139, 154, 198, 199, 209
  extraction 10, 109–16, 146, 207, 236, 245

Index

Great Flood 4, 30, 64, 71–4
Grove, Richard 43–4

H

Hall, Matt xiii, 190, 240
Hanawalt, Barbara 42
harm; harmful (to the river) 4, 6, 10, 19, 29, 33, 42, 59, 62, 105, 119, 124, 130, 132, 136, 137, 138, 142, 149, 150, 153, 154, 165, 168, 230, 233, 245, 248, 251
Hawley, Steven 194
Haydon Bridge 27, 73, 74, 114, 115, 139, 148, 225, 229
health
  environmental 3, 11, 18, 22, 23, 30, 32, 33, 62, 66, 89, 107, 116, 119, 126, 133, 141, 143, 144, 146, 147, 156, 158, 165, 168, 174, 176, 213, 214, 223, 226, 227, 228, 230, 244, 245, 247, 248, 251, 253
  human *see also* public health 157, 158, 171, 172, 189
Hebburn 27, 47, 77, 179, 188, 190
Hedwin Streams 35, 52, 73, 76, 94, 103, 117
Henderson, Tony xiii, 190
Hexham xvii, 4, 5, 26, 73, 133, 134, 139, 142–4, 189, 198, 200, 206, 225, 228, 241
Hoffmann, Richard 40
Holland 34, 39, 67, 68, 103, 251
Holyoak, Graham xi
Humber, R. 15, 19
Humphreys and Watson Report 32, 158
hydro-electricity 23, 98, 194–6, 198, 210–11
hydrology 19, 103, 183, 207
hygiene 89, 119, 141

I

improvement (works) 3, 4, 14, 22, 24, 28, 29, 30, 64, 65, 75, 76, 78, 79, 80, 81, 84, 86, 88, 89, 91, 93–7, 100, 102, 106, 109, 116, 117, 134, 137, 146, 166, 178, 192, 236, 239, 246, 247
industrialisation 15, 17, 20, 33, 38, 45, 72, 78, 87, 93, 94, 119, 180, 195, 238, 241, 245, 253
industry *see also* deindustrialisation 1, 10, 12, 22, 32, 39, 42, 45, 46, 47, 49, 51, 53, 66, 83, 91, 92, 116, 139, 142, 155, 159, 181, 186–91, 196, 197, 199, 210, 213, 217, 219, 220, 221, 222, 224, 227, 232, 237, 238, 241–4, 246, 247, 248, 250
infrastructure x, 12, 24, 31, 46, 66, 77, 84, 87, 90, 91, 102, 109, 114, 116, 174, 177, 178, 192, 221, 236, 239, 247, 251
Ingold, Tim 212
invasive species 4, 228, 230
island 44, 46, 49, 59, 93–4, 103–04, 117, 135, 139, 224, 230, 248

J

Jarrow 76, 105, 108, 117, 152, 172, 181, 241, 249
  Slakes 46–8, 123, 131, 132

K

Kaye, Joel 41–2
keel (boat) 1, 46, 49, 50, 53, 54, 60, 139
keelmen 50, 58, 60, 62, 250
Kempster, J. 51, 141, 175–6
Kielder 5, 29, 32, 187, 194–209
  Dam 197, 207, 210
  Hydro 195, 211
  Reservoir 32, 149, 195–6, 208, 210, 211
  Salmon Hatchery xii, 208, 209
King's Meadows 46, 49,59, 103, 139
Kiser, Lisa 42
kittiwake 8, 33, 233–4
Kraker, Adriaan de 34, 67–8

Index

L

Laing, Olivia 71
landowner 18, 56, 57, 115, 116, 143, 199
landscape x, xi, 6, 18, 19, 24, 27, 28, 38, 42, 74, 139, 195–7, 201–05, 209, 248
Laures, Robert 40
law; legislation; legal *see also* bylaw, regulation 17–19, 26, 27, 31, 32, 35, 36, 37, 38, 42, 51, 60, 63, 65–6, 103, 109, 113, 114–16, 119, 120, 127–8, 133, 135, 136, 141, 144–6, 156, 181, 186, 192, 194, 247, 249, 253
lead x, 6, 45, 49, 128, 138–9, 180, 197, 213–14, 233
leisure *see also* recreation; tourism 21, 28
Lemington 56, 102, 103, 124, 152
Lewis-Stempel, John 232
Lieshout, Carrie van xi
liquid highway 3, 10, 24, 25, 29, 35, 43, 45, 57, 64, 66, 246
Liri, R. 23, 87–8, 218–19
Little Ice Age xvi, 34, 66
Liverpool 15, 17, 76, 86, 90, 174, 195, 212
Ljubljanica, R. 213
London 1, 15, 35, 39, 44, 49, 53, 56, 60, 69, 76, 82, 84, 90, 94, 105, 119, 166, 169, 183, 203, 204
Low Light Heritage Centre xiii, 26, 188

M

MacFarlane, Robert 40
MacGregor, John 75–80
MacKirdy, Susan xi
Mah, Alice 218–19
management (human, of natural systems) *see also* regulation xi, xvii, 3, 10, 19, 22, 23, 25, 26, 28, 30, 42, 44, 49, 50, 52, 53, 55, 56, 61, 63, 64, 65, 69, 70, 77, 79, 82, 83, 85–8, 93, 94, 96, 118, 200, 224, 226, 228, 245, 247, 248, 253
manure *see also* excrement 50, 51, 56, 61
Marshall, Michael 13, 175, 210, 211
McCulloch, Christine 209
McNeill, John 36

Meeting of the Waters *see* Waters Meet
Mersey, R. x, 2, 15, 17–18, 86, 96, 176
Miles, Steven 217
mine; mining; miner *see also* lead x, xi, 6, 21, 41, 45, 54, 107, 138, 148, 167, 180, 196, 200, 213, 214, 232, 233
Ministry of Agriculture and Fisheries; Ministry of Agriculture, Fisheries and Food 149, 152, 155, 159, 164, 167, 179, 187, 206, 207, 208, 209
Ministry of Health 155, 157, 170, 171, 182
Mississippi River 22, 25, 92
mitigation (in natural systems) xi, 39, 40, 210, 228
monopoly 3, 22, 29, 30, 35, 64–6, 69, 70, 218, 247
Moon, David x
Moore, Andrew xii
Morgan, John 39
music; musician 8, 11, 33, 217, 220, 221, 248

N

Nail, Jimmy 33, 221–2, 238
National Grid x
navigability xvi, xvii, 1, 2, 4, 30, 35, 37, 47, 50, 64, 75, 81, 82–3, 88, 90, 102
navigation 19, 22, 30, 62, 66, 70, 76, 82–3, 108, 110, 116, 181, 192, 218, 222, 246, 247
Nef, John 46
Nent, R. 138, 148, 180, 233
Netherlands *see* Holland
Newburn 48, 74, 102–04, 110, 111–14, 122, 124, 137, 139, 146, 179, 191, 236–7, 241, 252, 169
Newcastle *see also* Port of Newcastle 1, 4, 14–17, 30, 45, 46, 47, 50, 52, 54–7, 58, 61, 62, 63, 65–70, 72, 73, 75, 76, 82–4, 86, 91, 94, 96, 98, 102, 104, 108, 109, 119, 122, 125, 129, 139, 142, 149, 152, 154, 160, 162–3, 166, 180, 183, 187, 190, 195, 197, 200, 217, 219, 221, 226, 231, 234, 236, 238, 239, 242, 243

Index

Newcastle and Gateshead Water Company 52, 143, 144, 173
Newcastle Corporation 26, 29, 30, 33, 35, 43–9, 52–7, 62, 64–70, 74, 76, 78, 80, 82, 85, 86, 88–9, 94, 103, 144, 214, 240, 247, 250
Newcastle Council 26, 78, 79, 80, 84–6, 183, 192, 214
Newcastle-Gateshead Quayside 5, 11, 213–18, 220, 222, 234
Northumberland 4, 5, 6, 13, 26, 32, 49, 61, 98, 103, 112, 138, 142, 152, 153, 159, 183, 195, 199, 206
  Dock 94, 121, 140
  Duke of 90, 110–13, 145, 146
Northumberland and Tyneside River Board xvii, 31, 32, 115, 127, 156, 173–4, 177–8, 181
Northumbrian Angling Federation 32
Northumbrian River Authority 32, 125, 156, 177–8, 185, 186, 197–200, 201, 206, 208, 209
Northumbrian Water xii, 4, 11, 25, 26, 156, 186, 228, 236, 245, 248, 253
North Sea 2, 4, 6, 39, 50, 120, 157, 180, 184, 209, 234, 246, 248, 253
North Shields xiii, 27, 65, 67, 70, 82, 86, 97, 106, 188, 189, 237, 239, 240
North Tyne 4, 5, 6, 32, 142, 154, 168, 187, 195–8, 201–02, 205, 206, 209–11, 231

O

oil xvi, 130–3, 150, 154, 190, 220, 243
oligarchy 3, 26, 64, 65, 70, 78, 88, 218, 247
Oliver, Stuart 10
oral history 26–8, 33, 187, 237, 245, 249–50
'organic machine' 3, 14, 23, 24, 106, 248
Ouseburn 48, 217
outfall, sewage 119, 122–3, 125, 126, 136, 141, 164–5, 170, 172, 179
oxygen *see also* deoxygenation 11, 51, 62, 119, 151, 159–65, 168, 178, 179, 192, 210, 213

P

Parliament *see also* Act of Parliament 48, 57, 70, 79, 90, 95, 108, 116, 128, 133, 134–5, 153, 167, 168, 183, 192, 200
Pattinson, J. and H. 129, 148
Payne, Jill xi
Pennines, North 4, 5, 233
pier 30, 94–101, 105, 107, 110, 111, 120, 137, 143, 239, 245
pilot, river 24, 50, 52, 66, 73–4, 90, 92
plant *see also* flora, flower 4, 6, 7, 11, 17, 19, 20, 31, 33, 91, 139, 207, 220, 228, 230, 235, 237, 243
plantation *see also* forestry 196, 200, 202
Pollard, Aidan xii, 224
pollution xvii, 11, 16, 18, 26, 31, 32, 39, 60, 62, 124–8, 135, 138, 141–56, 158–70, 175–9, 181–2, 184–93, 200, 220, 225–8, 233, 241, 244, 247, 250, 251, 253
Port of Newcastle 3, 14, 35
Port of Tyne xii, xvii, 3, 4, 26, 94, 109, 226, 228, 236, 248, 253
Porter, Dale 8, 92, 96, 142
power
  electric *see* energy; hydro-electricity
  river 1, 2, 9, 10, 14, 15, 19, 21, 22, 27, 32, 45, 48, 49, 50, 71, 73, 86, 92, 103, 118, 119, 137, 211, 213, 233, 240, 246, 247, 250, 251
  socio-political; legal 32, 59, 70, 86, 125, 126–8, 145, 174, 177, 178, 181, 185, 209, 229
  steam 21, 30, 47, 69, 75, 76, 79, 101, 105
Power and the Water Project, The x, xi, xii, xvi
power station 179, 195
Pritchard, Sara 14–15, 24, 37–8, 118, 158, 176, 244, 248
productivity 1, 3, 4, 11, 22, 84, 88, 113, 167–8, 214, 218, 222, 243–4, 250
public health *see also* health, human 89, 119, 141, 155, 157, 168, 170, 171, 183, 185, 192, 247
Public Health Act 141

Index

Public Inquiry 152, 155, 197, 200–03, 205

Q

quay *see also* Newcastle-Gateshead Quayside 53, 60, 74, 77, 79, 80–1, 104, 106, 109, 116, 125, 131, 135, 191, 241

R

Ramblers' Association 201
Rangeley-Wilson, Charles 9, 213
recreation *see also* leisure xi, 8, 10, 11, 21, 22, 25, 33, 96–7, 175, 181, 196, 201, 205, 207, 219, 223–6, 228, 230, 237, 239, 244, 245
regulation *see also* law; management x, xvi, xvii, 3, 4, 8, 9, 10, 11, 14, 16, 17, 19, 25–31, 35–8, 44, 45–63, 80, 120, 126, 128–33, 136, 138, 142, 149, 154, 175, 181, 186, 203, 207, 248, 251
Reisner, Marc 23, 193, 247
religion 8, 38, 41, 249
Rennison, R. 13
resources, natural 2, 10, 14, 17, 19, 20, 30, 36, 40–3, 51, 61, 62, 88, 89, 109–10, 113–14, 127, 199, 224, 243, 244
Reynard, Pierre-Claude 37
Rhine, R. 23, 37, 93, 251
Rhone, R. 15, 24, 118, 176
Richards, John 40
Richardson, Charles 1
Ritvo, Harriet 194
riverscape 1, 3, 10, 18, 22, 26, 27, 31, 33, 77, 91, 94, 124, 138–9, 142, 187, 188, 191, 195, 196, 204, 205, 212, 213, 214, 217, 218, 223, 226, 230, 237, 238, 240, 245, 248
Rosenthal, Leslie 18–19, 119–20
Royal Commission 16, 30, 64, 81–6, 101, 141, 192
rubbish *see also* waste 53–4, 57–8, 61, 120–1, 130, 133–6, 189, 190
Ryton 59, 91, 103, 106, 112–14, 117, 145, 188, 191, 239

S

Saddington, Pearl xiii, 188, 241
Sage Gateshead Music Centre 2, 50, 6614, 223, 237
sailing; sailing ship *see also* yacht 1, 45, 49, 224
salmon *see also* angling; Tyne Salmon Conservancy xvi, xvii, 2, 6, 8, 10, 11, 22, 25, 32, 33, 48, 59, 60, 138–56, 161, 167–9, 173, 175–7, 184, 185, 187, 190, 192, 194, 206–09, 213, 219, 220, 228, 232–3, 235, 237, 248, 250
Salmon Acts 31, 141, 146, 156, 206
Salmon River 194, 232
salt 47–9, 53
sand 48–9, 53, 55, 61, 74, 77, 87, 109–14, 117, 124, 138, 146, 199, 214, 229
sandbank 50, 66, 75–7, 96, 106, 248
Schmid, Martin 37–8
Schneer, Jonathan 15, 19
Schwagerl, Christian 21
science; scientist 8, 28, 31, 41, 42, 47, 97, 128–30, 147, 152–3, 156, 158–61, 165, 178, 187, 188, 192, 209, 210, 226, 227, 228, 229, 232, 237, 247, 251
Scotland 7, 16, 17, 27, 34, 51, 69, 88, 93, 96, 147, 240, 251
seal 179–80, 220, 224
sediment; sedimentation *see also* settling; silt 9, 58, 87, 96, 109, 154, 164, 165, 172, 183, 185–6, 228, 230, 236
sensory experience *see also* smell 27, 243, 245
settling 122–4, 148–9, 164
Severn, R. x, 15, 19
sewage *see also* waste 18, 31, 32, 52, 61, 120, 122, 123, 125–8, 141, 144, 152–3, 155–7, 159, 161–2, 164–73, 175, 177–80, 182–6, 190, 191, 225

Index

sewer 18, 25, 28, 32, 35, 51, 54, 56–7, 119–20, 122–9, 136, 141, 144, 152, 155, 157–8, 165, 167–9, 171, 172, 177–8, 182–3, 185–6, 192–3, 214, 236, 245, 250
  interceptor 157, 186
Sheail, John 15
sheep dipping 31, 145, 153–4, 178
Shepherd, Nan 232
shipbuilding 14, 91, 96, 13, 189, 219, 220, 221, 250
shipyard xiii, 1, 13, 108, 189, 219, 221, 238, 240, 241, 242
shoal *see also* sandbank 50, 66, 101, 102, 139
Silent Spring 63, 144, 150
silt *see also* sediment 29, 43, 44, 60, 69, 77, 103, 105, 106, 123, 217, 228, 230, 246, 250
Site of Special Scientific Interest (SSSI) xvii, 99
smell 26, 27, 140, 141, 157, 184, 186, 188, 189, 190, 191, 238, 239
smoke 124, 139
smolt xvii, 144, 145, 149, 151–2, 154–5, 159, 161, 168, 206–09
Smout, Christopher 6, 16, 17, 19, 34, 45, 51, 59, 88, 93, 169, 180–1, 229
socio-environmental relationships 7, 11, 16, 17, 22, 25, 26, 36, 61, 65, 174, 196, 205, 21, 220, 244, 246, 249, 253
socio-technical system 3, 15
Sörlin, Sverker 36
Souter Point 120, 172, 184
South Shields 4, 30, 53, 64, 65, 66, 75, 94, 96, 97, 104, 105, 106, 110, 111, 124, 130, 152, 181, 188, 189, 191, 221, 237, 247, 248
South Tyne 4–6, 27, 74, 114, 135, 138–9, 143, 147–9, 153, 178, 180, 225, 230, 231–3, 245
staith 46, 47, 48, 56, 66, 77, 81, 97, 105, 134, 140, 212, 235
Standing Committee on River Pollution (SCORP) xvii, 31, 152–3, 156, 157–61, 165–71, 247, 248

Stark, Martin 210, 230
steel industry 102, 104, 224, 225
stewardship, environmental 29, 43
Stewart, Mairi 16–17, 19, 169, 180–1
Sting 221, 223
Stradling, R. and D. 244
straightening (of river) *see also* canalising 30, 116–17, 137
Summers, Gregory 21
Sunbeam Dam 194
sustainability 4, 40, 41, 51, 110, 119, 141, 150, 181, 212–13, 248, 253
Swan Hunters xiii, 126
system, natural 2, 3, 7, 11, 15, 19, 20–2, 23, 25, 27, 36, 40, 2, 50, 56, 58, 62, 63, 65, 66, 68, 71, 77, 87, 89, 102, 107, 119, 138, 144, 213, 235, 245, 247, 248, 249, 250, 253

T

tar 131–2, 141, 151, 154, 160–1
Tay, R. 20, 93 27, 240
Team, R. 118, 122, 136, 160, 173, 234
technology 3, 17, 21, 24, 29, 30, 31, 45, 47, 50, 51, 62, 69, 75, 89, 92, 119, 197, 199, 200, 241, 250, 251
Tees, R. 19, 159, 161, 176, 197–9, 200
Teesside 32, 196–7, 210
temperature (of water) 125, 129, 160–2, 179, 210, 228, 231
testing (of water) 11, 26, 28, 31, 47, 128, 130, 157–64, 178–9, 183–4, 228
Thames, R. xvi, 2, 8, 9, 10, 15–17, 19, 60, 77, 92, 94, 96, 119, 142, 177
Thomas, Keith 43
tide; tidal xvi, xvii, 4, 12, 14, 19, 31, 35, 44, 49, 56, 58, 59, 62, 73, 75, 76–8, 82–3, 87, 94, 102–03, 106, 106–08, 111, 118, 120, 122–3, 127, 133–4, 137, 142, 149, 151, 152, 160, 162–3, 167, 172–3, 178, 179, 183, 184, 185, 199, 217, 227, 232 234, 238, 239
toll, shipping *see also* ballast toll 30, 35, 50, 53, 56, 62, 64, 66, 67, 69, 94, 95, 99, 101, 112, 117, 143, 163, 218

Index

tourist; tourism 3, 8, 11, 25, 33, 196, 203, 210, 212–14, 217, 218, 220, 222, 224, 237, 240, 243, 250
toxicity xiii, 28, 32, 123, 125, 141, 174, 177, 187, 188, 192, 213, 214, 248, 250
trade *see also* commerce xvii, 3, 12, 14, 34, 35, 42, 45, 47, 48, 53, 62, 64, 67, 68, 69, 75, 76, 77, 83, 90–3, 96, 102, 106, 113, 131, 137, 140, 168, 172, 213, 218, 221, 222, 235, 240, 241, 244, 246, 247
transport 13, 22, 24, 34–5, 42, 67–9, 220, 238, 239
Trent, R. 176, 230
tributary 4, 5, 6, 8, 9, 22, 31, 35, 45, 48, 49, 54, 76, 94, 109, 118, 132, 133, 142, 143, 145, 147, 149, 154, 173, 177, 178, 180, 194, 207, 208, 217, 225, 228, 230, 231, 233, 236, 249
Trinity House
  London 53, 56, 69
  Newcastle 50, 52, 53, 62, 66, 73, 95
trout xvii, 60, 142, 147, 150, 153, 164, 178, 208, 219, 220
Tryweryn Reservoir 195
tunnel 108–09, 167, 186, 200, 228, 238–9
Twain, Mark 92–3
Tweed, R. 2, 101
Tyne Dock xii, 94, 97, 98, 109
Tyne Improvement Commission (TIC) xii, xvii, 1, 2–4, 10, 11, 18, 26, 28, 30–1, 33, 64, 65, 70, 76, 79, 81–9, 90–137, 141, 143, 145–6, 151, 154, 155, 164, 168, 172, 177, 178, 181, 185, 186, 192, 195, 205, 218, 233, 235, 240, 247, 250, 253
Tyne River Court 11, 14, 30, 35, 36, 43, 49, 55, 61, 63, 78, 80
Tyne Rivers Trust xi, 4, 11, 25, 26, 33, 156, 210, 227, 228, 230, 231, 233, 236, 248, 251
Tyne Salmon Conservancy xvii, 10, 26, 28, 31, 32, 121, 138–156, 161, 165–6, 169, 170, 173, 174, 177, 181, 247, 248
Tyne Sewerage Scheme 157–8, 165, 167
Tyneside Joint Sewerage Board 32, 186
Tynesider 8, 11, 26, 32, 33, 51, 142 158, 175, 188, 193, 218, 220–3, 235, 237, 244, 248–9, 250, 253

U

Uglow, Jenny 44, 61, 223
unemployment 33, 136, 155, 166–8, 170, 218
urban 12, 16–19, 34, 35, 50, 119, 178, 218, 219, 237, 241, 253

V

Venice 39, 44
vulnerability 4, 11, 212, 246

W

Walker Riverside 219–20
Warde, Paul x, 36, 56
Warden Rock 4–7
waste *see also* rubbish; sewage 18, 19, 28, 29, 30–2, 50–4, 56, 58, 62, 64, 89, 91, 105, 119–23, 125, 128, 132–3, 135–6, 141–2, 148–50, 152, 155, 157, 159, 161–5, 168, 170, 172, 174, 175, 177–8, 181–6, 192, 193, 226, 236, 245, 250
  liquid 35, 45, 51, 56, 89, 119, 129–30, 185
  solid 3, 35, 50–1, 56–7, 133, 164, 172, 183, 184, 185
waste water xii, 32, 130, 174, 175, 245
Water Bailiff 35, 54, 55, 62, 78, 80
water closet 50–1, 89, 119, 141, 182
water mill 10, 45, 149, 151, 181, 198, 206, 208
Waters Meet 5, 6, 7
Watson, Fiona 42, 49, 59
Wear, R. 15, 20, 32, 56, 63, 104, 176, 185, 197, 198, 199
Weileder, Wolfgang 212
weir 31, 48, 54, 55, 59, 106, 115, 118, 141, 147, 198, 206
wharf 47, 53, 78, 124
White, Gilbert 232
White, Richard 3, 7, 14–15, 20–1, 23–4, 42, 106, 194, 209, 248

Index

White, Walter 6, 138–41
Whitehill Point 77, 80, 81, 94, 116
wildlife *see also* birds; fauna 4, 5, 6, 7, 11, 14, 17, 19, 31, 33, 59, 60, 91, 105, 199, 207, 226, 228, 230, 231, 237, 240, 243, 250
Wildlife Trust 199, 234
Windrush, R. 8
Woelfe-Erskine, Cleo 232
World War One 148, 149
World War Two 24, 32, 158, 172, 174, 82, 183, 192
Wright, James xii

Wright, Peter 13–14, 75
Wye, R. (Bucks.) 9
Wylam 4, 25, 73, 103, 112, 142, 148, 150, 152, 163–5, 172, 173, 198, 220, 227

Y

yacht 96–7

Z

zinc 6, 138, 180, 233
Zupko, Ronald 40

www.ingramcontent.com/pod-product-compliance
Lightning Source LLC
Chambersburg PA
CBHW021820300426
44114CB00009BA/259